THIS BOOK BEGAN

as a small bit of advertising history. Along the way, it became something more... Along the way, we discovered that a book about Howard Gossage wasn't just about advertising.

It was about love and magic – friendship and joy.

It was about how to live – and how to die.

If you're reading this, our journey is complete. 🕊 And yours is just beginning. 🕊 Spend some time with *"The Socrates of San Francisco."* Share his thoughts – and the memories of those whose lives he touched.

We hope this book touches your life. 🕊 We hope it inspires you to host a lunch for the finest minds you know. 🕊 We hope you write a letter just for the heck of it, throw a party full of *"Flahoolick,"* or find a cause to champion.

Most of all, if you're in advertising, we hope it inspires you to use your talents to enrich other people's lives – instead of just trying to sell them something.

🕊

Welcome to *The Book of Gossage*

[*Is This Your Book?*]

THE BOOK OF GOSSAGE

- A Compilation -

{
Which includes
"Is There Any Hope for Advertising?"
by Howard Luck Gossage
}

[*IN WHICH WE PRESENT PUBLISHING INFORMATION OF VITAL IMPORTANCE TO LAWYERS & LIBRARIANS*]

ABOUT THIS BOOK

The Book of Gossage is a compilation of *Is There Any Hope for Advertising?* by Howard Luck Gossage plus additional material. *Is There Any Hope for Advertising?* ©1986 was edited by Prof. Kim Rotzoll, Jarlath Graham, and Barrows Mussey and published by the University of Illinois Press. It is reprinted with permission in its entirety. [A slightly shorter version by Barrows Mussey originally appeared in German as *Ist die Werbung noch zu retten?*]

Additional articles, materials and commentary have been contributed by: Carl Ally, Dennis Altman, Bruce Bendinger, Stan Freberg, the estate of Robert Brewster Freeman, Jeff Goodby, Sally Kemp Gossage, Wayne Hilinski, Warren Hinckle, Jay Conrad Levinson, Alice Lowe, Jerry Mander, Dagmar Mussey, Professor Kim Rotzoll, Dugald Stermer and Tom Wolfe. All are used with permission. Other appropriate permissions have been granted by: *CA Magazine,* Lewis Lowe, and, if *Ramparts Magazine* was still around, we're sure they would have given permission, too. John Steinbeck's correspondence with Howard Gossage ©1995 by Elaine A. Steinbeck reprinted by permission of McIntosh and Otis, Inc.

The Book of Gossage is published by: The Copy Workshop - a division of Bruce Bendinger Creative Communications, Inc. • 2144 N. Hudson • Chicago, IL 60614. Voice: 312-871-1179 Fax: 312-281-4643 • copywork@aol.com • copyworkshop@adworld.com

Library of Congress Catalog Card Number: 95-68128

©1995 • ISBN 0-9621415-3-4

This book is dedicated to the memory of
Marget Larsen & Robert Freeman.
Love & Magic in the Age of Gossage.

ಶಿ

- PART TWO -

This is the original book [using the original negatives],* originally published in German as *Ist die Werbung noch zu retten?* and then set in 12 point Century Schoolbook and published in the original English as

Is There Any Hope for Advertising?

by Howard Luck Gossage

* We did re-do the plates for as many of the original ads as we could find.

How to
get your husband
to fasten his
Rover 2000  safety harness:

Tell him it's a Sam Browne belt
and he looks like a World War I aviator

Years before seat belts were mandatory, Howard thought safety should be fashionable in car advertising. He even saved his clients a modeling fee. What a guy!

[10]

- PART THREE -

This part of the book is about the man who wrote the book you just read & extensions of his ideas & articles that didn't make the previous collection & whatever else showed up by press time...

FAMOUS LAST WORDS

Howard's heritage lives on in two major forces

★ those who aspire to the best in advertising

★ those who have serious concerns about advertising.

Both are represented here in articles written by people whose lives he touched – and a few final thoughts from Howard.

Here is a love story. Robert Freeman and Marget Larsen – two of the unique creative individuals who worked with Howard. This originally appeared in *CA Magazine*. Introduction by Dick Coyne.

Two chapters from the memoirs of Alice Lowe, Office Manager, confidant, President of Shade Tree and Ring Mistress of Howard Gossage's Firehouse Circus.

Includes instructions on How to Throw a Party on the Spur of the Moment for Your Favorite People [Mariachi band not included].

The author of *Guerrilla Marketing* tells us about his early days with The Original Guerilla – as Howard's secretary. Today, Jay's books help small businesses around the world with a very Gossage-like spirit.

Start here...

(In which a guy clearly does not set out to change the world, but does so, then denies he ever did, and has a whole bunch of people over for drinks who will all go on to become famous and miss him for the rest of their lives.)

ST. HOWARD
AMONG THE
SADLY SERIOUS

by Jeffrey A. Goodby

Howard Gossage treated advertising as if it were radioactive waste. He hated it. He was fascinated by it. He wondered why more people weren't concerned about its effects. And he entertained the almost but not quite oxymoronic notion that it could somehow heat our homes, dazzle us, make a better future for our children. ❧ Amazingly, he operated out of a time when the fickle god of American business sported a crewcut and seemed to be forever saying "You bet!," a time when Vance Packard and David Riesman were still floating up diatribes about how package designs contained hidden cues and how "conformity" was a fate worse than death or communism. Howard conducted business in a city that was not only a total advertising backwater, but that most of the country had always found hard to swallow, a city that saw his career begin amidst beat, hip, beards, and coffee house poetry and end in free speech sit-ins, the big black Jefferson Airplane house near Golden Gate Park, and the passing around of mind-altering substances in Kool-Aid jars at the Fillmore West. The Victorian firehouse in which Gossage did business was just a couple of big hills away from some of the best—and worst—

windowpane acid on the planet, from Love Street and the snarling cops on their horses and all those sixteen-year-olds with eyes like cigarette burns. Howard never seemed to judge or even acknowledge them. Yet looking back, he seems more like them than unlike them, a tiny, laughing, downtown outpost of it all. ❧ Other than Gossage, there weren't a lot of people openly pondering the aesthetic and moral implications of business in those days. But then, there never have been. Business in general—and advertising in particular—has resisted self-examination somehow. It has never attracted the most expansive writers, showing itself instead to be more comfortable with a mind-numbing avalanche of shallower, B-school analyses, a kind of self-blind statistical hors d'oeuvre that for the most part avoids larger questions about what all this stuff is doing to our heads. ❧ To make matters worse, advertising people have always been sickly proud of the way they can ignore the aesthetic implications of what they do. (An art director in New York once glowingly told me how he had offed a woman who told him one of his ads was ugly and offensive by retorting: "You noticed.") In a tradition going back to Claude Hopkins and "The Science of Advertising," advertising people have approached the selling of toilet paper and beer like hired gunfighters who could care less about winging innocent bystanders or even taking out whole towns so long as their purposes are served. David Ogilvy, whom we now think of as one of

❧

...advertising people have always been sickly proud of the way they can ignore the aesthetic implications of what they do.

❧

the most urbane of the bunch, crowed about how he had doggedly exorcised his own "pseudo-literary ambitions," finally "concentrating (his) thoughts on the obligation of advertising to sell." Although he is a humorous and delightful man himself, he loudly declaimed against the use of any kind of humor in advertising. And about Bill Bernbach, the founder of Doyle Dane Bernbach, the agency many believe to be the most *most* in the history of advertising, Mr. Ogilvy somewhat bitterly "wondered if his output would have been less elegant if, like me, he had started as a door-to-door salesman." ❧ (All this feigned insensitivity would be a little easier to handle, by the way, if the feigners weren't so apt to immediately turn around and claim painfully precious sensitivity to the smallest detail about whether or not we ought to have a drop shadow on the headline type. But that's another story.) ❧ In the face of all this, Gossage stood as a kind of Far West prairie moralist, a man of principle, a human being. He hated the deeper, venal mission of his business, calling advertising "a multi-billion dollar hammer hitting a thirty-nine cent thumbtack" and announcing in *Time* magazine, "I don't know a first class brain in the business who has any respect for it." Advertising exhibited, he said, "a disregard for the decent opinion of mankind." It was "thoughtless, boring, and there (was) simply too much of it." He despised the way advertisers felt compelled to repeat communications over and over, rather than spending

❧

Gossage stood as a kind of Far West prairie moralist, a man of principle, a human being.

❧

any time paying heed to their quality: "How often do you have to read a book, a news story, or see a movie or play? If it is interesting, once is enough; if it is dull, once is plenty." While the industry lamented that advertising seemed to work less and less well with each repetition and each passing year, Howard had the nerve to suggest that maybe that was because the stuff was no damn good. ❧ A lot has been made of Gossage's writings about First Amendment issues—specifically, his belief that freedom had been sold down the river when publishers owed more financial loyalty to their advertisers than to their readers. But Howard also saw that the First Amendment would benevolently protect advertisers who were inflicting the most reptilian, dimwitted, cynical crimes upon the general populace. And given the abhorrent nature of most ad communications, he wondered aloud how far this kind of consumerism ought be to allowed to go, where it would take us, and what kind of people we'd all be when the dust cleared. ❧ Howard's fears about what advertising was doing to the brainpans of the nation were accompanied by a nagging irritation over what it was doing to *him*. He resented the fact that he was painted with the same poisonous brush used on his hacky, unthinking advertising colleagues. "When you consider the delicacies of timing and footwork required to be a creative man and the many years of practice it takes, it is appalling that the rewards, outside of money, are so few," he lamented. "I mean, outside of the

❧

He resented the fact that he was painted with the same poisonous brush used on his hacky, unthinking advertising colleagues.

❧

advertising business almost nobody gives a damn. Among other writers and artists we have almost no stature at all." He felt outrage at the general public's blindness to the little amusements and ephemeral beauties the trade had created now and then, and wondered aloud to us whether, if we kept acting this way, he'd really have the energy to take it to the levels of fun, silliness, and insight he suspected it was capable of. ❧ From the depths of this advertising swamp, Gossage hoisted an oddball integrity. It was perhaps best captured, in a different context, by the poet Michael McClure: "Maybe it's okay to use people as long as you use all of them." ❧ Gossage struggled to make advertising something that involved people at the upper levels of their capabilities, that searched for the audience's highest common denominator rather than its lowest. He advocated and created a kind of work that invited involvement from the audience, that went out to them on their own terms and got them to laugh, think, send something in, make a suggestion, appreciate something they might never have noticed. Howard went so far, in fact, as to suggest that there was a formula to his approach: ask the client what his biggest problem is, then write an ad asking readers to help solve it, providing a coupon for that purpose. He liked this participatory approach partly because the advertising that resulted from it simply worked better. "In baiting a trap, always leave room for the mouse," Howard would quote from the work

❧

. . . ask the client what his biggest problem is, then write an ad asking readers to help solve it . . .

❧

*Our first duty
is not to the old
sales curve, it is
to the audience,"
Gossage wrote.*

ea

of the short story master Saki. (Or not. Gossage was famous for attributing stuff he made up to more credible sources.) ea There was a greater reason for Howard's desire to involve all of the audience's capabilities, however, one that was more than anything else ethical. ea "Our first duty is not to the old sales curve, it is to the audience," Gossage wrote, delivering a rather stinging nose tweak to the Ogilvy School of Insensitive Advertising He-men. "It is simply not right," he said, "to treat an audience in (that) fashion. If we can't look at it from a broad, ethical point of view then we ought to look at it personally, to please ourselves. We are all members of the audience, too, and are bored or irritated right along with everybody else." Howard knew and loved the projectile nature of advertising—or any communication, for that matter (about his experience as a navy flyer, he wrote: "I wasn't a very good pilot, so I picked bombers"). With his zealot's stammer and what Warren Hinckle once described as a "cock-a-hoop" laugh, Gossage gregariously relished the sheer joy of doing things to people. But they would have to be things that, in the end, worked because the people didn't mind having them done. ea All in all, it was an attitude that has always struck me as curiously environmentalist. There was, of course, Gossage's widely-publicized grumpy distaste for certain "involuntary" forms of advertising: billboards, sound trucks, and telephone solicitors. But beyond those particulars, Howard thought of advertising as a physical and psychic landscape that we all had little choice but to travel through. (Predictably, Gossage was so taken with Marshall McLuhan that he funded a barnstorming media theory lecture tour with several thousand bucks of his own money.) For the most part, this advertising environment was invisible to us, like water to a fish, yet it quietly shaped and reshaped our perceptions, our values, what we thought was right and important, our views of ourselves. It was one of those powerful things that could irreversibly jerk the compass, make us lose our places forever, and that made it important enough to think about. ❧ It was, at the same time, an environment we created for our children to live in, a place that would be passed on to them. The things that we erected on this landscape, he believed, contributed mightily to an impression of what we thought was important to us as a civilization. It could, at its best, convey a sense of grace, humor, responsibility, even beauty. At its worst—well, we know all too well what kind of tawdry, lurid, toxic storm the machine is capable of belching up. ❧ It was a commonsensical, human approach to something that had either been ignored or rationalized away as being too precious for the tough guys of paid media to lose any sleep over. To Howard, making the kind of advertising that worked and that ought to exist in the world was always an act of faith. Faith in the basic goodness and intelligence of the people out there. Faith that one respectful or humorous or beautiful act

❧

To Howard, making the kind of advertising that worked and that ought to exist in the world was always an act of faith.

❧

. . . the best of Howard's best is arguably the finest stuff advertising has ever seen.

could be worth hundreds of cynical, assaultive ones. Faith that the world was a place worth saving and not just something to use up and throw away. ❧ Certainly, Howard's own body of advertising and marketing work is in some ways less important than the gleaming intentions he left us all. On the whole, the creations of others from his era, Bill Bernbach in particular, will probably be remembered over Gossage's. This is partly because Howard's work was simply seen by fewer people. He was never given a budget anywhere near the size of Bernbach's famous client, Volkswagen. (Ironically, Gossage's agency was considered for the VW account, but passed over.) And Howard did not, to my knowledge, ever work in television. ❧ Yet the best of Howard's best is arguably the finest stuff advertising has ever seen. The campaign he created for Eagle Shirtmakers snaps pleasurably across wide synapses of sense and nonsense. The idea would have been remembered as remarkable if only because it actually convinced you to respond to the ad twice—once when you sent for that strange shirtkerchief broadcloth-and-button thing, and a second time when you endeavored to tell Miss Afflerbach what it was. It was an apparently serious fabric sampling, based upon an absolutely useless, absurd, and sublimely indescribable item. And damned if the thing wasn't free. ❧ Along with Eagle, I direct the first time Gossage reader to Howard's Scientific American Paper Airplane Contest, one of the most successful magazine promotions of all time, and all the more amazing because it was created for a rather dour, unfunny journal and directed at a readership of grim academics and science nerds. There was Howard's kangaroo giveaway for Qantas, and the underappreciated leap of silliness (actually, an idea lifted from Charles Schulz's *Peanuts*, with unblinking acknowledgment) that led him to depict classical composers on sweatshirts as part of a scheme to save a destitute classical radio station. And of course there was his charity work for the Sierra Club, along with the quixotic efforts he made to end the Vietnam War with ads in the paper. His public service work was always aggressively smart and convincing, never moralistic, never just emotionalism. It had to really piss off the bad guys to find that the opposition could appear this reasonable. ❧ Naturally, it was Howard who brought Stan Freberg's intelligent, evocative radio work to the fore. Freberg used radio in ways that hadn't been heard since the great radio dramas of the thirties and forties, painting vivid mind pictures of alien planets, endless chorus lines, even a vast ice cream sundae being built in one of the Great Lakes. If you are too young to remember the mid-sixties, you can't imagine the ubiquitousness of Freberg's style then, the number of advertisers attempting to rip him off, and the ways in which he defined what we all thought was funny. You can't imagine it but Gossage, of course, could. And did. ❧ In purpose and appearance, Howard's advertising had a

❧

His public service work was always aggressively smart and convincing, never moralistic, never just emotionalism.

❧

[21]

quality about it that can only be described as transcendent. It looked and sounded better than other advertising because it set out so explicitly to hit you on a higher plane. This stuff was light years away from the brain-dead, tranquilized universe of "whiter than white" and The Man From Glad, and somehow it put its contempt for such lower forms of life right in your face. In fact, in its abilities to get past your suspicions, pleasingly thwart your expectations, and evoke deeper emotional responses, Howard's advertising worked in ways we usually associate with art. 🙞 Forgive me, Mr. Ogilvy, but it's not too big a word for it. As you leaf through this book, notice how a few decades have added a surprisingly sad note of ephemerality to the products advertised, a distinct unreality. A lot of their shrill presence is gone now, leaving the brilliance of Gossage's writing in hard relief. These are documents designed to evoke telling, funny, unpredictable responses through mechanisms indistinguishable from what we have now come to call performance art. This is the work of a man who operated inside business, but thought outside it. He is after something more, something bigger, something that will get inside your head and make you wonder why you see the world the way you do. 🙞 But to enjoy Howard solely on the basis of his advertising output would be like loving Paris because the subways seem to work pretty well. It's part of the deal, maybe an impressive part of it, but in the end, it's only a portion of what's important.

Although his campaigns clearly contribute the most to Howard's appeal beyond the business world (the writer Steve Emerson told me, "Gossage is the only guy with a body of work you could show people outside advertising and expect them to enjoy and respect it"), there is something attractively frail and yet brash, considerate and yet abandoned, trivial yet vital, comic and tragic—something very human—about Gossage that makes him more lasting and poignant than his work would suggest. ❧ Howard was palpably a guy in the world with a day in front of him and a buck to make, just like all of us. He was, however, able to imbue all that with such a sense of possibility, perspective, and fun that it became the stuff of legend. Against all odds, Howard had a way of making you feel that you were probably a lot better than you thought you were, that if you really had fun you'd somehow survive financially. He convinced you that you owned the airwaves and had just as much right to exult in them as the next guy. And he made you feel that he appreciated the hell out of you, and that time was passing so we'd better get on with it, whether it was perfected yet or not. ❧ Or so I've heard. Sadly, I never met Howard, but I feel I've come to know him through the people and things he left behind, the way a vacuum is defined by the container around it. I know him through his former partners—Bob Freeman, all frail and soupboned, and Joe Weiner, a mound of overcoat always hurrying through the rain to something

❧

Howard had a way of making you feel that you were probably a lot better than you thought you were . . .

❧

*...he seemed to live
so damned well,
sparking a kind of
hope, a faith in
possibility...*

really big. I know Howard through his magical deer of design, Marget Larsen. And I know him from walking the narrow rooms of the firehouse his agency inhabited on Pacific Avenue. ❧ Through all these media, from somewhere on the other side, Gossage has given me power, made me see fun. When the San Francisco columnist Herb Caen told me that Howard was "holy" to him, I understood. Gossage resists rational assessment. That's no doubt partly because, in the flesh, he was such a character. But it's also got to be because he seemed to live so damned well, sparking a kind of hope, a faith in possibility, a feeling that whatever the everyday fabric might be, it could be torn open with mischief and laughter and, well, just the sheer desire to tear it open. (His middle name, which he was noticeably fond of employing, was Luck.) It's something we all want very much and gobble ravenously whenever we come across it. ❧ My wife Jan once told me of a wonderfully sweet childhood memory. She grew up on a farm in California and remembers her father, in winter, listening to the radio frost report, with predictions of low temperatures reported for each and every city and town in the area. Redlands 34, Indio 38, San Bernardino 38—she would listen with him until, magically, the name of her very own town and the worst it could expect in the world that night would ring from the official belfry of the radio. And I got to thinking about how a lot of those farms are gone now, how Top 40 and talk show and all-sports formats have probably replaced the frost report, how the prices and demographics of commercial radio had almost certainly legislated it out of existence. There are so many such very silent tragedies in the modern world, and for the most part the people that feel them are not the people who know what to do about them. ❧ I like to think that Howard would have saved the frost report. He would have done it, goddamit, just for the hell of it and because there was nothing better to do this afternoon, because things like that were leaving the modern world all too fast these days, and so that the little girls could all be safe and hold the memory of these moments for the rest of their lives. Howard *could* have done that, if he felt like it. And he would have done it, with work that all sides would have to admit was a real kick in the pants, just so we could tell the story and laugh about it and feel good about what we'd just done. That's the kind of guy he was. That's what we should remember.

❧

His middle name,
which he was
noticeably fond
of employing,
was Luck.

❧

This chapter was designed by Rich Silverstein,
in admiring homage to Marget Larsen.

PROFESSOR ROTZOLL'S
PREFACE

by Professor Kim Rotzoll, Ph.D.

Why, in the mid-1990s, should we concern ourselves with the words and deeds of a man whose entire advertising career spanned less than two decades through the '50s and '60s?

A DOZEN EMPLOYEES AT FLOOD TIDE

Why, in this day of international mega-agencies should we care about an agency small enough to fit inside an elderly San Francisco firehouse – with a dozen employees at flood tide?

Because, unlike the other advertising giants of the '50s and '60s, who often sought their immortalities in corporate success and large ad agencies with their names on the door, Howard Gossage left us two very personal and very compelling legacies:

(1) Some decidedly unconventional advertising.

(2) A body of criticism of advertising structure and practice sweeping from the general (advertising as an institution) to the specific (billboards). He was, as David Ogilvy acknowledged, *"Advertising's most articulate rebel."*

His advertising was an expression of his communication philosophy, it set records for responses in magazines like *The New Yorker* and developed cult status in Europe. ☙ Almost as an afterthought, it was honored in this country by his posthumous induction into the Advertising Copywriters Hall of Fame.

How To Kill An Elephant

But in a business that likes to believe bigger is better, there was always an underlying discomfort with the Gossage approach. ❧ As Howard said, *"You don't have to bruise an elephant all over to kill him. One shot in the right place will do."*

There is much in Gossage's writing that is clearly relevant to contemporary concerns. Unlike others in advertising, whose speeches and writings are usually confined to trade journals, Howard wrote for magazines such as *Harper's* and the *Atlantic Monthly.* And, of course, he was also a guiding force behind the short-lived but zesty *Ramparts.*

Wit, Panache & More...

It is easy to celebrate Gossage for his wit, panache, and general ongoing irreverence and to position him as one of those madcaps who seemed reflective of the anti-establishment fervor of the '60s. But there is much more than that. ❧ For, clearly, a dispassionate reading of these pages reveals much of pressing relevance to contemporary thought and practice in advertising as well as the larger multimedia environment in which we all "swim." For, ever the extra-environmentalist, Gossage was fond of observing,

❧

"You don't have to bruise an elephant all over to kill him. One shot in the right place will do."

❧

"We're not sure who invented water, but we're pretty sure it wasn't a fish." (As you read these pages, it will be abundantly clear how Gossage came to "discover" Marshall McLuhan.) ❧ With his unquestioned gift of taking the larger view, he offers us a catalog of critical analyses of the structure and performance of the advertising business that seems destined to persist due to its unrelenting focus on enduring elements in the system.

BY WAY OF EXAMPLE:

❧ We hear speakers hailing the era of "Integrated advertising/ marketing communications," which, as you will observe, Gossage practiced effortlessly, with an "as any fool can plainly see" élan long before it had a name.

[As to the name itself, or the "IMC" monogram, I feel certain that Howard would have kicked the whole thing off with a contest that would have had a much better result.]

Meanwhile, his comments on the commission system no longer seem at all revolutionary – merely prescient.

❧ We observe the demise of daily newspapers with circulation in the hundreds of thousands and note that, once again as Howard lamented, no one asked their readers.

HUMAN BEINGS & BEAN-COUNTERS

As we seem to see our media options multiplying, we might ponder whether these new channels are there to serve us or are merely there to deliver us to the bean-counters of marketing – more concerned with Cost Per Thousand than Cost Per Thought.

We are reminded of Howard's line, attributed to press critic, A.J. Liebling (he didn't like quoting himself), *"What good is freedom of the press if there isn't one?"*

ﾑ We turn the pages of trade papers, where advertisers bemoan less bang-for-the-buck, and we are reminded of Gossage's doubt of the wisdom of the "big stick" advertising budgets, *a billion dollar hammer pounding a ten-cent thumb tack.*

ﾑ We note ongoing evidence of viewer disenchantment with commercial television and sardonic articles on the "commercialism of just about everything," and are reminded of Gossage's searing insights into advertising as an unwelcome guest. As he said, *To ask consumers how they like ads is like asking a galley slave what he thinks of his job calisthenics-wise.*

ARMOR-PLATED FISH IN A BARREL

As media audiences demonstrate a growing "immunity" to the wiles of advertising, he reminds us that while it may seem like shooting fish in a barrel, *there is some evidence that the fish don't hold still as well as they used to and they are developing armor plate.* ﾑ Gossage wrote more than ads. He probed these and other issues of contemporary concern while he attempted to raise the consciousness of the advertising community – a daunting task, given his perception that *To explain responsibility to advertising men is like trying to convince an eight-year-old that sexual intercourse is more fun than a chocolate ice cream cone.*

ﾑ

"To explain responsibility to advertising men is like trying to convince an eight-year-old that sexual intercourse is more fun than a chocolate ice cream cone."

ﾑ

KLH & LOVE

A recent survey sponsored by KLH has proven beyond doubt that when you buy KLH stereo equipment you will love your wife (or husband) more.

Admittedly this is a flamboyant claim. However, let us review the facts:

This survey asked each respondent to assume that he was for some reason to be deprived of his wife (or husband), and to assume that dollars could somehow prevent the catastrophe.

We asked *how many* dollars it would be worth to keep her (him). Well gentlemen, the findings showed that owners of KLH equipment said, on the average, $541,616.23.

Owners of other sorts of equipment said a mere $362,615.59. There is, then, a difference of $179,000.64 in favor of the average KLH spouse.

Now if this difference in marital value is not attributable to the fact that KLH owners become more loving people, then what is it attributable to? The statistics offer us no other answer.

Oh, there will be cynics who will rationalize that these scientific findings are inconclusive.

But to us it is abundantly clear that when you buy a Model Twenty Four three piece stereo system at $320†, or a Model Twenty at $400†, and the full dynamic range of a symphony orchestra or a rock and roll group, as the case may be, or a crooner, even, is heard, as if for the first time, throbbing out from our famous speakers, you are bound to be a happier and more loving person for it, aren't you? You certainly are.

Yes.

ADDENDUM: *For complete survey data (scientific findings on other things: toothpaste, wives, mechanics, tv programming, etc.), drop us a line, saying, "Love," at KLH, 30 Cross Street, Cambridge, Mass., 02139. (If you also would like a catalog, put it this way: "Love" "Catalog.")*
Yes.

†SUGGESTED RETAIL PRICE

And From My Lecture Notes...

I had the privilege of knowing Howard Gossage when I was a young professor at Penn State. Howard took time off from his agency to teach a course called *"The Nature of Paid Propaganda,"* the mere title of which caused a highly defensive reaction in the trade press. 🕭 I remember his first lecture, when he took his place at the front of a classroom of curious studets, brushed back his silver locks over the sides of his eyeglass frames, peered at the multitude over the lenses, cleared his throat, and in his dramatic baritone intoned ... *"Are there any questions?"*

When Howard Met Sally

I remember another class when his wife, the stunning Broadway and movie actress Sally Kemp, entered the classroom in mid-lecture to a collective gasp from the student body. Howard watched silently as she made her riveting passage to the rear of the room, then explained, *"That's my wife Sally. Her external flamboyance conceals... an internal flamboyance."*

I also remember Sally speaking of the moment she first saw Howard: *"I was waiting at a restaurant when this divine man entered. He stopped and gazed over the place as if he was deciding whether or not to buy it!"*

🕭

"I was waiting at a restaurant when this divine man entered. He stopped and gazed over the place as if he was deciding whether or not to buy it!"

🕭

And, perhaps above all, I remember social occasions in the presence of a first class mind and a wonderfully engaging human being.

Over the years, I have exposed hundreds of my students to Howard's insights on both the advertising message and the advertising business's place in the society it inhabits. ❧ Not uncommonly his words strike a chord with some.

The torch is passed.

HOW THIS BOOK BEGAN...

My co-conspirators on the initial book, *Is There Any Hope for Advertising?* were **Jack Graham**, a treasured friend and professional colleague of Howard's and **Barrows Mussey,** who spread Howard's gospel through Europe as general facilitator and translator for the German book *Ist die Werbung noch zu retten?,* that still serves as the foundation for this effort. ❧ The German predecessor had been put together by Howard and Barrows from speeches, articles, correspondence, and excerpts from other published material, particularly *Dear Miss Afflerbach.*

With Barrow's help, Jack and I secured the English manuscript, which had been expanded by Barrows and Howard to include material after the German edition appeared, in addition to Howard's *Atlantic Monthly* article reflecting on the news of his leukemia. I added an earlier *Harper's* column on billboards to augment his ongoing concern with the media and advertising in general.

To this group of conspirators, we must add:

❧ **Jeff Goodby,** who works to keep the flame of Gossage burning in San Francisco, where Howard's memory lives on.

❧ **Bruce Bendinger,** the driving force behind this edition, who has added additional pieces from those who knew Gossage and gives credit to the unique graphic abilities of Marget Larsen and Robert Freeman.

Both Bruce and Jeff are examples that creativity, integrity and business success are all simultaneously possible in advertising. They honor Gossage's principles and his memory in their work and their daily lives.

&. **Herb Caen**, writing the day after Gossage's death in the *San Francisco Chronicle,* entitled his tribute, *"A Singular Man."*

And so he was. And singular, it can be argued, is his legacy to contemporary advertising thought and practice.

For all those who remember, welcome back. For those new to the man and his ideas, we expect your curiosity to be generously rewarded.

Kim Rotzoll

Urbana, Illinois

Professor Kim Rotzoll is Dean of the College of Communications of the University of Illinois Urbana-Champaign.

He is author of: Advertising in Contemporary Society *(with James Haefner and Charles Sandage),* Media Ethics *(with Clifford Christians and Mark Fackler),* Advertising Theory and Practice *(with Charles Sandage and Vernon Fryburger), and an editor of the original* Is There Any Hope for Advertising?

He is past president of the American Academy of Advertising (1991) and was named the American Advertising Federation's Distinguished Advertising Educator (1992).

[by Howard Gossage]

AFTER FREBERG, WHAT? *

The Summer of 1957 witnessed radio's first real triumph since the advent of TV. ★ *Sputnik's signal, however, was not expandable to a half-hour weekly show. Freberg's was.* ★ *In some ways his triumph was greater than Sputnik's; he never had to share billing with a dog act.* ★ *Freberg orbited 15 weeks on the CBS Radio Network, unafraid, undaunted, unsponsored; alone except for the 6,000,000 foolhardy souls who joined him each Sunday at the outer-humor launching pad.* ★ *Why unsponsored with 6,000,000 listeners? Well, you have to look at this with advertising logic: six million is only about 3% of the total U.S. population and you'll certainly admit that 3 is an awfully dinky little number, won't you?* ★ *Besides, everyone knows that nobody cares about humor, satire, and touchy subjects anymore. Nobody except you, CBS (it was radio's highest budgeted new show in ten years), and Freberg.*

[Liner Notes from The Madison Ave. Werewolf and other hilarious moments from "The Best of the Stan Freberg Show." *An actual © Capitol Records record album. This pre-CD artifact was recently unearthed from the Editor's basement — Mr. Freberg's basement didn't quite make it through the Earthquake.]*

[by Stan Freberg]

MY BEST FRIEND

★ ★ ★ ★ ★ ★ ★ ★ ★ ★ ★ ★ ★ ★

Howard Gossage, while he was alive, was my best friend. ★ He came into my life circa 1956, as I wrote in my book: *It Only Hurts When I Laugh.* [fade up on page 93 . . .]

"One day in 1956, I received a call, totally out of the blue, from the creative director of a San Francisco advertising agency. ★ The caller's name was Howard Gossage. ★ How do I describe his voice? He had an endearing stammer that gave e-e-e-extra emphasis to the vowel sounds.

It sort of went like this...

SFX: Telephone.
FREBERG: Hello.
GOSSAGE: Stan Freee-e-e-berg?
FREBERG: Yes...
GOSSAGE: Have you ever done any aaaa-aaadvertising?
FREBERG: No.
GOSSAGE: Good. Juuu...just the man I want.

★ ★ ★

Feeling the way I did about advertising, hating the hard sell I was assaulted with from my car radio each day, I felt I suddenly had been given the opportunity as a consumer to, in effect, answer back, to create some commercials that didn't take themselves so damn seriously. I decided to try it as a lark.

Gossage flew down to Los Angeles, and we had lunch at the Brown Derby. Within minutes I realized I had met a rare bird indeed. As a radio and television performer, I had been exposed to many agency people in the sponsor's booth. To a man, they all acted like every word of their commercials was straight from the Bill of Rights. ★ The hard and boring sell they were responsible for were holy words. Worse, they took themselves as seriously as if they were delegates to the United Nations.

I could detect no qualities of any other ad man I had ever met in Howard Gossage. In fact here was an advertising man whose contempt for the content of most commercials and ads easily equaled my own. ★ Gossage, a brilliant copywriter, had his own unique sense of humor and a terrific sense of style. He showed me a copy of a recent *New Yorker* magazine. It contained a full-page ad he had written for QANTAS, the Australian airline. The headline was surely a first for an airline, "BE THE FIRST ONE ON YOUR BLOCK TO WIN A KANGAROO." I realized I had met what for me was a first: an ad man who refused to take himself or advertising too seriously. ★ That day at lunch, I knew I was talking to a fellow iconoclast.

From that moment on, even though he lived in San Francisco, and I lived 500 miles to the south in Beverly Hills, we spoke on the phone almost daily. We shared the same sense of humor, and the tears would roll down our cheeks as we reduced each other to helpless laughter, hundreds of miles apart.

So many memories crowd my mental hard disk. One of the first Freberg/Gossage collaborations was an ad I produced for him for Qantas Airlines. He had run that famous "WIN A KANGAROO" ad in *The New Yorker*. ★ Now we had to select a winner from the minor avalanche of entries that had poured in.

He asked me to put an incongruous panel of judges together, including myself and arrange to have us photographed for the next *New Yorker* ad. I assembled the following: seated in evening clothes were: Olympic Champion Pole Vaulter, Rev. Bob Richards, holding his pole aloft; CEO of Abbey Rents, Stanley Slotkin; actress Anna Mae Wong; myself; and a live kangaroo. (A black bow tie on the kangaroo.) ★ The marsupial wouldn't sit still and bounded about the studio, gouging up the photographer's expensive hardwood parquet floor with his long toenails. We finally got the shot and Howard got the bill for a new floor.

Meanwhile, I was working with Howard on that radio campaign. [Cut back to *It Only Hurts When I Laugh*, page 96.] ★ Gossage had an immediate problem with one of his clients, Contadina Foods. After being successful for years, this little tomato-paste packer was suddenly in danger of being buried by the giant Hunts company. He wondered if I could create and produce some radio commercials and later, TV. "Only if I can do them as unorthodoxly as possible," I said. He assured me that he would be disappointed with anything less. ★ Howard was

The radio commercials I created were immediately questioned by everyone at his agency. The first thing they heard was a song I had written, which never mentioned the sponsor's name.

a fan, he said, of my records and television appearances. He said he had a hunch that humor might help. He said he thought he could talk the agency and client into a radio campaign, but he didn't want the ordinary type of "straight" radio spots. ★ He said that was why he was coming to a professional comedy writer who had also been successful creating humor for the "ear."

The radio commercials I created were immediately questioned by everyone at his agency. The first thing they heard was a song I had written, which never mentioned the sponsor's name. ★ Upon learning from Howard that there was the equivalent of eight tomatoes smashed down into each can of Contadina Tomato Paste, I came up with a jingle: *"Who Puts Eight Great Tomatoes in That Little Bitty Can?"* I sang it myself with the Buddy Cole Jazz Quartet, and after repeating the question three times, I ended the song not with the sponsor's name, but with the line, *"You know who, you know who, you know who!"* After an embarrassing pause, an announcer cleared his throat and straightened it out: *"Ahem … in case you don't, it's Contadina Tomato Paste."*

Although I was not present when the agency heard my commercials, Gossage gave me a blow-by-blow report. ★ When they first heard them, he said, they were more or less stunned. *"Where are the recipes the client wanted demonstrating how to use tomato paste?"* they asked Gossage. *"How come he didn't tell how much thicker Contadina is than Hunts?"*

Howard just smiled and played the next Freberg spot. Would they get those recipes now? Not likely. The scene was a quiet conversation taking place on the wind-swept top of the Empire State Building.

FREBERG: Now look, you got it straight what we want you to do?

MAN: I think so, uhh, you want me to take down the tower from on top of the Empire State Building here and put up a three-hundred-foot can of Contadina Tomato Paste.

FREBERG: That's right.

MAN: (NERVOUSLY) Look, have you checked with the Empire State Building people? I mean … is it all right with *them?*

FREBERG: Wel-l-l, there's always somebody working on the building… They won't know the difference.

MAN: Yeah, but that tower was put there to moor zeppelins to.

FREBERG: Let's face it – how many zeppelins have moored there in the last week?

MAN: Well… not many, but I'm not sure I want to get involved.

FREBERG: You want us to get another contractor? Is that it?

MAN: No, but we could be arrested!

FREBERG: Suppose you let me worry about that, okay? Now, don't forget to have the can blink day and night the words "There are many delicious uses for Contadina Tomato Paste."

MAN: Wait a minute! I thought you wanted it to blink "Eight Great Tomatoes in That Little Bitty Can?"

FREBERG: Hmmmmmmmmmmm.

MAN: Which do you want?

FREBERG: Well, let me sleep on it. Okay?

MAN: Okay.

After a long silence, the head of the agency spoke: "That's it? That's the end of the commercial?" Gossage pointed out that Contadina's main competition, Hunts, was using normal advertising. Maybe the way to get people's attention was to use *ab*normal advertising. ★ "It's not *any* kind of advertising, as far as I can see. What the hell *is* it, anyhow?" muttered one old-line account executive. "It's just two guys talking on top of a building! How can we play *that* for the client?"

How indeed. They just got on a plane for San Jose the next day at Howard's insistence and played it for the Marrici brothers, who owned Contadina, and their staff. ★ Everyone hated the commercials. Everyone except the president, Marty Marrici, who happened to be the only one who laughed. "Let's see what the brokers say," Marrici shrugged. They were played for his food brokers and salesmen. To a man, they hated them, too. In spite of this avalanche of negative opinion, and over the protesting of his staff, Marrici okayed the campaign, and the first Stan Freberg commercials hit the air. ★ They were an immediate smash hit with disc jockeys, who went on talking about them on the air long after the commercials had ended, and after a few weeks sales were up dramatically.

Within three months Hunts had cut its price twice, and six months later it was giving away one free case with every ten to the grocers in an effort to catch up. Contadina recovered from the staggering blow Hunts had dealt it originally and raced way ahead of its competitor. ★ *Advertising Age* magazine later that year picked the two most outstanding marketing successes of the year. One of them was the Contadina campaign based on Howard's "hunch." ★ Suddenly, I was established as some new kind of advertising problem solver. Howard had started me in the world of advertising. Ultimately, I forgave him.

I continued to create more radio campaigns for Howard's various clients. After leaving Cunningham & Walsh, he formed his own agency. Twice. First with Joe Weiner, and finally with Bob Freeman, the art director who brought the equally brilliant art director Marget Larsen aboard Weiner & Gossage, which later evolved into Freeman & Gossage. ★ The exquisite taste of Marget Larsen transformed an old San Francisco firehouse into a beautiful place to work. The brass pole was preserved, and the second floor conference room became a place where some of the city's famous people would frequently gather as Howard held court in a kind of salon. ★ Herb Caen, legendary *San Francisco Chronicle* columnist; Warren Hinckle III, editor of the wild and influential *Ramparts Magazine,* to which Howard had become a kind of unofficial advisor; Cyril Magnin, department store major domo/philanthropist; writer Jessica Mitford [*The American Way of Death*]; bullfighter and novelist Barnaby Conrad [*Death in the Afternoon*]; Dr. Gerald Feigen and, when in town, me.

It was in this room that Howard would introduce the press to a then obscure University of Toronto professor named Marshall McLuhan whom Howard discovered and flew in from the University of Toronto. ★ Howard had happened upon McLuhan's brilliant but scholarly textbook, *Understanding Media,* and some sort of lightning bolt crashed in his brain. ★ McLuhan would later say that Howard was one of the first people to understand the point of his book.

As soon as Howard figured it out, he explained to McLuhan what he, McLuhan, was trying to say. And now Howard was going to explain McLuhan to the world. I was there that day.

Mostly, I remember Howard staring aghast at the professor's legs. Between the tops of his droopy socks and the bottoms of his tweed trousers, was a no-man's land of sickly white ankle. ★ The press, everybody from the AP to novelist Tom Wolfe were due within the hour and here sat *"possibly the most important thinker since Newton, Darwin, Freud, Einstein and Pavlov: what if he is right?"* – as Tom Wolfe would later write – here sat this media mega-guru with ankles flashing like white neon mailing tubes. ★ *"Cooooome with me!"* Gossage said, and rushed McLuhan to Brooks Bros. where he traded in his droopy gray nylon anklets for black over-the-calf socks. Then Howard paraded him back in to meet the press. And the rest is history.*

McLuhan apparently considered such things as long hose and properly tied neckties too trivial to bother with. He was given to popping on a cheap pre-tied tie suspended by two plastic pieces that slid under his collar. ★ In the time saved by not tying a tie he could figure out another "extension of man." ("The car is just an extension of your legs," etc.) But back to Gossage, the discoverer of McLuhan.

★ ★ *HOWARD'S HIDEAWAY* ★ ★

It turned out Howard was unable to actually write in that brightly lit, second floor conference room. He thought best at night. So Marget designed a tiny darkened third floor hideaway office in the top of the Firehouse. *"I've made this as close to perpetual night-time as possible,"* Howard told me as we sat in the gloom.

*You can read more about that particular escapade in "What If He's Right?" by Tom Wolfe.

An Irish green glow from a green desk lamp the only light in a room with windows blocked from sunlight by thick velvet drapes. "I have to trick my brain into thinking it's night-time or I can't produce anything." ★ In the last years, now married again to a beautiful redhaired actress, Sally Kemp, he abandoned the distractions of even that hideaway Firehouse office, and continued to write his beautiful ads for Irish Whiskey and Eagle Shirts in the relative quiet of his home.

Howard, more than anyone, influenced the way I think about advertising. Not a day goes by, that I don't think of him in some way, and miss him dearly. Even the part of Howard that was, at times, curmudgeon-ish. ★ Once, when Howard was staying at the Garden of Allah Hotel in Hollywood, I wrote with him in his room, until the wee hours, and was too tired to drive home, so I got a room next to him. In the morning, I loaned him a can of Aramis underarm deodorant from the toilet articles kit I'd dragged from my car, as well as a can of Aramis Hair Spray. ★ Unfortunately, the line of toiletries had been designed by some smartass art director in identical brown colors, and the only way you could tell which was which, was to read the fine print on the bottom. Before I could point this out to Howard, he had, of course, sprayed his long silver hair with deodorant, and his armpits with hair spray. Gossage – a man not overly pleasant first thing in the morning anyhow – was not pleased to find the hair in his armpits as stiff as a wire-haired terrier. ★ Repeated splashing of his armpits did no good, and three days later, after multiple showers, he walked around holding his arms out like he was a DC10. As time went on, he got a lot of laughs telling people what I had wreaked (my fault of course) upon his armpits.

One day, on a trip to San Francisco, Howard invited me to lunch. We ate at Barnaby Conrad's restaurant, not far from the Firehouse. ★ Present were Howard, Herb Caen, Conrad, myself and John Steinbeck. ★ Steinbeck had just completed his book *Travels With Charley,* an account of criss-crossing America in a motorhome, with his dog, Charley. ★ At one point, I asked Steinbeck which part of America Charley liked best. The Pulitzer Prize-winning novelist thought for a minute and answered, *"all things considered, I guess he liked the redwood trees."* Big laugh.

"*Gee,*" I said, *"what is there left for a dog once he's pee'd on a redwood tree?"* Long pause.

Then Howard said, *"Wel-l-l-l-l, he could teach."*

Howard Gossage left us all too soon. But he even turned that into an event. There was his *"Tell Me Doctor…"* article which appeared in the *Atlantic.* ★ And, when he passed away, there was a fairly lengthy piece in the *New York Times* written by another Pulitzer Prize winner and F.O.G. (Friend of Gossage), Seymour Hersh. I remember getting the call. ★ I knew Howard was counting on me to do my part. Seymour was on the line, and it just came out.

"*Well,*" I said, *"Howard finally got out of advertising."*

© *1994 Stan Freberg*

Send This Ad Man to Camp.

As Stan Freberg remembers it…"We were doing a photo shoot, and Howard found this canoe paddle … and the hat.

He said, 'Let's do a photo for an ad called Send This Ad Man to Camp.'

So we did.

I really don't think he had an ad in mind. I think he was referring to one of my gags where I showed a bunch of thin Vogue *fashion models — all cheekbones and angles — and suggested that we send these thin young women to camp.*

We never really got around to doing the ad, but I always loved the photograph. Howard had a great sense of humor."

Stan Freberg is the creative force behind [and in front of] some of the most popular comedy in audio. His classic satires of pop music. His revolutionary radio show [we thought the acrobats were a nice touch]. His modestly titled audio epic Stan Freberg *presents the* United States of America, *as well as his uniquely entertaining advertising have become a part of American culture. From iconoclast to cultural icon. We see that we're running out of room on the page, so we will quickly mention that you should make a general nuisance of yourself at your local book store — or with Times Books in New York to get yourself a copy of* It Only Hurts When I Laugh. *If you're of the MTV generation, you might want to grab a* Collector's Series: Stan Freberg *CD or cassette. Probably found under Comedy. His …United States of America album is also available on CD. Check out the classic "Everybody Wants to Be an Art Director."*

★ ★ ★ *by Bruce Bendinger* ★ ★ ★

[As the millenium approaches, strange and slightly magical forces appear with San Francisco at the epicenter. Is this "Flaithiulach" at work?]

CITIZEN GOSSAGE

★ ★ ★ ★ ★ ★ ★ ★ ★ ★ ★ ★ ★

WHERE did it begin? Was it Goodby's office? Or maybe halfway through *That Old Black, White, or Pango Peach Magic?* Frankly, I have no idea. ★ But somewhere along the way, I have become most thoroughly and delightfully *haunted* by a laughing Irish ghost.

And now I see the world in a brand new way.

[THE POWER OF PARENTHESES]

Howard Gossage is with us. Never met the man. But I hear his laugh. ★ And you know something, Tom Wolfe? Howard was right!

McLuhan's media prophecies have all come true [though they seem to look like a channel changer]. ★ San Francisco is turning into a city state [by fault line or default]. Parentheses are popping up in the latest ads [just saw some more in Hal Riney's ads for Saturn]. ★ Dingbats instead of paragraphs. And everywhere you turn, the Hot Dog Vendors have taken over every game in town.

Howard warned us. But did we listen? Nah!

SLIGHTLY HINDU

Remember *Citizen Kane?* A reporter wanders through the screenplay asking actors what Orson Welles was like. ★ Hey, it can happen to you.

At first, you feel in control – with a featured role in your very own movie. Then, somewhere along the line, you realize someone else is writing the script.

You begin to go slightly Hindu. ★ And, like a good movie, you discover that a life can hold up through another viewing – and another. ★ You see things you didn't notice the first time through. Early scenes take on new meaning. Subplots unfold. You begin to share it with friends. ★ Putting this book together was something like that. Magic at work – Pango Peach or otherwise.

A PLAIN BROWN WRAPPER

For example, when it was time to write this piece, a book showed up on my desk – in a plain brown wrapper. ★ The package was from a book search specialist in Moscow, Idaho by way of an advertising professor then living in the state of Washington [Thanks, Bill Huey]. ★ The book was [and still is] Warren Hinckle's memories of *Ramparts – If You Have a Lemon, Make Lemonade.*

"Gossage was the Socrates of San Francisco. (He) operated the Firehouse as if it were a French court, and he the captive king."

> *"He believed every man should be comfortable while engaging in the necessary business of rescuing the world."*

The book's title is based on one of Howard's classic lines – which was also, upon occasion, his philosophy of life. ★ I pick it up. The pages open to the moment Howard enters…

WARREN HINCKLE

"Gossage was the Socrates of San Francisco. ★ Visiting lions from Tom Wolfe to Terry Thomas came to call on him in the magnificently restored old firehouse on Pacific Street that was his place of work, and for a time, when Howard and his buddy Herb Caen were both between marriages and batching it about town, place of residence. ★ Gossage operated the Firehouse as if it were a French court, and he the captive king. ★ He did everything first class – he ate, flew, wrote, talked, traveled first class. ★ He believed every man should be comfortable while engaging in the necessary business of rescuing the world.

He was at the same time as open and innocent as a doe-eyed calf and as crafty as a raunchy old owl. ★ Howard was, nominally, in the advertising business. That at least was how he made his living, but he did it wholly on his own terms – first class – and with an originality of purpose and imagination that staggered the redundant minds of his profession."

[48]

The book goes on to talk about Howard bringing *Ramparts Magazine* a new art director – Dugald Stermer *"a Southern California beach boy turned to talent whom Gossage had singled out when judging an art director's contest in Houston."*

Today, Dugald Stermer is a well-known San Francisco artist and designer [he designed the medals for the LA Olympics – among other things]. ★ I got his phone number and called him…

DUGALD STERMER

I'm talking to Dugald on the phone – fingers flying across the keyboard – watching the words scroll across my computer screen – not much of a movie scene – but Howard's spirit comes alive as Dugald digs deep into a drawer full of memories…

"He was unsurpassed as an advertising copywriter and as a talent scout. ★ I met him in Houston and moved to San Francisco to do Ramparts *– largely at his instigation. He had a hobby of saving people – even if they weren't drowning. ★ He called me one day and said, 'Let's go to lunch. I think we need to re-do* Harper's Magazine.' *We have an eight hour lunch and then he calls his friend Bill Blair, the publisher of* Harper's. *Bill says, 'Let me think about it.' ★ A day or so later, Bill calls back and says 'Fly Dugald in.' That was the beginning. I designed maybe two dozen magazines after that."*

Dugald pauses and continues … *"He had this great talent to stop people, find out what they wanted to do and then the means to help them do what they wanted to do. I thought of something the other day and I looked for someone to tell it to. ★ Howard was the one to call and say 'let's raise hell here.' That's why people miss him."*

A few days later, some material arrives from Dugald - including a small leather bound book – about three inches square – with "HLG" embossed on the cover. It was a private publication Stanley Marcus had done in memory of Howard (©1984 by The Somesuch Press). ★ I page through it… there's Herb Caen's column, Howard's *Tell Me Doctor…* piece for the *Atlantic*. Then there's a piece I've never seen before.

It's by Jessica Mitford, author of a number of books, including *The American Way of Death,* a popular book on the exorbitant cost of funerals. ★ Naturally, Howard put her in charge of his funeral. ★ This wasn't Howard's way of keeping expenses down – never a Gossage trademark – it was just one more way to extract one more bit of humor from his fate. ★ I look up at the bookshelf, and see one of my wife's favorite books, *A Fine Old Conflict* by Jessica Mitford. I start paging through her memories of Howard…

JESSICA MITFORD

"Looking back, it seems incredible that I actually knew Howard Gossage for only five or six years; somehow during that time my husband Bob Truehaft and I, Howard and his wife Sally, managed to cram in a lifetime of friendship. We first met shortly after publication of The American Way of Death *in 1963. ★ Amongst the fan letters – mostly from well-intentioned readers deploring funerary excess – was one from Howard Gossage; a name unfamiliar to me, as advertising men apparently don't advertise themselves."*

How about that? Most ad folks need multimillion dollar ad budgets. Gossage uses a stamp. ★ He writes a letter and men [or women] of letters respond. His letter contained what Ms. Mitford *"came to cherish as the famous Gossage twist."* It recounted a memory from preparations for his mother's funeral…

"Howard was in the usual fog of misery on such occasions, longing to get the whole thing over with. He quickly chose a coffin. ★ The undertaker told him, 'Now you must choose the casket lining,' and he held up two

swatches of material which appeared to be identical. ★ 'This one is pure silk,' the undertaker explained. 'And this is rayon, cheaper of course. But we do find that rayon is more irritating to the skin.'

A few years later I fed this line to the film makers of The Loved One – who seized upon it, causing it to be repeated by Liberace, their inspired choice for the role of casket salesman. ★ Once in a while, on the late-night television, one can catch Liberace repeating Howard's deathless words."

She goes on to recount various tales of the days of *Ramparts* and McLuhan. ★ When Howard knew the end was near, he said, "*Go ring up Decca. She'll be able to ferret out the cheapest funeral in town.*" And she did. $150. ★ After the funeral, his ashes were scattered over Drake's Bay in an airplane flown by Howard's friend, Carl Ally…

CARL ALLY

Carl Ally is on the line – Advertising Hall of Fame and all that. Laughing, full of memories…

"*I was one of Howard's Cotton Pickers [New York chapter] – it was such a great little rat pack – always raising hell. I met him through Bob Freeman. In five minutes we connected – we were kindred spirits.*

"*Once in a while, on the late-night television movies, one can catch Liberace repeating Howard's deathless words.*"

He'd call up at strange times to talk about things like environmental stuff, human rights, fairness and justice. ★ *Howard wasn't that interested in advertising – he was interested in what was right, what was wrong, what was kind, what was cruel.*

He was an awesome figure in those days. Everyone in San Francisco knew who he was. In a business lacking in ornamentation, he was one of the ornaments." We talk. ★ Once again, Howard's name is the magic key that opens people up. Carl tells the tale of flying in from Switzerland and renting the plane – to scatter Howard's ashes over Drake's Bay. And the punch line. ★ We talk some more – about getting Howard Gossage into the Advertising Hall of Fame – about Bob Freeman and all the people at the Firehouse – like President Alice Lowe...

President Alice Lowe

It's Saturday morning. I'm driving through one of those parts of San Francisco where people are so dedicated to living there, they perch on the sides of hills. ★ I wind my way up streets, double back, and squeeze my rent-a-car into a parking place angled semi-sideways...

There, at the top of the stairs is President Alice Lowe. ★ She ran Howard's agency and was, at one time or another, President of all or part of his other intellectually far-flung enterprises. [See "The Shade Tree Memorandum."] ★ At this moment, she is Chair of the Asian American Art Museum of San Francisco [a promotion from President, I see]. Her Chinese name is, "Precious Jade." Howard called her "Presh." ★ She introduces me to her husband, Lewis, who was a designer with Walter Landor [another San Francisco legend – his design firm was on a ferryboat].

We sit and talk. Her voice has music in it – the words served up with an undertone of warm laughter... ★ *"It really was a magic time,"* she says. *"Maybe we didn't know it at the time, but it really was..."*

And the conversation begins. ★ Morning turns to afternoon and the sunlight turns golden as she shares memories from twenty-some years ago. ★ The magic seems contagious. Along the way, some of it rubbed off on Lewis.

Official Hat Day Photograph

We sit and enjoy his kit of avant garde paper airplanes [inspired by the *Scientific American* Paper Airplane Contest] and dig out some clippings of his appearance on *What's My Line* – as a "paper airplane designer." (Alan Alda guessed it. Go figure.)

We page through old photographs – the official Hat Day photograph – a magical shot of Marget with a parrot. ★ It all comes alive again. Name another agency in history that had an official Hat Day.

And then there was the story of how Howard met Herb Caen...

Herb Caen, Pen Pal.

Their friendship began shortly after Herb left the *San Francisco Chronicle* for the *Examiner* [he's back at the *Chronicle* for those of you who don't live in San Francisco]. ★ Anyway, people were accusing Herb of being a "fink, sell-out, rotten so and so." The usual.

Caen recalls, *"The letter that got to me was a one-liner from a man I had never heard of till that time. ★ On a distinctive piece of stationery headed 'Howard Luck Gossage' in a very distinctive handwriting, it said, 'Are you the same Herb Caen who used to work for the* Chronicle?'"

That was the start of a daily one-upmanship competition. By mail. ★ Herb continues, *"It got to the point where I was writing a column as fast as I could, getting it out of the way and spending the rest of the day trying to think of some great letter to Gossage which would top his.*"

By tacit agreement, they agreed not to meet.

Their letter-writing continued for four years. ★ One day, to their dismay, they found themselves seated at the same table at an Ad Club luncheon. They managed to avoid speaking to each other. ★ Afterwards, both happened to stop off in the same bar for a drink. Again, they ignored each other. ★ A mutual acquaintance, surprised that these well-known personalities seemed to be strangers, asked, puzzled, *"Haven't you two ever met?"* ★ *"That does it,"* sighed Howard, extending his hand.

The relationship grew from pen pals to a long rich friendship, including the legendary lunches where *"you'd find yourself building a pastrami sandwich next to Dr. Benjamin Spock. Or pouring a beer for John Steinbeck. Or listening to Buckminster Fuller. Or laughing at the bad jokes of Marshall McLuhan."*

THE POWER OF FLAITHIULACH

Alice Lowe mentions some memoirs she wrote right after Howard died. She promises to find them and send a copy to me. ★ Sure enough, a package arrives a few weeks later – they're carbons! Remember carbon paper? ★ I'm reading them, turning the pale green pages – what's this Irish word on page two? *Flaithiulach* [Fla-hoo-lik] ★ Hmmm… it means *"princely exuberance, generosity and lavishness."* I'm into it now – the gatherings at the Firehouse, the friendships – even the mail.

Alice mentioned letters from John Steinbeck. Ah, here they are…

JOHN STEINBECK

It started in typical Gossage fashion – Howard wrote a letter. The idea was to have John Steinbeck write ad copy for Rover. ★ Actually, no ads were ever done, but who cared – the relationship turned into a rollicking friendship. ★ Howard seemed to have that effect on people.

By the time Steinbeck writes this letter, he's clearly caught up in it. ★ He's ready to enter into a very Gossage-like enterprise.

We can surmise that Steinbeck has already been seduced by Howard's talk of the practical uses of magic… *"Dear Howard,* ★ *After you left I had an idea for a big business deal. We advertise the name PRAG-MAG but never say what it is nor what it is for. It is a new application of an old and tested formula… it is unbelievable and it works.* ★ *Its effectiveness is attested by doctors, psychiatrists, Duke University, and Madison Avenue.* ★ *I'll bet we could get millions of orders before we even decide on the packaging. Maybe it will be all packaging.* ★ *The name, of course, is a synthesis of pragmatic magic. People sell it all the time."* [For more about pragmatic – or practical – magic, turn to the "Black, White, or Pango Peach Magic" article Howard wrote for *Harper's.*] ★ Steinbeck continues…

"We would be the first to face the product squarely and know what we are dealing with. ★ *There's a fortune in it. And if we don't say what it is nor what it is for, we can't get in trouble with the AMA or FTC.* ★ *Let me know what you think of this. I think it would make our fortune. I never made a fortune and I think I might like one.* ★ *See you. And please put*

"Dear Gossage: I see no reason to beat about the bush. I have an invention that can and will make our fortune."

"It has everything — vanity, laziness, status, horse shit and it works. It can also be used only once and is disposable so that it clogs the plumbing in the good old American way."

PRAG-MAG in the works."

Name another ad man in history who spent time goofing around with his buddy the Nobel Prize-winning novelist. ★ This "Flahoolick," or whatever it is, is seductive stuff. ★ Here's another letter…

"Dear Gossage: I see no reason to beat about the bush. I have an invention that can and will make our fortune. It has everything — vanity, laziness, status, horse shit — and it works. ★ It can also be used only once and is disposable so that it clogs the plumbing in the good old American way.

Its market is women who control 97.81615% of the national income. ★ As we know, 94% of American women don't know their ass from a hole in the ground, a natural error. ★ This is six percent better than men.

A good invention should be 1. unnecessary. 2. 50% flap doodle, 37% advertising, 90% packaging, and $1/_2$% actual ingredients." ★ Steinbeck proceeds to outline his idea — a cellophane bag with a little bit of detergent in it. It's perfect for washing *"the dainties."* The product even has instructions…

"My lady puts her stockings, her bras and her panties in the dry bag, adds approximately a quart of warm water, twists the top of the bag and seals it with the rubber band. ★ She is now

able to rub, to massage, to soak her dainty things without wetting her hands, hereinafter known as her prehensile glories."

Steinbeck exhorts Gossage to join him in his venture, "asking for the order," like any good ad man. *"I propose that we go into business. ★ We can call the parent or holding company, Horse Shit and Sons. ★ This is only the first of many aids to loneliness. I think I have something pretty important here, particularly now with the Bomb and all. …will you get onto this? A tie-in with Lever Bros. would take all the work out of it. ★ …if this should go, I have eight others for exploiting our natural infirmities for pleasure and profit. Yours, John."*

There's more – and it's not all light-hearted. Here's an earlier letter on planned obsolescence, advertising in general, and Detroit in particular. ★ Steinbeck writes…

"If you in advertising could teach people to demand, to recognize and take pride in a good job rather than in a bunch of status junk, then advertising could be a respectable profession again, and it sure as hell isn't now. ★ Well, that's it. If you want to buy copy from me, I'll give you the best copy I can write but I won't write it about a bad product. ★ That would put me on a level with the slop that is packaged and delivered in this country. Iron poor blood, my ass!

"If you in advertising could teach people to demand, to recognize and take pride in a good job rather than in a bunch of status junk, then advertising could be a respectable profession again, and it sure as hell isn't now."

"If you want to buy copy from me, I'll give you the best copy I can write but I won't write it about a bad product. That would put me on a level with the slop that is packaged and delivered in this country. Iron poor blood, my ass!"

And if this means anything to you, make the most of it. ★ *Actually, standards of excellence have been so muddied and distorted for the sake of a quick buck that all objective approach is abandoned in despair.* ★ *But far from being wary – we seem to be increasingly drugged.* ★ *If Detroit could build a car that would melt and run out through your fingers they would. And people would buy it too."*

★ Sure were a lot of interesting people hanging around the Firehouse. ★ I smile and remember Stan Freberg's story about Steinbeck's dog, Charley...

STAN FREBERG

"Stan Freberg's on the phone!" Lorelei and Mairee call out and I dash in from the balcony. Celebrity Alert! ★ The phone seems to glow slightly with the magic of celebrity. ★ Jeez! Stan Freberg – the guy who did all those records – I loved those records – played the grooves off them. I pick up the phone and hear his voice. Wow! It sounds just like him.

"Hi, you don't know me," I say, stating the obvious – and I stumble through my well-rehearsed synopsis – telling him about the book that seems to be putting itself together. ★ Suddenly, the conversation changes – the sarcasm leaves his voice... ★ *"He was my best friend,"* Freberg the Famous says softly.

"I think about him every day."

Once again, I am caught up in friendships and memories from twenty-five years ago. ★ There's almost a bond. I'm an ad guy. Freberg hates ad guys. He's being nice to me – sort of.

I feel comfortable enough to kid him about *"Oregon! Oregon!"* a little known mini-musical comedy done to celebrate and commemorate the 100th anniversary of Oregon's statehood. [Blitz-Weinhard paid for it.] ★ It was one of Howard and Stan's flights of fancy – Jeff Goodby told me about it – among other things...

JEFF GOODBY

Watch out for this guy Goodby. ★ Not only does he know how to succeed in one of the toughest businesses in the universe – but he goes home to spend time with the kids – not a strong suit in the world of advertising. ★ I met Jeff through a mutual friend, the generous and gregarious George Burrows. Almost instantly, Jeff and I found ourselves caught up in a very Gossage-like scheme – this book.

What is going on here? I don't know him. He doesn't know me. But hey, we both know Howard. ★ *"Sure, I'll write the intro,"* says Jeff. ★ *"Hey, I'll publish it,"* says Bruce. ★ Jeff turns and opens a drawer. *"This might help."* He hands me one of the only copies in the known universe of Bob Freeman's memoirs.

I look at the hand-made book called *Sometimes It's an Ad.* ★ I sip wine and quietly page through this vintage labor of love and friendship, sensing, I think, what was to come. ★ I learn more later. Bob Freeman wasn't a writer, he was an art director and a loyal friend – sort of the graphic glue that helped the Firehouse Gang hang together, helping people like Howard and the legendary designer, Marget Larsen, hit the heights.

In the years after Howard and Marget left us, Bob Freeman put this book together. ★ It was the beginning of this project and the *CA* article on Marget Larsen is excerpted from that book. ★ But that was to come. Meanwhile, I was in Goodby's office as the early evening rolled on.

George decants just a bit more of a particularly well-selected red wine. Rich Silverstein wanders in with some new *New Yorker* ads. Gorgeous. ★ We talk about Gossage's ads in *The New Yorker*. ★ I decide it's a great idea to produce a line of TV Trays made from *New Yorker* covers… more wine. ★ Rich rolls his eyes and decides it's time to go look at some type mechanicals. Children appear. ★ Jeff's daughter autographs an article on advertising that she helped her father write and Jeff goes home with the wife and kids. ★ George and I stare at Bob Freeman's memoirs, *"Sometimes it's an ad"*…

True fact. ★ For many years, a photo of Howard hung high in the entrance way of Jeff and Rich's agency. ★ And while it was always clear that Goodby and Silverstein's success was a result of their talent and intelligence, I'm starting to have this funny suspicion – one that grows with every bit of good fortune that happened with this book. ★ Did that picture of Howard Luck Gossage in the lobby sprinkle a little extra Irish good luck on the good folks at Goodby's? Is it "Flahoolick" at work? Makes you think.

So I'm thinking.

For me, one more piece of the puzzle remains. Dugald and Alice and Freberg mention that Tom Wolfe was at that famous funeral, too.

★ ★ ★ ★ TOM WOLFE! ★ ★ ★ ★

What the heck was he doing there? My daughter gets me his phone number [she won't tell me how] and I call him.

Tom Wolfe & the Firehouse Gang

In 1965, Clay Felker sent Tom Wolfe out to San Francisco to cover "The McLuhan Festival," which was Howard's introduction of Marshall McLuhan to the world of media. ★ When the dust settled, another character had joined the gang. Here's what Mr. Bonfire of the Right Stuff had to say upon meeting Howard – it's in an article called "Maybe He's Right."

"This Gossage has a certain wild cosmic laugh. His eyes light up like Stars of Bethlehem. The laugh comes in waves, from far back in the throat, like echoes from Lane 27 of a bowling alley, rolling booming far beyond the immediate situation...

Alice tells me Howard and Tom became great friends after the McLuhan caper and that he visited the Firehouse and stayed at Howard's place in San Francisco. ★ Freberg says he spoke at Howard's funeral. ★ Ah, here it is… Wolfe talks about the party Howard threw in New York to announce his [Howard's] upcoming demise…

"I'll never forget his telling me how many people were angry with him for not telling them first. They seemed to be really put out and so he had me laughing with him. He had on a marvelous crazy necktie and we went down to dinner at the Carlyle dining room in New York. Not until then did it really sink in, like a blow to the back of the neck, what he was telling me. ★ At the time, I thought he was just trying to spare me the embarrassment and the agony of his own tragedy but I think he was doing a lot more.

That dinner had ended in the Carlyle dining room, with this fancy fancy vaulted ceiling. The hour had been growing late and the maitre d', by way of showing the gravity of overstaying our leave in the Carlyle dining room, had come up and put the bill on the table. ★ Howard turned to him, fixed him with a stare that he could summon up whenever he felt like it, and said, 'I don't remember asking you for the check.'"

"The maitre d' looked at him with absolute, total perplexity because obviously, never in his forty-five years reigning in that little swatch of Madison Avenue, had anyone ever talked back to him on any subject. ★ *Then, Howard broke into his cosmic laugh and it went rolling through the Carlyle Hotel."*

The laugh. I can hear it. Can you? ★ Wolfe continues…

"And, as he said it, just as he so often did when discussing his doctor's assessment of leukemia, that it was fatal but not serious, he would break into laughter. ★ *I realized weeks after that meeting in the Carlyle Hotel that Howard was really making that statement to us about death — that it's fatal but not serious.* ★ *And I think that from now on, death and darkness are going to have a much harder time because death is going to have to work its side of the street alone.* ★ *I think Howard put darkness out of business for a long time."*

This Gossage person — he busts across time zones. ★ Now it's dinner in New York with Tom Wolfe, Carly Ally, Bill Blair [the publisher of *Harper's*], and more. ★ I think of the old much-used line that "he was the party who knew how to throw one" and the twenty-five year echo on that "cock-a-hoop" laughter comes ringing through.

I see Wolfe has a few more things to say about his friend…

"Howard was a person who somehow imparted a fantastic energy to anything that people around him wanted to undertake. ★ This is a quality beyond assessing, whether it was in terms of the magazines he was involved with, or the personality he was involved with, or with various things in the lives of each of us. ★ He somehow made you able to soar a little higher and do it with a kind of zest for your own life that you probably had not had before. ★ He exulted in whatever other people could do with their lives. In fact, that was one thing that Howard insisted on — that you somehow get on the Dionysian plane with him and if you could do it, no one would applaud louder than he. ★ It was a dare which he handed you, a dare you could not forget."

HOWARD LUCK GOSSAGE

After wandering through someone else's life, we are left with a rather large thought, one that has no doubt been thought of before. But it seems worth thinking again. ★ The thought — it's sort of important what we do with our own lives.

"He somehow made you able to soar a little higher and do it with a kind of zest for your own life that you probably had not had before…
It was a dare which he handed you, a dare you could not forget."

*The lesson
seems to be,
that as we
work to make
the world a
better place,
it's sort of
important to
have as good a
time as possible
doing it.*

I'm not sure if it matters whether or not we introduce the world to important concepts it doesn't quite understand - there are enough of those already. Or whether or not we succeed in establishing a new country in the Caribbean [Howard almost pulled this off] – there are already plenty of those as well. ★ Or if it matters whether we win some big advertising award – or even have a medium-sized one named after us.

★ ★ A CHEERING THOUGHT ★ ★

The lesson seems to be, that as we work to make the world a better place, it's sort of important to have as good a time as possible doing it. ★ And, building on that thought, it's probably a pretty good idea to make as many friends as you can along the way.

This, I think, is the lesson of Howard's life. It is a cheering thought for the vast majority of mankind. ★ It's not about immortality. It's about making the absolute very most of that little bit of mortality given to each one of us.

Now, I have nothing against immortality, but on this plane of existence, few of us will achieve it and it's a cinch none of us will be around to enjoy it. ★ Howard had the right idea. ★ He made the most of every opportunity. He promoted virtually every worthy cause, every worthy thought, and every worthy human being that entered his life – with princely exuberance.

When it was time to do a little honest work, he served the interests of his clients brilliantly. ★ And in the creation of one of those all-too-perishable works of art that is a human life, he left us some lessons.

Were any of those lessons about advertising? Quite a few, actually. ★ When this book began, we were all set to position Howard as the first creative guru of *Integrated Marketing Communications*. And maybe that's useful – but we think we'll leave that job to someone else, because it really diminished the larger truths. And what were those larger truths? ★ As Howard said, *"I shall get around to them in a minute..."*

I flip back to Hinckle's book to see if good fortune will favor me one more time with a closing quote. ★ Here's one...

"He had made his living making lemonade out of lemons, and he didn't see why he should treat dying any differently. ★ His was the rarest breed of one-upmanship, life laughing literally in death's face, a gut instinct beyond bravery, a final act played with great style but without bravado. ★ He simply refused to accept

"He simply refused to accept death's own unimaginative terms, and made of the experience a love song to the innocent merriment of existence."

death's own unimaginative terms, and made of the experience a love song to the innocent merriment of existence." I sit quietly for a while.

I hear Alice saying softly, *"He made people think."*

Near as I can figure, he's still at it.

FLAHOOLICK

[VOL. A № II]

FLAIⱄIÚLAꞆ is an Irish word meaning openhanded generous expansive and Oh much else. It is pronounced "Flahoolick," which we 〖The Whiskey Distillers of Ireland〗 admit looks a bit earthy; English is a simply wretched language that way. However. ☞ Anything can be flahoolick under certain conditions. Even water, supposing you were crawling on your hands and knees across the desert and in the broiling sun and came upon a waterfall though what it would be doing there we are not prepared to say. Lemon squash can be flahoolick if you are nine years old or inordinately fond of lemon squash. Draught beer is flahoolick; large linen napkins are flahoolick; long nightshirts are virtually always flahoolick. ☞ Tea bags, on the other hand, are unflahoolick, and so is one lambchop. Wrapped sugar cubes, tiny glasses of orange juice, doormats without "WELCOME" on them, and wire coat hangers are, for one reason and another, not flahoolick. Irish Whiskey is flahoolick; O it is the acme of burnished, emphatic flahoolickness. And so is Irish Coffee with its luscious collar of chilled, frothy cream. ☞ *People* can be flahoolick, as well. Still, bear in mind that:

"All of the people are flahoolick some of the time
Some of the people are flahoolick all of the time
But all of the people are not flahoolick all of the time."
—Anon

To this end we are putting out the very nice badge pictured below and in our next install-

ment we shall include a coupon so you may send off for one. Oh, we have a bit of room so it will do no harm to put it in here, too,

> The Whiskey Distillers of Ireland
> Box N186T, Dublin, Ireland
>
> Gentlemen:
> Please send me my Flahoolick/Unflahoolick badge. I'll read next week's installment to find out what it's all about. (I am printing this so you can read it.)
>
> Name_____
> Address_____
> City_____ State_____ Country_____

and tell you more about it later. ☞ Now, those of you with sharp eyes will notice that

(concluded next week)

Howard Luck Gossage

Is There Any Hope for Advertising?

edited by Kim Rotzoll, Jarlath Graham,
and Barrows Mussey

University of Illinois Press *Urbana and Chicago*

The following publishers and authors have generously given
permission to use extended quotations from copyrighted
works: From *The Pump House Gang,* by Tom Wolfe. Copyright
1968 by Farrar, Straus & Giroux. Reprinted by permission
of the publisher. From "A Singular Man," by Herb Caen.
Copyright 1969 by Herb Caen, columnist, *San Francisco
Chronicle.* Reprinted by permission of Herb Caen.

Library of Congress Cataloging-in-Publication Data

Gossage, Howard Luck, 1917-1969.
  Is there any hope for advertising?

  Bibliography: p.
  Includes index.
  1. Advertising. I. Rotzoll, Kim B. II. Graham,
Jarlath. III. Mussey, June Barrows, 1910-
IV. Title.
HF5823.G625 1986   659.1   86-11277
ISBN 0-252-01278-X (alk. paper)

To Sally and Sarah Luck Gossage.
And to Barrows, for keeping the faith.

A Note on the Editors

Kim Rotzoll is a professor in and head of the Department of Advertising at the University of Illinois and knew Howard Luck Gossage while he was at Penn State.

Jarlath Graham is currently Director of External Relations for Crain Communications. He knew Howard as a reporter and then as an editor of *Advertising Age*.

Barrows Mussey, who wrote the introduction, was the German translator of *Ist die Werbung noch zu retten?* (Can advertising be saved?) and was a writer himself. He died in Germany in July 1985.

Contents

Illustrations

Preface

Kim Rotzoll

In the summer of 1969 the following appeared in *Newsweek*'s "Transition" section:

> Died: Howard Gossage, 51, witty, cultured, talented mainspring of the San Francisco ad agency of Freeman, Mander & Gossage, famous for unorthodox campaigns in which he dreamed up everything from Beethoven sweat shirts to an international paper-airplane tournament; of leukemia, in San Francisco, July 9. He was also noted as the discoverer of Marshall McLuhan and as a stinging gadfly of the ad game—though personally he was so well-disposed that his unkindest comment about anyone was, "Well, I can take him or leave him—not necessarily in that order."[1]

So? Why, in the mid-1980s, should you concern yourself with the words and deeds of a man whose entire advertising career spanned less than two decades and whose agency was small enough to occupy an elderly firehouse with a dozen employees at flood tide?

Because, amid the Reeves, Bernbachs, Burnetts, Ogilvys and other advertising giants, Gossage offers us two compelling legacies: (1) a body of criticism of advertising structure and practice sweeping from the general (advertising as an institution) to the specific (billboards) that is clearly relevant to contemporary concerns, and (2) his decidedly unconventional advertising communication philosophy, which developed cult status in Europe and which was honored in this country as evidenced by his posthumous induction into the Advertising Copywriters Hall of Fame.

It is easy to celebrate Gossage for his wit, panache, and general ongoing irreverence and to offer him and his era (the anti-establishment decade) as an anomaly in advertising history. But there is more here than that. For clearly a reasonably dispassionate reading of these pages reveals much of pressing relevance to contemporary thought and practice in advertising.

Throughout its history advertising has been subjected to criticism from without—and within. Indeed, some of the more devastating indictments have been offered by former practitioners.[2] But much has been uninformed, often focused on specific elements within the larger confines of advertising, such as the large advertising agency, and frequently given to fits of pique and ensuing manic extrapolation.

But Gossage stayed in the trenches. With his unquestioned gift of stepping back from his environment, he offers us a catalog of critical analyses of the structure and performance of the advertising business that seems destined to persist due to its unrelenting focus on enduring elements in the system. For example, today we are confronted with the topical "children's advertising," which can be illuminated so clearly through his concept of "audience." We turn the pages of trade papers where advertisers bemoan soaring budgets while the academic journals begin to offer empirical evidence that perhaps advertising operates with *diminishing* returns, thus casting doubts on the wisdom of "big stick" advertising budgets, which Gossage had assailed decades before. We note ratings evidence of viewer disenchantment with commercial television and sardonic articles on the prostitution of the "Highway Beautification Act." We observe the demise of urban daily newspapers with circulations in the thousands and note that—once again—no one asked their readers. We hear speakers at advertising gatherings lamenting government "interference" and casting their eyes skyward at growing evidence of "consumer" indifference. Gossage penetrated them all, probing these and other issues of contemporary concern while he attempted to raise the consciousness of the advertising community to address them.

I knew Howard from his days at Penn State; Jack Graham was a treasured friend and professional colleague of Howard's; and Barrows Mussey spread Howard's gospel through Europe as general facilitator and translator for the German book that serves as the foundation for this effort.

Ist die Werbung noch zu retten? had been put together by Howard and Barrows from speeches, articles, correspondence, and excerpts from other published material, particularly *Dear Miss Afflerbach*. With Barrows's help Jack and I secured the English manuscript, which had been expanded by

Barrows and Howard to include material after the German edition appeared, in addition to Howard's *Atlantic Monthly* article reflecting on the news of his leukemia. I added an earlier *Harper's* column on billboards to augment his ongoing concern with the media and advertising.

Herb Caen, writing the day after Gossage's death in the *San Francisco Chronicle,* entitled his tribute "A Singular Man." And so he was. And singular, it can be argued, is his legacy to contemporary advertising thought and practice. For all those who remember, welcome back. For those new to the man and his ideas, we expect your curiosity to be generously rewarded.

> For his distinguished and consistent contributions to the craft of advertising writing and for the strong and positive influence he had on advertising as an industry, The Copy Club elects Howard Luck Gossage to the Copywriter's Hall of Fame.
>
> —March 26, 1970

NOTES

1. Transition, *Newsweek,* 21 July 1969, p. 74.

2. See, for example, Frederic Wakerman, *The Hucksters.* New York: Rinehart, 1946; Paul Stevens, *I Can Sell You Anything.* New York: P. H. Wyden, 1972.

Introduction

Barrows Mussey

Howard Luck Gossage as a Creator of Art Forms

Nobody reads advertising. People read what interests them; and sometimes it's an ad.

Advertising is not a right, it's a privilege. Our first responsibility is not to the product but to the public.

I don't know how to speak to everybody, only to somebody.

What I can really do, I can convince these gurus like Marshall McLuhan and Leopold Kohr that their ideas will actually work.

There, encapsulated, are pertinent thoughts of an impertinent genius who did with his left hand something the right-thinking have always maintained was impossible: make "advertising" into a true, if unassuming, art form. The late William Bernbach of Doyle Dane Bernbach was better known and more influential for much longer within the advertising profession, but hardly in the world at large. David Ogilvy probably offered a closer parallel.

Howard Luck Gossage's two books besides the present posthumous volume—launched, like his agencies, as "collaborations," with his own name last on the masthead—were sparkling narratives of memorable campaigns.[1] One was for Eagle Shirtmakers, the other for *Scientific American,* and they will be as entertaining ten years hence as they were the day the first ads ran in 1961 and 1967, respectively.

"Art form" should not, of course, be taken to signify graphic perfection. Chapter 9 contains accounts of Gossage's struggles with art directors to keep ads from being too beautiful.

He impressed the intellectuals (what F. A. von Hayek calls "the second-hand dealers in ideas") by spending his own money to make Marshall McLuhan partially intelligible and thus alluring. Gossage's friend Tom Wolfe described the process in a piece called "What If He Is Right?":

> One day in New York, McLuhan was staying at Howard Gossage's suite at the Lombardy Hotel. Gossage is a San Francisco advertising man. McLuhan was staying there and representatives of two national weekly magazines called up. Both offered him permanent offices in their buildings, plus fees, to do occasional consulting work. . . .
>
> "What should I do, Howard?" says McLuhan.
>
> "Take 'em both!" says Gossage. "You need offices on both sides of town. Suppose you get caught in traffic?"
>
> McLuhan looks puzzled, but Gossage is already off into his laugh. This Gossage has a certain wild cosmic laugh. His eyes light up like Stars of Bethlehem. The laugh comes in waves, from far back in the throat, like echoes from Lane 27 of a bowling alley, rolling, booming far beyond the immediate situation, on to. . . .
>
> McLuhan is at the conference table in the upper room in Gossage's advertising firm in San Francisco, up in what used to be a firehouse. A couple of newspaper people are up there talking about how they are sure their readers want this and that to read—McLuhan pulls his chin down into his neck:
>
> "Well . . . Of course, people don't actually *read* newspapers. They get into them every morning like a hot bath."
>
> Perfect! Delphic! Cryptic! Aphoristic! Epigrammatic! With this even, even, even voice, this utter scholarly aplomb—with *pronouncements*—
>
> The phone rings in Gossage's suite and it's for McLuhan. It is a man from one of America's largest packing corporations. They want to fly McLuhan to their home office to deliver a series of three talks, one a day, to their top management group. How much would he charge? McLuhan puts his hand over the receiver and explains the situation to Gossage.
>
> "How much should I charge?"
>
> "What do you usually get for a lecture?" says Gossage.
>
> "Five hundred dollars."
>
> "Tell him a hundred thousand."
>
> McLuhan looks appalled.
>
> "Oh, all right," says Gossage. "Tell him fifty thousand."
>
> McLuhan hesitates, then turns back to the telephone: "Fifty thousand."
>
> Now the man on the phone is appalled. That is somewhat outside the

fee structure we generally project, Professor McLuhan. They all call him Professor or Doctor. We don't expect you to prepare any new material especially for us, you understand, and it will only be three talks—

"Oh—well then," says McLuhan, "twenty-five thousand."

Great sigh of relief. "Well! That is more within our potential structure projection, Professor McLuhan, and we look forward to seeing you!"

McLuhan hangs up and stares at Gossage, nonplussed. But Gossage is already off into the cosmic laugh, bounding, galloping, soaring, eyes ablaze—¡mas alla!—¡mas alla! just over the next skyline!—El Dorado, Marshall! Don't you understand!—

Looking back, I can see that Gossage, but not McLuhan, knew what was going to happen to McLuhan over the next six months. Namely, that this 53-year-old Canadian English teacher, gray as a park pigeon, would suddenly become an international celebrity and the most famous man his country ever produced. . . .

McLuhan's pivotal trip to the U.S. came in May, 1965. As I say, American corporations had already begun to import him for private lectures. The publication of *Understanding Media* in 1964 had prompted that. . . .

McLuhan's May, 1965, trip to New York, however, was at the behest of two rather extraordinary men from San Francisco, Howard Gossage and Dr. Gerald Feigen.

Gossage is a tall, pale advertising man with one of the great heads of gray hair in the U.S.A., flowing back like John Barrymore's. Feigen is a psychiatrist who became a surgeon; he is dark and has big eyes and a gongkicker mustache like Jerry Colonna. He is also a ventriloquist and carries around a morbid-looking dummy named Becky. Gossage and Feigen started a firm called Generalists, Inc., acting as consultants to people who can't get what they need from specialists because what they need is the big picture. Their first client was a man who was stuck with an expensive ski lift in Squaw Valley that was idle half the year. They advised him to start a posh and rather formal restaurant-nightclub up the slope that could be reached only by ski lift. So he did. It was named High Camp and immediately became all the rage. One thing that drew Gossage and Feigen to McLuhan was his belief that the age of specialists (fragmentation of intellect) was over.

Gossage and Feigen invested about $6,000 into taking McLuhan around to talk to influential people outside the academic world, chiefly in the communications and advertising industries, on both coasts. Gossage says they had no specific goal (no fragmentation; open field). They just wanted to play it "fat, dumb and happy" and see what would happen.

So in May 1965 they had a series of meetings and lunches set up for McLuhan at Laurent, Lutèce, and other great expense-account feasteries of the East Fifties in Manhattan. . . . The first meetings and a cocktail party in Gossage's suite at the Lombardy were set for a Monday. McLuhan never showed up. Gossage finally got him on the telephone in Toronto that evening. Marshall, what the hell are you doing—

"I'm grading papers."

"Grading papers?"

"And waiting for the excursion rate."

—the midweek excursion rate on the airlines. He could save about $12 roundtrip if he didn't come to New York until Tuesday morning.

"But Marshall, you're not even *paying* for it!"

—but that was the English prof with the Pre-Tide tie. He had a wife and six children and thirty years behind him of shaving by on an English teacher's pay. So there he was in the bin, grading papers, scratching away—

"Listen," says Gossage, "there are so many people willing to invest money in your work now, you'll never have to grade papers again."

"You mean it's going to be fun from now on?" says McLuhan.

"Everything's coming up roses," says Gossage.[2]

Gossage was born August 30, 1917, in Chicago; he left at age six months; growing up in Queens, New York (the late Henry Miller, originally from Brooklyn, sounded a bit like him on a TV program I once heard), Denver, New Orleans, and Kansas City.

He entered the University of Kansas City in 1935. Inspired by *Huckleberry Finn,* he took a canoe trip to New Orleans that ran from July 17 to August 31, 1936. In 1938-39 he was publisher of the K.C.U. *Kangaroo.*

He was next heard of as a navy pilot. ("I wasn't a very good pilot, so I picked bombers.") In early 1945 he had his flat-hatting flight 23 feet above enemy-occupied Hong Kong harbor. In 1946, as a lieutenant entrusted with decommissioning the Naval Air Station at Quonset Point, Rhode Island (home of the eponymous semicylindrical metal huts), he had his papers filled out to become a regular officer but thought better of it at the last moment.

At 30 he became promotion manager for radio station KLX in San Francisco. Possibly the first professional act that foreshadowed the later firehouse gang came late one year at appropriation time. He sent out to the names on the station prospect file an empty calendar of the current year with a covering letter that said in substance, You've let this year go by without using any of its opportunities to make money. Don't you want to catch up next year?

As Howard told me, "Several ad managers bought time. I think the calendar must have brought them to it because they projected their own ideas.

My appeal certainly didn't move them; it was probably the memory of their own successes and failures over the year."

One of Gossage's favorite rules was from Saki (the short-story writer Hector Hugh Munro): "In baiting a trap with cheese, always leave room for the mouse." Another way of putting it, which Gossage introduced and later got sick of hearing, was *reader involvement*.

In 1949 he went to Europe with a food shipment, stayed a month or two, then returned to work for a couple of years at CBS and elsewhere.

He took his then wife with him for a year and a half while he studied sociology at the Universities of Paris and Geneva on the GI Bill. As Howard explained it, "I didn't pursue the doctorate; I am a P.U. dropout. I am not really very good at French at all. Lovely pronunciation, though. . . . *Il y a longtemps depuis j'ai eu besoin de Français sauve à épater les vachements bourgeois.*"

And at age 36, in 1954, he joined the small San Francisco advertising agency of Brisacher, Wheeler & Staff. Within a year he was vice president (less of a commonplace there than in the Madison Avenue factories). In 1957 Cunningham & Walsh of New York bought the shop, chiefly because of the ads he had been doing for clients like Qantas and Safeway frozen foods. In 1955, the year the Qantas account came in, he fetched the comedian Stan Freberg to do radio commercials—Freberg's first contact with advertising.

He left Cunningham & Walsh because he "couldn't stand the sight of blood" (i.e., referring to firing inadequate colleagues) and did a cameo bit at Guild, Bascom & Bonfigli before going into partnership with Stan Freberg.

"All of the jobs I have had since the Navy (and three before)," he often said, "have either resulted in firing or leaving in dudgeon, save two, I think. Which is why I am in business for myself."

This began in earnest with J. Joseph Weiner as partner in 1957. The famous original San Francisco Firehouse No. 1 belonged to Weiner, who continued as landlord after selling out of the agency to pursue non-advertising interests, a role he retained even after Gossage's death. Art director Robert Freeman, an old friend, replaced Weiner on the nameplate.

Blitz-Weinhard beer went along to Weiner & Gossage; their first brand-new client was Paul Masson.

The year 1958 brought the Irish whiskey account to Gossage. Consultants who do advertising for hotels and resorts are sometimes encouraged to take part of their pay in trade; the Gossage family spent a "sabbatical" in Ireland, soaking up atmosphere, reinforced by study of the *Book of Kells,* the famous eighth-century Irish illuminated manuscript. According to Howard, "You will note in the Irish ads that I would sometimes make a sentence of two hundred words with no punctuation whatsoever, and it worked, because I wrote the way they spoke; breathlessly."

The campaign was unique in another way as well: in Howard's words, it "blandly assumed that people would be interested enough in an advertisement to follow it from week to week even when it stopped in mid-sentence. To show you how this kind of revolutionary invention comes about: I'd simply written too much copy for the first ad. So I said, 'Hell, let's stop here and continue next time.' What we ultimately got was one ad consisting of four chapters that ran for four weeks. Originally I wasn't even trying to be cute. And people actually read the serial."

This may have been the ultimate extension of his procedural rule, "Only use enough string to go around the package; sometimes it takes quite a lot."

The *New Yorker* campaign was popularly perceived as continuing seven or eight years after it had accomplished its mission and disbanded. ("By the way, the Irish government quietly got the Ulster distillers into the act, although there was no financial advantage to Eire.")

One enthusiastic reader, S. Miller Harris of Eagle Shirtmakers, responded by becoming a prize client and remained so until Gossage's death. The book the two of them wrote about the Eagle Shirt campaign, *Dear Miss Afflerbach*, sold splendidly in hardback. It was published in 1962, the same year that Gossage was a visiting professor at Pennsylvania State University, lecturing on "The Nature of Paid Propaganda." This was his first pulpit for reflection on the moral plight of the media.

Among the other successful campaigns of the early sixties, Pink Air put Fina gasoline on the map. In 1961-62 came Rainier beer with Beethoven sweatshirts ("a brewer's idea of culture" that was originally devised to help an ailing San Francisco music radio station Gossage liked) and Coach Stahl's march to Seattle, a classic Gossage performance of three ads setting the world abuzz and the local newspapers doing the rest. It was also typical in that the advertising "propaganda" generated an excitement beyond the client's marketing ability to exploit. Gossage, for all his far-out genius, was still an extremely shrewd marketing man. Giving advice on airline advertising, for instance, he would say, "Remember, your biggest customers are the other airlines." In 1963 Rover Motor Company came over—which began one of those glorious partnerships where a client urges the adman to do the outrageous things he's spoiling for a chance at.

The February 3, 1964 issue of *Advertising Age* reprinted a talk that caught my eye in Germany. I asked a prominent American copywriter working in Duesseldorf at the time if he knew who Howard Gossage was.

"Yeah, he used to be with Cunningham & Walsh in San Francisco. Did that Irish whiskey campaign." What about him? "Oh, I don't know, he sounds to me like somebody that's always telling dialect jokes."

Gossage might have taken the dialect as a compliment, although he disliked people's telling jokes; said he had total recall and had heard them all. Anyhow the editor and the publisher of the German marketing monthly *Absatzwirtschaft* shared my delight in the article, and my request to Gossage for permission to translate and reprint it brought on a correspondence. I harried him for further material and was overjoyed to find he didn't need much harrying. I soon learned, as I told him, that his letters read like his ads—higher praise I could not imagine.

In the end *Absatzwirtschaft* ran a couple of articles that generated the idea of adding more to make a book for publication by the parent company, Econ-Verlag.

Shortly after work on the book began (we fancied we had a deadline to meet because Gossage was also under an American contract for a book that never took shape), John Shea issued his "Memo from a Dallas citizen" (with which Gossage was intimately connected); there was an uproar at Fina, over which Shea and Gossage offered their resignations. In November Shea became chairman of Freeman, Gossage & Shea; he left to go into real estate in June 1966.

In 1965 Gossage began his efforts for *Ramparts*, originally the five-times-a-year leftist Catholic hobby of a rich convert, Edward M. Keating. Gossage and Feigen, acting as Generalists, Inc., told Keating he would have to change his focus—"take an extra-environmental view," in Feigen's words. Generalists, Inc., accepted pay for their advice in stock of the magazine. Warren Hinckle, who had been handling public relations, became editor. Later he took the title of his reminiscences from Gossage's motto: "If you have a lemon, make lemonade."[3]

During 1966 Gossage undertook two campaigns of relatively major proportions. First David Brower, head of the Sierra Club, whose handsome photo books Freeman & Gossage had been advertising, asked for help to block the damming of the Grand Canyon by the U.S. Department of the Interior. Jerry Mander wrote the ads in the Gossage posture. Nine newspapers reprinted them free, and in the end Commissioner Floyd Dominy of the Bureau of Reclamation was beaten. John McPhee's magnificent book about Brower, *Encounters With the Archdruid*, described a Grand Canyon boat trip McPhee arranged with Brower and Dominy, on which they became great friends without ever convincing each other. It also tells of Brower's later downfall at the Sierra Club because he had spent so much money without authorization on the campaign and had thus multiplied the club membership elevenfold, from 7,000 to 77,000 (letting in, one assumes, just anybody). Gossage appears anonymously in the book as an "advertising writer with a Beethoven haircut." Brower thereupon launched his own organization, Friends of the Earth, with offices in the firehouse.

Between the Grand Canyon campaign and the next blockbuster, paper airplanes, Gossage went to Frankfurt at the invitation of the Art Directors Club of Germany, and on November 5 gave an all-day seminar for the annual meeting. He delivered half the morning's talk in very creditable German (which he had been boning up, using my translation as a text), then went on in English. An interview with a reporter led to a story in the newsmagazine *Der Spiegel* on the Grand Canyon campaign. Of "Howard Luck Gossage, 49, monocle-wearer from San Francisco," it said that he "cultivates an appearance blended of Hollywood star and Prussian cavalry captain of the guard."

Not only Gossage's ideas but also his typography (the no-nonsense 1930s magazine layout of the paper airplanes, not the Irish elegance) long served as models for the German agency GGK and Swissair as well as a growing number of other European disciples. One of his trademarks was the "skyline," the deadpan subhead bracketed and shifted above the headline; it became a regular badge of his German disciples. For example, confronted with a new ad lacking a skyline, Swissair would shyly ask if they couldn't have one.

Hardly was he home from Germany when he launched the paper-airplane launching for *Scientific American*. The first ad appeared December 12, 1966. That day, 160 reporters—the most since the pope's visit two years before—gathered in the offices of the magazine and had to be adjourned to the roomier Harvard Club. On December 15 the *San Francisco Chronicle* (its editor, Scott Newhall, an intimate of HLG's) devoted a banner head and half the front page to "Paper Airplanes—A Global Test." This alone generated over 3,000 of the nearly 11,000 entries. American Airlines provided paper-airplane facilities aboard its planes. French, German, and British papers commented on the event; *Der Spiegel* ran a column and a half, with illustrations from the ad and the address for submissions; a German tabloid put on its own contest. *Time* waited for the fly-offs, which it reported on March 3, 1967.

Meanwhile, back at the firehouse . . .

In keeping with the way they had launched McLuhan, Gossage and Feigen organized a seminar to showcase Leopold Kohr—lawyer, economist, college professor, and "the apostle of shrinkmanship"—at the firehouse from February

27 to March 3, 1967, coinciding with the arrival of the first copies of *Ist die Werbung noch zu retten?* (Can advertising be saved?), the volume from which this book takes off. The seminar began with a session on "the city-state" (San Francisco: A City-State), giving the *Chronicle* a chance to front-page the headline "A Modest Idea for S.F. Secession." The audiences for the ten sessions were carefully sifted from the all-embracing acquaintance of the firehouse gang. There were several architects, a novelist, magazine writers, public TV, lawyers, art directors, a college president, a theologian, a drama critic, and research and development executives. Those present, in proper Gossage fashion, put in their two cents' (or more likely their two thousand dollars') worth after Professor Kohr and the hosts had set the theme. Some of the reports were at first suspicious of Kohr and his Austrian accent because a previous firehouse seminar with comedian Mort Sahl doing a dialect bit had been a put-on, or lark.

"The droll but indefatigable economist," Michael Grieg wrote in the *San Francisco Chronicle,* suggested that "eventually, San Francisco might have its own Senate and the right to coin money or to decide whether or not to send its young men off to war. . . . Whimsical and serious at the same time, the far-ranging scholar even foresees a special currency design for the time San Francisco mints its own money—a design in keeping with the city's topless tradition. 'You should follow the Austrian example, with its alluring coinage depiction of a quite topless Empress Maria Theresa,' he pointed out. 'This has a marvelous anti-inflationary effect—it's often so much nicer to keep the coin than to spend it.'"

By late 1967 the Gossage wave in Germany, Switzerland, and Austria was now beginning to swoosh—he was widely quoted in ads and press, even in a book-review section.

When the Gossages got back from Europe in February 1968, he was "so debilitated I went into hospital immediately." On Valentine's Day he got the news: "I . . . have leukemia and was about two quarts low blood-wise, which is enough to enervate anyone. . . . My reaction to this interesting news was typical of a man who has delighted in finding lemons to make lemonade out of—I was elated: just to think! I said, here I am alive (one generally doesn't realize this outside of Reader's Digest). And I have used it like a bludgeon to get things done. I have never been one to harbor secrets and why start now."

He was told he probably had six months; he stretched it to eighteen. *Ramparts'* Warren Hinckle:

Gossage reacted to that as if they had given him a license to shoot ducks out of season. 'Who-who-who do you think I should tell first,' he stammered at Feigen. Feigen said he didn't think Howard should tell anyone. 'People will treat you differently if they know,' he said. Of course, said Gossage— that would be the only way he could squeeze something out of the grandslam lemon of leukemia. . . . 'Just think,' he said, 'now nobody can tell me, wait until next year. . . .'

Howard made great sport of telling his friends, a performance which was part Shinto ceremony, part Miracle Play, part barroom hijinks. 'Hey, no shit, I'm really going to die,' he would insist, somewhat impatiently, to those who failed or refused to accept his technicolor announcement of his own doom. . . .

He used his fatal disease as a club to get what he wanted. He organized his advertising agency for a six-month dash to perfection to get his associates in condition for the lonely mile ahead. If someone objected to a particular point of order, Gossage would glower, and say, 'You don't have leukemia —who the hell are you!' And then he would laugh, a triumphant, cock-a-hoop laughter that filled the room and seemed to echo from the sky, a laughter that suggested what fools these mortals be, that life was but one good joke and the man laughing alone knew the punch line.[4]

During the first six months of 1969 he: took Leopold Kohr on a grand tour of San Francisco, Houston, New York; delivered the speech that forms part of chapter 2 on the unwanted responsibility of advertisers; planned a new magazine to be called *Scanlan's* for fall publication (counting on Hinckle's help because *Ramparts* folded); ran the Ford Maverick Renaming Contest for Eagle Shirts; did a page-and-a-half newspaper ad for a Harper & Row book attacking the anti-ballistic missile and comparing it, as a safety measure, to the fallout shelters of the 1950s; and produced a two-page spread in the *New Yorker* for "The Random House Sweat Shirt of the English Language," an offering from Eagle bearing, across the chest, a choice of entries from the *Random House Dictionary*.

On July 8 behind a curtain at the Presbyterian Hospital, he took leave of those closest to him; next morning at 4:30 he was gone.

Herb Caen's column in the *San Francisco Chronicle* of July 10, 1969, read:

A Singular Man
Yesterday I mentioned that Howard Gossage's middle name was Luck, and that he'd need all of it he could get. Well, it ran out for him at 4:30 a.m. yesterday in Presbyterian Hospital. He died of Leukemia, a kidney

infection and other complications, but mainly, I think, he died because he didn't want to live as a vegetable, never having had any experience at it.

If there were any justice, the flags would be at half-staff all over town, for he was one of the most valuable of San Franciscans. He would have understood why they aren't, though. As he once said in that wild Irish[5] way of his: "Of course there isn't any justice, buddy, and isn't that wonderful? We'll never run out of things to be angry about."

Only, the buddy would have come out "b-b-buddy." He had an ingratiating stammer, along with a dramatic appearance that made him an unforgettable figure around town: flowing white hair, a perpetually gaunt, drawn and handsome face, the sad-sweet smile that seems to be the signature of so many Irish philosophers.

Nominally he was in advertising — he hated the business, incidentally — but realistically, he was the archetypical San Francisco Renaissance man. Like most of the best men I've ever met, he never haggled over a bill and overtipped recklessly. Money meant nothing to him and he probably died broke. But he knew more about classical music than most musicians, he was better-read than most critics and he composed more graceful prose than most writers. I never met a more unbigoted man, even about bigots; the worst he would say about anybody was "Well, I can t-take him or l-leave him — not n-necessarily in that order."

What was important about Howard Gossage? It's a matter of style. There was nothing cheap or shoddy there, and his everyday presence made you feel that just being a San Franciscan was important. If a guy like Gossage picked this place above all others — in the face of constant offers from New York and Europe — then San Francisco had to be okay, b-b-buddy. Editors, authors, tycoons and advertising men were forever seeking his advice, and he'd say, "If they want to see me all that much, they'll just have to come HERE."

And come they did, to his firehouse on Pacific. Talk about style: he was the first to buy an abandoned old firehouse and convert it into offices that were the last word in cool modern elegance. His lunches there were lengendary. He'd call up David's Deli, order a ton of everything, ask you to drop in at the last minute, and you'd drop everything to be there.

You'd find yourself building a pastrami sandwich next to Dr. Benjamin Spock. Or pouring a beer for John Steinbeck. Or listening to Buckminster Fuller. Or laughing at the bad jokes of Marshall McLuhan. (Gossage, more than any other person, was responsible for the launching of McLuhan as a household name — a job he took on, like so many others, just for the hell of it, "let's see if it works.") Robert Manning, editor of *Atlantic Monthly*, was a Gossage luncheon regular. And Writer Tom Wolfe, who invented a new style of reportage.

Along with Ogilvy and Doyle Dane Bernbach, Gossage was responsible for changing the whole concept of American advertising. Before they came along in the '50s, the approach was serious, heavy, bombastic. Gossage was the first to inject sophisticated humor and even—amid cries of "Sacrilege!"—the poking of fun at one's own product. His first ads for Qantas, long ago, are still classics. For the then unknown airline, he devised a contest he headed: "Be the First Kid on Your Block to Own a Kangaroo!" And when a winner was finally selected, his headline read "Bronx Girl Wins Her First Kangaroo." The style won the accolade of instant imitation.

Did I say he had no interest in money? In '53, Volkswagen was ready to begin advertising heavily in the U.S. and narrowed the competition to Gossage and Doyle Dane. Howard's final presentation to VW's directors lost him the million-dollar job: "I've been driving your car for years, and it's a great little product. I don't think you NEED any advertising." Later he confided wryly: "I've always hated automobile accounts—but wow, I had no idea they were going to advertise THAT much!"

I saw Howard for the last time on Tuesday afternoon. He looked worn and dazed, but he was trying bravely to keep up the old style. Marshall McLuhan had phoned him long distance to say "I can't send you flowers, you've read all the books, so I'll give you a joke." Then followed a typical McLuhan pun that made no sense. "For a genius, he sure tells lousy jokes," Howard mumbled. A couple of hospital technicians wheeled in a complicated kidney gadget. "That's okay, boys, you can have the machine tonight," he grinned weakly. As I started to leave, I said, "I'll be back to see you tomorrow," and he sighed "W-why would you w-want to do that?" And when I reached the door he called out "Hey, b-buddy, you're not going to be m-mad at me, are you?"

It just dawned on me that I don't even know Howard's age. I guess he was 50-something, but he never talked about it, as he never talked about his years as a Navy combat pilot in the South Pacific and a lot of other matters he considered trifling. But to answer his last question, yes, I'm mad that he died. Damn mad.[6]

One of HLG's last requests (superseding his wry instructions that his friend Jessica Mitford, author of the biting best-seller *The American Way of Death,* negotiate with the undertaker) was that his ashes be scattered over San Francisco Bay from the plane of his old friend and fellow aviator Carl Ally, the New York advertising man. Ally and the widow did as they had been asked.

There was a memorial service at the firehouse, which his right hand, Alice Lowe, described: "It was very Gossage-like. . . . The members of the quartet are all from the San Francisco Symphony and Mr. Krachmalnick is the concertmaster. . . . We wanted to include the mariachis because Howard loved them so. After the program, Sally thanked people individually for attending—we served food and drink and then we had a band of 16 bagpipers come marching down the alley facing the firehouse—pipes and drums—parade slowly to and from the front of the building—march in through that long corridor—form a circle in the rear office facing the garden—with the drummer in the middle surrounded by the pipers—after which they played a Scottish lament, and other Scottish songs. Then they marched to the front gallery, did a similar thing, and then tropped up the alley again—sounds fading as they disappeared up the top of the hill. I think he would have liked it."

A friend wrote, "Instead of the conventional remarks about what an aching void he leaves, we can contemplate the lives he filled fuller. Not optimism, faith, or teleology, this; merely the observation of an uncommon fact."

A few months later Freeman, Mander & Gossage paid their bills and went out of business.

NOTES

1. S. Miller Harris and Howard Luck Gossage, *Dear Miss Afflerbach*. New York: Macmillan, 1962; Jerry Mander, George Dipple, and Howard Gossage, *The Great International Paper Airplane Book*. New York: Simon and Schuster, 1967.

2. Tom Wolfe, *The Pump House Gang*. New York: Farrar, Straus & Giroux, 1968, pp. 139–64.

3. Warren Hinckle, *If You Have a Lemon, Make Lemonade*. New York: G. P. Putnam's Sons, 1973, 1974.

4. Hinckle, *Lemonade*, p. 355–56.

5. The Gossage family was English, but evidently his work for the Irish identity had left its mark on him. –ED.

6. Herb Caen, "A Singular Man," *San Francisco Chronicle*, 10 July 1969.

Howard Luck Gossage

Is There Any Hope for Advertising?

edited by Kim Rotzoll, Jarlath Graham, and Barrows Mussey

"Gossage [had] a certain wild cosmic laugh. His eyes [lit] up like Stars of Bethlehem. The laugh [came] in waves, from far back in the throat, like echoes from Lane 27 of a bowling alley, rolling, booming far beyond the immediate situation, . . . bounding, galloping, soaring, eyes ablaze." — Tom Wolfe, in *The Pump House Gang*.

"He had an ingratiating stammer, along with a dramatic appearance that made him an unforgettable figure around town: flowing white hair, a perpetually gaunt, drawn and handsome face, the sad-sweet smile that seems to be the signature of so many Irish philosophers." — Herb Caen, *San Francisco Chronicle*.

GOSSAGE ON ADVERTISING

Is advertising worth saving? From an economic point of view I don't think that most of it is. From an aesthetic point of view I'm damn sure it's not; it is thoughtless, boring, and there is simply too much of it.

I long for the day when advertising will become a business for a grown man. But before we can find out whether it is possible we must remove the obstacles that confine it to being the well-known multibillion-dollar sledgehammer to drive an economy-size thumbtack.

Advertising is as curiously innocent of the shape of evil as a ten-year-old. There is no real comprehension of sin. The industry, it is true, is awash with condemnations of bad practice, but one gets the same feeling as when a child evangelist preaches against fornication. It is unlikely that he knows what he is talking about.

Advertising is by nature a very limited art form. But like any other form, it requires superlative talent, if the results are to be superlative. The upshot is, that a large talent will have to settle for a small, if precise, outlet. It is like making Steinways which will only be used for playing Chopsticks.

The real fact of the matter is that *nobody reads ads*. People read what interests them, and sometimes it's an ad.

Most good copywriters are very strange people who have only reached copywriting after eliminating every other means of making a living through writing. . . . If he is praised by outsiders for his copywriting on artistic grounds he is likely to cringe a little.

Advertising men *pretend* to like one another, but down deep inside they don't really. Advertising men find other advertising men a rather dull lot, and for good reason. We *are* a rather dull lot collectively, without much to say. No, that's not true. We have a great deal to say and we say it over and over again, possibly to convince ourselves that it is true.

If I have any "the-man-who" trademark in the ad business, I suppose it's the idea of breaking off in the middle of an Irish whiskey ad and picking up in the next where I left off. To show you how this kind of revolutionary invention comes about: I'd simply written too much copy for the first ad. So I said, "Hell, let's stop here and continue next time."

Photo by Skelton Photography

ISBN 0-252-01278-X

Chapter 1

Is Advertising Worth Saving?

One time, on a trip through southeast Asia, I landed at Bangkok. As the passengers got off the plane the distinctive odor of the Orient hit us smack in the face. A woman passenger standing next to me asked, "What's that awful smell?"

"That's, uh, fertilizer," I answered.

"Yes, I know," she said. "But what did they do to it?"

Being an old fertilizing agency man myself, I am not anxious to push this analogy too far. I was going to say that I didn't want to run it into the ground, but that's exactly the thing to do with fertilizer—or advertising—if you want to make anything grow. The trouble comes when you lay it on so thick that you can't see the forest for the fertilizer. At which point it starts to attract flies and even fish; minnows, at any rate. And the neighbors begin to complain; the smell is always more noticeable inside the house; particularly near radio or TV sets.

It would be splendid if we could work out a formula for the amount of fertilizer needed to grow a crop. It's very hard to find agreement on this because, apparently, some products need a great deal more advertising than others if they are to sell. Their sales picture is almost pure fertilizer; 99-44/100 percent, anyway. The products that need the most fertilizer are precisely those that nobody would conceivably be without anyway. I dwelt on this point on a TV panel show and therefore questioned how necessary advertising really was to our economy since the bulk of big advertising seemed to be devoted to such products. Another advertising man took sharp exception to my conjectures and said that he knew for a fact that if Procter and Gamble, for instance, stopped advertising their sales would fall off 25 percent the first year. I asked him, "Do you suppose anybody would be any dirtier?"

The answer is, of course, that people wouldn't be any dirtier if soap advertising were stopped. And people would still be able to handle their headaches, upset stomachs, or symptoms of neuralgia just as well if all of the aspirin derivatives and compounds were to quit advertising. And we would get through to lunch just as well if our children weren't incited to yammering us into closets full of breakfast foods. And we would manage to get a snootful on occasion without being reminded to do so by whiskey, beer, and wine advertisers. And I suppose we would shave regularly and brush our teeth, and our womenfolk would remember to grease themselves up like channel swimmers before they go to bed and put on fresh faces the next day without being gigged about it 24 hours a day.

I think we can go further and say that if these businesses were to fold entirely the net effect on the gross national product would not be terribly important. I daresay we'd all look a lot crummier until we learned how to make do with salt on a fuzzy stick and how to shave with a super-honed ax, but the whole lot do not really count for much in the economic scheme of things. And yet, I would guess that they spend well over 50 percent of our yearly advertising expenditure.

Which brings us to the subject of this chapter. Is advertising worth saving? From an economic point of view I don't think that most of it is. From an aesthetic point of view I'm damn sure it's not; it is thoughtless, boring, and there is simply too much of it; but we'll get around to the point of aesthetics later. For the moment I'd like to talk about the sheer economics involved.

I have no objection to relatively nonessential items being advertised. I can't afford to object; that's most of our firm's business. Oh, if our clients were to stop advertising tomorrow it would, naturally, inflict severe hardship in some quarters; I would have to go to work, for one thing. But the total loss would not be very great, even to the advertising business, for the simple reason that our agency does not believe in spending too much money for advertising. We try to keep budgets as low as we possibly can and to say what we do say in as interesting a manner as possible.

These two concepts seem to go hand in hand. If you have something pertinent to say you neither have to say it to very many people — only to those who you think will be interested — nor do you have to say it very often. How many times do you have to be told that your house is on fire? How often does your wife have to read that a coat she has been lusting for has been reduced from $200 to $79.50 before she is off and running? How often do you have to read a book, a news story, or see a movie or play? If it is interesting, once is enough; if it is dull, once is plenty. Wild horses couldn't drag you back again. But advertising, working on the theory of the captive audience, and having in effect bought you, can bring the wild horses—straining mightily to deliver an aspirin, or 10,000 filter traps, or eight draining sinuses—right into your living room.

You see, the trouble with advertising, as with fertilizer, is not in itself, but in how it is spread around. The unalterable fact of the business is simply this: there is only so much fertilizer. There is only so much radio or television time and only so many newspapers or magazines, and their pages are only expandable to a certain point, regardless of what you think when you pick up the Sunday paper. Most of all, there is only so much human attention span; we only have so much time to absorb the advertising messages which assail us. But since ours is a competitive business in an open economic system, our services and facilities are for sale to the highest bidder; and the highest bidders are just those who have the highest profit margins—usually because they have little intrinsic worth—most of their value is contributed by the advertising they buy so freely.

Thus we see that consumer advertising will tend to be more and more dominated by products which, by the size of their budgets and the fatuity of their messages, tend to make advertising more and more objectionable. In turn, the advertising media they dominate tend to become degraded as well. Then the Federal Trade Commission (FTC) comes in, a few poor quislings are disgraced for life, the government forbids Ted Bates to throw baseballs at our television screens, and we have to go back to pumping digestive juices through our livers all by ourselves. Carter's Little Pills just aren't the same without that dear old middle name.

Where will it all end? Well, I imagine it will get more and more trivial while at the same time getting more and more boring until we are left with nothing but police calls, satellite signals, and the exquisite pleasure of heaving mail addressed Occupant into the wastepaper basket as acceptable entertainment.

Except for one thing: the whole thing is becoming so uneconomical that even the most lavish advertisers are bound to be getting a little nervous about it. After all, there's no use in going to all the work and expense of putting on the world's dullest show if nobody's going to look at it. Me, I'm so leery I wouldn't turn on television to see Rosser Reeves and Marion Harper, Jr. playing touch footall with a porcupine. Because I know that afterwards I'd have to watch the victor delivering a Gillette commercial from the locker room.

It used to be you could rely on kids; you remember the fiction of the twelve-year-old mentality? I suspect that it was not so much that twelve years old was the age they were shooting at with their advertising as the age that they had to settle for. I don't know what the age is now, but it must be considerably lower. I have a seven-year-old son, so it must be six they are working on nowadays. The reason I say this is we were out riding here recently and we saw a gasoline billboard showing two rabbits looking wistfully down the road after a car, and the larger rabbit was saying, "It's no use, son, you can't beat methyl power." I asked my boy what he thought of that; whether he believed that ad or not. And he said that sure he did, "Look Dad, no rabbit can beat any car, no matter what kind of gas it's using."

I told this story in a speech at the San Francisco Advertising Club and the advertising manager of the company involved, who was present, was considerably miffed about it. "Look," he said, "we don't put out advertising for seven year olds; grownups seem to get the idea just fine." I'm sure he's right, and I imagine that the message did get across to adults.

Which raises a frightening conjecture: maybe grownups—ourselves—are the only people who are still willing to put themselves out to grab conventional advertising messages. Perhaps children, the whole new generation coming up, simply are not taken in by such cute fantasy. I believe this is true; how else could you account for the success of such magazines as *MAD* and others who spend a great deal of their space ridiculing advertising? It's the business of the emperor's new clothes all over again. A child—only in this case it seems to be millions upon millions of children of all ages—sees right through the whole thing; and he or she is not amused. How awful!

So it seems probable that in the future, if present advertising is to continue, it will be directed not to the twelve-year-old mentality but to us senior citizens. And one day, despite the benefits of Geritol and other life-prolonging devices, we will eventually die out, leaving nothing but a few peeling barn paints as monuments to our gorgeous receptivity as an audience. I suppose it will be like the GAR; there will eventually be one last man—or probably a woman—alive, who still likes commercials, and Mr. Clean will be playing to him or her alone. A poignant thought.

Well, the big boys know about this, you can bet; sure they do. You can't tell me that they can have 10,000 captive Ph.D.s locked up there on the thirty-third floor without one of them somehow tripping over the horrid truth. It's like the roomful of monkeys banging away on typewriters. By the law of mathematical probability one of them is bound to have stumbled onto the fact. Yes, our leaders know what's going on and are probably already making plans to get more entertaining. Even though it means that they'll have to knock five or ten million dollars off the budget. Because when you get entertaining or interesting or pertinent, you simply can't repeat the message so often.

People can stand any amount of boredom or routine. You can say L.S./ M.F.T. or Flip-Top Box at them for years on end after the first shock and it doesn't really bother them. Until the day comes when they are so unbothered that they decide not to bother about turning on the set at all; or about buying the product. But when you say something interesting you can't say it all that often, and this means that you will just have to spend less money on your advertising, hard though it may be. It's a tough thing to decide to stop spending money when you've been flinging it around like a drunken account executive all these years.

Oh, there is one thing I want to interject here as a fortifying argument. It is this: the very bulk of advertising is its worst enemy because somewhere along the line an immunity starts building up against irritation. This is one of the reasons people aren't bothered more by annoying advertising than they are. If they had to absorb it all they would go mad. Thus we see that as the immunity builds up it costs more and more to advertise every year. It's like narcotics, it must be taken in ever-increasing doses to achieve the same effect. Until one day the patient dies, or goes crackers and is led off to some nice quiet place away from advertising while he undergoes the difficult withdrawal symptoms.

Anyway, I like to imagine a better world where there will be less, and more stimulating, advertising. I suppose all of us would like to see this come to pass. It would certainly clear away some of the confusion from advertising's murky picture and make it easier to comprehend. In my experience, sales personnel are almost as baffled by the structure of advertising and its various justifications as are advertising men.

I have a confession to make. For years I was very humble; I thought I was the only one who didn't understand. I used to go to luncheon clubs all the time hoping to get the word from the speaker of the day. I was also more naive; I believed the poop sheets that they put out beforehand with a picture of some hotshot on the cover and a glowing rundown of what he was going to talk about. And afterwards I would walk back to the office, still belching from the breaded veal cutlet, chicken à la king, or roast turkey, bemused by all the words of wisdom and feeling inadequate because I *still* didn't understand.

I might have gone on like that forever except that one day I picked up an ad club bulletin that told about next week's speaker and how he was going to give everybody the word about advertising. You could see from what they said that here, at least, was a man who really understood what it was all about. Well, I got very excited, as you might imagine, and was on the point of calling up to make reservations when I happened to notice that the man in the picture—the one they were talking about—was me. Talk about agonizing reappraisal. Not only didn't *they* understand about advertising but they thought that *I* did. If I had had any moral fiber I would have refused to speak; but of course I did. I marched up there just like a little man and told them how to lead their lives. There is nothing so good for overcoming one's ignorance as the sound of one's own dear voice.

Anyway, to get back to salesmen, it is small wonder that *they* don't understand about advertising either. Now, I will admit that we in advertising do the very best we can to explain it to sales personnel. Every salesman, I suppose, has been to annual sales meetings where somebody from the advertising department or the agency presents next year's advertising program with slides, the ads blown up large enough to make post office murals, and bar charts showing the degree of penetration achieved by poster showings in Cincinnati as contrasted to the product distribution pattern. All good stuff.

But the fact of the matter is that it's mostly a waste of time, because salesmen, being very impractical, are really only interested in two things. One, they want to be able to walk into a store or an office and announce where they're from without people either saying Who? or getting that glazed look they get when they know where you're from but don't give a damn. The salesman reasonably expects his company's advertising to be interesting enough so that the prospect's receptivity is a *little* stimulated; it puts him miles ahead in his sales talk. The only other thing that the salesman really wants from advertising is something to hold in his hand when he makes a call; something that solves a problem or has something to do with the matter at hand.

As we know, an awful lot of advertising doesn't perform either of these functions but is merely a few more acres of printed stuff he's got to carry around in his briefcase, and if it doesn't mean much to him the chances are remote that it is going to mean anything at all to the man he is calling on.

Another thing that I think baffles salesmen is how advertising agencies really work—how they make their money. This is not to be wondered at, for it is the most God-awful, ridiculous set-up imaginable. Until it is changed there is little prospect that advertising will ever achieve professional status or that the advertisements themselves will be markedly more effective, efficient, and pertinent.

The advertising business, as you know, works on what is known as the commission system. But, to a salesman at any rate, it is a commission system in name only. Looking at it coldly it is nothing more or less than a kickback system. When it pops up in any other field it is not only roundly condemned from a moral point of view but the feds also crack down on it faster than you can say Bobby Kennedy. The bare bones of the matter are that advertising agencies are paid not by the client for whom they are supposedly working but by the newspapers, magazines, and television and radio stations who sell them space and time.

The agency is given a kickback of 15 percent for buying, not for selling. This would have some justification if, as it was when the system began, the agency really performed a selling function for the advertising medium. But this is no longer true, nor has it been for fifty years.

In actuality the medium must maintain a sales staff to sell *to* the agency, thus incurring, on the face of it, a double sales cost. They have gone along with it because, if it suits the agency and the client, it's no skin off their nose. All they've done is hike their prices to cover the 15 percent.

The client goes along because it looks like a good deal. They, in effect, get the work for no more than they would have to pay for the advertising without an agency.

And this brings us to the really sly element in the whole business: there is no alternative for the client. Whether he goes through an agency or buys direct he pays the full price; he doesn't get the 15 percent himself, only the agency can do that. So you see why advertising agencies have clung to the system. It effectively forces advertisers to deal through them, if for no other reason than the economics involved; 15 percent is a hell of a lot of money.

Well, the defenders of the system will point out that it has worked pretty well despite the logical defects, which they don't bother to deny. And they will say, with some justice, that the dishonest restraint of trade overtones are simply not borne out in operation. And yet, you show me a business where one's income is dependent on the amount of money spent rather than on the amount of money that comes in and I will show you a business that is doomed, even with the very best of intentions, to mutual distrust and enormous psychological barriers. It is as though your corporation were to engage a law firm on the basis of how many lawsuits it could instigate rather than on how many it could keep you out of, and, to top it off, drawing its fee from the other party rather than from yourselves. There are, now that I think of it, lawyers who work on a basis somewhat like this, and we call them ambulance chasers.

So we see that the advertising agency's compensation is based upon what they spend rather than on the services they perform. Not only is this psychologically wrong, because it makes their financial recommendations suspect, but it puts the entire question of advertising expenditures in the wrong perspective. Instead of starting out the way you would with any other project, by defining the problem and *then* deciding what to do and *then* allocating the money, the procedure is reversed. The advertising recommendation is based on money to be spent rather than problems to be solved. In most companies, first a budget is approved, and then eager minds provide justifications for spending it in this or that fashion. And then the rest of the year every other department in the company devotes its spare time to thinking up ways to carve off pieces of the advertising budget; and, as we know, they are remarkably successful. And the next year it's the same thing all over again. Is it any wonder that most advertising has the efficacy of a butterfly's belch? And that salesmen are often discontented with their company's advertising programs? The system had them beat going in.

Well, what are we to do about it? I can tell you what we and our clients do about it. We work for fees. The fee is substantially more than the 15 percent commission would be. There are a couple of reasons for this. In the first place we believe our work to be superior to that generally available and therefore worth more. In the second place, we find that our clients can easily afford it because they get more out of it, and also because we tend to spend far less money in total than is usual. So they make out and we make out. In addition, we write contracts with them in which our fee increases each year as their business increases. This does not necessarily mean that their total advertising budget need increase; indeed, it could conceivably decrease. Oh, one other thing; since the industry hasn't yet been enlightened enough to jettison the commission system, we go along with it to the extent of crediting commissions against the fee so the poor client won't have to pay twice.

Now, this not only gives *us* a psychological advantage and enables us to act as professionals, but it is reassuring to the client as well. We are not forever in the position of having to sell him something. He can take our recommendations at face value; we are his men. Incidentally, we generally have money left over at the end of the year, and you'd think a client would be happy about that, wouldn't you? Not always. We have found there is nothing that a department head detests so much as having money left in his budget at the end of the fiscal year. Because then the comptroller, or whoever the eagle eye for the company treasury is, will think they don't need it and cut if off beforehand next year; that's what they're afraid of. We urge clients to keep an open mind on this subject because, despite everything you have heard about the value of repetition and keeping forever lastingly at it, there are some problems that can be solved with one ad if it's the right ad. And there are some problems that won't be solved by any ad or any number of ads; you should simply save your money. Maybe there is some way to go about it that won't cost you anything.

Well, that's the sort of advice you get from people who don't have to sell you something before they can eat.

There's another thing we are able to do because we're not dependent on selling a big media recommendation with ads to fit. We can do one ad at a time. Literally, that's the way we do it. We do one advertisement and then wait to see what happens; and then we do another advertisement. Oh, sometimes we get way ahead and do three. But when we do, we often have to change the third one before it runs. Because if you put out an advertisement that creates activity, or response, or involves the audience, you will find that something happens that changes the character of the succeeding ads. It's like a conversation. You say something and then the other person says something; and unless you're a bore, you listen to what they say and respond accordingly. This, after all, is the only polite way, when you come to think of it. It's amazing how much fresher and more to the point the ads seem when you approach them in this fashion.

People like to be treated as human beings rather than as consumers, and they react very well to it, particularly when it comes to trotting down to the store, gas station, or saloon and buying some. Every one of our clients has enjoyed notable sales increases. This is in answer to the unspoken question that we have been asked ever since we did our first interesting ad: "Yeah, but does it sell?"

Now, back to the question: is advertising worth saving? Yes, if we can learn to look at advertising not as a means for filling so much space and time but as a technique for solving problems. And this will not be possible until we destroy the commission system and start predicating our work on what is to be *earned* rather than on what is to be *spent*.

Chapter 2

Advertising and the Facts of Life

Instead of the customary witty story, I shall start off this chapter with a reading from Scripture. Not that I have anything against witty stories. As a matter of fact, since this particular quotation is about Adam and Eve, I suppose I could have begun with "that reminds me of an allegory." Or even, "A funny thing happened on the way out of the Garden." However, to establish an appropriate and improving moral tone I shall stick to the original. Genesis III, then:

We recall that Eve, an inexperienced young housewife, has been approached by a glib-tongued spokesman for the Fruit of the Tree of the Knowledge of Good and Evil Advisory Board. He was a snake, true, but it didn't make so much difference before TV. Let us proceed:

> And when the woman saw that the tree was good for food, and that it was pleasant to the eyes, and a tree to be desired to make one wise, she took of the fruit thereof and did eat, and gave also unto her husband with her; and he did eat.
>
> And the eyes of them both were opened, and they knew that they were naked; and they sewed fig leaves together, and made themselves aprons.
>
> And they heard the voice of the Lord God walking in the garden in the cool of the day: and Adam and his wife hid themselves from the presence of the Lord God amongst the trees of the garden.
>
> And the Lord God called unto Adam and said unto him, "Where art thou?"

And he said, "I heard Thy voice in the garden and I was afraid because I was naked; and I hid myself."

And he said, "Who told thee that thou was naked? Has thou eaten of the tree, whereof I commanded thee that thou shouldst not eat?"

At this point we see some of the fanciest buck-passing in history, unsurpassed until the recent Federal Communications Commission (FCC) investigations:

And the man said, "The woman whom thou gavest to be with me, she gave me of the tree and I did eat."

And the Lord God said unto the woman, "What is this that thou hast done?" And the woman said, "The serpent beguiled me and I did eat."

Well, you know the rest of the story: the snake was condemned to crawl upon his belly, which makes you wonder how snakes got around before that. And Adam and Eve were expelled from the Garden of their innocence and ignorance with these words: "Behold the man is become as one of us, to know good and evil."

Well, this is a very useful allegory and not nearly as sad and dreadful as is often supposed. To know good from bad—the critical faculty—may be our greatest blessing; but it is also our greatest burden for it embodies our sense of personal responsibility.

The nice thing about allegories is they are so applicable; you can apply them to almost anything. Here I'd like to apply this one to advertising, though with a few twists I suppose it would work just as well for the United Nations, the United Automobile Workers, or even the United Presbyterian Church. No, not quite as well, for advertising seems to be a peculiarly fertile field for this particular allegory.

Advertising, being a very young thing, is as curiously innocent of the shape of evil as a ten-year-old. There is no real comprehension of sin. The industry, it is true, is awash with condemnations of bad practice, but one gets the same feeling as when a child evangelist preaches against fornication. It is unlikely that he knows what he is talking about.

You see, before personal responsibility can come into play one must have some notion of what the score is. There is shocking little evidence that our industry does know what the score is, or even what game it is playing, or even which side it is on.

There is some vague notion that a team exists. It is called Advertising, and any blatherskite can play who brings his own ball. This ought to be very confusing to the cheering section, which for some reason or other is almost entirely made up of the players themselves. But no, we solve it neatly by rooting for everybody, even when they run the wrong way.

Our industry's outward solidity under the vague banner of advertising is more than I can fathom. The indiscriminate loyalty we show for anyone who identifies himself or his works with our business is not only foolish, it is injurious. Never to criticize openly, never to reject overtly, is to have no standards, no real morals.

I cannot recall the time when our industry has taken a public stand on anything that anybody gave two whoops in hell about. Oh, we come out foursquare for schools and against forest fires, but that's about as far as it goes. Do we ever do anything except mumble piously about the all too evident abuses within advertising—abuses inflicted on every man, woman, and child in this country? No, we content ourselves with such bold ventures as Advertising Recognition Week, as though anyone could help recognizing it.

Not only are we extremely loath as an industry to make forthright public stands with teeth in them, but we disapprove of anyone else who does. When Mr. Minow, Chairman of the FCC, says that the advertising abuses on television are terrible, everybody from General Sarnoff and Dr. Stanton on down har-rumphs and gets out the old bar charts and surveys to prove that they aren't so terrible. This, when all anyone has to do to prove that they *are* so terrible, is turn on the set and wait awhile.

Another example: a while ago the *San Francisco Chronicle* ran some pictures showing how outdoor advertisers were lousing up the freeways. Now this was perfectly evident to anyone who has ever driven on the freeways; outdoor *does* louse it up. So what happened? Half the agencies in town signed some sort of petition circulated by an interested party protesting that this was a threat against the advertising industry—against *all* advertising. Poppycock.

I don't know where the justification for this sort of action stems from. Perhaps it is a perversion of the remark attributed to Voltaire, "I disapprove of what you say, but I will defend to the death your right to say it."

I can think of a lot of things I won't defend to the death. I won't defend Dristan's right to drain sinuses all over my living room or the right of all those silly, grinning, preposterous hair preparation commercials to make me want to rip the set out of the wall. And I won't defend to the death a station's right to lure me into seeing a movie and then clobbering me all during the last half of it—after I'm hooked—with triple spots every ten minutes, as happened the other night. And I won't defend to the death outdoor advertising's right to stick up an ad along the freeway built with my tax money so that I have to look at *it* instead of at my beautiful city.

However, our gutless, formless industry, while it tolerates such opinions as these within its ranks—having no choice—gets exceedingly wroth when they are made to the general public. It's as though the people we advertise to aren't supposed to think about it. Or perhaps it's just that we aren't supposed to disturb the animals when consuming.

I wrote an article for *Harper's Magazine* a couple of years ago which expressed dissatisfaction with some aspects of advertising. The trade press had a marvelous time; everybody jumped in with both feet. I recall one treasured comment from the head of one of our advertising trade associations: "This is no time to be playing with matches when the house is burning down."

I hope it seems as obvious to you as it does to me that unless we, as individuals, as companies, as an industry, reject the things we don't like and fight for the things we do like, we shall, as a business, become more and more discredited. We shall all go down with the ship; not even the rats are deserting it.

Advertising as an industry has always been morbidly preoccupied with its own "image"; largely, I think, because it has little notion of its real identity. So it is not surprising that many of us have grave reservations about the system generally, even though we may find satisfaction in our own work.

I didn't realize how widespread these reservations were until a few years ago when advertising was having one of its recurring attacks of chronic imagitis; which is like Madison Avenue flu except that you only lose face, not the account. I can't recall exactly what brought on this particular attack. Either the feds had caught some of the boys trying to make a piece of non-sandpaper look better groomed through better shaving or the Food and Drug folks had taken exception to frosting an angel food cake with brushless lather on TV.

At any rate, *Time* decided to do a roundup story on how advertising men felt about advertising morals. Eventually they got down to me, and a *Time* reporter came by and interviewed me for forty-five minutes, during which time, knowing me, I probably didn't shut my mouth once; thousands and thousands of golden words. The next week *Time* sent by a photographer *and* a reporter who wanted to clear up a few points from my earlier filibuster. He was wonderfully attentive and respectful as I blatted out my brains for another forty-five minutes.

A couple of weeks after that the story appeared and, with feverish fingers, I opened to the business section of the book, wondering how many pages they had devoted to my world-shaking opinions. My picture was there, all right, but out of ninety minutes of talk, just one sentence, a direct quotation; it was this: "I don't know a first class brain in the business who has any respect for it." That was it in its entirety: "I don't know a first class brain in the business who has any respect for it."

Well, I almost fainted. I'm an outspoken man, and I'm sure I said it, but that's a pretty blunt statement to see in print with nothing to soften it or qualify it. And I had no wish to overtly offend all the people I know in advertising. And I was certain that I'd get a lot of telephone calls and letters from people who were offended. A day passed, a week passed, a month passed, and not one call or letter attacking me. I didn't broach the subject myself, of course. Then one day, I was riding in a plane from New York with one of our industry's most eminent spokesmen, also quoted in the *Time* article, and I asked him if he'd noticed my published comment. He said, of course he had. I told him I hadn't gotten one beef from it and I wondered why. He said, "Well, Howard, I guess it's true, isn't it?"

Is it true? If it is, I can think of several reasons why. They aren't secrets; they are perfectly evident to anyone inside the business. The first to come to mind is the general level of ethical hypocrisy. The Four A's (The American Association of Advertising Agencies), and other associations, have rules condemning speculative presentations—which is advertisingese for stealing—at least, not from one another, and yet, I wonder whether there is an agency man who hasn't at some time been party to stealing an account from some fellow member. I don't know what the answer to this is except to abolish the association. But that would be even worse. It's nice to be able to keep your eye on a lot of your competitors at one time, even though it's only once a month at dinner.

Another thing that is likely to breed a certain amount of disrespect for advertising among its practitioners is the triviality that constitutes most of big advertising—a multibillion dollar hammer hitting a thirty-nine cent thumbtack.

A third factor that is apt to affect our regard for the business we are in is the abuses of public trust and public taste. These will range from incidents smacking of downright fraud, accompanied by action from the Federal Trade Commission (FTC), to simple bad taste and a disregard for the decent opinion of mankind. The industry tries to pretend that these incidents are few and far between and that, when they do occur, they are committed by fringe or fly-by-night operators. It just isn't true; they happen all the time, and the bulk of intelligence-insulting, banal, tasteless advertising is done by the biggest agencies for the biggest clients. If you doubt this, just watch television objectively, especially during the day or late at night. That a great many of these abuses can be laid at the door of the media makes little difference, for it is advertising and its system that bears the blame and is, in fact, ultimately responsible.

I have suggested that a sense of personal responsibility is not unconnected with a knowledge of the facts of life. Well, how can advertising become more personally responsible? The same way children become personally responsible, by being thrust out into life, by direct experience.

Someone has said that the difference between children and adults is that the world happens to children; adults happen to the world. We develop stability and then momentum—we start to become mature—when we start happening *back* at the world and accept the responsibility for our actions.

I think the reason advertising seems to lack this personal responsibility is because most advertisements are so protective, safe, and, yes, even introverted. Certainly they are shielded from real life; they rarely engage their readers on a direct basis or attempt to involve them.

An advertisement that sticks its neck out in a forthright manner, as though it expected to be spoken back to, is rare indeed; and it is too bad. For this attitude is the beginning of reality, of experience, of personal responsibility. It is as necessary for corporations—who are, after all, legal persons—as it is for individuals.

Most advertising, by playing it safe, by never sticking its neck out, is sort of an eyeless mask that effectively prevents the people behind it from talking to the people in front of it, or from even seeing them. The audience remains out of contact; you never know whether you got through to them or not, or whether they applauded, booed, or simply looked the other way. The cash register is no substitute for this sort of response, for, as we know, many other elements enter into making a cash register ring. Until advertising really believes that there is someone out there and talks to them—not in advertisingese, but in direct, well-formed English—we will never develop the personal responsibility toward our audience, and ourselves, that even a ninth rate tap dancer has. The audience is our first responsibility, even before the client, for if we cannot involve them what good will it do him?

Let's see, we were talking about snakes. The snake in the Garden of Eden, whom I mentioned earlier, I regard as a pretty good fellow, a benefactor to mankind, for without him we would still be little more than animals.

Perhaps we, each of us, make our own snakes simply by sticking our necks out far enough. Of course, they can be chopped off, but that's the chance you take. Come to think of it, I'm not sure we have any alternative; it's not much harder to chop off a short neck than it is a long one. And there seems to be more and more guys with axes hanging around every day.

Amen.

Chapter 3

When Will Advertising Become a Business for Grown Men?
(Or "How to Want to Do Better Advertising")

The other evening we had a professor and his wife over for dinner. In addition to teaching, he has also been the chaplain of the university for a good many years. He is a delightful, intelligent, witty man with a broad, perceptive view of the world around him. During the conversation he said that the greatest obstacle he encountered in talking to people was the label of clergyman. As soon as it was known that he was a man of the cloth, people clammed up, or became defensive, or in some cases, offensive. So if he wished to discuss anything that might have to do with religion he often had to mention all the things he *didn't* stand for before he got around to what he *did* stand for.

I thought to myself, "Why, that's what advertising men do, too!" I mentioned this to him, and he immediately started talking about advertising in terms of the things he didn't like. I thought, "Oh, here we go again."

In my teaching[1] I also find I must spend half my time clearing away the deadwood before I can begin to talk constructively about advertising and what it can do, and occasionally does do. And I am sick and tired of it; I am not primarily a critic, I am an advertising man. And I long for the day when it will become a business for a grown man. But before we can find out whether it is possible we must remove the obstacles that confine it to being the well-known multibillion-dollar sledgehammer to drive an economy-size

---

A version of this essay appeared in the *Penn State Journalist*, January 1963.

thumbtack. And I'm afraid that the people in advertising are the ones who must do it. Before advertising can become better, we must *want* to do better at it, and do the things to make it so.

Many of you have something to do with advertising, even if it is only creating it, or paying out the money for it. If there are any of you who neither support advertising financially nor are supported by it, but are reading for other reasons—possibly morbid curiosity—you have the greatest stake in advertising; you are its audience.

Now, the word "audience" is widely used in advertising and in very strange ways; at least they do not correspond to what the rest of humanity understands by the word. No, we use "audience" to mean a group of prospective consumers who have been gathered together by someone else—a magazine, newspaper, or radio or TV station—for some other reason. Then, when they are comfortably seated, we get in there and make our pitch. Ideally, we think it better to get on and off fast before they can budge.

This gets harder and harder to do, with television particularly. A new, speedier race is developing; eventually we may be born wearing tennis shoes. The record for intra-commercial activities is currently held by my twelve-year-old nephew, Stephen Bowerman, who, on May 10 last, during a program break went to the bathroom, thence to the kitchen where he prepared a peanut butter and jelly sandwich, drank half a pint of milk directly from the bottle, was scolded by his mother for this, promised he wouldn't do it again, and got in a fight with his fourteen-year-old brother as he fell over his feet while reentering the darkened room; all in fifty-two and three-tenths seconds; moreover, arriving in time to join in the last eight bars of the jingle that concluded the fourth spot. A memorable feat.

At any rate, when advertising talks about the audience, it doesn't mean its audience, it means somebody else's, gathered there to watch or read something else. Advertising hopes to snag this audience as it flips through the pages or watches or listens its way through a show. This seems reasonable, doesn't it? Nobody looks at advertising on purpose, do they?

Yes they do. Most women find the department store ads much more interesting than the front page. I daresay that the *New Yorker*'s advertising is read on purpose, in most cases before settling down into the editorial matter. I think a great deal more advertising would be read on purpose if it was more interesting. In the few instances where it has been tried, extraordinarily interesting or entertaining advertising has commanded its own audience and has sold well, too.

However, the real fact of the matter is that *nobody reads ads*. People read what interests them, and sometimes it's an ad. What I'm getting at is this: we should think of the audience out there as *our* audience, not as a group of people we must collar simply because we have some sort of concession we have bought. I was going to liken our role to that of a hot dog hawker at a sports event, but that's not particularly flattering to the weenie salesman; after all, he adds to the enjoyment of the proceedings and we usually don't. As a matter of fact, we rarely have anything to do with the proceedings at all. So, all we can do if we feel any duty to the audience at all—or to ourselves, for that matter—is fabricate our own proceedings within the time or space limits. And do it as interestingly and entertainingly as possible.

But before we can even begin to do this we must get it into our heads that the buying of time or space is not the taking out of a hunting license on someone else's private preserve but is the renting of a stage on which we may perform. Advertising is not a right, it is a privilege. Our first duty is not to the old sales curve, it is to the audience. Until we conceive of this clearly our advertising will not be better than it is, nor will the results improve. As it stands, each year advertising becomes less effective because people simply pay less attention to it. In consequence the advertising bill goes up and up every year, quite aside from inflationary factors. An immunity sets in. As with narcotics, it takes more and more to achieve the same effect.

Advertising men often find the thought that anything should come before duty to the product heretical. Strangely enough, most clients don't, once it is explained to them. Any salesman will get it right off the bat. They are used to regarding their audience first and foremost, because if they don't please them they won't get the order. I'm sure that salesmen for companies who put out boring, offensive, or repetitious advertising would not dream of using those techniques on *their* customers. Unless they are masochists who simply love being tossed bodily out of places, including their jobs. Then why the double standard about advertising? Because they think of advertising as something different, as beyond the rules of ordinary behavior toward audiences.

Well, there is no arguing that even awful advertising is effective if it is craftily done and you have enough of it. So is a knock on the head with a baseball bat or shooting fish in a barrel, but neither one of them is very sporty. And there is some evidence that the fish don't hold still as well as they used to and are developing armor plate. However, what is more important than these practical objections is that it is simply not right to treat an audience in this fashion. If we can't look at it from a broad, ethical point of view then we ought to look at it personally, to please ourselves. We are all members of the audience, too, and are bored or irritated right along with everybody else.

It is not an unusual thought, this matter of responsibility to one's audience. It is the first principle of the theater, newspapers, magazines, political speeches, or indeed any other form of communications except advertising—and those media dominated entirely or in part by advertising. I can only think of one major medium entirely dominated by advertising and that is outdoor advertising. Consideration of the audience has never been a factor at all, except for some primitive attempts at public service messages against forest fires or for going to church. And, oh yes, for advertising; you know the sort of thing I mean—that plugs advertising as a bulwark of democracy and so on.

But aside from that, outdoor advertising doesn't bother with the audience at all; except to count it as it goes by. I don't really know what more they could do to please the audience except tear all the billboards down. I don't know anyone who really likes billboards, except presumably those in the business. I doubt very much whether they even constitute a proper advertising medium. A medium to me is one that communicates something else and *also* communicates advertising. Outdoor's medium is the out-of-doors, I suppose, and that is not theirs to sell. To be sure, they are standing on private property, but they are broadcasting into the public road, projecting their messages on citizens without their permission. There is no freedom of choice involved whatsoever. I think this is quite wrong, because it is not the outdoor advertiser's street or highway; it is yours.

Mind you, I am not concerned with the aesthetics at all. I have seen lots of locations where the billboard was the nicest looking thing around. As a matter of fact, I *like* outdoor advertising; I just think it has no right to be outdoors. I also have a hunch that a successful citizen's lawsuit could be waged against billboards on the grounds of invasion of privacy.

Now this sort of talk always throws my advertising colleagues into a flap because, they say, if you encourage the public to act against one part of advertising, why, what's to keep them from acting against the rest of advertising about things they don't like? What indeed? And why shouldn't they? It's their communications media we are using or abusing, as the case may be. As far as that goes, why should I, an advertising man, feel compelled to identify myself, much less protect, every rag-tag, bob-tailed creature or practice that crawls out of the woodwork of our far from perfect house?

We have two other media that are dominated, at least in part, by advertising: television and radio. Advertising dominates our broadcast media and it's not a condition that works very well for anyone; not for the audience, the stations, or the advertisers. Our programming has gone to hell, and—disaster of disasters—spot announcements are crammed one on top of another so they aren't really very good buys.

Now, this all started back with radio. Before the advent of TV, the big programs were mostly produced by the agencies. When television came along, the big networks announced that all that was going to be changed. From then on, they, the networks, would produce the shows or ordain what was to go in the time slot and then make it available to advertisers. Of course, despite a valiant try, it didn't work out that way. It couldn't possibly work out any way but that advertisers would continue to dominate programming whether they really wanted to or not.

You see, anytime you are able to buy a specified block of time on a station it immediately assumes a market value in comparison with a competitive block of time on another station. The value of these blocks is not based on cost so much as it is on comparative ratings. So, to keep these times commercially desirable it is necessary to keep the ratings desirable, too. So the station will do whatever is necessary to keep the ratings competitive, which means, in effect, that its programming is determined not by what it thinks it should be but by what the advertiser will buy. The predictable result, as you can readily confirm by merely turning on your set, is blah mediocrity for the most part competing with everybody else's blah mediocrity. This is in accord with an advertising Gresham's Law. Just as bad money drives out good, so bad programming will drive out good programming.

The only possible way around it is to do what the English have done with their commercial television: sell rotating spots only, not sponsorship—the magazine concept. Now this makes sense for everyone, I think. Advertising certainly has more value when it is not fighting another ad. And certainly it can afford to be more ingenious and, yes, thoughful of the audience when it is not struggling to make itself heard.

If this sounds outrageous to you, merely ask yourself whether the best print media would be nearly as good as they are, or would give advertisers the platform they do, if advertisers were able to sponsor their editorial matter. Certainly not. There are, of course, papers who *do* permit advertiser influence on or in their editorial matter; and you know how we look at them. They are precisely the least valuable papers on the list.

It is all the more surprising that this effective advertiser domination should occur in broadcasting, because broadcasting is more demonstrably a public utility. It is piped in just as is electricity, gas, or water, on a flow basis. Moreover, its channels are so much a part of general, public ownership that no one would ever think to challenge a national government's right to control them. And yet, in the States at any rate, the concept of public interest has never been developed much beyond doing dull programs or making recruiting announcements in such peak hours as 8:30 Sunday morning. It is only recently that the Federal Communications Commission, in the person of its chairman, Newton Minow, has bestirred itself at all. And I'm afraid that his just accusations that TV is a wasteland have fallen on apathetic public ears. It has been so long, people don't really know that they have a choice.

Let's see if I can give you a parallel. Suppose the water supply were privately owned by virtue of a franchise granted it long ago and that it were profitable for the water company to sell—in the sense of selling broadcast time—segments of its flow to advertisers in hour, half-hour, and fifteen-minute periods. The advertisers would then have the right to color the water during these green, purple, red, or whatever color they wished. Once this practice was established I'm quite sure it would be accepted as normal and even be defended against wild-eyed radicals as an example of free enterprise working for the public weal. After all, they would point out, we are getting the water free. There would, of course, be a Federal Water Commission (FWC) to rigidly control pumping facilities and ensure that a water company did not use anyone else's pipes.

So the water would come out in stretches of pink, orange, or chartreuse; interspersed with twenty-second, puce pumping station breaks or eight-second, scarlet water signals. And since people would naturally develop color preferences we would see the more popular ones during the peak drinking or flushing periods. I imagine competition would arise in the form of other water companies entering the field.

They, naturally, would not wish to buck the trend—I suppose there would be rating services—so that their colors at any given hour would be variants of whatever hue the leader in the time slot was piping out. I don't mean there'd be anything off-color; no, whichever channel you switched the valve control to, it would all be pure enough.

However, to fight the competition it might be necessary to do other things. Can you imagine the edge you would have if you were first in the field with a faint lemon flavor in your yellow or raspberry in your red? Of course, your competitors would fight back with other flavors, and then stronger flavors. Eventually, all water except for public service programming—which would be a dull gray—would be flavored as well as colored.

At this point a public reaction would set in, first among intellectuals and other do-gooders, and then a broader, but by no means universal, discontent. After all, people would not realize that they had any choice in the matter. Rather let us say that they had so many dazzling choices that the real issue was quite obscured. So, do you know what the ensuing struggle would center about? Some red-hot would protest that he didn't want to take baths in lemonade. And then the industry, through its spokesmen would say he had freedom of choice, that he could switch the valve to another channel—to raspberry soda or root beer. And the dissidents would say that wasn't the issue; that the issue was such strong flavors during peak bathing hours, right? And then someone would call for more rigorous policing by the FWC. And *Ad Age* would be full of statements from the National Association of Watercasters and advertising industry leaders. And Rosser Reeves would say his research showed that people didn't really care, and he'd probably be quite right, they wouldn't be aware that they had a choice of caring or not caring.

You see, lost in the shuffle would be the real heart of the matter: not whether the water ought to be flavored so strongly, or even whether it ought to be flavored at all, or even whether it ought to be *colored* at all. No, the real issue is that the water does not belong to the advertiser, or even to the water company, it belongs to us. I have nothing against colored, flavored water, but I don't think it should dominate our water supply. Water is a public utility, and so is broadcasting. Until this concept is widely understood I don't think things will get much better for the public, for the stations, or for the advertisers.

I think this is a matter that we as advertisers can do something about—if we are enlightened enough. We could agitate for industry-wide conversion to the magazine concept of broadcasting and for the necessary controls and policing to make it possible. It would necessitate a good deal of adjustment in our thinking about availabilities, and rates, and sponsorship. But it is one of the things that we must face if we want to do better at advertising.

I have mentioned the dread word "policing." I think we ought to have—and ought to want—a great deal more policing than we have. No other industry or profession dwells in the formless anarchy that advertising does. One of my students once asked me how clients felt about their shoddy products. I said, after thinking hard for a moment, that I didn't believe I knew of a manufacturer who wasn't terribly proud of his product. You know, they all tell you—and I'm sure they believe it, or can even prove it—that theirs is the best thing on the market. As a matter of fact, most clients, left to their own devices, would think the best ad possible a full page with big words right in the middle saying: "My Competitor's Products are Shit." But I told the student that the chief reason this was so was that the manufacturer could afford to put out a good product without being driven crazy by shoddy competitors. And that this was so because his industry was so well policed by the government, by the Better Business Bureau, by trade associations, by his competitors, and by his customers. All of them would scream like eagles if he didn't put out a good item.

Advertising has no real policing by anyone; there are no real, enforceable rules of conduct except that you cannot tell an outright provable lie. This is too bad for us because it inhibits us from doing a better job. As Nicholas Samstag says, "As an advertising man, I should be free in my mind to scheme the most seductive schemes possible to get people to buy my product, but as a citizen I am in favor of a government that polices me and prevents me from telling untruths and injuring the public in demonstrable ways. If I don't have to worry about policing myself I can produce much better seductions. And if the government doesn't have to worry about cuddling up to business (or advertising) and openly acts as the policeman, it can do a better job of policing."

So here is another thing we must do. If we want to do better at advertising we must insist on it.

I hope that by now a pattern is starting to emerge in my writing. If advertising is ever to shape up as a prideful business or profession we must eliminate the frightful obstacles that stand in our way, and we must look at ourselves and our audience differently. Then perhaps the audience will look at advertising differently: as a public service.

We should accommodate ourselves to our audience as a first duty and *then* sell our wares. I mentioned this in class one day and a student asked: "Professor, how about doing it the other way around; make the sales pitch and then be charming?" I said, "Yes, I suppose you could, but I know an awful lot of guys who have struck out trying that technique on girls." And then I thought, why—that's Ted Bates's Unique Selling Proposition. You stand on the busiest corner and ask every babe that comes by the same question. Of course you get your face slapped a lot, but boy, do you make out. The only flaw being that you've got to be awfully indiscriminating.

Now, being aware of the audience doesn't mean you ought to go in there and Uriah Heep-it up. There's too much of that already. What there isn't nearly enough of is honest, forthright opinion. I see no reason why an advertiser shouldn't take a stand that may be unpopular with some people, or even a lot of people. People don't really mind that, even if they don't agree with you, as long as you treat them like human beings instead of consumers. I think there's a good deal more room for corporative expression than anyone realizes. It's very good for companies to speak out, and it's very healthy for them, too. Corporations are legal persons, but they can become sick or neurotic just like real people; and when they do they affect not only their own well-being, but the well-being of their employees. This business of corporate therapy through advertising is a pretty new subject—for all I know I invented it—and is too much to go into now. But it is another thing we ought to investigate if we are to want to do better at advertising.

The trouble with writing about advertising—for me, at least—is that there is always so much to be cleared away outside before I can get down to how to impove it inside. And I think we had better do something about that, too. I have suggested that advertising's public acceptance is not everything it ought to be. Well, business's acceptance of advertising isn't all that good, either. Part of it is because, in the light of the abuses I have mentioned, advertising just isn't as effective as it might be. That's why we'd better all get busy and do something about the abuses. And part of it is because we work under that ridiculous compensation system, with the money coming from the media instead of from the client. This is not a situation exactly designed to bolster client confidence. As daddy told us when we were children, you appreciate things more when you buy them with your own money. Remember?

Well, this situation doesn't do much to build up an agency's confidence either. The client looks at you as though you have your hand in his pocket—which you have—everytime you bring in a new, which is to say bigger, media recommendation. It's really a hell of a note. Here you are on your hands and knees, under a cloud of suspicion, and it isn't even costing him anything; as far as he's concerned, you're doing it for freebies. Under these conditions it's a wonder there are any good ads at all, and there aren't an awful lot. It's an impossible situation.

Disregarding these difficulties, there are some things to be done. They aren't infallible, but they are a good deal better than firing everybody. Look, the chief reason ads aren't better, I think, is that they pass through the hands of advertising managers and account executives. Now these people have valuable jobs to do, but the creation of advertising is not one of them, not usually. In every company there is usually some red-hot who has wild creative ideas. In many firms we have a name for him; we call him the president or owner. This is more likely to be true in newer firms. In older firms he is often the one just under the president, pawing the ground until the president retires. At any rate this wild man is the one to talk to. And who talks to him? The copywriter, the art director, whoever the agency's wild man is. These two will be able to say more to each other in five minutes than they could say to anyone else in a week. And while they're in there, the advertising manager and the account executive can talk to *each other*, which they would be doing anyway, about things only they can handle.

Now aside from the fact that these two creative types will possibly stimulate each other and come up with some good directions, there is also this: you won't have to fight so hard to get whatever it is through the agency *or* through management. It is a boon all around. It makes everybody's job easier—and is likely to result in much better and more pertinent advertising. However, too often the trouble with this procedure is this: they get so carried away in their creative ecstasy they forget to tell anybody. So you have to fasten a milking machine on each of them immediately after the meeting breaks up or the whole thing will have only been unsupervised activity.

You see, the machinery of both advertising and business is subject to a lot of waste energy through slippage. And nowhere is this more apparent than in the traditional lines of communications that I'd like to see circumvented. By the time an idea has passed through several layers, committees, etc., at the client's, it either isn't the same idea or it may not be what The Man really wants, but can't quite verbalize why. So the advertising manager passes it on anyway. Then the account executive starts feeding it through his machinery, committees, etc., and the work gets under way, passing through a few more hands in *that* process. Then it starts back, but chances are that it goes through the same layers at the agency on the way out. So what actually gets to the account executive is probably a watered-down version of a thought based on an idea that may not have been much to start with. And we aren't even back to the advertising manager yet. But enough. All this could have been avoided by eliminating the middle men and making their lives happier, too.

Well, to get back to home theme, I think the best way to want to do better at advertising is to think of the audience out there as your audience and play to them. Once you do, you'll never again have to worry whether you put out a lousy ad or not. They'll let you know.

NOTE

1. Gossage was distinguished visiting professor in the School of Journalism at the Pennsylvania State University for the Fall term, 1962.

Chapter 4

That Old Black, White, or Pango Peach Magic

Magic is mankind's oldest continuous belief. It antedates either religion or science, and although both appear to have sprung from it, neither has supplanted it entirely or is soon likely to.

By magic I don't mean pulling a rabbit out of the hat or sawing a woman in half or other such edifying spectacles, but magical thinking as it has been thought by man for a million years and still is. To be sure, we do not subscribe to the total and literal beliefs of either our remote ancestors or the Australian aborigines. And the higher one goes in the intellectual order the less susceptibility to magical thinking one will encounter.

But even where faith has faded, the imagery of magic remains. For so broad and basic are its points of reference that it is difficult to avoid them in human intercourse. The language of magic is truly the universal tongue.

Magic, moreover, is the most adaptable of creatures; it moves in, makes itself at home, and fades into the wallpaper. It so thoroughly identifies with its surroundings as to be unnoticed by the inhabitants. This is to say that magic is never an isolated phenomenon, it is invariably germane to its period. This is why such now obvious performances of magical thinking as the Inquisition, the Dutch tulip craze of the seventeenth century, the stock market boom of the late twenties, Couéism, McCarthyism, and chain letters escaped recognition at the time. It is possibly too early to pass final judgment on farm surpluses, credit cards, filter tips, and the theory of an ever-expanding economy.

Originally printed in *Harper's Magazine*, March 1961, under the title "The Golden Twig."

Magical stewardship in every age resides at the heart of the era's chief concerns: hunting, agriculture, religion, politics, commerce, nationalism, or whatever. James Webb Young, the dean of American advertising men, tells me that the magical authority of the Egyptian priesthood was founded on their knowledge of the rise and fall tables of the Nile. This amounted to more than a paltry prediction trick to amaze the fellahin, for the river's timely flooding was the source of Egypt's wealth. The chief concern of our era is the consumption of goods and services. It is a big job, but to assist we have the biggest propaganda force the world has ever seen, advertising.

One of the characters in Christopher Fry's play of the Middle Ages, "The Lady's Not For Burning," says, "Religion has made an honest woman of the supernatural." Someone is always ready to make an honest woman of her. Today advertising is her most ardent—or most affluent—suitor.

Advertising is a brand new instrument, unique to our age, but at the same time it plays mankind's oldest themes. The reason is this: in an advertisement's effort to persuade people of the justice of its cause, whatever it may be, it invariably seeks a common denominator. The more people it attempts to persuade, the more common the denominator, the more basic the appeal will be. When, in addition, the product advertised is virtually identical with its competitors, or when the product's value to its user is largely subjective, the appeals become so basic that they slide away from fact as we know it. They go beyond reason into something more basic, the most common denominator of all, magic.

Sir James Frazer in his classic on the subject of anthropological magic, *The Golden Bough,* divided the field into two general parts: theoretical magic and practical magic. Theoretical magic has to do with natural law, the rules that govern the sequence of events throughout the world: the rising of the sun, the changing of the seasons, the moving of the heavens, the surging of the tides. Only recently in human history have we discarded theoretical magic as an explanation of these phenomena. If we wonder why it took so long, it is well to remember that there are still people who believe the world is flat and that to this day our senses testify that the earth circles the sun rather than the other way around.

Practical magic, our chief concern here, is a body of rules for human beings to follow in order to achieve desired ends. Its techniques are still very much with us, and advertising—itself devoted to satisfaction of human desires—has availed itself of them.

Frazer divides practical magic loosely into what he calls *imitative* magic and *contagious* magic. Imitative magic assumes that objects which have been in contact will continue to act on each other at a distance after the physical contact has been severed. Examples of imitative magic might be the sticking of needles through wax figures or hanging in effigy. The underlying rationale is probably the same as that of the rejected swain who tears up his girl's picture. The objective mind might detect an application of imitative magic in an airline advertisement of a couple of years ago which consisted of a picture of the sea with a strip torn off it and the word, "Starting Dec. 23 the Atlantic Ocean will be 20% smaller."

Another example of imitative magic—in that it is based on the assumption that effect will resemble cause—is the use of powdered rhinoceros horn, which I understand is highly prized in the Far East as an adjunct to virility; look how powerful the rhino is! I don't know what powdered rhinoceros horn costs but its users probably find it worth the price. Analogous to this was the recent rage for queen bee jelly. One supposes that it served to satisfy a womanly urge to extreme, uncompetitive femininity; to be the only queen in the hive. Or could it be that women have some deep, unconscious impulse to mate in midair?

Closely akin to imitative magic but somewhat different in its application is contagious magic. The idea here is that an object that has been associated with one person will continue to be associated with that person. His fingernail parings, hair, etc., will thus do nicely in preparing a love philter to be used on him. But it works another way too; a thing can also carry with it whatever qualities the person who owned it, or touched it, or used it had. Thus, relics sanctified by a witch doctor, or a lock of Elvis's hair, or autographs, or Miss Rheingold, and all testimonial advertising are examples of belief in contagious magic. For instance, I can buy Gillette razor blades just like the ones used by that star athlete on television the other night . . . although I am always a little fearful the whole thing might backfire and, instead of acquiring his physical powers, I might end up with his vocal prowess.

All toiletry advertising draws heavily on practical magic for its substance. Like the love philter, it promises that you will be irresistible. If you use most hair preparations or after-shave lotions you are taking your chastity in your hands. If a girl uses virtually any advertised facial soap she is triumphantly assured of a glorious marriage to a pimple-free, vibrant youth, six feet four inches tall with gleaming teeth and perfect elimination; their respective toiletries have brought them together.

Also implied in the above examples is the suggestion that whatever benefits the product may bestow will be denied you if you don't use it. If you do not use Brylcreem all the girls may not pursue you. More explicit is the threat contained in mouthwash advertising: not only will the girls not pursue you, but you will drive them away unless you gargle. This is even more magical than the other threat because while you can see by looking in a mirror that your hair looks wretched, it is very difficult for you to smell your own breath. You have no real way of knowing whether you are ruining your love life or blasting your career. The mouthwash thus becomes a charm by which you may avoid *possibly* dire consequences; and the beauty of it is that you will never know whether it worked or not since even your best friend won't tell you.

This brings us to another aspect of magic: taboo. Here we see advertising actually creating and naming taboos. The most famous, B.O. and Halitosis, are archaeological specimens from an age that we might fix as either Late Iron Tonic or Early Soap. It is doubful whether such epidemics are really catchy today; the Gray Sickness has never achieved plague proportions despite best efforts. Bad breath and body odor have always existed, of course, but as individual matters. To transfer them from personal idiosyncrasies into tribal taboos is a magicianly trick indeed.

But we are frittering around in very trivial taboo territory; let's get into the deep stuff. Cosmetic advertising. According to Freud, "the basis of taboo is a forbidden action for which there exists a strong inclination in the un-conscious." That is to say we have a deep-seated desire to violate taboo and to put ourselves above it, beyond the reach of its strictures. The cosmetic industry plays this line for all it is worth. Consider the names of perfumes: Forbidden Fruit, My Sin, Shocking, Sortilege, Black Magic, and even Tabu, and many others that I am too frightened to remember.

Revlon must keep a staff witch if we are to judge from certain of their advertisements. I don't know which taboos Miss Fire and Ice wished to violate, but they must have been honeys. Ravishment seemed to be the very least she had on her mind.

Miss Pango Peach, on the other hand, seemed to take a more tempered view of the subject. Her voluptuous demands, though probably excessive, did not appear to include either whips or cannibalism. You will recall my men-tioning, in connection with queen bee jelly, the mating habits of bees. You know, of course, that the successful bee suitor explodes immediately following the happy event; the altitude or something. I predict that some day someone will make a fortune by marketing praying mantis marmalade. Some brassiere advertising also obviously exploits the desire to violate taboo. However, fash-ion advertising as a whole seems to dwell in another magical area.

Have you ever wondered why fashion models look the way they do? A couple of years ago, Stan Freberg, the humorist, swept by compassion, pro-posed that a fund be established to send the girls to camp to fatten them up a little and put the roses back in their cheeks. If you ask a woman why models look like that she will say that skinny girls show off clothes better. I find this next to no answer at all; for the real essence of their unearthly appearance is simply that: they are unearthly. Their attitudes are trancelike, as though they were frozen in those bizarre poses by a spell. They are supernatural representations, and I defy you to account for them in any other fashion.

Nor are these the only supernatural figures in advertising. I should point out here that the heart and soul of the magician's power has always been his command of what we might call the "nearby supernatural" as opposed to the "remote supernatural." The magician does not pray or implore these approachable supernatural forces to aid him; he dominates them through his superior knowledge and power. He is their master and they perform at his direction. Advertising invokes supernatural entities in many forms and some of them are pretty obvious. Mr. Clean, for example; he materializes at man's—or in this case, woman's—bidding and works like magic. Think of the number of times you have seen the words "like magic" in advertisements. These devices are effective because command of the supernatural is one of mankind's oldest dreams—and the basis of literature from man's earliest myths to the *Arabian Nights, Faust, Superman,* and *Damn Yankees.*

Some of these supernatural manifestations are, of course, far more subtle than Mr. Clean, Elsie the Cow, or Mr. Coffee Nerves. Some of our most stimulating advertising summons what I can only regard as Mephistopheles-like figures. Mephistopheles, you will recall, is suave, imperturbable, of-the-world-worldly but not really a part of it. His presence is not to be accounted for by ordinary standards; he is simply there, he has materialized. And he usually bears the sign by which we know him: a mark that sets him apart from mere mortals, whether it be a cloven hoof, beard, tattoo, or a black eye-patch. He is a fascinating chap and you can say this for him, he likes people. Mephistopheles grants a boon: eternal life, youth, prowess, togetherness, unfulfilled dreams. His price is always something. When it is such a small thing as a pack of cigarettes, or a soft drink, or a lipstick, why should not one take the chance?

As distinguished from our accessibility to the nearby, workaday supernatural is our helplessness in the face of the remote supernatural. The remote supernatural is that force quite beyond our control: death, disaster, the vagaries of fortune. The remote supernatural is nobody's plaything; it cannot be evoked at will or used as a tool. There is nothing man can do about it and yet he must do *something.* So he performs rituals, makes sacrifices, builds monuments, fathers many children, keeps his fingers crossed, saves his money for a rainy day, and buys life insurance. Surely it is reasonable to save and have life insurance, but the reasons for doing so are likely far beyond reason.

32

First off, saving for a rainy day is quite a different matter from saving for a purpose like buying a house or taking a trip. People save for a rainy day without, in most cases, any certainty when the rainy day will arrive or even whether it will arrive. And we all have known people who would not touch their savings even when the rainy day *does* arrive. This, it seems to me, is an act in appeasement of the remote supernatural, a bribe to fortune, an act beyond mere prudence.

Similarly, the buying of insurance is in part an art to propitiate Providence and rests solidly on primitive instincts and emotions way at the back of the mind. The first of these is pure anguish in the face of the unknowable; the second is a belief in luck. An insurance policy is more than a highly sophisticated bet against odds, it also assumes the properties of a talisman to counteract disaster or stall off death.

It may be easier to see this when we apply it to, let us say, fire insurance or accident insurance. I think there is no arguing that a definite feeling of courting disaster exists when one is uninsured; it is positively unlucky — you are just asking for it. This magical instinct may influence the buying of *any* insurance, whether it be life, plate-glass, or the coverage you get when you stuff quarters in the machine at the airport. This last, while apparently life insurance, is not the same thing, really. One buys life insurance because one knows one is going to die — the only question is when. One does not expect to be wiped out in an airplane accident — the odds are enormously against it. The quarters buy a cheap charm to carry you through to the end of the journey.

Incidentally, in the field of credit we see financial institutions venturing into magic in more pointed ways. Installment credit buying is surely a tacit invitation to think magically about money. The English term for such buying is revealing: the Never-never. The most flagrant example is seen in the recent rise of the credit card. According to one motivational researcher quoted in Vance Packard's *Waste Makers,* "Credit cards are magic since they serve as money when one temporarily has no money. They thus become symbols of power and inexhaustible potency." And, may I add, with the rainy day built in.

By now I hope it is apparent that there is a broad field of human susceptibility to magic. Advertising, abhorring a vacuum, has rushed in to fill it. In doing so it produces some magic on its own.

Through advertising, a product will acquire what Martin Mayer, in *Madison Avenue, U.S.A.,* called "the added ingredient" and what I must regard as a magical property, beyond natural and ordinary logic. This property is frequently so pervasive that all of the product's being and authority reside in the advertising; the product *is* its advertising. And what do we call an object that carries magical properties? A charm. A product will tend to be a charm to the extent that its authority exceeds bare fact.

Let me give you a parallel. A red traffic light is a piece of colored glass with a bulb behind it. It means stop. But, as S. I. Hayakawa, the semanticist, points out, in practice it often *is* stop. Recall how guilty you feel when you run an obviously stuck light, even late at night with no one in sight for thirty miles in either direction. Another example: if you were to take a piece of cloth and jump up and down on it in public you would be mobbed or at the very least arrested—provided the cloth in question were the American flag. The flag in this instance not only symbolizes the United States, it *is* the United States and as such is a charm.

Similarly, such humble items as toothpaste, soaps, and cigarettes are charms. Advertising has imbued them with prowess quite beyond any reasonable assessment of their plain-Jane natures. Now, to do this sort of charm-school job—and have it take—is not as easy as you might think. Usually there is nowhere to go but up; to the supernatural. Their slogans, therefore, will be suprafactual ("contains new XXK-140"), supralogical ("You'll wonder where the yellow went"), or merely supradooper. Moreover, with repetition any slogan will lose whatever sense it had to begin with and only the magical litany will remain; it will become an incantation pure and simple. Given enough exposure it may attain the ultimate symbol meaningful/less/ness of L.S./M.F.T. Even a slogan containing such sound—for a cigarette—reasons as "Filter, flavor, flip-top box" will assume, after the first few hearings, the properties of an incantation. This is true of all jingles if they are any good.

Speaking of Marlboro, I understand that they introduced the original tattooed man because they wished to change the "product image" to a masculine one. That sounds logical except that as it turned out his hex-signed presence was an argument beyond any logic I know of. It is magic—a seemingly pertinent but logically irrelevant association of ideas. We may see a different application of this principle in a recent series of Shell gasoline advertisements. They feature famous works of craftsmanship in the shape of shells. These ads are done with great dignity and point out that they, Shell, do good work, too. Here we note imitative magic (their Shell and Cellini's shell) and also contagious magic (his craftsmanship bestowed by association on their craftsmanship).

By extension it could be argued that Texaco's admirable sponsorship of the Metropolitan Opera broadcasts—or any sponsorship for that matter—has a contagious magic aspect. The same might be said of Container Corporation's magnificent series on "Great Ideas of Western Man." If guilt by association is a magical technique (and it is) then so is quality by association.

This is not to say that the facts behind these associative devices are magical or illusory, they are real, they are supportable in practice. The Indian tribe performing a corn dance never forgot to plant the seed either.

Now it is reasonable to ask whether advertising is likely to employ magic of one sort or another. I suppose so, in the sense that every person alive — even one who makes all his purchases on the basis of Consumers Union recommendations — employs magical symbolism in some fashion. If it is more apparent in advertising, it is because advertising itself is most apparent. However, we should distinguish between advertising's white magic and black magic. The difference depends chiefly on whether the technique is used as a means of illustrating a point (Chase Manhattan Bank's nest egg) or constitutes a point itself ("9 out of 10 witch doctors approve"). The former we could call magical imagery; the latter, magical thinking. If some advertising is more blatantly guilty of magical thinking than others, it is because some audiences are more simple-minded.

But, whatever its form, advertising's magic is relatively lucid in that it never confuses the main issue, what it has to sell. The same cannot be said for the economy advertising represents. Perhaps it is just the way it is explained, but the stability of our economic system apparently rests squarely on a magical device, the pyramid club. This is not, I regret to say a private, crotchety view of my own; both of the candidates in the recent election seemed to embrace it vigorously. Both parties swore fealty to ever-expanding production; this presumably based on ever-expanding population and ever-expanding consumption. Not only are all of these terms plainly impossible, but unnerving as well. Put like that, our economy sounds like nothing so much as the granddaddy of all chain letters. All you can do is hope to get your name to the top of the list, or die, before something happens (like peace) and the whole thing collapses.

Is our economy really so magically conceived? I don't know and I'll wager you don't either. But there must be some sounder prospect than that of endlessly consuming more and more, force-fed, like so many Strasbourg geese. An explanation of the economic system to its people (and what strange abracadabra turned us into consumers anyway?) in sensible terms might be a fitting project for advertising and its clients to undertake as a public, and private, service.

Chapter 5

Environment and Creativity
(Or "Ninety-nine Non-Zebras")

Dearly beloved, we will now discuss creativity.

Creativity is quite a different matter from creation, which occurred a long time ago. One seventeenth-century educator, the Reverend John Lightfoot, even fixed the exact moment. He said, "Heaven and Earth, center and circumference, were made in the same instant of time . . . the twenty-sixth of October, 4004 B.C., at nine o'clock in the morning."

At 9:30 the account executives came in and started talking about creativity. They haven't stopped yet, and neither has anybody else. Creativity may well be the most popular subject of our time. Everybody either wants to be creative or wants to know what he should do about people who are already creative. But what people *really* mean is either "how to get good ads out of lousy copywriters" or "how to get good ads out of good copywriters without actually paying them twice as much as I make."

But, I will try to find some new slant on the creative process. Goodness knows the old ones have been chewed over often enough. The only comment on creativity that has managed to stick in my mind is Ernest Hemingway's dictum, "It is a good thing for a writer to have a built-in crap detector." This, however, does not tell us how to build one.

I have a notion that what we call creativity is a process that begins when a person becomes aware of his environment. By "environment," I mean that accustomed set of conditions which limits an organism's world at any given moment. In the ordinary course of events we are not aware of our environment any more than a fish is aware of his. We don't know who discovered water, but we're pretty sure it wasn't a fish.

Imagine a series of clear plastic domes, one within another. One can only see them from the outside; from the inside they are invisible. You become aware of an environment—one of these domes that surrounds you—when you get outside of it. At that point you can see it; but you can't see the one that is *now* above you.

To put it another way, let us suppose that an ant has lived all his young life inside an anthill. He is not really aware that the anthill is his world, it simply is his world. So one day they send him off on an important assignment; to drag back a dead beetle, say. He goes outside the anthill. Two things happen: (1) He sees the anthill for the first time; (2) he becomes aware that the world is a very big place. Does this mean that he is aware of his environment? No, because what he doesn't know is that his anthill is inside a greenhouse. The only way he'll become aware of the greenhouse is if he goes outside of it. And even then it won't do him much good, because, you see, the greenhouse is inside the Houston Stadium, and so on.

So awareness is becoming conscious that there is something bigger controlling us than we had thought. The catch is that we can never catch up; we are always one step behind, for everything is contained by something bigger. All we ever see are things inside our environment, things inside the anthill; or if we are outside the anthill, the anthill, but not the greenhouse. If we are outside the greenhouse we can see it and the anthill but not the domed stadium, and so into infinity.

There are many sorts of environments besides the simple one of physical space that I have mentioned: business, political, social, cultural, communication, etc. But for the moment I'll just call it all environment. We can get more specific later.

Two things make us aware of an environment; either it changes or we do. One imagines that if a new glacial age began and stretched down toward the tropics that the natives of, say, Miami, would become aware of their environment and do something creative, such as using the indoor swimming pool. We also become aware of our environment if we change. A man who has lost a leg will become aware of steps. A man who has had five martinis may see things he has never seen before. A man who has had *ten* martinis may see things *nobody* has ever seen before. This does not necessarily lead to creativity, however.

As far as I can see, what we call creativity begins with the ability to recognize what is already there. If this sounds like too glib a definition, let me remind you that not only beauty but everything else is in the beholder's eye. Some people behold better than other people.

The ability to behold takes several forms. The first is largely acquired through experience. It is being able to tell the difference between one thing and another. It is seeing a hundred horses run by and saying, "Hey, that one there is a zebra!" This is the beginning of what we call the creative process. What happens from here on depends on what sort of person the beholder is.

The conservative beholder might say, "What the hell is that zebra doing in there?" We all know men like that. I used to have one for a client when I worked on a bank account many years ago. I remember one time we ran a series of ads that attracted a great deal of new business. After the second one ran, he called up and said, "Howard, I think we ought to cancel the rest of the series." I asked him why, and he said, "Because it's bringing too many people into the bank when the officers are out to lunch."

The pragmatic beholder might ask, "What the hell do you do with a zebra?" He'd really like to know, too. The first thing he does is call up the advertising agency. No, that's the second thing he does. The first thing he does is to check zebra futures in the *Wall Street Journal* to find out whether he ought to sell now, or hang on to it for awhile.

The imaginative or zebra-oriented beholder—and there are quite a few of them around—might ask, "What are we going to do with those ninety-nine horses?" These are the people who are always coming to me for jobs. They tell me that where they work now they just don't appreciate creativity. But the type of beholder I rather fancy not only is imaginative and practical but has a plan, too. He says, "OK, here's what we're going to do with those ninety-nine non-zebras."

A second type of observation that sometimes leads to creativity is apparently due to an innate deficiency. That is to say that some people are simply unable to see things in a normal fashion. On the other hand, they will see things that normal people can't.

During the Second World War, I understand that some aerial observers were recruited because they were color-blind. Their color blindness made them unable to distinguish things designed for normal eyes, such as camouflage. They'd look down at a quite ordinary stretch of landscape and say, "Hey, there's a gun emplacement!" Because of their disability, their impairment of vision, their eyes were not taken in by the camouflage; all they could see was the thing itself.

Now this is an example of our normal unawareness of environment, which camouflage is certainly meant to simulate. It is only the person who is for some reason alien to the environment who will be able to detect its shape. The extra-environmental man—we might as well give him a label—has a great advantage in the creativity race. For one thing, his mind isn't cluttered up with a lot of rules, policy, and other accumulated impedimenta that often pass for experience. I think that if there is anything overrated, it is experience of this variety. It is experience for experience's sake; what we might call "experience" experience. It is the sort of experience they ask you if you have when you go to look for a job in advertising. Do you have food experience? Do you have farm machinery experience? If any of you are asking advertising job applicants if they have bank experience, I would suggest you quit it. What if somebody answered "Yes" and started turning out bank ads for you? What you really need is a nice, extra-environmental; someone who will look at your environment with fresh eyes.

You have noticed, I am sure, that talented immigrants to our shores do very well indeed and in a remarkably short time. I think it is mostly because they are extra-environmentals. They see things that we don't and are not stuck with our load of "experience" experience. There is also another factor: in any environment you have a system of checks and balances that constitutes what we call stability. When an organism moves into a strange environment it will prosper because it has no natural enemies; there is no one to say, "You can't do that."

As a matter of fact, one of the most interesting developments in the banking business took place because an extra-environmental saw something that had existed ever since balance sheets were invented. The result was the leasing business. The pioneer in industrial leasing, Henry Schoenfeld, tells me that when he first started out, bankers were dumbfounded because they couldn't think of a reason to say no. As you know, banks do not like to lend money on plant equipment, machinery, or other non-liquid items below the line, because if a factory is not working it is a dead loss. However, banks are delighted to lend money on inventory, receivables, cash, and other items above the line; especially cash. Unfortunately, people who want to borrow money usually want to borrow it against items below the line, which is usually why bankers say no.

So along comes a leasing company and says to the manufacturer, "Sell us all of your plant equipment for cash and we will lease it back to you over 5 years. You will have all that nice cash above the line, and the bank will be happy to lend you even more money on top of that." Then the leasing company goes around to the bank and shows its statement with all of that machinery represented as receivables under the lease and the bank lends it money, too.

Now, you can see why a banker would be suspicious; it all sounds kind of tricky. Until it occurs to you that the reason the whole thing works is not because it tries to get around the banking system, but precisely because it goes along with it; there is no reason to say no.

Still, it is doubtful that this creative solution would have originated within the conventional banking environment; there was too much "experience" experience against it; though, of course, many banks have gone into leasing since.

The big advantage the extra-environmental has is that he has no rules to hamper him doing things the environmental not only wouldn't think of doing but also wouldn't be caught dead doing, even if he could. However, once they are done and accepted within the environmental power structure, then he will do them, and do them, and do them. They have become part of the anthill.

You can see this with ads. An outstandingly successful ad will be extra-environmental. I am not referring to the sort of ad that achieves success by repetition; that type is successful simply because it is environmental—it becomes part of the environment the way a wallpaper pattern becomes part of a room. The way you achieve success with wallpaper-type advertising is the same way a wallpaper manufacturer does, by repeating it over and over again.

You will have observed that advertisers tend to do what other advertisers do; they merely repeat the other fellow's wallpaper some more. I think the reason is this: that they look at one detail—one ad—one cabbage rose in the pattern—as though it is an original, and they copy it. Their justification for this is, "you can't argue with success." Unfortunately, success in the wallpaper biz is not one cabbage rose, but the repeat. And the upshot will be just some more cabbage-rose wallpaper.

Now every wallpaper design was once an original piece of artwork. If it was very effective as a single picture it was because it was, at the time, extra-environmental, something no one had seen before. The best art, the best ads, still are. And the people who do them will tend to be extra-environmental, too; they will be men from outside the prevailing environment. They will either come from another culture, another country, or be men who got into the business late in life after doing much else, or they will be "color-blind" in the sense I mentioned earlier. Often they will be a combination of some or all of these things. At any rate, they will do things that seem normal to them but that will seem extraordinarily perceptive to us. More than that, they will heighten our own perceptions. A good example of the extra-environmental message that is at once perceptive and heightens our own perceptions is someone shouting "Fire!"

Let me give you instances of what I regard as extra-environmental ads:

do you recall the Hunt's Ketchup ads of a few years ago that featured a high-style photograph and setting with a ketchup bottle standing out like a sore thumb? Recall also that these ketchup ads ran in *Vogue,* which made them doubly extra-environmental. Commander Whitehead was certainly extra-environmental, and so was Baron Wrangel, the man with the eye-patch. Most of David Ogilvy's best-known ads seem Englishly extra-environmental to Americans, though some of them might not be considered so in England. There they might seem like pieces of their environment fixed up for export.

This is not to suggest that if everyone forsook his present specialty and went into some other line of work he would automatically garner the creative advantages of extra-environmentalism. For unless he can also comprehend the structure of his new environment and see what is missing, all that will happen is that he will carry his tendency to specialism with him the way a snail does his shell. A born specialist will tend to interpret all experience in the light of his own expertise.

One time a cloak and suit manufacturer went to Rome, and while he was there managed to get an audience with His Holiness. Upon his return a friend asked him, "What did the pope look like?" The tailor answered, "A 41 regular."

Since we are developing nomenclature we may as well try to nail down another term: the process of approaching a problem from outside its environment. We might call it generalism, as opposed to specialism. A generalist starts from the outside; a specialist works from the inside. There is a time for specialism of course, but it is not at the onset of a problem, I think. Because once you take a problem to a specialist you are wired in to a specialist solution. The result may be splendid, but it may not be what you really need.

Let us say that your company is having growing pains and is uncomfortable in its present quarters. So you go to an architect. Let us also suppose that he is a very good architect, one dedicated solidly to the proposition that form follows function. So he inquires after your needs, your ambitions, your hopes, your fears, what sort of people you have working for you, etc. Do you know what you are going to end up with? A building. Now a building, however nice, may not be the answer to your problem at all. Perhaps the real answer is to stop expanding, or to go into some other line of business, or that the president should do something about his liver condition, or that everyone should stay home and do cottage work connected by closed-circuit TV. These are generalist solutions, not the sort of thing you expect an architect to come up with; and, if he did, you'd probably think he was a busybody.

In my own business I am always running into would-be clients who think spending money on advertising is the answer to their problem, when it really isn't. Unfortunately, being extra-environmental both by nature and professionally—I didn't go into advertising until I was in my middle thirties—and being a busybody to boot, I can't resist giving them the benefit of my generalist wisdom. This rarely deters them from spending their money on advertising, but elsewhere. They generally don't have far to look, since many of my colleagues in the agency business seem to share this overweening faith in advertising; and money.

Mind you, these clients are the same people who wouldn't dream of having an operation without first getting a general diagnosis, which in effect is what I had been trying to give them. So the upshot has been that some months ago I started a generalist consulting practice with another man, Gerald M. Feigen, M.D., who, appropriately enough, is already a diagnostician as well as being an eminent surgeon and psychiatrist. We keep office hours on Wednesdays and on Friday afternoons. We also take night calls if you have an emergency. The name of the firm, not surprisingly, is Generalists, Inc. Now please don't think that I'm trying to deliver a commercial. I debated whether to mention it at all but figured that if I didn't, and you heard it from the kids on the street, you'd think that I had been trying to keep something from you.

Back to our subject. What I have said about specialism seems to run counter to the prevailing belief that this is the age of the specialist. It is and it isn't. This is to say that our social and economic organization charts are still predicated on specialism, but our technological environment isn't and hasn't been since the dawn of the electronic age. Marshall McLuhan of the University of Toronto has an interesting and plausible explanation of this: specialism came into being with the start of the machine age. The machine is a sequence of mechanical linkages from cause to effect: A acts on B, which acts on C, which acts on D, on down to the end of the line and the finished product. With the production line the whole process became fragmented into a series of functions, and for each function there was a specialist.

Nor was this methodology confined to making things; it pervaded our entire economic and social system. It still does; our thinking pattern continues to be based on mechanical linkages and people handing things one to the other, from cause to effect. The fact of the matter, as we know, is that with the electronic age cause and effect have become simultaneous; what McLuhan calls "instant speed." You don't even have to say "Let there be light." You push a button and there *is* light. Electric circuitry has bypassed mechanical linkages, and specialist linkages, too.

This is not to say that we don't need specialists, but that a specialist is not in a very good position to understand what is going on; especially when both the man above him and the man below him are likely to be machines. This is quite literally true; he gets his work from one machine and puts it into another one. I spend a lot of my time doing that.

So unless a man has a generalist comprehension of processes, not functions, he will only be a sort of electronic jigsaw-puzzle solver, with one piece of his very own and *no* notion of what the environmental picture is.

Chapter 6

The Shape of an Idea and How to Draw One

I have always enjoyed talking to and working with artists. I have often wondered why, especially when being thrown bodily out of an art department, as sometimes happens. On those occasions when I have been lucky enough to address a group of artists I have tried to explain this one-sided love affair. I say one-sided because, although writers always want to meddle with the artwork, no artist really wants to do anything about the copy except perhaps leave it out. This wholesome notion, while entirely warranted in most cases, has nothing to do with literary judgment or even logic as we know it.

I used to think that an artist's attitude toward writing was this: that deep in their hearts they knew that they could express it better than I could. And that was the reason they liked to put the copy in orange type on a red background or in 4 pt. Microbe Condensed italics set 7 inches wide, with inch-and-a-half line spacing, so the reader needed a magnifying glass and a bloodhound to make his way through it.

However, when I accused art directors of trying to sabotage the writing I got such blank, uncomprehending stares that I eventually formed another theory: that artists don't read, or at least not very well. This thesis was nullified when I noticed that the most intellectual art directors were precisely those who tended to come up with classy layouts in which the copy is printed white on white.

The truth of the matter, I have finally concluded, is not that they don't read the writing, *it's that they don't think of it as writing at all,* not when they are working. What do they think of it as? Who knows? Squiggles, a lot of little forms that they can push sideways, or make fat or skinny, or write on the head of a pin, or blow up so big that nobody can read.

"What," one might ask, "does an art director *think* he is working on?" I have often wondered. But I think that the art director's childlike innocence should be preserved as long as possible. Too soon they grow up and start nagging you about the facts of advertising. You can't put them off by telling them about birds and bees forever.

Many people feel that you should tell art directors the facts of advertising as soon as they are old enough to understand and that you should run around the office naked, so to speak, so there won't be any sense of shame. I personally think this is ill advised, for it is likely to lead to early precocity and even a client-fixation: one morning you come to work and find that the two of them have run off and shacked up somewhere—possibly in what used to be your office.

On the whole I think that you should answer the art director's questions about the advertising act simply and naturally, but without too much realistic detail which might lead him into morbid fantasies; such as asking for a raise. This is not to say that one should be evasive with art directors, for they notice a great deal more than you would think.

For example, in the sixth or seventh month of a new account a normally bright art director will observe that your billing is getting noticeably larger, that your expense account is swollen, and that you are sending out for dill pickles during client meetings.

If you have encouraged him to speak frankly to you—which is probably a terrible mistake—the art director will ask you about this in that cute way they have. The only thing to do is to take him off to one side, away from the others and say something like: "You see, deep inside daddy's pocket, he has this account which is growing, growing; and someday when it is big enough you will have a brand new baby assistant art director. If you are a good boy, he will work for you." It is not necessary, I think, to tell him at this time what will happen if the new art director is better than he is.

Back to what art directors see in an ad. Science does not tell us, so I have set out to explore the field myself.

Since the problem is apparently that of words and the abstract or subjective ideas they represent, I have wondered first of all how they look to me. I don't mean the appearance of the word or how it feels, or even what it means, but how the idea behind it looks—what shape it is.

If I have lost you at this point perhaps I ought to tell you that I have a wife who thinks in colors. Being an actress she is very aware of words, but

I don't know how many actresses think of a color every time they hear a word. She does and has done so all of her life, so that it is no effort for her. Until she was in her teens she believed that *everybody* thought in colors and was quite surprised to find out different. I mention this because it may be that some of you think or register ideas in colors, shapes, and sizes. If so, I would like to hear from you, perhaps in a plain envelope.

While preparing these pages I gave her a list of random words so I could give you an idea of how it works. *Idea* is white. *Dallas–Fort Worth Art Directors Club* is white and red; however, it breaks down: *Dallas* is white, *Fort* is dark blue, *Worth* is maroon, *Art* is red, *Directors* is white with slashes of orange, and *Club* is yellow; all together they are white and red. *Ben Mead* is blood red and yellow and *Tom Young* is puce. On the political front, *Johnson* is brown, *Goldwater* is bright yellow, *Russia* is maroon, and—surprise—*Red* is maroon, too. *Orange* is white, *blue* is raw sienna, *chartreuse* is yellow, *Pink Air* is beige with burgundy splotches, and *burgundy* is yellow.

I find this concept interesting though baffling. It is not the color part that baffles me, but the word part. As far as I know I do not get abstract visual impressions from words; although now that I think of it *abstract* looks like a picket fence, *visual* is a figure eight on a Jello skating rink, and *typewriter* is a bucket full of fresh ice cubes. However, for me it is ideas that have shapes. The word *year*, for example, to me has a definite, drawable shape. *Year* is an irregular figure closer to a triangle than anything else.

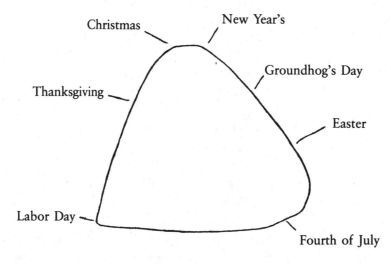

Up at the top is a little straight stretch representing the week between Christmas and New Year's. The line then slants diagonally down to the right past Groundhog's Day, St. Patrick's Day, and about a week after Easter it starts a gentle curve around through Memorial Day and flattens out again at the Fourth of July to form the bottom; it keeps going left until it gets to Labor Day where it makes a sharp corner and zooms straight up like a bat out of hell for Christmas again. I have always thought of the year this way but kept it to myself for fear nobody else would understand until I read a *New Yorker* article by a man who drew it exactly the same way. I doubt that it is a universal concept because at least one person I know sees the year differently.

My wife says I have it all wrong; that in the first place the year is a circle—like a child's hoop really—with the rim divided into brightly colored segments representing months, weeks, and days. Holidays have special colors: Christmas is yellow, New Year's is brown, her mother's birthday is orange, and Halloween is black. I should mention that only the holiday Halloween is black, the word *Halloween* is green. Also, she points out that it is all wrong for me to put New Year's at the top, for that is not where her visual year begins. Can you guess when her year begins? August 2. The reason for this is that it is halfway between the Fourth of July, which is fittingly pink and orange, and my birthday, which is emerald green. I myself am navy blue but my name, I am happy to say, is gold.

I have found the most practical use of shapes to be in the description of processes. I'll tell you a little about this because it has, in my experience, been a good technique not only for bridging the communications gap to artists but also to clients. Our firm doesn't have any account executives, but if you do I don't see what harm it would do to give it a try; there must be something that works. At the very least it may give them the feeling that they are somehow in touch and that there is a reason behind those pretty pictures art directors tuck under their arms. Also, it will give them something to think about out on the golf course, between putts.

The first of these shapes has to do with how to place an idea so that someone will accept it. Artists and writers continually have to produce ideas which are applicable to the problem before them. Unless they have independent means or don't give a hoot about getting into print, they must, in addition to producing ideas that make sense to them, also consider whether they make sense to all those others, all of them eager to toss in their two bits' worth. Since one can't take into consideration all of these people and still do a good job, there is only one way to beat the system: present an idea that they must simply accept without quite knowing why. This, I admit, is easier said than done, but there is a trick to it—you start with yourself. On any given problem you will have a lot of ideas; try and pick the one that *you* can accept without quite knowing why. The chances are good that after you have executed it the others will accept it the same way. If they reject it at least it will be nice and clean, without all that usual picking it to death and amateur criticism.

Now here is the way you think about this sort of idea visually. Imagine that a person sits in the center of a circle that represents his comprehension. He can comprehend anything within the perimeter, but the farther it is from the center the fainter his ability to criticize it will be. However, anything outside the perimeter is beyond his comprehension; he won't criticize an idea placed out there because he simply won't know what you're talking about. So the trick is to place an idea close enough in so he gets it but far enough out that he's not able to flyspeck it, only accept it.

The ideal placement would, of course, be right on the circumference of his comprehension. Perhaps it is just as well that it is impossible to determine where this is in other people, for you would probably waste more time worrying about them than you do now even. The only possible way to work this process is starting with yourself; if it doesn't work, they'll let you know soon enough and you can take another crack at it.

A very good example of this type of idea and its placement was Pink Air. When we got the account the first thing I did was institute an extremely efficient research project: I came to Dallas and asked the client, J. M. Shea, Jr., what the problem was. I had never met him before, but I figured that a man smart enough to have built an oil company from just an idea to one of the country's 300 largest corporations in five years and sure enough of what he wanted to hire us sight unseen probably could tell me about it better than a consumer panel could.

I told him I didn't know anything about the oil business. He said that was OK, because he did and there was no point in duplicating effort. He then said that there were only a handful of facts that mattered in the job we would have to do and I could take my pick of any or all of them; and that I would recognize them as soon as he said them. Now, the funny thing about these facts was that they all were of the sort I have just described: they were so placed that I knew them to be true without thinking it over.

> Nobody likes to go to gas stations; having your car serviced is about as much fun as getting your pants pressed while you wait.

> People don't really expect all that service oil companies promise them. Part of it is because we're really not as good at it as we say we are, but mostly people just want to get in and get out of the station. They're happy if the attendant wipes the windshield and remembers to put the gas cap back on. Therefore, all those advertising campaigns that show beautiful young men with beautiful smiles in beautiful crisp uniforms are not very

convincing. Besides, anybody in the oil industry knows that the only thing harder than hiring pump monkeys that look like Rock Hudson is getting them to change their shirts once a week.

No motorist in his right mind really believes there is any difference between one reputable brand of gas and another. Therefore, any ads built on the premise that they *do* think so are recognizably hooey.

You can save yourself an awful lot of time and trouble, and you can save us money, if you won't waste it in ordering people to always drive in to one of our stations. What if there are six cars waiting? The fact is that people will stop at a gas station when they have to, and if they're aware of our name and think kindly of us they'll stop at one of ours . . . if it's convenient. (This point resulted in the hard sell punchy slogan: "If you're driving down the road and you see a Fina station and it's on your side so you don't have to make a U-turn through traffic and there aren't six cars waiting and you need gas or something, please stop in.")

It is probably either useless or half truthful to make any additive claims. Everybody has pretty much the same additives, and everything in a car—including the driver—is chock-full of them already. The last secret ingredient anybody cared about was invented forty years ago: clean rest rooms.

While we used all of these points in our subsequent ads, it turned out that Mr. Shea had been wrong about one thing. Nobody had thought to make an additive for tire air. We did. Since there wasn't much you could do to tire air except color it, we staked out pink. Pink Air was one of those ideas that one simply accepts, knowing it will work but not knowing why. When we presented the campaign to our client he looked at the big pink headline and said, "Good Lord!" I asked him, "Don't you want to run it?" He replied, "Sure I want to run it." "Why?" I asked. He thought for a moment, shook his head, and said, "Beats me."

We got just about the same reaction at every sales meeting in every city as we presented the campaign. They couldn't think of any reason why, and they couldn't think of any reason why not, they just accepted it. I'll admit they weren't terribly demonstrative; you should have seen them three months later.

Thus we see how thorough research paid off, even if we only researched one man. This, incidentally, is the way we usually go at it. We prefer to work from the inside out—a process I will draw for you presently—starting with the client himself, seeing it through his eyes. I find this method so much better that I have made it a rule that I have yet to violate: never go through the

"IF YOU'RE DRIVING DOWN THE ROAD AND YOU SEE A FINA STATION AND IT'S ON YOUR SIDE SO YOU DON'T HAVE TO MAKE A U-TURN THROUGH TRAFFIC AND THERE AREN'T SIX CARS WAITING AND YOU NEED GAS OR SOMETHING** PLEASE STOP IN."***

* *We know it isn't very pushy as mottos go, but it's realistic and Fina doesn't expect you to do anything that isn't reasonable or convenient.*

** *Like oil. And 1503 other items your car might need.*

*** *Meanwhile, if you're missing a valve cap (and you probably are) and would like a pink one we will be happy to send you one free and post paid. Just fill out the coupon. If you'd also like a Fina credit card application just put an X in the right box.*

------------------[COUPON]------------------

American Petrofina, Dallas, Texas

Dear Fina:

☐ Please send me a Pink Valve Cap.

☐ Please send me a Fina Credit Card Application.

Name_____ Address_____

City_____ State _____

FINA

© 1962, AMERICAN PETROFINA, DALLAS, TEXAS

Plate 1. Reprinted by permission of Fina Oil and Chemical Company.

PINK AIR!

The following news item appeared in the San Francisco *Daily Commercial News* for March 21st, 1961:

Gasoline service stations will be filling your tires with tinted or brightly colored air in the foreseeable future, according to R. G. Lund, marketing consultant.

Detecting a strong trend in the industry, Lund said, "The oil companies are already adding additives to additives in their efforts to win motorists' favor in this highly competitive field. They have added extra ingredients to everything connected with an automobile except the air that goes in the tires. An additive for air will definitely be the next major advance."

It will take ten years, the Portland, Oregon marketer estimates, before the research and manufacturing problems are solved. Existing facilities will have to be converted to meet the public's demand for more colorful presentation of products. "But then," he concludes, "stations will feature air in decorator shades of green, blue, purple and even pink."

A word to the wise if we ever saw one. Fina's not the kind of company that has to be told twice. Pink sounds like as good a color as any and besides it's short and catchy. This is to serve notice we have settled on Pink Air.°

Not only that, but as of right now we are starting a crash program: the Fina Five Year Plan. If it is going to take everybody else ten years we'll do it in half the time.

So look for Pink Air at the thousands of Fina stations on May 12th, 1966! Give or take a few days.

The reason we're in such a rush is, as the man says, if you want to stay on top you've got to have a little something new from time to time.

But Fina's gas, oil, and accessories are already just exactly as good as the best. We wouldn't want to add more things to them just so we could say we did. (Oh, we've got additives, all right, we just can't think of any good names or numbers for them.)

And that's why we're so pleased to have a brand new additive of our very own: Pink Air. If you see anybody else claiming it, just let us know and we will deal with them for sure. Keep your eyes open.

Meanwhile we'd like to be able to give you a better idea of what the air in your tires will look like on P.A. Day, May 12th, 1966. And right now we're trying to make up a few experimental batches of Pink Air. By the time our next ad comes out we'll be able to mail you a sample if we can just figure how to keep it from leaking out of the envelope.

Now, before we go here is a picture of our Fina emblem:

 . . . so the next time you see a Fina station you'll recognize it. And if it's on your side so you don't have to make a U-turn and there aren't six cars waiting and you need gas or something, please stop in.

Plate 2. Reprinted by permission of Fina Oil and Chemical Company.

factory. One time I was visiting another client of ours, Eagle Shirtmakers in Quakertown, Pennsylvania. The production manager implored me to step ten feet over and inspect the world's most modern sewing plant. I declined, saying that I thought of their shirts as being made by little old Pennsylvania Dutch ladies with gnarled fingers and didn't want to be disillusioned.

Now I'd like to tell you about another drawing. This one is a picture of how you solve a problem. I just figured it out a couple of weeks ago and I'm not quite sure how much help it's going to be in actually doing the work. However, I suspect that it will be useful in other things; such as explaining to clients why they must not monkey around with the artwork, for instance. I see no reason why it shouldn't work with account executives and other people like that, too. Here goes:

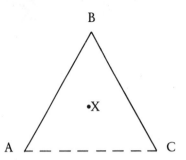

Every project will have at its core a central relationship, which I think of as a triangle. One one point (A) of the base is the man who does the project, on the other point of the base (C) is the man the project is being done for; the point at the top of the triangle (B) is not the project itself, but the involving idea about the project that both the buyer and the seller share.

The thing itself, the result of the project, is the dot in the center of the triangle (X); it will not change hands until the project is completed. Actually, all that is ever bought or sold is an involving idea about a thing. It is only after the buyer has taken delivery that it becomes anything more than an involving idea.

Despite the fact that this is the basic structure of any relationship at all, whether it be between a man and a woman, an actor and his audience, or the members of the New York Stock Exchange, we generally tend to think of it in another way. We visualize it as a straight line with the seller on one end, the buyer on the other, and the thing itself somewhere in between. It's a good enough way to look at it, I suppose, except that it doesn't take into account *why* people do things.

The reason I like this triangle representation of the market is because it is the only one I've ever seen that shows advertising's function while still making it perfectly evident that the seller has got to do his job too. It is my own belief that advertising weakens its case enormously by trying to be all things to all angles, by getting away from its unique talent of involvement and dabbling in the marketing line at the base.

Now, at various distances from the central core of the project let's place a number of random dots.

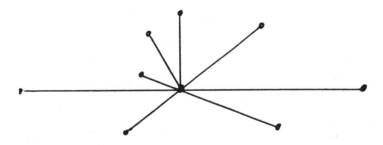

These represent problems, facts, limitations, and other known factors affecting the project. If we connect these to the center by radii we see that they are not only of unequal length

but that most of the problem areas are not accounted for at all. I mention this because there is a deplorable tendency to start to solve a problem by working in, which hardly accomplishes anything; sometimes you don't even get to the center. Almost as bad is working out along the radials, for no matter how good a job you do on any given line you stand the danger of going beyond what the rest of the project can reasonably achieve. And of course you leave all those other areas quite untouched.

Probably the most sensible, cohesive procedure is first to draw a circumference at the extreme of your shortest line

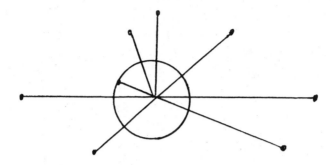

and work outward from the middle in concentric circles; better make that a spiral, since, being chronological animals, we do one thing at a time

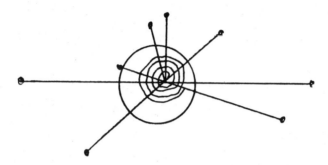

so you are in control as you proceed and when you reach the minimum circumference you have a solid entity. I suppose that one could apply this diagram to a continuing process as well, so that by increasing the limits of the shortest radius—which, in the case of a company, might represent capital, production, or distribution—you could illustrate growth. However, the intention here is merely to show the process of solving a given problem without exceeding the limits of a medium. I wish that I could figure out a way to apply it to advertising.

Advertising, because it is ill defined, is constantly being lured into seemingly allied fields that have little to do with its unique talents and often interfere with them. Advertising is many things to many people, of course. But there is one job it does well that no other communication form does at all: the controlled propagation of an idea with a defined objective through paid space.

Advertising is many thing to many people. If it does not have a defined objective, so that the effort has a beginning, middle, and end, but goes on and on in a continuous exploitation flow, it is something else; probably marketing. I realize that advertising has always done this sort of thing, but the

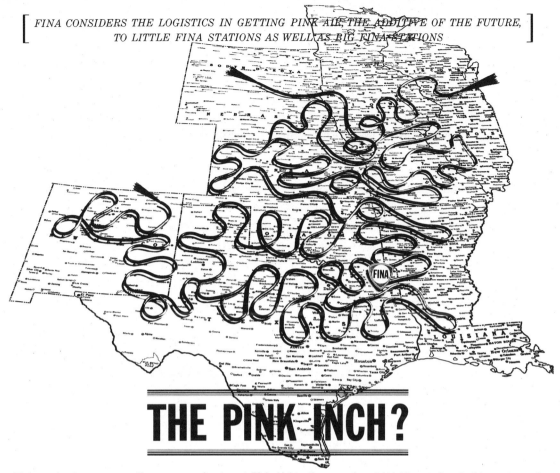

THE PINK INCH?

The question has come up: How are we going to get Pink Air® to the more than 2,000 Fina stations by May 12th, 1966?

(Pink Air, if you recall, is Fina's additive of the future; the secret ingredient which will color the air in your tires. It is the only possible additive left; everything else in your car has already been taken care of. So Fina can be first, we have started a crash program, The Fina Five Year Plan.)

There are two answers:

1. *That we transport Pink Air the same way we do our gasoline;* from our refineries in Mount Pleasant, Wichita Falls, and El Dorado to distribution points where our trucks would pick it up and deliver it to Fina stations who would then put it in your tires. This is impractical because the pink air might mingle with and color the gasoline. Our gas doesn't need any more additives; it is already as good as the best and we wouldn't want to gild the lily — not even pink.

2. *That we build a special pipe line for Pink Air:* The Pink Inch. (See map above.) This isn't as easy as it sounds; it would be a lot of hard work and would probably cost a pretty penny. You know, you don't just get out there and lay pipe across the countryside. You've got to ask people's permission and pay them something to boot. Still, if we have to do it we have to do it.

Maybe the easiest thing would be to make it a *hose* line, out of air hoses like we use in our stations, only thousands of miles long. And a little bigger: The Pink Inch Hose Line. We don't suppose people would mind so much having a hose strung across their front yards except they might trip over it.

The real advantage to the proposed Pink Inch Hose Line is that it would be fair. It would make Pink Air available at the big Fina stations and the little Fina stations at one and the same time, without fear or favor.

[BIG FINA STATION]

A big Fina station has, in addition to lots of pumps you can see, lots of underground storage tanks; and lots of attendants to keep check on them. So taking care of Pink Air would be no problem at all to them.

[LITTLE FINA STATION]

But a little Fina station might be just two pumps in front of a general store and the proprietor not only has no extra storage space but is plenty busy as it is, what with slicing bacon and all. You might have to honk twice, not that he doesn't give you good service once he knows you're there. So you can see that a direct hose from the refinery would be a real help to him.

There are still a few details to be worked out in laying that much hose; such as how to get it across highways. Maybe when we come to a road we could string it between poles. If the telephone company people will cooperate. Well, we have five years to iron out the kinks and we'll probably need every minute of it.

Meanwhile, if you are driving down the road and you see a Fina station and it's on your side so you don't have to make a U-turn through traffic and there aren't six cars waiting and you need gas or something, please stop in.

(We've said this so often now that it's gotten to be sort of the Fina motto. It isn't very pushy as mottos go but it's realistic. We don't expect you to do anything that isn't reasonable or convenient.)

Plate 3. Reprinted by permission of Fina Oil and Chemical Company.

difference is, that before nobody *else* was doing it. Nowadays other forces are engaged in mass exploitation selling, and possibly doing it better. It is my belief that advertising as an efficient exploitation medium is obsolescent, if not obsolete, for all but the lowest cost–highest profit items.

However, advertising as a medium for propagating an idea still stands by itself, when it is allowed to. Our firm has tried to confine itself to projects of definite, realizable objectives. Without these limits, advertising is a race with no finish line; you never know whether you have won or even whether it is possible to win.

I mentioned earlier how Jack Shea outlined the limitations we faced. At the same time he described his objectives. Fina, a new company, was not distinguished in any way; indeed, most people vaguely felt it to be an off-brand gas. He wanted an identity for the company. He wanted to project its vigor, size, and diversification without being stuffy and without hammering away at it in the usual advertising style.

As to diversification and size, it may surprise you to know that that was the subject matter of at least half of the ads we put out. Do you recall the ad proposing the Pink Air Pipeline with a map showing how it would work? It managed to tell in detail about every one of Fina's refineries, its network of pipelines, its producing properties, and the largest gas trucking fleet in the Southwest. Do you recall the time we offered a prize of 15 yards of Pink Asphalt (which was eventually won by a mother of five)? The subject matter of that ad was that the company was also the second biggest manufacturer of asphalt in the country.

It may also surprise you to know that the company had the lowest percentage of advertising cost against gross sales of any firm in the petroleum industry. They spent less money the first year we had the account than they had spent the year before, and this figure decreased each year thereafter until it was about half of what it was before we took over. We were able to fly in the face of usual prudent agency practice because we were working for a realistic fee. It is much easier to save money for your client if it is not coming out of your own pocket, so to speak.

As to the prestige that Jack Shea wished for his then company, it is a very hard thing to measure. Perhaps the most solid indication that Fina had achieved it occurred when the president of the most prestigious store in the United States, and some people say the world, came into my office in San Francisco and proudly announced that he, Stanley Marcus, had scooped us on Pink Air—he was offering a carnation-scented spray with the same name.

This brings us full circle or irregular triangle—depending on how you draw a chapter—back to color again. On behalf of my wife and myself may I wish you all an emerald green Halloween and a yellow Christmas.

YOUR CHANCE TO WIN 15 YARDS OF PINK ASPHALT

PINK ASPHALT?

Why not? *As you may remember Pink Air, Fina's Additive of the Future, was invented to make the insides of your tires look prettier because everything else that goes into your car already has all the extra additives it needs; sometimes more. And we started our Five Year Crash Program so as to be sure of getting it to all of our thousands of big and little Fina stations by Pink Air Day, May 12, 1966.*

WELL you know how it is in a company when one department gets something special; it's like with kids. Right away the TBA* Department wanted a Pink Program too. So the Pink Valve Cap ("the accessory to help you through the difficult withdrawal period from Regular Air to Premium Pink") was invented.

Then somebody in Trucking said: "How about painting a few of our trucks pink so people will know we're ready to transport the Pink Air from our Fina refineries in case the Pink Air Pipeline** isn't completed by P.A. Day?" And so we did.

Meanwhile back in the Asphalt Department people were feeling Left Out. It isn't an ordinary little old stick-in-the-tar asphalt department, either; we are one of the country's big manufacturers of asphalt. And it is good stuff, sort of an asphalt man's asphalt. But only in basic black—until our boys made some revolutionary experiments.

Which is why we now have 15 yards of very high-quality Pink Asphalt to give away to the one who can think up the best way to use it. (15 yards is a whole heap of asphalt; pink or otherwise it weighs about 30 tons and, if you win it, it'll take us two double-dual wheel dump trucks or semi-trailers to haul it to your house.) After we roll it out for you, it'll cover around 270 square yards which is enough to pave a pink driveway plus a pink badminton court plus a pink patio. Or about ⅞ths of a doubles tennis court; O.K., O.K., we'll pave the whole court.

Although nobody here knows how cows might feel about having their barn floor redone in wall-to-wall pink, we do know that asphalt is gentle on their feet; and neat. We suppose it would also be swell for paving sundecks on roofs; if only we can figure out how to get the steamroller up there. So if you happen to have anything you'd like paved for free with Premium Pink Asphalt just fill out part one of the coupon below and tell us what you want it for, and why. The best answer wins.

Meanwhile if you're driving down the road and you see a Fina station and it's on your side so you don't have to make a U-turn through traffic and there aren't six cars waiting and you need gas or something, please stop in.

* *For Tires / Batteries / Accessories; Fina stations sell several things besides gas and oil; hundreds.*

** *This is so complicated it took us a whole ad to explain it last time; but if you'd really like to know, just drop us a note and we'll be glad to send you a copy.*

[PINK ASPHALT COUPON]

Pink Asphalt Department
American Petrofina
Dallas, Texas

Dear Fina:

☐ Why I want 15 yards of Pink Asphalt is (you needn't limit yourself to 15 words or less. Use another piece of paper if you want):_____

_____

_____

☐ While you're at it, I would like an application for a Fina Credit Card. I understand I can use it to buy any TBA item with no money down and six months to pay; is that right?

Cordially,

Name_____ Address_____

City_____ Zone_____ State_____

P.S. Also, while you're at it, you might as well send me one of your Pink Valve Caps [ ], *too.*

Plate 4. Reprinted by permission of Fina Oil and Chemical Company.

MOTHER OF FIVE WINS
15 YARDS OF PINK ASPHALT

THE great Fina Pink Asphalt contest has ended in an unexpected three-way tie. We didn't say anything about what we do in case of ties so all three of the winners will each receive the Grand Prize, 15 yards of Pink Asphalt laid down where they want it. (This, you recall, is what the contest was about; to find the most interesting use for a batch of Pink Asphalt our asphalt division whipped up to match Pink Air – Fina's additive of the future coming May 12, 1966 – as well as our pink gas trucks, pink valve caps, etc.) The entries were so stimulating that the judges couldn't make up their minds, so we have had to scrape up an additional 30 yards to cover the other two winners.

GRAND PRIZE goes to Mrs. Bernie Rohling of 3407 Belmont Blvd., Nashville, Tennessee. This poses some problems, being outside our marketing area; we may have to smuggle the stuff to her. She says "For years I have been tying pink ribbons on bassinets, all to no avail, – I have five sons. Your contest has brought new hope into my life. How could old man stork miss leaving the right bundle if our house was plainly marked with 15 yards of beautiful pink asphalt driveway?" And she concludes, "Here's hoping, or should I say expecting?" Good luck, Mrs. Rohling!

Consolation Prize goes to Valley Center High School, Valley Center, Kansas – a new suburb of Wichita – 86 of whose students wrote rousing letters. Several wanted a pink tennis court. "Which we badly need," says one, "since there isn't a tennis court, or swimming pool, or park even in the whole town – yet." Another states: "We have done so poorly at football this year there must be *something* we can excel in; maybe it is tennis." Still another: "The old school spirit at V.C.H.S. (established 1958) can't be beat. But we haven't ever done anything anybody has heard about. It is hard to brag under such conditions. A pink tennis court would make us famous. Also it would match the trim of our building, which is pink. Maybe we will even change the school colors from purple and gold to purple and pink." Four of the 86 thought they needed a pink drag strip more, however. Well, fight it out among yourselves and congratulations all!

A Special Pink Prize goes to Mr. W. H. Moseley of 3901 Sockwell Blvd., Greenville, Texas. We found Mr. Moseley's entry especially noteworthy since he happens to be a Fina dealer; the first known instance of a company man winning a contest; we forgot to make a rule against it. You may remember that one time we mentioned in an ad that not all Fina stations were big super-stations? That some Fina stations were more modest? Mr. Moseley's is one of them, but he is anxious to improve himself. He was about to repave his driveway when he heard of our contest. He has stalled off in the hopes that his could be the first Fina station paved pink; with the result that the drive is beginning to collect a bit of water in the wet weather while he waits to find out whether to go to pink or black. He ends on a somewhat familiar note, "Meanwhile if you are driving down the road and you see this station and it is on your side and there aren't six cars (or rowboats, if you don't hurry) waiting please stop by." So, congratulations to you, Mr. Moseley, and best wishes for a dry, Pink 1962!

Our sincere thanks to all of you who wrote in; we enjoyed the fun and we hope you did, too; and that we will hear from you again sometime.

Plate 5. Reprinted by permission of Fina Oil and Chemical Company.

How to Be Creative about Next to Nothing at All

People are always asking me to teach other people how to be as creative as I am.

I've written a little about it already. But there are various other things to consider. For instance, being able to think of something at the last possible minute. In anybody else it would be called lack of foresight; in creative men it is called creativity.

For example, I was born in Chicago. I left it at the age of six months and could never seem to remember that it has two seasons of the year, January and August. Consequently I have probably made more impromptu purchases of fleece-lined overcoats, galoshes, ounce-and-a-half cheesecloth suits, and armpit ointments—depending on the season—than any other San Francisco copywriter; or creative man as we prefer to be called nowadays. This, you must admit, is a much nicer way of looking at it; when I go to Marshall Field's in January to get a pair of earmuffs it is not merely a purchase. No, I have solved a problem, in this case how to keep my ears from falling off; it is creative buying.

There is almost no limit to creativity when viewed in this fashion. You see, the essence of this sort of creativity is its last minute spontaneity. I seriously doubt that an idea is really creative unless it is thought up just before everything goes to hell, or your ears fall off, or something. It is not enough to have a good idea; you've got to have the idea, whether it is good or not, just before it is too late.

There is considerable evidence to indicate that an idea becomes less creative the longer it sits around. Unless it is acted on even a marvelous idea begins to lose its creativity; within twenty minutes in a small meeting, within twenty seconds in a large meeting. To halt this decaying process—creativity's worst enemy—I am thinking of marketing an electronic device that turns on a light bulb over your head and simultaneously calls for a vote before anybody has had a chance to think about it.

To sum up this section of our discussion, I think we could say that the creativity of an idea works in inverse proportion to the amount of time available and the number of people involved.

When you consider the delicacies of timing and footwork required to be a creative man and the many years of practice it takes, it is appalling that the rewards, outside of money, are so few. I mean, outside of the advertising business almost nobody gives a damn. Among other writers and artists we have almost no stature at all. So it is small wonder that we huddle together in advertising clubs, art directors' clubs, copywriters' clubs, and such. Or that such recognition as we have is for the most part bestowed on us by one another.

There is, no doubt, some satisfaction in this sort of recognition, but it is pretty thin stuff. It reminds me of a conversation I had with a young woman I was taking out many years ago in Houston. She was very despondent this night and was telling me her troubles. She concluded with a brave, teeth-clenched statement: "But there's one thing they can't take away from me." "What is that, Virginia," I asked politely. She replied defiantly, "That I'm the best castanets player in Harris County."

Well, if that sort of self-imposed accolade is the best we can hope for—until a younger, better castanets player comes along, that is—why in the world do we do it? What's so great about being a creative man? I don't think most of us have any choice about it. We took a flyer at several other more legitimate things and flunked out, before we ran into this peculiar thing that just happened to fit our bizarre talents. It isn't absolutely necessary that one be embarrassingly terrible at everything else, but there are certain eccentricities in the personalities of most first-rate creative men that render them unsuitable for other employment, except perhaps acting. From my cursory observations I would say that the same ego-drive is present among top creative personnel and top actors. I will go further and say that a strong ego is probably a necessity since, as we have observed, public and professional recognition is likely to be minimal. I'll go further than that and say I can't remember ever seeing a really outstanding ad that couldn't be traced to an outstanding ego.

Aspiring young copywriters come to me for advice from time to time;

that is to say they are looking for jobs, but when they find out my own ego is so strong I can scarcely bear to have other copywriters around at all, so it shouldn't be a total waste they ask polite questions to fill in the remainder of the time. After warning them that a career in advertising is like skin-diving in a barrel of piranhas, I generally advise them to get a job wherever they can. Then, I tell them to look around until they see an account that nobody else in the place gives a hoot about and grab it and run like hell back to their own cubicle. Since nobody else cares about it they can do it just their way, and, if possible, smuggle it out the back door direct to the client so that nobody else's hands taint their lovely child. Actually, this is a very good way to start, but, in fact, my recommending it is simply a waste of good breath. Because anyone capable of following such advice would do it naturally anyway, with no more thought than a dog uses to wag his tail.

The nature of the creative process itself is a never-ending source of discussion and has received a rather thorough going-over. I regret to say that I have no creative philosophy myself to impart to you. If you'd asked me a few years ago I could have given you a few thousand well-chosen words, I'm sure, but not any more.

This isn't to say that I've quit thinking about what I'm doing. As a matter of fact, I've developed a couple of techniques over the past years, and I'll give them to you for whatever they're worth.

The first is "role-playing." That is, playing the client's role, just as an actor would, expressing the client's personality and point of view. Role-playing ads will all be written in the first person; I can't remember the last ad I wrote that wasn't in the first person. This is a very handy form because it enables me to identify with the client as I'm writing—in a sort of venal Stanislavski method—and so maintain consistency of attitude. It makes for a certain spontaneity of style and one, moreover, that the client can also identify with without too much effort. This identification is desirable since the closer advertising policy is to corporate policy the more efficient it is likely to be.

This projection of identity is not, I hasten to say, the same as the word "image" implies. This word is very popular in advertising, though not with me. I prefer the word "identity," what one *really* is; whereas "image" only means how one appears to other people. "Image" also has a somewhat fraudulent sound, as though you are trying to put something over, which isn't entirely true. There's another, practical reason for preferring "identity" over "image"; it requires much less upkeep. Identity is like the sun, it radiates energy from a solid mass. Image, on the other hand, is like a balloon, all surface, and spends far too much of its time avoiding pin pricks.

Role-playing as a technique also has this advantage: that the audience tends to believe messages so delivered. At least they believe that the company really means what it says and that there is someone in back of the ads who can be talked to, or talked back to. To encourage this feeling of accessibility we frequently stick coupons or other response forms in ads. It is not so important whether they really send in the coupons, as that they feel that they can. A visible invitation to respond, whether it is used or not, adds another bit of believability to the characterization. These responses are also useful to the client in establishing his relationship to those previously faceless people out there. He feels differently about them and about himself, too. Once a client has got the idea that there is really somebody out there who cares, who is interested, he no longer feels quite so driven to advertise his gasoline as though it were rocket fuel or his beer as though it were holy water.

Another technique we have worked on is closer to journalism than anything else, I guess. It consists of planting an idea through an ad and then waiting to see what happens before you do another ad. This runs counter to the usual procedure of preparing a whole year's campaign in advance, which, of course, is a much more convenient way to do it but commits you to more or less static advertising. The conventional type of national advertising will center around a theme or a technique that acts as the vehicle for whatever it is we have to say about the client or his product. Journalistic advertising, on the other hand, has for its theme how the client feels about things or happenings. The product's flavor, or whatever other properties it has, are projected through the company's attitudes and the manner in which they are expressed.

When I told you about our campaign for Fina gas, I cheated on the research angle; I not only questioned the client, I sent the copywriter, Niels Mortensen, out to work in competitive stations for a couple of weeks—he worked at seven of them two days at a time. He confirmed that neither station attendants nor their customers had any illusions left. Nobody likes to go to gas stations. So we said that in our first ad and announced a crash program to develop Pink Air for tires and distribute it by May 12, 1966.

The second ad offered a sample of Pink Air; not really Pink Air *itself,* you understand, since it hadn't been invented yet, but a pink balloon inside of a transparent balloon so you'd get an *idea* of what it would be like.

You've already heard how the campaign succeeded. Despite its seemingly erratic course it had a definite pattern from a creative point of view. It was based on what we might call the "five thousand acres of hollyhocks" theory. What it amounts to is this: if you start off with a ridiculous assumption but develop it henceforth with fastidious logic, you don't have to dream up things, they simply evolve as you go along.

SEND FOR YOUR FREE SAMPLE OF PINK AIR!

*(A*s we know, there is a strong trend in the gasoline station industry toward adding a coloring ingredient to the air which goes into your tires. Like blue, purple, green, crimson, and others. The reason is: additives have been added to everything else connected with your car. Now it is air's turn. But authorities estimate that it will be ten years before the switchover from ordinary air is completed and colored air is in the hoses.

Meanwhile Fina, an alert young oil company, has staked out Pink Air.° And has started a crash program so they can beat everybody else by five years: the Fina Five Year Plan.)

WE are happy to report some progress. Our Pink Air Research Laboratory at Mount Pleasant, Texas is hard at work on the secret ingredient which will turn air pink. We are still confident that we will be able to get it to our more than 2,000 Fina stations by May 12, 1966. About 4:30 P.M., we figure; some of our trucks don't get around until late in the afternoon.

We will keep you posted.

However, a technical question has been brought to our attention: "How is anybody going to know what Pink Air looks like when it's inside a tire?"

That is a good question and to answer it we will send you a sample as we promised in our last ad. A Free sample.

Naturally, for security reasons* we won't be able to send you any *real* Pink Air. Besides, what would we mail it in? No, the best answer is a pink balloon,** so when you blow it up Regular air will look like Premium Pink.

And there'll be a Fina emblem on it so the next time you're driving down the road and you see it and the station is on your side so you don't have to make a U-turn and there aren't six cars waiting and you need gas or something, please stop in. And see for yourself that our products are just exactly as good as the best.

And when you're through looking at the Pink Air give it to the kids, they'll like it. How many children do you have?

*It might float into the wrong hands. Enough said.
**Actually, TWO balloons, one inside the other. Don't worry, we'll send directions.

- - - - - - - - - - - - - - - -

Fina Pink Air Development Division
American Petrofina
Dallas, Texas

[**FREE PINK AIR COUPON**]

Dear Fina:

I would like to see what Pink Air looks like. I have_____children.

Name_____Address_____

City_____State_____

© 1961, AMERICAN PETROFINA, DALLAS, TEXAS

Plate 6. Reprinted by permission of Fina Oil and Chemical Company.

Let us suppose that a farmer has five thousand acres which he has plowed and harrowed and fertilized and it is all ready for seeding. Well, the seed arrives. However, through some awful mistake they sent him hollyhock seeds instead of corn. It so happens that either he has no money left, or it will be impossible to get the seed corn in time; at any rate he is stuck with the hollyhock seeds. Now, his problem is whether to sow the hollyhock seeds or not. If he doesn't, he won't have anything. So, in spite of the fact that he doesn't want the hollyhocks and has no possible use for them, so it shouldn't be a total loss he goes ahead and sows them.

From here on out you don't have to indulge in any fantasy whatsoever, all you have to do is report what happens. You see, as long as the farmer has committed himself to hollyhock farming he has to take it seriously. But still with a certain amount of bafflement as to what to do next.

For instance when the hollyhocks bloom, is he going to send out his farmhands and harvesting machinery to gather the flowers, or is he going to wait until they go to seed and gather the pods and really go into hollyhocks in a big way the next year; maybe become the hollyhock king of the world?

And after that he has to send out his binders to gather the stalks into shocks. And so on. This technique is almost foolproof if you retain a logical mind throughout and don't attempt to improve on nature. The trouble with most efforts to use the light touch in advertising is that they can't resist adding extraneous elements once the project is launched. They do what our agency's founder, Joe Weiner, called, "putting raisins in the matzohs."

This journalistic technique is even more interesting when you use real people launched on some interesting enterprise. Because then they will produce their own variants and problems and quandaries as they go along; all you have to do is to report them. For instance, one day a few months ago a little old man came into our office, which at times resembles a newspaper city room, to announce that he wished to walk to Seattle, a thousand miles away, to promote the Seattle World's Fair and would Rainier Ale, a Seattle firm, sponsor him? He said he was seventy-nine years old and wanted to reach Seattle on his eightieth birthday; that he was a retired postman, retired for physical disability in 1935, and had been a professional walker—all over the world—ever since. When he was discharged from the postal service he had walked from the Canal Zone to Austin, Texas, about 3,500 miles. When he got there the government, suspicious, made him take a physical to see whether he deserved his retirement pay. He flunked it.

We thought this man, whose name was John F. ("Old Iron-Legs") Stahl, had a very interesting idea. But since we wanted to make it more involving of Rainier's total audience we decided to make him the coach of a three-man team and let the four of them walk to Seattle. So we ran an ad with a picture of Coach Stahl wearing a Beethoven sweatshirt pointing his finger like James Montgomery Flagg's World War I recruiting poster—Mr. Stahl had a nice white beard, too—with the headline "Coach Stahl Wants *You* to Walk to Seattle."

We drew over 700 entries and of these selected three: a twenty-eight-year-old Scotch bagpiper in kilts, a sixty-two-year-old millionaire with five children under ten years of age, and a thirty-eight-year-old professional adventurer. The interesting thing about this campaign was that it wasn't necessary to run an ad from the middle of February until late in May, after the hikers were off and well on their way to Seattle. The newspaper, television, and radio coverage on the coast was enormous. Front page stories with pictures—sometimes five-column pictures—and absolutely no reluctance to mention the client's name. I have a notion that this last may have stemmed from the fact that we didn't mention the product's name in the news releases except as an address to show the origin of the handout.

If it had been necessary to run ads reporting the progress of the walk we would have told exactly what happened. If one of them had been thrown in jail for violating village maidens along the way I feel sure we would have mentioned it with deprecating sentiments. No one would have deplored that sort of behavior more than our client. But, you get my point, it wasn't necessary to embroider an already interesting story—one that got more interesting as it evolved. All we had to do was what any newspaper editor does—keep abreast of the situation and tell what happened.

Perhaps out of all of this you have got some idea of my own attitude toward the advertising audience. They are to be considered first and always. They are to be involved. They are to be pleased for the same reason that an actor plays to an audience—because they paid their money in one form or another, and their time and effort, to get it. They bought the magazine, or newspaper, or television or radio set, and they turned the page, or turned them on; you are there at their pleasure.

This, incidentally, is the thing that distinguishes proper advertising media from bastard forms such as sound trucks, telephone solicitation, and billboards, all of which intrude themselves upon you without your permission. They inflict their messages without so much as a by-your-leave, and they do it at inappropriate times and places, without giving anything in return. Even a triple-spot of Gardol, Dristan, and Nair has the good grace to bring you a 1933 all-talkie.

As you know, I have been unjustly accused of not liking outdoor advertising. This isn't true; I *do* like outdoor advertising, I just don't think it

COACH STAHL WANTS YOU TO WALK TO SEATTLE!

Yes, this is your chance to win a free trip to Seattle's Century 21 World's Fair! And the beauty of it is you will be able to enjoy the great out of doors every step of the 1000 miles from the Opera House in San Francisco to Seattle and the Space Needle. What finer way to reassure man that he will still be able to fill his lungs with fresh air amidst the marvels of the 21st Century?

However, man does not live by breath alone.

Plate 7. Reprinted by permission of G. Heileman Brewing Company.

In line with Rainier Ale's policy of combining the cultural with the vigorously masculine, you will, of course, be wearing one of our Beethoven, Bach, or Brahms Sweatshirts* as the glorious miles trudge by. Expenses en route will be paid; you will be fully equipped from sweatshirt to shoes. On arrival at the Fair each of you will receive a crisp $1000 bill from an official (at the very least) of the Seattle Fair in recognition of your services to music.**

All this if you can qualify as one of the three man team to leave San Francisco the day the fair opens, April 21, 1962, and arrive whenever you get there. Applicants must be between 21 and 65 and have about three months to spare so they won't have to hurry; this is no race. Coach Stahl, shown at left, is against walking for any reason except pleasure and physical improvement. He moreover feels that this project, in line as it is with the President's fitness program, would be self-defeating if the walkers arrived too pooped to have a nice time at the Fair.

We are fortunate indeed in having John F. (Old Iron Legs) Stahl, Rainier Ale's Athaletic Director, as mentor of our squad. Coach Stahl, the dean of American walkers, has already made the arduous trip himself in a "dry run" (a figure of speech, since he gratifyingly believes Our Product to be an adornment to the training table). Mr. Stahl, 79 — he intends to spend his 80th birthday on the road to the Fair — has made walking his career since being retired from the Postoffice for physical disability in 1935. He has covered 17,832 miles the hard way during the last 27 years. His walking feats on three continents include a 3000 miler from the Canal Zone to Austin, Texas and from Fatima, Portugal, via Lourdes, to Rome. He has received many honors in recognition of his prowess, viz., he is a Papal Knight of St. Gregory and an Honorary Texas Ranger. He credits his longevity and excellent physique to walking and is anxious to inculcate an appreciation of its pleasures in young people. "The Twist is no substitute," says he, "the action is faulty."

Of the Seattle Walk Coach Stahl says, "Hitch-hikers need not apply; we do not need their sort." Those of you who are interested in joining him at the San Francisco training camp should have your applications in no later than April 9th. Write: Mr. John F. Stahl, c/o Rainier Ale, Seattle, Washington. Coach Stahl will require the data customary in affairs of this sort — age, occupation, photograph, shoe size, previous experience in long distance walking, if any; and, without seeming to pry, a report on the general condition of your health. In a pinch he would be willing to accept your say-so in this area, however a report from your personal physician would be preferable. We like to acknowledge the primacy of the medical profession in corporal matters whenever we can. It only seems fair. Oh, one other thing: men only.*** Happy Walking!

*You may still buy one—and we now have Mozart, too—by sending $4.00 plus 50c postage and handling to: Sweat-shirts, Rainier Ale, Box S3134N, Seattle 14, Washington. Specify composer and size; either Male or Female.
**Since you are making the trip anyway perhaps you won't mind doing a service for us, too: return a Rainier Ale empty to the brewery; a purely symbolic gesture to remind you who put up the $1000.
***Rainier Ale itself is for men only, or so we like to think. It has a strong male flavor and a strong male color. Therefore it should not be swilled down, but drunk with the same respect as a highball. Our Product is now available on the West Coast only, but soon N.Y., and after that who knows?

OUR PRODUCT

COACH STAHL AND TEAM OFF AND WALKING!

Yes, by now the three man team headed by its playing Coach John F. "Old Iron Legs" Stahl, Rainier's Athaletic Director, is well on the long walk from San Francisco to the Seattle World's Fair, "Century 21."

Chosen from over 700 applicants who answered our appeal, the three finalists selected by Coach represent a broad if interesting cross-section of American manhood.* They include a Scots bagpiper, a millionaire, and a soldier

Plate 8. Reprinted by permission of G. Heileman Brewing Company.

of fortune. They are:

CHARLES KNOWLES, 28, 6 feet 4 inches tall, Secretary of the Clan Campbell and Pipe Major of the Fraser Highlanders. Charles, not an inhibited man, will play your favorite selections at the drop of a *piobreach*. Since he habitually wears kilts anyway he is marching northward in them at a stalwart gait. At last report he was in the lead by several furlongs.

Not too far behind, however —and we must repeat that this is no race, the Coach feeling strongly that walking is for healthful, manly enjoyment— is *HERBERT HASCHE,* 62, a millionaire whose fortune is based on an invention which gives solace to each of us who rides in a car since it apparently has to do with the springing system and no American car is without one or however many it takes of whatever it is. Herb, as he has asked us to call him, is also the father of 5 children under 10 years of age. They (Gina, Nina, Tina, Herbert, Jr. and Henry II) and his pretty blonde wife (Evelyn) were at the Golden Gate Bridge to wave a cheery, teary goodbye on getaway day, May 9. (Oh, the excitement! The press was out in force and all the TV stations and newsreels; it was glorious.)

Our third man, *ROBERT LE MAIRE,* 38, is a professional adventurer-explorer who has spent his life seeing the world the hard way. Immediately he reaches Seattle he will head an expedition to certain lost cities in Central America, an area he knows well from previous scientific forays.

And, of course, there is *COACH STAHL* of whom we talked in detail last time. The Coach has done more walking than all the rest put together and will have totalled over 18,000 miles by the time he reaches the Fair; this exclusive of his pre-retirement U.S. Postal miles. He plans to coincide his arrival with his 80th birthday on August 13. Projected individual schedules by the others will have them coming in the 27th of June (Knowles), Fourth of July (Hasche; his and the nation's birthday), and the 15th of July (Le-Maire). However, the road is long and who knows what hardships and adventures may await our boys and alter their well laid plans?

They are each proceeding alone and by different routes as we see by the accompanying strip map. We hope that any of you living along, or driving along these roads to Seattle will wave or honk a friendly hello should you see any of the four. But please do not offer them a ride; it would only embarrass them since they have taken the pledge.

This concludes the news, now on to our footnote:

COACH ——
KNOWLES ··········
LEMAIRE — — —
HASCHE ·—·—·—·

SEATTLE

SAN FRANCISCO

ought to be outdoors. Now, some spokesman for the outdoor industry is sure to say that my remarks about outdoor inflicting itself on the public are unfair; that lots of people *like* billboards. To forestall this and to avoid any suggestion that I am discriminating against a minority, I would like to propose a plan devised by Bill Tara, the advertising artist and consultant. The Tara plan calls for the establishment of billboard parks, outdoor museums with hundreds of posters in tasteful surroundings where aficionados can browse to their heart's content. These to be situated well off the highway and away from disturbing traffic noises. He concludes, "What an artistic treat this would be!"

Our business, advertising, is plainly dominated by what even the least objective bystander must regard as trivia. So much so that we never take a strong stand on anything of real significance—unless it is perfectly safe. We are for schools and against forest fires. All of the courageous statements made by the advertising industry could be inscribed on a 5-milligram Dexamyl tablet.

I am sorry it is so; I would like to think of the better part of the world's greatest propaganda machine and its best minds involved in something more important. But since it is so, and there seems little prospect of immediate change, I think the least we can do is to start thinking of the audience more as we peddle our trinkets. Unless we do, some day we may find that we have been tuned out.

Now, let me examine some of the basic assumptions on which advertising has rested until now. I happen to believe that they are nowhere near basic enough, and that they must be broadened.

John Steinbeck once said, "Culture is a lousy word to describe what mankind is all about." Similarly, I would say that advertising is a lousy word to describe what advertising is all about. The advertising industry understands everything about advertising except where its real authority rests. For that reason it is obsolescent, both as a marketing tool and as a propaganda medium. To say that a thing is obsolescent does not necessarily mean that it will become obsolete.

A thing will start to obsolesce when its underlying assumptions no longer pertain. The time lag between obsolescence and obsolete depends on how much has been committed to the continuance of whatever it is. In the case of hula hoops, this commitment may not be very much at all. One awakes one morning to find that they have vanished as suddenly as they appeared.

However, where the obsolescent thing is an institution involving a great many people and much power and wealth—such as pyramid building, freeways, advertising, or Detroit—it may take a long time to become truly obsolete. Indeed, its practices will continue to be observed as long as there are

70

those who profit from them or who are so committed to them by reason of conditioning that they cannot, or will not, change.

This resistance to change is not, interestingly enough, due simply to bullheadedness, or greed, or lust for power. Often as not it is based solidly on what one calls common sense, drawn from actual experience. One imagines, for example, that if someone with what today is ordinary knowledge of the solar system had sought to impart this information to a Druid priest, he would have been dismissed as a wild-eyed radical.

The Druid—conservative and pragmatic as all primitives are—might have said: "Your theories may be all very well, but do not expect me to fly in the face of experience. When I light my two-penny candle each morning, does not the sun then kindle his great torch in the East? These are facts, plainly observable to all who have eyes. I am a practical man who must stick with the tried and true. I have no time for unreality in theorizing."

Does this line of reasoning sound familiar? The interesting thing about it is that it is sound, as far as it goes. All it proves, though, is that it is possible to begin with verifiable data and end up with a conclusion that is absolutely provable but irrelevant. It will become obsolescent as soon as its premise is supplanted by a more basic one.

Even then, the sun will continue, effectively, to rise in the East and things will go on as before. However, knowledge will progress no further, for any thinking based on this surface fact will run into a dead end. Until we probed beyond this self-evident truth, no science was possible. It is hard to imagine that we would have even discovered America, much less the structure of an atom, had we stuck with the effectively true.

Advertising, similarly, is obsolescent, and limited in its scope because it concerns itself with effects rather than causes. It apparently disregards the central fact of its existence: the media that make it possible. Now, this may seem very strange to you, since advertising devotes a great deal of time to analyzing media. That is true, but it does it in a peculiarly subjective fashion, the way the Druid examines the sun coming up in the East.

Let me try to explain. We know that if there is one indisputable fact in advertising it is that every advertisement must have a medium. This is true whether it is a print ad, a commercial, skywriting, or "Jesus Saves" on a culvert.

We also recognize that an advertisement cannot exist without a medium— a place to happen—any more than weather can exist without a place to happen. One does not simply have rain, or snow, or fog; they must happen *somewhere*: the weatherman reports rain in Spain, or fog in London, or snow in Sweden.

However, it is doubtful that the weatherman thinks of Sweden as existing solely to be snowed on, or London as merely something to be fogged on. This, I think, describes advertising's attitude toward the media that accomodate it and permit it to exist. In all my years in the business I don't think I have ever heard anyone use the term "communications medium"; it is always "*advertising* medium."

"Well," you might ask, "why should advertising think of media in any other fashion? Is the weatherman responsible for London?"

Unfortunately, there is a difference here, too. The weatherman does not make weather, nor can he control it. He cannot make the countryside flourish by bestowing his favors or starve it to death by withholding them. Advertising, as we know, can and does do the equivalent to the media it uses — or doesn't use.

I don't believe that advertising should have this life or death power over our media, nor am I suggesting for a moment that it seeks it. But whether it wants it or not is beside the point. The fact is that *it has got it.* Advertising has the stewardship of our communications media for the simple reason that economic control, however unwillingly assumed, constitutes de facto control. The effective test is: will the patient *die* if support is withdrawn? Yes.

What is equally true is: if there are no media, then advertising will die, too. Conversely, the more healthy a medium is, the more effective it is for advertising. So shouldn't we concern ourselves with improving our communications media?

Now, when you get this far you begin to try the advertising Druid's patience. Not only does it go against the conventional wisdom, but it violates his conventional loyalty, which, as we know, is to his client and prospective consumers. Not people, *consumers.*

I once got into a discussion of advertising's responsibility to the audience with an eminent advertising practitioner of the Sweden-is-for-snowing school. He said, "Look, what is the worst television commercial you can think of?" I said that I thought Dristan would probably take the prize. He said, "All right, there are 12 million people in this country who suffer from sinus trouble. Don't you think that they deserve relief from their ailment?"

I said, "There are 195 million people in the United States who have bowel movements every day, but I don't want them to do it in my living room."

In retrospect, I believe that my argument was beside the point. Whenever you veer off into aesthetics or value judgments you effectively block other more basic avenues of approach. It is like starting out to talk about whether the sun really rises, and then being sidetracked into arguing about whether it is too hot today for a topcoat.

You see, the real issue with the Dristan spot was not whether it helps some people or was offensive to others—or even whether it sold well. The real issue was the medium—the process which enabled it to be there at all. Once you have analyzed the process, the aesthetics tend to sort themselves out.

As a general rule it is useless to apply an aesthetic yardstick to a thing apart from the medium which carries it. To take this one step further, unless we examine media as processes rather than things, we will constantly be led astray by what appears to be perfectly good evidence.

To summarize, advertising's blockages in thinking—creative and otherwise—may stem from its disregard of the media it employs as processes of which it is an integral part. That is to say that the medium and the advertisement are not separate things but part of a total process just as the car and the road are. This relationship would exist even without the medium's economic dependence on advertising; that, of course, makes the intercommitment that much stronger.

The joker in all this—and probably the greatest obstacle to improvement of either our communications media or advertising—is that the recognition of this process is one-sided. The media certainly recognize their dependence on advertising for it was they who allowed it to happen. But advertising utterly fails to recognize its dependence on, and responsibility for, the media whose very existence it controls.

Chapter 8

How to Be an Art Director

As an advertising man writing for artists, most of what I have to say will bear directly on business. It's not so much that I am particularly beguiled by business as that I wished to be thoughtful to my readers. It is only common courtesy that I write about a subject of vital concern to them.

It is generally thought that artists are interested in hearing about art. Nothing could be further from the truth. Artists are interested in money; it's the rest of us who are interested in art.

This tremendous fascination by art is evident in every level of advertising, from the client's wife right up to the copywriter. Everybody wants to be, or is, an art director. While I've done a good many things in advertising, the thing that I do best—to my own mind—is art directing. I am possibly the world's greatest unrecognized art director. Occasionally, I have even gotten away with it.

My greatest feats in the art world have not been achieved either through sheer force of personality or through talent. Nor has the fact that my name is on the door helped all that much. Robert Freeman's name is also on the door, and he is an art director, which cancels out that advantage. No, my real artistic ace in the hole is simply that I am sneaky. I learned long ago that the only way to win was to hold the copy until the last minute, announce a crisis at 4:45 on Wednesday afternoon, and present some poor devil with a thumbnail sketch, telling him the plates have to be in New York by Saturday morning.

I used to think that this was an exclusive formula, but then I found out that about half of the ads are produced this way; which is probably why half of the ads look the way they do. The other half go through an orderly process that takes about three months, during which time the art directors, artists, and everybody else—and I do mean everybody else—have plenty of time to fiddle around and disimprove what probably wasn't a very good idea to begin with. This is why the other 50 percent of the ads aren't much to write home about, either.

Let's see, that adds up to 100 percent. That can't be true, of course. Nothing is perfect, not even mediocrity.

A few ads will beat the system, sometimes by accident, but usually it's on purpose. I think it's quite possible to beat the system a good deal of the time if you use your resources wisely. I'll say more about this presently.

For the moment, out of deference to artist readers, we ought to get back to discussion of business. If artists are to understand more about the advertising business, they ought to know something about its health. Let's start there.

Possibly the greatest fact about advertising's health is that it suffers from a disease of plague dimensions. We have all sensed that the disease exists and that we have it, but we have blamed those frazzled nerves, morning sickness, and quadruple spots before our eyes on other things. We have thought it was the international situation, trouble at home, unhappy childhoods, or simply that we were growing old. Incidentally, when is medical science going to do something about the most troubled and awkward age of all, middle age?

H. F. Ellis, in his series of articles in *Punch* a couple of years ago, suggested that, while pediatrics and geriatrics were all very well, what was really needed was mediatrics: a field of medicine specializing in the problems and diseases of the middle aged. At no time in a man's life does he work harder, worry more, or have less than in his middle years. Everything he has is set aside for his family, including his house, life insurance, and cars. Man's home is no longer his castle but a sort of giant do-it-yourself kit. There is nowhere for him to be alone. If there are small children in the house, chances are that even the bathroom doors will not lock for fear a toddler might imprison himself.

The mediatrics case who is also an advertising man will be particularly hard hit by the raging disease which I mentioned earlier and which now, thanks to medical scientists in California, has been identified and named. The name of the disease is *Mouse Shock*.

An Associated Press story of November 2 reported that Los Angeles was overrun by field mice. Because of a spell of unusually warm, pleasant weather, ideal for mice, "the population has increased tremendously," the story reports, "the total number would be astronomical. In the hills where they normally live they can't sustain themselves. So they are moving on." When this happens, the mice descend from their natural habitat and invade other areas. Even then, they continue to multiply at a fantastic rate until nature asserts itself in another phenomenon: Mouse Shock.

"When the population grows so great that living becomes difficult, mice suffer a shock disease similar to a cataleptic seizure." Now, I want you to pay attention to the symptoms of Mouse Shock as they are described: "The stress gets too much for them. They quiver and shake, and then start running in all directions." I hope that this is not too much for you to bear. If any of you feel an attack of the old Mouse Shock coming on, by all means put down the book and start running in all directions.

I doubt that our Mouse Shock stems from there being too many advertising men. Possibly, however, there are too many people in advertising; people who think they're in advertising, but really do something quite different. It's remarkable, when you think of it, how few people in advertising actually have anything to do with ads or the making of them. Even in a very large agency, only a handful of people will be involved in making ads. The rest do something else, and the proportion of the something elsers to the ad makers grows larger every day.

This is not a criticism, but the fact is that the advertisements themselves are becoming less and less important to what we still call advertising. Basically, this is due to the fact that advertising's role in marketing has been misunderstood, confused, and overextended. It has been overemphasized as an exploitation tool; it has been underestimated and under-used as a propaganda medium.

A word of explanation of what I mean by "exploitation" and "propaganda"; both of these words have an undeserved derogatory sense in this country. This is too bad, for they are perfectly good words, and I know of no others that serve the same broad purpose. "Propaganda," to our ears, sounds like something you tell to the natives, and "exploitation" sounds like something you do to the natives, which is unfortunate, for they mean much more than that. The same sort of thing has happened to the word "politician." Because we think of a politician as one who propagandizes and exploits the natives, a great many people who should go into politics don't. We therefore tend to leave government to those politicians who are the most likely to use propaganda and exploitation of the wrong sort.

"Propaganda" simply means the dissemination of instruction and information by an interested party. "Exploitation" merely means the follow-up that makes it pay off. If a fellow tells a girl he loves her, that is propaganda. If he kisses her, that is exploitation.

Advertising is propaganda; marketing is exploitation. Incidentally, I caused Pennsylvania State University a certain amount of trouble when I spent a term there as a visiting professor. I taught a course which I called, "The Nature of Paid Propaganda." The purpose of the course was to explore advertising as a communications medium—as an economic and cultural phenomenon—as distinct from the techniques, the nuts and bolts of advertising. Now this rather unusual title might have remained an item of limited local interest at the Penn State Journalism School except for the fact that Peter Bart, advertising editor of the *New York Times,* somehow got wind of it—possibly because I told him—and printed it.

A year later, outraged letters and cautious, steely inquiries were still pouring in to Penn State. Perhaps "commercial propaganda" would have been more tactful, but "The Nature of Paid Propaganda" had an alliteration that no copywriter could resist using. I'll tell you one thing: that title drew an overflow crowd.

Advertising, by which I mean media advertising, is at its best and most efficient when it is confined to propaganda of the better sort; that is to say, when it is informative and instructive by being fresh and interesting. All the very best, most effective ads are, by definition, propaganda, whether they are retail ads, national magazine ads, or—much less frequently—television and radio commercials.

It is when media advertising shifts from propaganda over into exploitation that the trouble begins. Here's how you can tell the difference: an advertising message that possibly wasn't very informative or interesting to begin with will attempt to achieve its goal by sheer repetition. This not only makes it inferior propaganda but also the most dubious sort of exploitation.

Entirely aside from the human consideration that it is quite wrong to clutter up our communications media in this fashion, and that all of advertising's flagrant abuses are attributable to this practice, it is an absolutely uneconomic procedure for all but a small handful of advertisers. These advertisers, however, spend most of the money that is spent in advertising, national advertising at any rate.

Now here is a curious thing: with a couple of notable exceptions, the biggest spenders in advertising—the categories that dominate the industry—are economic pipsqueaks. Soap, aspirins, compounds, toothpaste, beverages, tobacco, cosmetics, breakfast food, and so forth comprise a ridiculously dinky percentage of our gross national product, but they spend most of the advertising money. And the way they spend it is mostly in the repetitious extension of propaganda into exploitation, which I have described. The reason they do it is that they are the only ones who can afford to.

To be able to indulge in such economic profligacy one must have a product with an extremely wide profit margin and an exceptionally broad market. Moreover, because such a product will be lagely undifferentiated from its competitors, it will seem necessary to spend so much money in this fashion. They don't spend it because they want to, but because they think they have to, which I seriously doubt.

Apart from the fact that I disapprove of this practice on ethical grounds and because of what it is doing to our communications media, there is some evidence that it isn't working as well as it used to. The law of diminishing returns seems to have set in some time back. Advertising of this sort seems to have less and less effect, undoubtedly because people pay less and less attention to it. The traditional remedy, as we know, has been to pile on more and more of the stuff. This is probably why advertising budgets go up and up every year, even after full distribution is achieved. Common sense, or even natural law, suggests that it should take less energy to keep a thing going after you have got it off the launching pad, rather than more and more. It is my belief that, for simple economic reasons alone, the bulk of product advertising as we know it is obsolescent.

What will take its place? It's happening already: a clear division between propaganda and exploitation. Media advertising will increasingly tend to confine itself to its propaganda function in the effective presentation of ideas. Exploitation will be properly left to marketing and promotion. This distinct separation of function is not only more efficient, it is less confusing too. I think that the exploitation function ought to be moved right out from under the umbrella of advertising. Either that or we develop a new concept which includes only the creation of commercial propaganda and the actual making of advertisements to express it.

As it stands now, the wrong things are expected of ads, and in trying to fulfill these expectations, advertising men—like the field mice I mentioned earlier—have migrated from their natural habitat into areas that have nothing to do with advertisements. And how they have proliferated! They have spread out all over the place, overlapping each other so that they aren't quite sure who they are, where they are, or why they are there. No wonder Mouse Shock has set in.

It's very hard to avoid being infected. Although my own firm tries mightily to do so, it is tough to keep from being caught up by the general confusion. After all, we're in a business where everyone else, the media included, still works on an outmoded system. I hope the day will come when I don't have to talk myself blue in the face just to explain what seems to be only common sense.

It is peculiarly difficult, for instance, to explain to a client that if he presents fresh ideas that will involve his audience and does it with a new ad every time—for the same reason that the newspaper or magazine puts out a brand new issue every time—he won't have to spend so much money. This for the simple reson that he won't have to repeat the ad any more than a newspaper has to repeat its front page next day. And that therefore this sort of advertising is worth much more than the other sort, and that therefore I am going to charge him more; and that he can easily afford to pay me more because he is not only getting more effect, but his total budget will be far less than it ordinarily would be.

Now, since every argument for fresh, stimulating advertising is always questioned on economic grounds of the "Yeah, but does it sell?" variety, let us start from there. The best argument I can offer is that if it didn't sell department stores would have given it up years ago. Can you imagine Neiman-Marcus or Macy's running the same ad every day? Or, if they did, can you imagine that it would pay off; even if they upped their budgets to ten times what they are?

Lest you think that a retail example does not apply to national advertising—or if it does, only to certain exotic products—forget it. You can do it with anything and do it for less money—provided the client is able to recognize the difference between propaganda and exploitation, is willing to regard them separately, and is ready to do each sensibly and well. This is a lot to ask of a client, I know, but very few people ever ask them. Most clients don't know they have a choice. Nor do most agencies.

The important thing to know is where propaganda ends and exploitation begins. The chief thing that advertising can do for a product is grant permission to buy it. If you do more than a certain amount of this without the requisite follow-through in distribution, sales effort, and other exploitation, people will not buy the product because they can't find it or because they are disappointed. If you do more than a certain amount of permission-granting with the necessary follow-through, you are brainwashing. Either one is bad, unbelievable, or wasteful.

In my own experience I have had some fine successes with most of the categories that any of you are likely to come up against: banks, beer, gasoline, automobiles, shirts, wine, whiskey, airlines, motion pictures, toilet paper, tomato paste, and other bulwarks of our economy. However, I can think of a couple of these cases where our job finally ground to a halt, even though sales were up, because there was no more that propaganda could do without the necessary exploitation. The bride was beautiful, admired, and left waiting at the church.

On the pleasant side, I'll give you a short case history of a client of ours in Texas who has not only achieved a certain amount of fame through its advertising during the past couple of years, but spends far less money on advertising than it used to. I think we have only run six ads for them this year, but each one has been different—each one has caused at least some commotion, so that it seems that they are doing much more than they are. As a matter of fact, American Petrofina spent less money in 1963 than it spent in 1962; less in 1962 than in 1961, when they first came to us; and far less than they spent the year before that.

At this rate, if we were on the commission system, we'd be out of business pretty soon, for that's the way it is with most of our clients; they spend a great deal less than their competitors. Usually there is money left in the budget, because there was no logical reason for spending it. When you're working for a fee that is much larger than the commission would be anyway, you can afford to take your hands out of the client's pockets and really be Joe Altruistic instead of just pretending to be.

Look, do you know what causes a lot of the Mouse Shock in the advertising business? It's this terminological nonsense of agency and client: that we provide a service, that we represent the client. Represent him to whom? Not to the media, surely, or vice versa; that hasn't been true in over fifty years. The truth of the matter is that we are not go-betweens at all, but producers of an end product. Even the space in which the ad appears is supplier-provided just the way production is. An advertisement is a commodity whose price should vary according to its worth comparative to other similar commodities. As it is under the zany commission system, the best ad in the world has no price tag at all; it is sort of tossed in for the privilege of collecting 15 percent on all of the customer's money you can spend. If this sort of thing happened in any other business they'd either have us all in jail for extortion or in the funny farm for acute simple-mindedness. Dear Abby: Can they commit you for Mouse Shock? Signed, Worried.

The awful part of this no-price situation on ads is that it discourages any real examination of what an idea and its competent execution are worth. All of you have at some time, maybe often, brought forth some really effective thing that has made all the difference in the world to a client's future. Well, it is very hard to know how to evaluate this, though I think we should try. I simply can't accept that our reward is in heaven. But what is more discouraging, especially to an artist, is not being given a real chance to bring forth anything.

80

I have known very good artists who spend most of their time filling in high-level coloring books; taking some art director's explicit roughs and making them more pretty or less pretty, depending on how gorgeous the art director was. The best art directors, in my unlimited experience, either can't draw or pretend they can't. The very best art directors will just give you an idea in the form of a question and let you go to it, provided you are one of the very best artists. There's that.

Let's discuss artists for a while. I have always been very fond of artists and art directors, possibly because they are the only people in advertising who aren't chronically afflicted with Mouse Shock; only sometimes. They have always seemed an uncommonly happy lot to me, leading well-balanced lives. Their digestions seem to be in good shape and they keep regular hours. They arrive promptly at nine, go out to lunch promptly at noon, and leave promptly at five. When I say promptly, I mean exactly; not 5:01, but 5:00 on the dot, and sometimes 4:58. The reason for this is all artists and art directors belong to car pools. Car pools are one of their two major hobbies; the other one is lunch.

If you want to know how the world will look after the big bomb drops just walk into any art department at one minute after twelve. That sound you heard was not thunder, but the art staff stampeding to lunch. The desolate scene that greets your eyes is reminiscent of the final shot of "On the Beach," everything left exactly where it was when they thundered off to take their temporary red and white pills.

Aside from this compulsive nourishment neurosis, artists have very few quirks that cannot be overcome by love, understanding, and discipline. I would like to dwell on a couple of these characaeristics for a moment since they bear directly on the problem of coexistence with the artist.

In these days of enlightenment, we Americans are making a genuine effort to understand the mentalities of people who are different from us, both abroad and at home. I am sure we are all sympathetic with those who work with minority problems through such groups as the Peace Corps, the American Civil Liberties Union, the Anti-Defamation League, the Republican party, and the Petroleum Club. Nobody, however, has made any real effort to understand the thought patterns of the artist or art director. What sort of a world does he live in? What are his ambitions and hopes? What does he really see when he looks at something?

Let me give you an example. A few months ago, I bought an electric typewriter with one of those modern type faces so fashionable these days. Marget Larsen, one of the finest designers and art directors in the world, came into my office and admired it. I typed out a few words and asked her what she thought of the type face. She looked at it thoughtfully and said, "It's very nice, but never use the capital M."

Another example. Several years ago I did a series of airline ads and the art director made a beautiful format, the top of which depicted an airplane in reverse against a black sky. I took it off with me to Australia to show the client. For some reason or other he simply could not stand that black sky— it spelled doom and destruction to him—perhaps his mother had been frightened by a tint block. I don't know.

So I immediately called San Francisco from Sydney and asked the art director to please reverse it all back and turn the sky to white. When he asked me why, I said that it had something to do with an airline's morbid fear of air disaster and I was sure he understood. He said he did, and I hung up, confidently assuring the client that he would not be going into public mourning. When I got back to San Francisco I told the art director what a smashing success his ads had been and warmly congratulated him. He smiled gratefully and modestly.

Time passes; about five weeks, as I recall. One morning I opened an issue of the *New Yorker,* and there, in glorious black and white, was my ad with the little reverse airplane winging its way through the stygean murk. Thinking there must have been some horrid mistake, I hurriedly checked *Time, Holiday, U.S. News & World Report,* the *Wall Street Journal,* and every other book on the list. All of them were top heavy with Australian gloom and doom.

Exercising great control, I called my colleague on the intercom and asked him to come visit me in my office. This was not because I was too haughty to go to him so much as that I didn't think my legs would support me at that moment. He appeared presently, all gracious smiles, and asked what was up.

I measured my words carefully: "Er, you do remember me calling you from Sydney about this, don't you?" (Sweeping gesture encompassing fourteen ads in basic black death.) He nodded pleasantly.

"And you remember that I said that Australians had a superstitious dread of black skies?" He said, yes he did.

"Well, then, of course you remember that on account of all this I asked you to change the sky to white?" Sure, he remembered.

"Would you mind telling me, for Christ's sake, why you didn't change it!"

"No," he answered, "I don't mind telling you."

Now then, I'd like to ask—what do you think it was that he replied? Bear in mind that disaster was facing me, and that just as soon as the magazines reached Sydney I would probably receive a cable informing me that we were fired: this from a man who had, with tears in his eyes, extracted a solemn promise that I would change the ad. Would anybody like to guess what the art director told me when I asked him why he didn't change it?

He said, "Because it looked better the other way."

The upshot was not as dreadful as one might fear. The agency wasn't canned; however, one thing led to another as they often do. And shortly thereafter I decided to go into business for myself.

Do you know what the real lesson in this morbid tale is? It is that I went about the thing in all the wrong ways. And so do most copywriters and account executives. The art director I have mentioned is one of the most capable in the business. He has done a great deal of really excellent work and undoubtedly you have seen much of it. In retrospect I can see that the fault was mine in not starting all over again with the layout. It was his mistake that he did not do so on his own initiative. The fact of the matter is that the ad was better the way he had it originally and the way it actually ran. To have changed one element in an ad that was mostly composed of art would have made it a pretty mediocre thing, as he showed me later. The ad as it appeared was extremely effective, and it also won art awards all over the country, for what that is worth.

The only thing to do in such a situation is to start over from scratch. Sometimes it is better to scrap the idea entirely. I've seen too many ads over the years that have been disimproved by deletions, additions, and other changes, supposedly for the better.

"Disimprovement" is a wonderful word invented by an Irish client of ours. It means making things worse by trying to make them better. Cars have been disimproved of their head room so that a man can't wear his hat in the car and a woman can't get into one at all without unladylike skootching. As far as that goes, girls have been disimproved of their lovely jiggle by girdles; and hair sprays disimprove their hair so that it's no longer possible to run your fingers through it unless you want to pick up splinters or love the feeling of excelsior.

Art work, and copy too, are disimproved every day if you allow them to be. One way to prevent this from happening is to refuse to allow any alterations or editing. If someone objects to something in an ad, do not let him fool with it, but go back and start all over again. I know this makes a lot of work, but it is the only way to avoid mediocrity. Your implicit attitude must be: "You have a perfect right to reject or accept it, but not to change it. Because if you start to change it you have set a process in motion which has no master and no end."

One time several years ago when Saul Bass was still an agency art director in New York, he attended a presention in a client's office high in the Empire State Building. The client, a rather assertive type, looked at one piece of art and said, "I don't like this, what I think you should do is. . . ." At this point Saul picked up the comp and tossed it out an open window. Everyone in the office, aghast, ran to the windows and watched the layout as it idly fluttered and swirled its way down to Fifth Avenue far below. As luck would have it, it landed in the middle of the street and a big truck immediately rolled over it.

Saul says that the effect was electrifying. The client turned to him and said, "Gee, you shouldn't've done that, that was a wonderful piece of work!" Saul just shrugged ruefully.

I, of course, approved heartily of Saul's dramatic gesture, but commented that it was a shame that he had to throw away a good piece of work to make his point. "Oh," he said, "it didn't make any difference. When I picked out that piece the day before as the one I was going to heave out the window I made another copy of it."

Chapter 9

How Can an Art Director Become an Advertising Man?

As I was saying in the past chapter, being an art director must be the most wonderful job in the world because everybody wants to be one. You will recall that I was advising account executives, copywriters, and other fringe operators on how they, too, could become art directors.

Now, by contrast, I should like to suggest how art directors can become advertising men. This may be gratuitous advice. It is likely that most art directors have no desire to improve themselves. Still, it has not escaped my notice that art directors admire certain aspects of advertising. They do not wish to become copywriters, for copywriters have all of the disadvantages of art directors—cubby holes to work in, inferior social position, etc.—without any of the advantages, such as free colored pencils to steal and take home to the kids.

However, most art directors envy account executives, for a most interesting reason: free lunch. To understand why this is so you must appreciate that eating is the most important thing in the world to an artist. All his life, from the time he is a small boy he dreams of two things: (1) to be an artist, and (2) to eat, though not necessarily in that order. In time, since he is purposeful in his pursuit of the muse, he becomes an artist. But with all his success, he never forgets the other goal: to eat as often as possible, and as promptly.

But, aside from the free lunch aspect of being an advertising man, the art director does not care to become one. Of all the people in an agency, art directors are the only ones who seem reasonably content with their lot. In comparison with the rest of us they lead rather regular lives. Except when expressly commanded to do so they are not given to working overtime. How often, at five o'clock, I have said, "Hark! a peal of thunder!" only to realize it was the art department stampeding homeward to dinner.

In eerie contrast to this noisy departure is the folding-their-tents-like-Arabs-and-silently-stealing-away technique. This occurs on evenings when they suspect that there might be some last-minute rush job. God knows how they can sense this, but my guess is that some animal instinct warns them—they are earth creatures and live closer to nature, you know—possibly a raven flies by their north windows croaking out a warning. At any rate they *know;* just try walking in an art department at 4:58 on those evenings and see how many you find. Gone, vanished. How do they do it? Apparently when they receive their diplomas from the Famous Artists Course or wherever, they also get secret instructions on how to dematerialize. The other alternative is that this talent is passed on from artist to artist; probably at some secret initation ceremony where Fred Ludekens, Bill Tara, Saul Bass, and Jack Roberts hold up candles with one hand and clients with the other. After which everybody eats.

Now, please do not think I am being bitter. It is envy, pure and simple. Why? Because art directors enjoy themselves so much. They also enjoy one another's company. This is not true of advertising men; they *pretend* to like one another, but down deep inside they don't really. Advertising men find other advertising men a rather dull lot, and for good reason. We *are* a rather dull lot collectively, without much to say. No, that's not true. We have a great deal to say and we say it over and over again, possibly to convince ourselves that it is true.

This is particularly true of account executives. What do account executives have to talk about, really? When you have discussed the best way to carry a piece of paper over to the client's office *once,* the subject is about exhausted, isn't it? Now, if account executives were to wear distinctive uniforms sporting their agency colors, and with epaulets or other insignia of rank, or wear ribbons—campaign ribbons—they would have things to talk about. But as it stands I doubt there will ever be an account executives' club.

Copywriters are not much better off. In the first place, most good copywriters are very strange people who have only reached copywriting after eliminating every other means of making a living through writing. Once a man becomes resigned to making a good living by writing a few words at a time and writing them over and over again in various combinations, he is likely to think of himself as a professional copywriter. He dismisses the idea of winning the Nobel Prize. An art director, on the other hand, remains an artist; that is the way he thinks of himself. On weekends he paints pictures for his own pleasure. Deep in his heart he never dismisses the possibility that one day he may be recognized; a wealthy old man will come up to him and say, "I like your work. It has a quality I have never seen. I will arrange a one-man show for you at the Metropolitan."

A copywriter has no such illusions. That is why copywriters' clubs are such dismal flops for the most part. They last a couple of years and then dwindle away. Likewise, awards for copywriting never attract much interest because the copywriters themselves know that the stuff simply doesn't look all that good when judged comparatively. I mean, designs, art, will look good no matter what the subject matter is. Some of the dullest items in the world receive simply ravishing art treatment, but the copy is mostly just about what it ought to be, informative but not terribly stimulating artistically. Ads generally receive a good deal better art treatment than copy treatment. This is because there is much more freedom of expression in art than in copy. There are unlimited ways of making a lousy idea *look* brilliant, and almost any competent art director can do it and even win prizes at it. There is hardly any way at all to make a lousy idea *read* brilliantly; the most you can shoot for is writing it competently enough so that it doesn't rot the paper.

Even given a good idea, it is more difficult to do an outstanding copy job. The reason is this: any attempt at unusual excellence involves the risk of exceeding one's medium. The tolerances are much broader in art than in writing, probably because fewer clients can draw than can read and write. So, if an artist does a piece of work—an abstract, say—that no one understands, chances are he will get away with it, even though he has exceeded the medium. There is a much smaller chance that a writer will get away with it. People may not know much about art, but they do know whether they can understand writing or not. Consequently, most advertising copy never gets a chance to be adventurous the way advertising art does.

There is also the personal motivation of the artist as against that of the copywriter. The best artists in advertising will not regard their work as a thing apart from real art; everything they do is real art. Writers, even very good writers, will tend to divide their judgment, and consequently their work, sharply.

Advertising writing is not real writing, it is something apart. This is not to say that a copywriter doesn't take a workmanlike interest in it, for he does, but he doesn't confuse it with the real thing. Consequently, if he is praised by outsiders for his copywriting on artistic grounds he is likely to cringe a little. Indeed, the whole field of copywriting is likely to tend toward anonymity.

The intent of a piece of copy is to project the client's identity, not the writer's. This is true even when the writer's style is very distinctive. Even there the client's identity is projected, not the writer's, in a process very like an actor playing a role; except there are no screen credits. An artist, on the other hand, feels no necessity to submerge his own identity, and often—whenever he is allowed—he will sign the artwork.

I think most artists feel that their art, even in an ad, is a thing apart. This is not always to the good, at least from my point of view. It sometimes means that the idea of the ad is subordinated to its appearance. I have written a good many ads that are not *supposed* to look good; in some instances they are supposed to look absolutely awful, from an artist's point of view. I will say to him: "Look here, Charlie, or whatever your name is, I want to achieve a sort of vulgar, impromptu look here. . . ." At which point I may be interrupted by him saying, "Supposing you let *me* decide that, eh fellah? Do I come back and tell you how to write copy?" And I will say, "If you knew how to write copy you probably wouldn't be an art director," or something equally tactful. He sees I have him, so he changes his tack: "See here, Howard. . . ."

"Mr. Gossage."

"See here, Mr. Buttinsky, there's no reason why an ad—even a borax one like this—shouldn't be the very best I can do. I agree that totality of expression is important, but it involves elements of which I am a better judge than you."

When I was young and humble I was more easily intimidated by this split-level Bauhaus, half-Aspen sort of talk, but I soon got cured of it; not entirely, I still bite from time to time. When I get the layout back—from those art directors who allow me to look at a layout—I find, all too often, that the guts have been refined right out of it. It looks handsome, sure, but it's not the real thing. Usually the thing works out all right in the end, but sometimes it never does come out just right as an ad.

I have cited an extreme example; the difficulty becomes more pronounced and harder to define when we come to the projection of more subtle feelings. From my experience, artists are inclined to design something the way it *ought* to be rather than the way it *is*. This tendency is understandable, because their taste is superior. However, in doing so they sometimes produce an effect that exceeds the demands, or even the propriety, of the occasion.

I recall once seeing a young couple dancing; they looked like they were right out of the prom sequence of *West Side Story*. A rumba struck up and the girl broke away and started sashaying around by herself. Her partner grabbed her back and said, "C'mere, you're giving it too much class, which you ain't got."

I see a lot of ads that give it too much class, and I know that a lot of them are not the art director's fault. But some of them are. Mind you, these ads are good art, but they aren't fitting; they are excessive for one reason or another. I think part of this is due to something I mentioned earlier: art directors are artists first and advertising men second.

I don't know what the answer to this one is, and I certainly wouldn't recommend that they change it around. This very quality is possibly the thing that makes art directors as a group more attractive than any other in advertising. It is also entirely possible that if art directors were advertising men first our ads wouldn't be as good as they are. Advertising, although it hasn't improved markedly as a business—if anything it is getting worse—does produce better looking stuff all the time. The copy hasn't gotten much better, but the art certainly has. So, if art directors knew as much about writing as the copywriters think they do about art, just imagine how helpful they could be; and how much better the ads would be!

But before they get to that point they'll all have to start being more serious about advertising. In the first place, art directors will have to cut out this thing of admiring their work so much. Why should they be different from the rest of us? In the second place, give up eating or, at least, enjoying it; they might as well have upset stomachs like everyone else.

Ah, Art, what I have suffered at your altar! I won't bore you with whining recitals of the countless times I have been lied to, sneaked around, bamboozled by certain of that number. One thing about having grown old as a copywriter: sooner or later every art director in the world has outfoxed you or at least tried to. I say tried, because I assume that one of them must have failed at some time or another; nothing is perfect, not even the universal perfidy of art directors.

You'd think that now, when I am not a young man anymore, when I am a pillar, or at least a two-by-four, of the community that they would let up on me a little bit. But no. Only yesterday it was necessary to speak to Robert Freeman out of sheer self-defense. We were talking about a layout and I said: "Look, I'll tell you exactly what I want again so that when you don't do it I'll at least have the satisfaction of knowing that you knew what it was you weren't going to do."

Do you know what he said? He laughed uproariously and said, "Hey, put that in your book." I was incredulous. "You mean you don't care if other art directors know how two-faced you are?" He said, "Hell no, they're even worse." He's right, of course.

Chapter 10

Our Fictitious Freedom of the Press

Of all the concepts on which our republic rests, I should imagine freedom of the press to be far and away the best known. This is hardly strange, since those who are the most vitally interested in promoting freedom of the press are also those who have all the facilities for doing so, the newspapers themselves.

As a space grabber, any real or fancied violation of freedom of the press has it all over even such favorite contributions to our intellectual well-being as axe murders of teen-age girls, what's new with the Kennedys, or the Academy Awards.

Despite all the venerable sanctity accorded it and all the publicty, as concepts go, freedom of the press is a newcomer. It is a pretty new thing and for a pretty good reason: until just yesterday in man's history there was no press to be free or otherwise. Indeed, at the time the Constitution was written there were no newspapers as we know them. What there were were little better than politically slanted poop sheets that made small effort to separate editorial views from news matter. It may be argued that we could say the same thing of *Time,* which is quite unfair for as we know there were no four-color presses in those days. And of course there was nothing to compare with, say, the *New York Times,* which as we know gives us all the news that's fit to print. I sometimes wish that more of it were fit to read.

A version of this essay appeared in *Ramparts,* August 1965.

It is doubtful that the founding fathers, for all their wisdom, had the slightest inkling of the extent to which communications media would develop by our time. In spite of this, freedom of the press is still a vital concept today, long after certain other items in the Bill of Rights, such as those protecting citizens from Bills of Attainder or from having to quarter troops in the home, have ceased to be matters of intense concern.

In a way it is too bad that so much is made of our constitutional guarantee of freedom of the press from governmental control, for it tends to obscure other incursions on freedom of the press that are just as dangerous and much more immediate. That these incursions are economic rather than political makes them somehow more insidious and certainly much harder to recognize. This is because we are admittedly an economic society, with a long tradition of protecting our economic interests against political inroads. Economics is a *nice* word, politics is a *bad* word. So we are unlikely to look for invasions of our political freedoms in perfectly legitimate economic practices or to comprehend their enormous implications even when we find them staring us straight in the face.

What I am getting at is this: in this century we have seen effective control of our press shift from the public, for whom it presumably exists, to the advertiser, who merely uses it to sell his wares to the public. It has shifted so much that the life or death of a publication no longer depends on whether its readers like it but on whether advertisers like it.

If you doubt this, consider that well within our lifetime over half of the daily newspapers in this country have folded and that most of them have done so with their circulations more or less intact; that magazines with circulations into the millions have gone under not because their readers didn't love them but because advertisers didn't.

Well, there have assuredly been other factors at work. But I think it is unarguable that the central fact in this deplorable situation is that our press, by committing the overwhelming portion of its financial well-being to the discretion of advertisers, has done its readers, itself, and even advertising irremediable harm. If we are to do anything about it in the future perhaps we'd better take a brief look at how we got into this mess in the first place.

Originally, a publication was almost wholly dependent upon its readers for financial support and therefore charged them accordingly; if a magazine was worth five cents, they paid five cents for it. However, with the growth of advertising the publication enjoyed more and more income from paid space. Now this was a very pleasant situation indeed: the advertising revenue was, in effect, found money. Moreover, it provided yet another reason for getting new readers: more could be charged for the advertising as more people bought the publication—still at a profitable five cents. Now here was an incentive plan. My God, how the money rolled in.

But not for long. At some point two opposing economic spoilsports—rising production costs and competition—started to ruin the whole lovely thing. On one hand it was necessary to raise the price to the reader; on the other hand it was desirable to keep the price down so as to attract more circulation and more advertising dollars.

Well, the publication couldn't do both, so it made a decision, a fateful one as it turned out, for it thereby committed itself to an increasingly irreversible course, which it still pursues. It probably didn't seem like much of a decision at the time, however. Why antagonize the customers and help the competition by raising the price from a nickel to a clumsy figure like six cents? No, what we'll do is give the reader a break so we can keep up the circulation and get more advertising.

Some break. On the day the reader first bought a publication for less than it cost to produce he lost his economic significance and became circulation. Moreover, he traded off his end of freedom of the press. It was a forced sale; the publisher had already traded off the other end. Of course the editor was still free to write anything he wished without government censorship, but there are other freedoms upon which this freedom depends—the freedom to publish, for instance. Is freedom to publish really significant if the power to kill it has been assigned to outsiders?

It seems to me that any publication represents a contractual agreement between the publisher and the readers. He will undertake to publish something to their tastes and they, on their side, will support the publication as long as he does. Now, this is a perfectly just and reasonable arrangement embodying such sturdy traditions as democracy, free enterprise, and freedom of choice. But none of it means a damn as long as the rug can be jerked from under it by a third party.

The sad fact is that no matter how pleased readers are by a publication, no matter how many of them faithfully renew their subscriptions, they will be deprived of it if sufficient advertising is not forthcoming for the simple reason that circulation revenue is just not high enough to be of any real significance. In effect, the price the reader pays has been subsidized by advertisers, so that he gets a twenty-five cent newspaper for a dime and a seventy-five cent magazine for a quarter. Actually, he rarely pays anywhere near that much, for publishers, anxious to look good on the ABC, continually put out special offers that, in some cases, bring the price of a fifty-cent magazine down to about nineteen cents.

Well, the public has paid dearly for its cheap magazines; and there are fewer and fewer around for them to pick up at bargain rates. Nor are there many new magazines coming up, mostly for the reason that the subsidized, artifically low rate structure makes it extraordinarily difficult for any but the richest publishing ventures to get started. Advertisers, who could help—if only to make up for the old corpses they created by starving them to death— are extremely reluctant to go into new magazines. Advertising agencies are reluctant too, but for an additional reason: there's no money in it. Fifteen percent of next to nothing is just not worth the trouble.

But let's not get into the commission system or advertising agencies again here except to observe that, although the commission system is obsolete and the advertising agency obsolescent as concepts, they and the philosophy they represent continue to dominate and pervert our communications media. This is because they constitute a concentration of power that changes advertising from being an added service within a medium to being its control factor. I don't think this should be. While it is very nice added service to have hot dogs at a football game, I don't think they should interrupt play to sell them. This, of course, is precisely what happens on television. The only reason we tolerate this outrage is because we simply do. We allow it to occur on our most powerful communications medium—a medium that demonstrably belongs to us; it is only licensed to the operators—when we wouldn't dream of letting it happen at a football game. And yet, it already has; time-outs are routinely called whenever a commercial comes up.

Now, why would they interrupt a game to hawk razor blades on TV when they wouldn't do it to hawk hot dogs in the stadium? Simply because more money comes from selling razor blades than comes from the viewers, whereas the receipts from hot dog sales are minor compared to those from ticket sales. Let us suppose that the latter situation were reversed, that the proceeds from hot dog sales were greater than ticket receipts. Moreover, suppose that it was more profitable, hot dog–wise, to have a full stadium, even though the spectators got in free or had greatly reduced special introductory rates, than to have a smaller crowd at the full price.

Well, this might affect the constituency of the audience right off the bat, because it's not quite the same thing when you get in free, and many people would rather pay for their pleasures. But, since we are now interested in numbers, things are going along very well; the place is packed and everyone is happy even though they have been demoted from spectators to potential hot dog consumers.

However, here comes that economic spoilsport again. High football production costs make it necessary to bring in more money. Well, you certainly can't expect people to pay to see football games when they are used to seeing them for nothing. And you can't raise the price of hot dogs beyond a certain reasonable point either. So the only thing to do is to try to sell *more* hot dogs. A survey sponsored by the American Association of Hot Dog Vendors shows that the peak hot dog consuming period is the halftime intermission, which, as with most surveys, everybody knew anyway. It reminds me of Carl Ally's definition of a consultant: a man who borrows your watch and tells you what time it is.

Anyway, the obvious solution, brilliant in its simplicity, is ten-minute intermissions between quarters. But, so as not to extend the game so much that it runs over into the game that immediately follows in this stadium—the late show—five minutes is chopped off of each period.

With the advent of the ten-minute quarter the character of the game changes somewhat. Not that it makes much difference to the fans, because the fans have changed too. They no longer feel fiercely about football, they just come to watch it with varying degrees of interest. Sometimes they aren't very interested at all and attendance dwindles. However, the top-rated games pull very well indeed and are much copied for format. It is found, for instance, that the most popular game one season was a 29-to-27 struggle between Duke and Northwestern, decided in the last twelve seconds of play by a field goal kicked by a Duke pom-pom girl. The next year nearly every game gets down to the finish line 27 to 26 with an underdog pom-pom girl trying a field goal. Talk about your suspense! Thus football ends up a sort of open air television, except that if you want to escape the hot dog vendors you have to walk a half a mile to the bathroom.

I used this analogy when I was teaching at Penn State. Incidentally, if you ever want to stop conversation dead at a faculty tea just have yourself introduced as a Distinguished Visiting Professor and when they ask, "Really, of what?" you say, "Advertising." Back to the class. When I had finished the Saga of the Hot Dog Vendors we got into a discussion of the rights of advertisers versus those of the audience. One girl said she certainly thought that advertisers had the right to control television programming; after all, they paid for it. I asked her if she thought that hot dog vendors had the right to change football games. "Of course," she said, "if they paid my way in."

"But what right have they got to pay your way in?" I asked. "Whose football game is it? Whose stadium is it? Whose university is it? It's yours! It doesn't belong to the hot dog vendors, it belongs to you; and so do our communications media."

Well, it's very easy to kick the hell out of television, but to my mind the other media are just as culpable. Television's abuses are just more obvious, that's all. If you still doubt that the same destructive forces are at work on magazines, for instance, let's consider how a great magazine dies.

The process works something like this: at a certain point it is noticed that advertising revenue has slumped. Usually the cause for this will have occurred some time in the past—poor management, poor representation, poor whatever-it-is that causes confidence to start to sag—and has only caught up just now, so it is not always easy to find out where the trouble lies. At any rate, to stem the tide everybody is exhorted to get out there and sell, and the promotion department turns out a few gross more bar charts showing the magazine's overwhelming superiority in every field from baby pants to nuclear reactors.

They also turn out a brand new audience survey that proves incontrovertibly that their average readers are young marrieds, have 1.5 dogs, 2.5 children, 3.5 cars, own an eight-room house outright, go to Europe 2.3 times a year, drink enormous quantities of every kind of booze you can name, and have a high median income of $8,743 a year.

Well, no wonder they can do all those things, with all that money. Every time I see a survey like that I wonder why the internal revenue boys don't subpoena the magazine's circulation lists and swoop down on every one of the subscribers for tax evasion; they each must have about thirty or forty thousand a year that they're not declaring. But I digress.

Anyway the advertising revenue keeps on slipping until everyone from the publisher down to the mail boy starts getting flop sweat. Flop sweat is a show business term best described by a comic who becomes aware that he is laying an egg. Nothing works. The fewer the laughs the harder he tries. Sweat begins to stand out on his forehead and he becomes a ghastly sight, a shell. He stays on and on because he no longer has strength enough to move. So finally they bring the curtain down on him. It's a terrible thing to see.

Since the advertising side hasn't been able to do anything they decide that the editorial side must be at fault. So they hire a hot-shot research firm who, after three months and about a hundred thousand dollars, tells them that they ought to change their format. The editor vigorously protests that to change the format will change the character of the magazine and that's what the readers buy the book for. However, in desperation, he makes a feverish effort to mold a new team, this being a more acceptable alternative than involuntary resignation. It doesn't work, he is canned anyway. The new editor comes in, bringing his own boys with him from wherever he came from; this means that the rest of the top editorial staff is canned, too. By now flop sweat is so severe that everybody walks around in mental terry cloth robes.

Eventually, after much in the way of breast-beating announcements in the trade and consumer press, the new look is bestowed on a waiting world, loads of new promotional material are bestowed on waiting reps, and everybody goes about glowing with false confidence.

Sometimes all of this works, but mostly it doesn't. Maybe it's *never* worked, I can't recall. The chief reason it doesn't work is that, just as the old editor said, this isn't the magazine that the subscribers were subscribing to. So, they begin to drop off, cancel their subscriptions, or simply not renew them.

This drives the circulation department into a frenzy of activity. They come up with trick deals on trick numbers of months—I guess this is so you can't figure out the cost per copy easily. I imagine it's based on the sort of reasoning that prompts finance companies to do the same thing on car cards so that, unless you take out a paper and pencil and think real hard, it won't dawn on you that you're going to have to pay 37.5 percent simple interest on that $420 loan. Well, they replace the circulation all right, but they only accomplish it by spending more and more money per new subscriber. And each new subscription at the special, introductory, money-losing rate replaces one old time full-rater. So the circulation revenue starts a downward spiral too. Moreover, some of this circulation activity will be reflected in the ABC, and media buyers will spot this for just what it is and will chop back insertions even more.

By now the whole operation will have the smell of death about it. Morale will be utterly shot, another editor will have made further changes, they will have converted the publisher's office into a revolving door; and in the end, the publication is sold as a tax loss. The new owners, after a death rattle of activity, close the magazine down and buy more rock and roll stations.

And so a magazine dies. And hundreds of people are forced to look for new jobs in a dwindling industry. More than that, the most important group of all, the readers, millions of them, are robbed of a great magazine. Not that it was great when it folded, because in its flop sweat it had changed from a fine lady to a painted whore. So when she dies, nobody really gives a damn too much, which is a pity; especially since it needn't have happened at all.

Well, whose fault was it? It wasn't anyone's fault; no one did it on purpose. It's just that the system makes it inevitable. The only ones who could have remedied it, the advertisers, strictly speaking had no economic or moral responsibility to do so. The hard fact of the matter is that no publication should be in the position of having to depend all that much on advertising. It is all wrong that agencies should, by the negative act of simply not placing advertising, be able to kill off a magazine. But that's the way it is.

As an advertising man, I find this regrettable since we don't have enough first rate media as it is. As a citizen, as a human being, I find it deplorable, shameful, that the readers of a magazine should count for so little in comparison. There is no valid, just, decent reason why a publication should go down for the lack of support from any group on God's green earth except its readers. It is all the more shocking when one realizes that the life or death of, say, the *Saturday Evening Post* rests not in the hands of its six million subscribers but with surely no more than ten top advertising agencies.

Do you know what I'd do if I had a magazine that was in trouble? I think I'd change it back more or less to what it was before it got flop sweat. At least I'd try to give it the same feel. And then I'd let the readers in on the act: I'd write them all letters and explain to them what I was doing and why I was doing it. I think I'd level with them about some of the economic facts I've talked about here: of how effective control had slipped from their hands into the hands of advertisers, and that to readjust this imbalance we were going to cancel all trick subscription deals and raise the price from, say, twenty-five cents, to forty cents or fifty cents, whatever it took to do it. And I'd tell them that the net result might be that the circulation would go down to perhaps three million, but they'd be three million subscribers who really *wanted* the magazine; it would be *their* magazine, not something put out to cadge advertising revenue. If advertisers liked it, fine, but that was incidental to the purpose of putting out a magazine in the first place.

Do you know, I have a notion that *that* would work. It's courageous, it's economically sound, and it would certainly build up morale around the old place. Also, it's properly considerate of the reader; I think he'd rally around too.

If I were publisher of a magazine that's *not* in trouble, I think the first thing I'd do is get rid of those stiff insert cards that are used to get new subscriptions and forbid advertisers to use them. And I think I'd tell readers why I'm doing it: because they're a damned nuisance, because they inhibit page-turning, because they make people mad. They are probably the least-liked single item in the free world. It's not so bad with saddle-stitched books, because all you end up with is two pieces of cardboard that you haven't got any place to put unless you get up out of the chair and walk across the room to the wastepaper basket. But with a side-stitched book, unless you're careful, you're liable to mutilate it, and your fingers, to boot. Some magazines have so many cards from Book-of-the-Month Club, American Heritage, etc., that they feel like they're printed on 100-pound stock. I have cancelled subscriptions for less.

Well, I have painted a doleful picture indeed, but I think it to be a realistic one; and I also believe there are some remedies, or at least new approaches that may help in the long run. Before I get to them, however, there is one other economic encroachment on our freedom of the press that I'd like to mention. This one, it seems to me, is much easier to spot and much easier to do something about. It is hard to imagine a more flagrant abridgment of freedom of the press than closing it down entirely. But that's what happened in New York for three months, as we know. I can't understand why our government was not in there arbitrating right at the beginning, even before the strike actually began. Surely unfettered access to information is as essential to a free society as steel or shipping facilities, both of which have received recent federal arbitration.

Failing federal intervention, why didn't the advertising industry offer its good offices in this cause? Surely we have a good deal to gain, for if there is anything positive it is that if you want to run a newspaper ad you've got to have a newspaper to run it in. This would have been a splendid opportunity for the Four A's (the American Association of Advertising Agencies) to do something besides hold conventions where the members can eye one another like rival used car salesmen. It would have been an unparalleled chance for that bastion of our freedoms, the Advertising Council, to do something more contributory to our welfare than hating cancer or loving Smokey the Bear.

Let's see, is there anybody I haven't offended? Well, to sum up: what is there to do to get our communications media back in the hands of the audience, namely us? I will forbear to make any suggestions about radio or television because (1) I hardly know where to start and (2) it would take too long. For newspapers and magazines the cure is obvious and drastic: the reader must simply *pay* more for them and should understand *why* he should do so. This I see as an industry-wide effort, and one which will require a good deal of patience and skill in the telling. But it is a stirring story. If it is argued that there is the danger that advertisers may take offense, I see no reason why the help of the Four A's, or the Association of National Advertisers and other industry groups, should not be enlisted. They should certainly be interested in anything that makes our media stronger advertising media.

Magazine circulation income should be increased as well. As a starter they might cut out special offers. If they stuck to the full rate it would bring revenue up tremendously. I'll admit that it would also wring a lot of the water out of the circulation and reduce it for a spell. But why play the numbers game if it is deleterious anyway? The sturdiest magazines in this country are not the ones with the largest circulations necessarily. Here again I think that industry-wide cooperation would be very effective, especially when it comes to the matter of explaining why magazines should be priced higher per copy.

There is no reason why they should be priced as low as they are; it's just that people are used to an unrealistic price structure. And nobody has dared to come right out and broach the subject.

Something else the magazine industry might do, though I think there is small chance that they will, is simply quit paying agency commissions. As you know there was originally a reason for it: the agencies sold space for them, but they don't anymore. So in effect the magazine has a double sales cost; they must pay the 15 percent to the agency as well. Well, *that* will be the day, and I hope to see it. Come to think of it, most newspaper space is sold at a retail rate, so if they want to get on a sounder basis they might consider abolishing commissions on the rest of their advertising too.

As individual efforts, publishers might take a more realistic view of their publications as regards the readership. Some of the things they could do are small, such as eliminating those stiff cards and not allowing subscription salesmen to solicit me by telephone. But the most worthwhile thing would be a little harder for them to conceptualize, from my experience. It is this: that they take the same responsibility for the advertising matter in their pages as they do for the editorial matter. That is, that they exercise something like editorial control over everything between the covers. I don't know why they shouldn't. After all, the reader buys everything within the covers; to him that is the magazine. Once the publisher gets this firmly in mind he may find that he looks at his publication and the readers to whom it belongs differently.

Chapter 11

How to Look at a Magazine

When I first started in advertising I worked for a very small agency. It was so small that I had my choice of any title in the place except owner, art director, and receptionist, which were already spoken for. Not knowing any better I decided to call myself a copywriter. This was a mistake, and I had an uneasy feeling about it right from the start, but it took me awhile to discover just what was wrong.

The whole thing revolved about lunch: I was the only one in the place who had to buy his own, or in those days, bring it from home in a paper bag. The owner was always being taken out by media reps; the art director, who also doubled on production, lived high off the lithography hog; and the receptionist, while she didn't actually buy anything, was extremely well stacked. So I had a very lonely time of it munching my squashed sandwiches—I pressed them as flat as I could so they'd fit in my pockets; this made me look a little lumpy, but at least I didn't have to carry a paper bag.

Then one day, just as I was about to unwrap the wax paper, the phone rang, and since the receptionist had just taken off with the *Boy's Life* rep, I answered it. It turned out to be the advertising manager for, as I recall, some cemetery trade journal who was making a turn around the big territory outside the picket fences and wanted to leave no headstone unturned.

He asked for the media director. I didn't know who that was so I asked him to hold the phone a minute. I made a decision that was to put thirty pounds on me in the next three months. When I came back on the phone, changing my voice to suit my new title, I was the media director. He apologized for the lateness of his invitation and asked me to lunch, which I accepted as I dropped those damned sandwiches in the wastepaper basket.

I didn't get back to sandwiches again until I became an owner myself some years later. In the meantime I not only learned a great deal about lunch but also something about reps, though I suspect they learned more about me.

My definition of a rep is: a nice man who listens and eats lunch. A magazine publisher, on the other hand, is a nice man who talks and plays golf. A magazine editor is a man who doesn't have to be nice to advertising men and sits there wishing he were having lunch with John Kenneth Galbraith or Zsa Zsa Gabor, both of whom called him two minutes after he made the date with you.

I do not know how magazine readers feel about lunch, but presumably someone does. It is hard to imagine that this aspect has not been researched in depth along with the other vital characteristics of the reader's life. Magazines are very thorough about collecting and disseminating this sort of information. It makes it easy for an advertising agency man to evaluate the audience of any given magazine. All he has to do is ask the media department to send up the latest survey put out by the loving, lavish hands of the magazine's promotion department.

This document tells us that the average reader is thirty-two years old, is married to a thirty-one-year-old girl named Helen whom he met at an intramural lacrosse match, and they have 3.1 children. Presumably the interviewer got the happy news about five minutes after little 0.1 was conceived, which beats hell out of the rabbit test timewise. If you wonder why the couple were willing to blab about their intimate lives to the first person who rings the doorbell, they were probably drunk. At least that is what I would gather from looking at the section having to do with their liquor consumption. Those people drink bourbon, scotch, Irish, Canadian, gin, vodka, Slivovitz, aquavit, brandy, champagne, table wine, dessert wine, beer, ale, stout, rum, tequila, forty-three kinds of cordials, and Mennen's after-shave; they don't want to offend anybody. And they consume them in quantities that would stall an ox.

Part of this enormous consumption is accounted for by the fact that they entertain 2.1 times each week. The 0.1 in this instance may refer to the nights when they invite people over but have to call it off because he got boiled in the bar car and didn't come to until three hours after the conductor threw him off at Stamford. And, of course, they go out twice a week, which gives them a little more elbow-bending time.

While any magazine can point with pride to the amount of both gallivanting and lushing-it-up its readers do, *Playboy* stands in a class by itself.

According to last year's Starch study of the consumer magazine field, *Playboy* readers bought more booze than anybody. Not only that, they went to far more movies than any other audience except that of *True Confessions;* the girls just barely beat them out. Since there were no figures in Starch on number-of-pocket-flasks-owned-per-hundred, it is hard to tell whether the *Playboy* reader keeps up his drinking record by taking steady pulls clear through the double feature or whether he slugs himself before he goes and then gulps doubles at home afterwards as he looks at the gatefolds. At any rate, it looks as though we have a lone drinking problem here. Perhaps the solution is for Mr. Hefner to get his boys together with the *True Confessions* ladies; man does not live by gatefolds alone.

But I digress. In perusing a magazine audience's characteristics we will also note that they own 2.4 cars, go to Europe twice a year, belong to a country club, buy so much hi-fi equipment they have to sleep on the lawn, and do many other marvelous and expensive things.

If what I have said suggests that this sort of comparative audience measurement doesn't mean much to me, I should like to add that none of the others do either. Perhaps the least interesting are those employing sheer numbers, whether of subscribers or readers per issue. Nor do I find demographic breakdowns of more than limited significance. I have yet to see the magazine that cannot make a splendid case for itself with glowing competitive costs-per-thousand out of the same report. Simmons not only stands behind every bed but behind every publication as well. Say, do you suppose it's the same one? That would explain the speedy report on baby 0.1.

I think it is good and fitting that each magazine should have a convincing story about its audience. Now all I have to decide is the same thing I had to decide before—which one is more convincing.

As a matter of fact, that's not the way I decide about magazines at all. The way I evaluate a magazine is based on how its readers feel about it. I think this is a much more important factor than what they do, what they buy, or how many of them there are. These have their place, as do the reader's interests, influence, and attitude toward the world around him. But what I really want to know is his attitude toward the magazine itself; how he evaluates *it*.

It is hard to imagine anything more worshipful, servile, attentive, and obedient than a magazine audience as portrayed by its promotion. However, these readers are also shown to be vibrant, go-getting, adventurous, independent spendthrifts. They are always on the go. On the other hand, they never budge out of the house because then they wouldn't be able to enjoy happy family times poring over the magazine together, greeting each page with delighted ohs and ahs or furrowed brows, as the case may be, before passing it on to the 2.5 other readers waiting impatiently in the front hall.

While this picture sounds like a cross between a heroic canvas of a mob of French Revolutionists marching on the Bastille—except that *everybody* is leading—and a Norman Rockwell painting of Thanksgiving—except that the turkey is the magazine of your choice—I get another, simpler impression. Every time a rep tells me about his audience and how they are simply panting for my client's product, I imagine thousands and millions of alert, adoring cocker spaniels trembling for me to throw the stick; with 5 percent off if I throw it six times.

I suppose people do like some magazines better than others. If I didn't think so I'd simply say to hell with it and fling a flock of proofs to the peasants every now and then; throw them down the fire pole and see if anybody stoops.

Magazines try to be helpful in this respect. From time to time they will present surveys that show that their readers prefer them over rival publications. They sometimes get too helpful. *Time, Newsweek,* and *U.S. News,* for instance, are even able to show that among people who read all three, each of them is preferred over the other two. I imagine the same is true among competitive shelter books, service magazines, and the double-widget-maker's trade journals. Since all of this research is true, being done by independent research organizations, it makes a dreadful quandary for me.

But even if someone were to come up with an independent survey that everyone believed and that settled the matter once and for all about which magazines were liked better, and by whom, we still wouldn't have an applicable yardstick. We wouldn't know *how* much better, which is the thing you've got to know if you're going to make sensible comparisons. You have got to have a constant, verifiable factor expressible in *numbers,* so that it will work with the *other* numbers you have, such as circulation, audience composition, and cost-per-thousand.

Also, this numeral factor should be universal, so that it not only shows how much each magazine's audience values it in comparison with competing magazines, but how it compares with *all* magazines.

Do you see what I mean? This yardstick of subjective value—what a magazine is worth to the reader—should be universal enough so that you can compare *Boy's Life, Time, Advertising Age,* and *Vogue,* if you want to. While you're at it you might as well throw in the *Christian Science Monitor,* "The Beverly Hillbillies," the telephone book, and anything else that appears regularly.

I mention these last because if you are vying for the advertiser's dollar you are competing with everything else that is vying for it, too. What is more important—and this is the real point—if you are vying for the reader's attention you are competing with every other communications medium.

Circulation figures mean very little in this competition, for they do not tell the degree to which you command the reader's attention. By this I do not simply mean the *amount* of attention, but the *quality* of attention. I don't know how long you'll read this book today, and you may not recall a word of it later. But if I were to tell you that your house was on fire, I dare say that the quality of your attention would be very good indeed.

I only know of one yardstick that can measure subjective value in a way that everybody can understand and that is money. Because we live in a market society with a pricing system, we are able to use the same yardstick on every commodity whether it be a diamond, a garbage can, a bottle of whiskey, or an airline ticket. The price of these items is based not only on how much they cost to produce but also on how many of them there are and how much people want them—supply and demand.

Magazines carry price tags, too, but they don't mean anything. They neither reflect the cost of the item nor have they anything to do with the supply and demand. This is because magazines, like newspapers, have been subsidized for so long that no purchaser has any notion of their worth to him relative to other things he buys.

Every time I see a newspaper editorial slamming farm subsidies I wonder what sort of system the publisher thinks he is operating under. The chief difference between publication subsidies from advertising and farm subsidies from the government is that, whereas farm subsidies keep prices up, advertising subsidies keep publication prices artificially depressed.

People pay for publications the same way they pay utility bills, sort of grudgingly. If you doubt this, notice the way you react the next time the boy comes around to collect for the paper. There's no feeling of buying something you want; it's a necessary annoyance like paying the water bill—if you don't pay they'll cut you off. And it's never so much so that you ever have to think whether you really want it or not. I think that this must be the theory behind magazine subscription rates: keep them low enough so that it's too much trouble to say no. Also keep them incomprehensible enough—like 34 weeks for $2.78—so that nobody knows what in the hell you're talking about anyway.

There's another element enters into the matter, too, I think. While all of this has been going on, radio and television have developed. People know full well that the reason they get all that entertainment—if you can call it that—free is because advertising supports it.

I have an idea that most people rather feel that *anything* with advertising in it ought to be free, and maybe they have a point. There is pretty good evidence that controlled circulation magazines, as long as they have quality, a definite audience, and are really controlled, have excellent acceptance. Baldwin Ward's *Newsfront,* for instance, has as prestigious an audience as any you'll find anywhere, and its voluntary renewal rate among the top corporate executives of this country is fantastically high. Actually, I doubt that price or the lack of it makes a particle of difference where publications are delivered to the office. Most executives don't pay for them themselves; most of them never see the bills. So whether you charge something or nothing is academic; the only thing that is important is whether the man wants it or not.

On the other extreme we see that a good many people are apparently willing to pay a very hefty price indeed for a magazine without any advertising at all, if it is a magazine they want; especially if it has stiff covers. I suspect that we are going to see more of this sort of magazine without advertising and that we are going to see a great many more controlled circulation magazines chock-full of ads.

But what about all the magazines in between? Up until now they have been the only sort we have had. I think they are going to have to play the "want" game, too, if only because it is going to get harder and harder for them to operate unless they do. You see, as it appears to be shaping up now, conventional magazines are the freaks; the others have committed themselves one way or the other as to understandable price.

Now, I am not suggesting that magazines as we know them are going to go to the wall. However, the addition of two more categories of magazines—both of which defy the conventional, incomprehensible pricing system—make it desirable that a new measurement tool be developed. This yardstick should give us some idea, in dollars and cents, of how much any given magazine is valued by its readers; not how much it costs, not how much it sells for, but how much it is *worth*.

I became interested in this last January when the *New York Times* discontinued its western edition. I was so interested—perhaps incensed is a better word—that I wrote a quarter-page ad to appear in the last issue of the paper. As it turned out, they wouldn't accept it in the western edition. Perhaps they didn't want anything to rock the coffin. However, they graciously assented to let me buy a quarter page in the New York edition.

Sixteen-hundred dollars later, the ad, with the headline "What Good Is Freedom Of The Press If There Isn't One?" appeared. I attributed the quote to A. J. Liebling because he had just died and I had admired him greatly and also because I thought they might take a dim view of his original line, "Freedom of the press is only guaranteed to those who own one."

The text suggested that perhaps, before folding the edition for financial

"WHAT GOOD IS FREEDOM OF THE PRESS IF THERE ISN'T ONE?"

—A. J. LIEBLING

Today, Friday January 24, 1964, is a sad day: another newspaper has died. "I wouldn't weep about a shoe factory or a branch-line railroad shutting down", Heywood Broun once wrote, "but newspapers are different".

Well, it's happened before and I'm afraid it'll happen again, soon. But this newspaper was quite different. The New York Times, Western Edition represented a genuine effort to publish a national newspaper and get it to you before breakfast the same day. (A paper isn't quite the same thing if you get it four days late; a morning paper isn't at *all* the same thing if you get it after breakfast.)

90,000 OTHER DEAD

More than that, the New York Times is unique in our nation; there is nothing like it for either authority or sheer volume of information. If "All the news that's fit to print" isn't always as fit to read as one might wish, that's a small beef. Part of the Times's inestimable value is that, in a time when most papers are scared stiff of boring somebody, they have dared to be dull in the interest of thoroughness.

But that, as of today, is all gone, at least as a living part of my daily life. So while we are mourning the death of the New York Times in the West I hope you won't mind if I shed a few tears over my own corpse before I start the inquest. For I, as a Times reader, have died too, along with the other 89,999.

EPITAPH NICELY WORDED

The inquest then. The worst of it is I didn't even know I was sick. Just last week I paid the bill for the next month's Times. And then the following day I learned that there wasn't going to be any next month. It was a very nicely worded notice, regrets and all that sort of thing; and did anybody know of jobs for all the reporters, printers, stenos, punch card operators, etc.? Sadly, decently solicitous.

I know it's a nasty thing to lose a job in a dwindling industry; still, there are other jobs. But what about us, the 90,000 readers? What we've lost is irreplaceable: the peculiar community of a great newspaper and its readers. Why didn't somebody ask us before they threw us away, before it was too late? Maybe some of us out of 90,000 could have thought of something if the facts had been squarely presented. Was it money? (It was money.) How much? (Didn't say.) How much more would a subscription have had to cost to make up the difference? I would have been willing to pay it.

COULD HAVE ASKED

As a matter of fact I got my chance, after a fashion, the next morning. A mimeographed insert in Saturday's paper said that if enough of us showed interest the New York Edition would be delivered the *same day* for around $7.00 a month. I accepted with alacrity.

It was only after the wonder of it wore off that I asked myself why, if they could offer me the Eastern Edition at twice the price the day after, then why the hell hadn't they filled me in on the facts and offered me the Western Edition on the same terms the month before, or whenever it was they were weighing the decision? They could have at least asked. I'm a reader, I'm the one they put the paper out for; readers are the only reason for a newspaper's existence, aren't they?

...THAN A BILLY GOAT

Before we get into that, let me say that I have the greatest admiration for the Times's brave try, and the greatest sympathy for them now.

If I am critical, it is of an industry-wide system that has no more real notion of where its basic responsibility lies than a billy goat. It is my belief that it simply would never occur to a big publisher to take the readership into his confidence about whether a paper should live or die.

Perhaps publishers feel that they are conducting a private enterprise, and that such things are properly private. This I feel to be a highly dubious assumption. Freedom Of The Press must imply the public interest, otherwise why bother to guarantee it? If not for the citizenry, for whom is it guaranteed? The publisher? Then why circulate a newspaper? Just run off one bold, fearless copy for him to regard fearlessly. No, I think the Founding Fathers must have had the Freedom Of The Reader in mind, too. Maybe that's *all* they had in mind.

BUBBLE GUM CUSTOMERS

As it stands, though, the subscribers to a paper have less voice as to its conduct or policies than do the customers of a given brand of toothpaste, or hair oil, or bubble gum. And for a pretty obvious reason: whereas the customer's money means everything to a product's economy, the subscriber's money has very little financial significance to a newspaper compared to advertising revenue. That's why we can buy a 25¢ paper for 10¢. Some bargain! To get it, the reader has traded away the economic power to keep our newspapers alive. With the rise in production costs in the face of inadequate advertising revenue they are dying like flies — even though they have huge circulations.

You see, if a paper is losing money on each copy it sells (because it doesn't have enough ads), then the more readers it has the worse off it is. Isn't that ridiculous? If it's unlucky enough to have 800,000 readers, like the late New York Mirror, it loses so much money on each of them it has to fold up.

ADVERTISING CHANCY BULWARK

It seems quite wrong to me that a newspaper should go under while its readers still want it; what is a newspaper for if not for them? And yet, over half of our big dailies have shut down in the past generation, leaving monopolies in their wake. Only four major cities still have competing morning papers.

What to do about it? Well, two things seem to be evident: 1) On the record, advertising seems a mighty chancy economic bulwark for a free press; 2) Newspapers ought to belong to their readers.

PROPOSAL:

Since our press needs to be subsidized to survive, why don't the readers do it? Actually, it's not a matter of subsidy as much as paying for value received. Who says a paper should cost a dime? Why not a quarter? Why not 50¢? Surely a newspaper is worth more than a pack of cigarettes.

Unless we are willing to pay for the freedom of *our* press, the Constitutional guarantee isn't worth a damn. We will continue to have less and less press to be free.

But before we can do anything to help, some paper has got to give us a chance to be something more than circulation figures. Do you suppose one will?

Howard Gossage
451 Pacific
San Francisco

Plate 9. Reprinted by permission of Sally Kemp.

reasons, they should have taken the readers into their confidence since the paper was presumably being put out for them. As I recall the subscription price was three dollars a month. It seemed to me that they could have pointed out the financial realities of publishing and asked us whether, considering the alternative of no paper at all, we wanted it enough to pay more and, if so, how much more. In other words, what was the paper really worth to us?

Well, the ad ran and that was the end of that. Except that I was in New York the next week and Nicholas Samstag, with his beautifully original mind, carried the idea to its logical conclusion; one that had never even occurred to me.

He said, "What this means, and what you are really asking, is 'How much would you pay for the next issue of this publication rather than be deprived of it?'"

"Look," he continued, "you could ask this question about any publication, regardless of what the price per copy is, and get an accurate idea of what it is really worth to its readers individually and, by taking an average, collectively. Moreover, you could run directly comparable subjective value figures for every publication in the country. The trick," he concluded, "is to figure out the method."

Samstag's question, "How much would you pay for the next issue of this publication rather than be deprived of it?" is so stunning in its simplicity that perhaps I'd better give some examples.

Supposing you were to ask the subscribers of either *Newsweek, U.S. News,* or *Time* how much money they would pay rather than be deprived of their next copy, and then put the three figures side by side. One imagines one would get a pretty good idea of subjective worth. That is a comparison I would like to see very much indeed. I can't think of anything more significant than how much a reader wants his magazine—especially if my ad is part of it.

I would also be curious to see such an evaluation of other categories: general magazines, women's magazines, business magazines, trade journals, etc. Or even one that weighs a mixed bag—say *Fortune,* the *Bee Keeper's Guide, Seventeen, Scientific American,* the *New Yorker, Esquire, Printer's Ink, Jack & Jill,* and *Pravda,* for instance.

Approached in this fashion every publication has some value, even if it is zero. I can think of a couple—alumni bulletins, for instance—that may even have a negative value. That is to say I would pay a reasonable fee if I could be absolutely *certain* of being deprived of the next issue.

An important thing to note here is that this sort of research would have to be continuing and broadly based, for subjective value changes constantly and will vary from person to person.

We need a dollar yardstick badly not only for advertising but also so that publications can get a notion of their real worth to their audience in dollars and cents. It's something the rest of our market society faces; there's no reason why they shouldn't.

Chapter 12

How to Look at Billboards

While it is easy to see billboards, it is hard to look at them objectively without getting bogged down in trivial or secondary criticisms; nevertheless let me try.

It is so strange that billboards exist at all that the current controversy about whether outdoor advertising should be allowed along federal highways achieves the unreality of a debate on whether witch burning should be permitted in critical fire areas. Apparently no one has thought to wonder just what in the hell billboards are doing anywhere.

Why do you suppose this is? It must be that billboards have somehow acquired an easement across our minds just as they have gained squatter's rights on our visual air space. They've been there—everywhere—for a long time and we have grown used to them. It requires a conscious effort to recognize that a billboard has the same objective status as "Jesus Saves" scrawled on a culvert or men's room poetry; it is there by public sufferance. But there is this difference: while those other gratuitous messages are accorded the shrugging tolerance that we grant to eccentrics, outdoor advertising has come to be regarded as an institution like any other overtly respectable industry. This is where the confusion starts, for if one accepts this premise all sorts of preposterous assumptions seem worthy of consideration; indeed, it would be positively un-American to question them.

Originally appeared in *Harper's Magazine*, February 1960, in the column "The Easy Chair."

Outdoor advertising is most certainly an institution; but so was the open range. And just as the open range ceased to exist when private interest was no longer compatible with public rights, so it is with outdoor advertising. While it is unlikely that we shall have more than a smattering of midnight poster-burnings, it is inevitable that the billboard will eventually join such other relics of America's past as battleships, running boards, the language of flowers, flypaper, and two-a-day vaudeville. Perhaps our grandchildren will collect vintage Coca-Cola and Edsel billboards the way we do Toulouse-Lautrec and bullfight posters. They will do nicely to fill in unwanted picture windows; I am assuming that tomorrow's man will grow less interested in bringing the outdoors indoors as he again becomes emboldened to meet it halfway.

As a matter of observable fact, the billboard is already starting to vanish from the American scene because of zoning laws and new residential developments of one sort and another. This, of course, does not mean that you have to hurry to get in your field work; there are still plenty of collector's items around. But the market is starting to dry up, thanks to, of all things, the automobile. The automobile: the very thing that made possible outdoor advertising's greatest prosperity also contained the germ of its certain doom. The billboard, you might say, is dying of success. If only the horse had never been replaced, outdoor advertising, in modest flower, might have been tolerated indefinitely.

This is how it all came to pass: once upon a time, long, long ago, there was a blacksmith (say) in a small town. He didn't need a sign since everybody knew he was a blacksmith, and even if they hadn't known, they would have found out very soon, what with all the clanging. Still, he did have a sign of sorts: a horseshoe. Anything more would have been pure show, since nobody could read. Time passed; people learned to read, and so did the blacksmith.

One day an itinerant sign painter came by and made him a real sign, with letters; it said: BLACKSMITH.

I haven't mentioned that he was the only blacksmith in town, or was until (the place was starting to boom a little) another smith set up shop. At this point, you may be sure, the sign painter sold a new sign to the first blacksmith, let us call him Brown: BROWN THE BLACKSMITH/Quality Horseshoes since 1776, and to the new blacksmith (Green) one which read: GREEN THE BLACKSMITH/*Modern* Horseshoeing.

And so competition was born. That might have been the end of it, had it not been for our friend the sign painter, by now no longer itinerant. He went to Brown and tried to sell him a new sign. Brown said, with justice, that he already had a new sign. Oh, the sign painter said, he meant *another* sign. With all the new people moving in (not to mention drummers and other transit business) it might be well to catch the trade before it actually got into town. Just look at the Rotary and Kiwanis meeting notices. Brown fell for it and so, of course, did Green.

This was an important milestone in outdoor-advertising history, for it marked the first time a sign was not physically attached to a place of business. From there on it was just a matter of extension. The sign painter began to specialize, and as he did so the signs became larger and further afield. He expanded, but at first he was largely limited to the sides of country barns and city buildings. It was not until the advent of the automobile that he got a glimpse of the staggering potential.

His was a stirring experience, roughly comparable to commanding the only keyhole on Ladies' Night at the Turkish Bath. He saw Main Street become an arterial road along which the newly mobile population hopscotched to the suburbs, leaving vacant lots in its wake—enough traffic to warrant billboards, enough land to build them on! Moreover, his Main Street reached out, far enough to meet the next city's Broadway—a highway. To the sign painter it was one long vacant lot. End of story.

That is the end of my allegory but not quite the end. At this point people began to be aware of outdoor advertising not as a raffish collection of isolated phenomena but as an ordered, reachable institution. It is very easy to slide your mind over "Good Eats ½ mi." or "Repent!" even if you do not find them attractive. Besides, they are only one of a kind, you may not pass that way again and, above all, you have no recourse. I imagine it would be difficult to find the man who had scribbled an obscenity on a fence and, finding him, to get him to admit it.

There was no such difficulty about billboards. The outdoor advertising company's name was neatly, proudly lettered on a plaque, there for all to see, and the sign itself was devoted to the sales message of a large and reputable firm. Recourse galore, offered and taken up. But it was not taken up by as many as one might expect, for, as we noted earlier on, we have got used to billboards; they have become a part of our way of life. On the other hand, how many garden clubs, neighborhood improvement leagues, and Pro Bono Publicos are needed to constitute a vanguard? Not many.

It is not generally realized how sensitive large businesses are to even minor criticism. I have seen one of the world's most colossal corporations stopped dead in its advertising tracks by a single derogatory letter addressed to the president and forwarded by him without comment to the advertising manager who, horrified, immediately called the advertising agency and canceled the campaign in question. The aftermath of this incident is equally revealing: the agency then got *two* people to write the president letters that extravagantly

111

praised the ads, and they saved the day. Four cents' worth of postage sufficed to swerve the course of a billion-dollar enterprise; eight cents put it back on the tracks.

The outdoor-advertising industry has done its best both to defend itself and to placate its critics. It has maintained costly legal, public relations, and legislative advisory staffs. It has devoted many of its nicest locations to public piety, and it must be admitted that "The family that prays together stays together" shows progress over "The day of judgment is at hand!" The industry has even landscaped its billboards and put little picket fences around them. All, alas, to no avail. You just can't please some people.

In retrospect, perhaps, it would have been better if the outdoor-advertising folks had been content with their modest, ragtag-and-bobtail lot. It wasn't respectable, nor was it patronized by the mighty but, by heaven, it was anonymous. But who are we to question their choice? Is it better to spend eternity looking over your shoulder for the sheriff than to be king for a day? It is an idle question, for the headsman awaits; the billboard's day of judgment is surely at hand. Awareness of this fate seems to elude the still-embattled principals, i.e., the public and the outdoor industry, as it is called in the trade. ("The outdoor industry," what a splendid name! It conjures up visions of Thornton W. Burgess and of a host of dwarfs helping Old Mother Nature, Jack Frost, Johnny Woodchuck, and Reddy Fox to organize the countryside.)

Almost the only argument against outdoor advertising one ever seems to hear is that it blocks out the scenery and is unsightly. This isn't a bad point, but it isn't as good as you might suppose. The industry is quick to answer that less than 10 percent of all outdoor advertising is in open countryside, outside of developed areas. I am not sure what this means, for it is possible to drive fifty miles from New York, Chicago, or Los Angeles and never be out of a developed area of some type. As to unsightliness, the industry can prove that its billboards are well constructed and well maintained. We'll accept that, although it does seem a trifle immaterial. It is rather like a man who is accused of shouting in a hospital quiet zone insisting that he has shiny teeth and gargles after every meal.

The industry naturally also sticks up for the design values of the posters themselves. It is right; the designs are the best money can buy. Truly, from an aesthetic point of view, it is hard to see that most billboards are inferior to the property they obscure; usually they are markedly superior.

Do you see why it is a mistake to attack outdoor advertising on aesthetic grounds? The row then becomes a matter of comparative beauty and one can go on haggling about that forever. In a sense the garden clubs have led us down the garden path. For when the girls insist that they shall never see a billboard lovely as a tree it then becomes legitimate to consider all the things a billboard *is* lovely as. There are quite a few: ramshackle barns, flophouses, poolrooms, cheap lodgings for ancient ladies with orange-tinted hair. Since the world is absolutely stiff with arguably uglier objects it may be some time before the billboards come down; presumably the last billboard will stand on top of the last shack.

The other thing wrong with the aesthetic line of attack is its utter irrelevancy. It is like arguing that mice should be kept out of the kitchen because they don't match the Formica. What a billboard looks like has nothing to do with whether it ought to be there. Nor does the fact that it carries advertising have anything to do with it, either. It would be the same thing if it were devoted exclusively to reproductions of the old masters; just as the open range would have been the same thing if they had only run peacocks on it. The real question is: has outdoor advertising the right to exist at all?

The industry says it has. It claims two rights, in fact. In asserting the first of these it clasps the flag firmly to its bosom and, in cadences worthy of the late William Jennings Bryan, invokes the spirit of free enterprise. Now, it should be understood that the outdoor industry is fighting only against what it regards as discriminatory regulation. It seems never to have occurred to the industry to question its basic right to any existence whatsoever. Therefore, when it protests against operational restrictions, it is not effrontery, as one might think, but outraged indignation. Its reaction is that of an old-time cattle baron the first time a farmer dared to fence in his potato patch.

Outdoor advertising is, of course, a business and as such would ordinarily have a strong case against inroads on its domain. However, there is a very real question whether it has title to its domain. Outdoor advertising is peddling a commodity it does not own and without the owner's permission: your field of vision. Possibly you have never thought to consider your rights in the matter. Nations put the utmost importance on unintentional violations of their air space. The individual's air space is intentionally violated by billboards every day of the year.

But doesn't everything visible violate one's air space? Not at all. Visibility is not the only consideration. The Taj Mahal, street signs, the Golden Gate Bridge, a maze of telephone wires, even a garbage dump—however they may intrude on the eye—are not where they are merely to waylay your gaze; they have other functions as well. A billboard has no other function, it is there for the sole and express purpose of trespassing on your field of vision. Nor is it possible for you to escape; the billboard inflicts itself unbidden upon all but the blind or recluse. Is this not an invasion of privacy? I think it is, and I don't see that the fact that a billboard is out-of-doors make the slightest

113

difference. Even if it were possible for you not to look at billboards if you didn't so choose, why in the world should you have to make the negative effort? Moreover, this invasion of your privacy is compounded in its resale to a third party. It is as though a Peeping Tom, on finding a nice window, were to sell peeps at two bits a head.

Thus we see that what the industry has to sell doesn't really belong to it. It belong to you. So much for the free enterprise argument.

This brings us to outdoor's (as it is also known in the trade) second line of defense. I doubt if you would be aware of this line unless you were in the advertising business, for it is an intra-trade campaign of the united-we-stand-divided-we-fall type . . . with overtones of approaching doom. It is this: what threatens outdoor advertising threatens all advertising; what discriminates against one advertising medium discriminates against all advertising media. These propositions are interesting to me as an advertising man, and I would like to dissect them.

First, what is the difference between seeing an ad on a billboard and seeing an ad, even the same ad, in a magazine? The answer, in a word, is permission—or, in three words, freedom of choice. Through a sequence of voluntary acts you have given the magazine advertisement permission to be seen by you. You bought the magazine of your own volition; you opened it at your own pleasure; you flipped or did not flip through it; you skipped or did not skip the ads; finally, it is possible to close the magazine entirely. You exercise freedom of choice all down the line.

The same is true of advertisements in newspapers. It is also true of radio and television commercials though in a different way, I'll admit. Arthur C. Clarke, in *Holiday,* likened TV viewers to "readers who have become reconciled to the fact that the fifth page of every book consists of an advertisement *which they are not allowed to skip.*" The fact is that Mr. Clarke and you are allowed to skip—to another channel, to Dr. Frank Baxter, or to bed; you can turn it off entirely. Or you can throw the set out the window. You cannot throw U.S. 40 out the window, especially if you are on it. Nor can you flip a billboard over. Or off. Your exposure to television commercials is conditional on their being accompanied by entertainment that is not otherwise available. No such parity or tit-for-tat or fair exchange exists in outdoor advertising.

And this leads us to the other aspect of the intra-advertising controversy: do laws that discriminate against outdoor advertising discriminate against every other advertising medium? The answer is yes—if you regard Outdoor as an advertising medium, which I don't. It is not an advertising medium; it is isolated avertising. An advertising medium is a medium that incidentally carries advertising but whose primary function is to provide something else: entertainment, news, matches, telephone listings, anything. I'm afraid the poor old billboard doesn't qualify as a medium at all; its medium, if any, is the scenery around it and that is not its to give away. Nor is a walk down the street brought to you through the courtesy of outdoor advertising.

Having myself arrived at a point where the billboard no longer exists for me simply because I just can't see it, I wonder how many others feel the same way. So here is a ballot. Would you mind filling it in? And putting it in a stamped, addressed envelope and mailing it? We in advertising always feel we must make such instructions explicit so as to permit no misunderstandings. Otherwise you might stuff it in a hollow tree or twirl it around on a prayer wheel.

BILLBOARD BALLOT

Howard Gossage
451 Pacific Street
San Francisco, Calif.

(   ) There ought to be billboards.

(   ) There ought not to be billboards.

Remarks: _____
          (or use another piece of paper)

Name_____

Street_____

City_____ State_____

Chapter 13

How to Tell One Place from Another
(or "Today's Thursday, This Must Be Singapore")

Anyone who has traveled a lot, and over a lot of years, knows that the real trick in going from one place to another is not in coping with the differences but in finding them. It seems to get harder and harder each year to tell one place from another.

When this first dawned on me I thought perhaps I was just getting jaded. Or perhaps it was because I had flown so much for so many years, as a pilot and as a passenger. Airports do tend to look alike the world over; I guess they always have. But even airports look more alike than they used to.

Actually, now that I look back on it, airports seemed quite different from one another back in the old days. Landing at Kingsford-Smith in Sydney twenty-five years ago wasn't at all the same as arriving by China Clipper at Treasure Island. And do you remember Gander? I was quite surprised, and even saddened, when I made an unexpected stop at Gander four or five years ago and found they had built a brand new building, with escalators and everything. They had made it look just like every other airport. I realized then that I liked it better before, ratty as it was. I even felt a certain affection for it; maybe just because it was different from the others.

Oh, I do like differences, even when they involve a certain amount of inconvenience, for that's the only way I can tell I'm somewhere else. This

This is the text of a speech Gossage delivered before the Pacific Area Travel Association, Anchorage, Alaska, on April 21, 1969.

feeling of being somewhere else is a very precious thing when you are traveling; if you don't have that, why bother to travel at all?

Now, this seems very elementary indeed, this preserving and encouraging of peculiar local differences. One would think that people in the travel business, and government tourist bureaus, and chambers of commerce—those who stand to gain the most—would strive to make their particular corner of the earth quite different from any other corner. This is apparently not so, for the tendency seems to be towards uniformity rather than uniqueness.

It is true that places seem quite different when approached from the sea, which is possibly why I prefer to travel by ship whenever I can. But most travel these days is by plane, so that one arrives at an airport; that is where the dead hand of sameness is so pervasive as to make you wonder why you ever thought it worthwhile to leave home.

Nearly all airports are of a particularly sterile school of architecture which I call neo-obsolescent. Size doesn't seem to be much of a factor in alleviating the monotony. The only real difference between a smallish airport and a largish airport is the distance you have to walk. Those moving sidewalks don't help much either, except to accentuate the boredom.

I have often wondered why most airports are built around that gigantic central hall whose chief purpose seems to be a high ceiling. I used to think that airport planners secretly believed that heavier-than-air transport was just a fad and that sooner or later zeppelins would come back, in which case they could moor them inside, closer to the baggage check-in. I now believe that there is a much stodgier reason—transportation tradition. A good many architectural firms must have got their start designing railway stations and have never been able to kick the habit.

Well, there's more to foreign travel than airport terminals, to be sure. All you have to do is to walk outside and there you are in the exotic country you paid your money to visit, aren't you? You know the answer to that one. The fact is—baggage delays aside—that it is harder and harder to get out of airports. A good many people never make it at all. A lot of them have stopped trying. More and more conventions are being held at airport hotels exactly like every other airport's air-conditioned, swimming-pooled hotels; only the cocktail waitresses have been changed to protect the innocent. Thus we see the ultimate in tourism progress: the traveler not only is spared painful adjustments, he is spared seeing anything new whatsoever.

This all sounds so ridiculous that I have to keep reminding myself that it is the literal truth. What, then, is the attraction, the differentness, that makes these airport-confined conventioneers travel and, for that matter, pay out all that money? The obvious answer is that they have *traveled* somewhere. Let's see how this holds up in the light of reality.

I don't think that what we used to call travel exists when one takes a jet aircraft—except, perhaps, as a state of mind or a pleasant illusion. Travel in the old sense consisted of leaving one place and then passing through a series of geographical experiences, point to point, until you reached your destination. You still do this when you take a train or a ship and to a certain extent with driving, though with superhighways there is scarcely anything to experience except the hulk of the highway itself. You could even argue that a car becomes something else when it gets on a freeway and that the car—relatively speaking—doesn't move, the freeway does. If you care to test this, try to stop sometime during rush hour.

The change in transportation from travel to the something else it is now started with the advent of aviation. When I first started to fly it was still a point-to-point experience, even for pretty large aircraft. I can recall flying a four-engine plane across Hong Kong harbor in early 1945 at twenty-five feet off the water. That, I can assure you, was a travel experience.

But jet travel seems to me not so much an experience as a suspension of experience. To fly from San Francisco to New York is not travel, really, so much as a process with a beginning and an end but virtually no middle, except as a way to pass the time. You can't even see anything, usually. It is more or less like taking a horizontal elevator. I imagine that if we had buildings three thousand miles tall that there'd be young ladies on the elevators offering us coffee, tea, or milk.

This transitional process will, of course, become even less akin to travel as Mach 2, and faster, aircraft come into service. As this happens, the burden for providing enough stimulating differences to make travel worthwhile will fall more and more upon those at the end of the line, the destination. I think that this is the day we must prepare for, even if it means disregarding what people seem to prefer now. I say "seem to prefer," because such current gaugings of taste, if taken at face value, can be very misleading.

Just as the travel market changes, so does the traveler. This year's conventioneer is next year's old Pacific hand, even if only to gain face among the greenhorns who have never been out before. The man who yammered for tinfoil-wrapped baked potatoes with sour cream and chives is now Mr. Worldly leading the gang to the Kava bowl or gulping down hell's own quantity of raw fish and seaweed—with chopsticks yet, or should I say *hashi*. If we don't make things different for this man—and he is the backbone of the travel business—he'll find someplace that *is* different.

There are still so many of the others, the newcomers, I know. And I also know that it is very tempting to those who wish to build tourism to make their countries as easily acceptable to foreign visitors—and I guess I mean Americans—as possible. Unfortunately, once you start in this direction, it is very easy to make conditions *exactly* as acceptable; just the same as home. What is more, this process tends to extend and reproduce itself so that, for the most part, the tourist never really leaves home at all, except as a sort of supervised activity.

I mean, after you escape the sameness of the airport and the industrial sameness of the highway into town, there you are at the Attu Sheraton, the the Melanesia Hilton, or some other slab-sides chain hotel. Now, I like these hotels well enough, and I know—considering the difficulties they work under, carrying all that money to the bank—that they try very hard to be different, one from the other. According to whether they are in Vienna, or Sydney, or Tokyo, they will dress the help in dirndls and lederhosen, or have blowups of aboriginal bark paintings in the Boomerang Room, or offer flower arranging lessons and a crash tea ceremony course around the swimming pool. You've got to give them marks for trying. But you have to be pretty naive to find these small sops of local color enough reason for leaving Indianapolis to see them, at least a second time.

This sounds as though people spent most of their time in hotels. That's exactly what a lot of them do; some of them spend all their time there. At any rate, what they think of a place is liable to be heavily conditioned by where they stay.

I am acutely conscious of how even a highly individual environment can change character and lose character. I have seen my own city, San Francisco, change in just a few years from a place of charming variations with a considerable variety of architectural form to a freeway-clogged, slab-sided, high-rise mess. There's still a good deal of the old character left, but I wonder how long it can hold out. Visitors to our city are still ecstatic over what they see in their few days, and well they should be. But most of what they see is laid on for them specially; it has no great depth aside from the hundreds of restaurants and thousands of bars. We have our climate, of course, and our hills, and our bay. The tourists had better look at the bay while they still can. Do you know that, due to filling, the bay is only half the size it was a hundred years ago? But that is another matter.

The point is that San Francisco is so anxious to attract tourists and conventions that we spend more money on that endeavor than we do on maintaining and encouraging the splendid differences that have made San Francisco what it is. We have a hotel tax—a very modest affair of two or three cents on the dollar—which is purportedly for supporting our cultural institutions. But, in fact, most of this revenue goes to promotion and advertising for more tourists and more conventions. The business interests who stand to profit by this policy apparently see nothing strange in it, though it flies in the face of even the most ordinary financial sense. Even the owner of a whorehouse makes sure that the girls are in good shape.

The result is precisely what you would expect under these circumstances. The general quality of San Francisco goes down as the sales curve goes up. In the end I expect that the tourist is pleased, but more and more his pleasure will be of that variety we find in Disneyland, an engaging place of illusion where nobody lives—but without Disneyland's ingenious differentness.

I mention this doleful prospect because it can happen anywhere—in the most remote atoll or the greatest city—and happen very quickly. There is no spot, however distant and unique, that cannot be turned into the same old thing. Which brings us to this: what is the purpose of tourism anyway?

Let me put it another way. I can understand why carriers, hotel operators, and other service industries would encourage tourism in terms of the balance sheet first and the considerations I have spoken of second. That is their business, and these other things are somebody else's business.

Well, whose business is it? How about the government tourist offices, chambers of commerce, and so forth? No, it doesn't seem to be their function either. Their job, if I understand it correctly, is to get tourists in, make them happy, and make money from them, though not necessarily in that order. Isn't that enough justification for a tourist promotion program? Not by me it isn't. It makes me wonder whether we shouldn't reexamine the whole business of why a country would bother to encourage tourism.

Let's start with the reason countries start tourist programs in the first place. Obviously it's not for the pleasure of seeing a lot of sore-footed tourists around. No, the purpose is to get the money—what we smartly refer to nowadays as an "invisible export." I really can't accept that as a good reason either—at least not good enough. A genuine export, whether it's bales of cotton, hundredweights of copra, or machine tools, is not at all the same thing as changing over where you are, and what you are, and who you are, to accommodate a bunch of fly-by-nights. That's precisely what happens, of course, especially when the country in question is relatively underdeveloped or unspoiled, or—OK, let's say it—poor.

I'd like to suggest that the only reason—at least the only one that makes any sense to me—for a country's supporting a program to encourage visitors is that it will improve the lives of the citizens of the country. The sort of program I'm thinking of ought to do a great deal more than simply bring in money. It ought to make the citizen's life more interesting for him, more productive, more fun. Why shouldn't he get some enjoyment out of it? It's his taxes that pay for the tourist program, isn't it? I'm talking about something that goes beyond tourism and sightseeing and souvenir-hawking, something that involves the people of the country and makes them participants in a program rather than colorful natives to be gawked at from rubberneck buses.

When we start thinking like this, the first thing we throw out is the word *tourist*. Nobody likes tourists, and nobody likes to be a tourist himself. A tourist is a lonely guy, a pitiful creature, a paranoid dysentery prospect, a Kahala-shirted, camera-toting patsy. Moreover, the people who serve him tend to become something less than admirable themselves. It's rather like being in advertising, except you don't get Saturdays and Sundays off.

On the other hand, everybody likes to be a visitor. A visitor has things to do and people to see. He is a man with a mission, therefore happy. To qualify as a visitor, one need not necessarily be on a business trip, or there to interview the prime minister, or have just water-skied across the Pacific on one leg. But a visitor will have *something* to do. He'll be engaged in some enterprise that involves him with the locals, an event. It can either be a small thing like an International Nipa Thatch Weavers' Congress or a very large thing like the Olympics. People who went to the Olympics were not tourists, they were visitors. And the Olympics were very involving of the people who lived in Tokyo and, before that, in Melbourne. It involved them before, during, and after. They had a great time. They participated.

You can't have an Olympics every year, of course, and most places will never have anything of that magnitude even once. But in the life of every country there are activities, projects, pastimes, arts, and interests that go on all the time. Some of them are important and widespread, but the greater part of them are small and, often as not, local. These are the things that, in their collective, make up the life, tradition, and pride of a people and give richness and texture to its culture. Most of these cultural forms can be shared with, or performed for, people from outside the country as well as for those who live there. And this is where a national travel program should begin, I think—with participation.

Well, how would one go about starting such a participating program? Let me think as an advertising man here; it makes it somehow easier to describe what I mean. Let's say that the program is expressed as a series of ads, each of which dwells on some particular event within a given country. The purpose of the campaign is threefold. (1) It should encourage activity within the country—setting the juices running, and creating enthusiasm, too; these are real involving events, not hoked-up stuff for tourists. (2) Each event or festival or activity will also create its own foreign audience or group of delegates or participants; some of these will attract a lot of outsiders and some very few. Size here is of secondary importance to the overall scheme. (3) The cumulative effect of this effort, even after six months or a year, will show what the country is really like. We will find that the end result—dear old sales curvewise—will be just what I have been recommending against up till now: tourists, but on different terms. The reason they come is because they, like all the rest of us, admire and wish to visit places that think very well of themselves, know their own minds, respect their own cultures, and stand on their own feet.

If this sounds too simple—or too complicated—let me spell it out. Take Australia. All over the country they have beach patrols; it is a very large thing Down Under. I don't know whether they have ever had an International Lifesaving Congress or, if they did, whether it was any fun. I don't see why it shouldn't be nor why one couldn't do a whale of an ad telling about it and inviting delegates to come. This needn't be in glorious color with a square cut picture and a little bit of copy underneath; not necessarily. It might be lots and lots of copy because there is lots and lots to say that is interesting. But also, among all the nuts and bolts, the non-lifesaving reader might get the idea there's more fun to be had on Aussie beaches than just the latest mouth-to-mouth techniques. How many people would come? I don't think it really matters. There will be enough if it's a good ad. And in any event they've gotten the main idea, haven't they?

I wonder if anybody ever had a Sheep Shearing Festival? Or an Amateur Anthropologist's Conclave in the middle of an Abo reservation? I can think of a dozen things, and they'd all make splendid ads—providing the events were real and meant as much to the Australians as they did to the visitors. In the end others would have a real feel of Australia, and so would the Australians, for this would also provide a mirror for them to see themselves.

Indonesia. I wonder if anyone has ever thought of having a Gamelan Music Festival? I think I'd go. Gamelan orchestras inspired Ravel and Debussy and provided one of the brightest sparks of the French impressionist school. And then there are dancing, wood carving, volcanoes, and the durian season; durian eating is very involving, I hear.

Think of the genuine events based on arts, literature, or technology that Japan could have and think what interesting advertisements they'd make. I don't think you necessarily have to throw away views of Mt. Fuji by moonlight, or cherry blossoms, or even communal baths. But there's a great deal more—and more involving than all that.

And Hawaii—isn't there anything more stimulating to dwell on than another view of Diamond Head or those magnificent pictures of gorgeous stereotypes? Don't they *do* anything in Hawaii? What do the people there gain from all that tourism? Can money really compensate for more high-rises in Waikiki and land values that jump while you wait? What do the Fijians get out of it all? When will the New Zealanders get tired of being loved for their fourteen-pound trout alone?

How about Alaska? I should think that a new state and its people could stand a little of the stimulation and involvement I've talked about. I could use it, too. San Franciscans as a people get damned little out of their own expensive tourist huckstering. I'd like to feel something more in the way of involvement than standing in line to get into places I support twelve months out of the year. It occurs to me that one thing that distinguishes a cosmopolitan city is that the tourists and the locals go to the same restaurants. But it has its disadvantages, too.

Well, that's the idea, and I'm sorry I'm not able to be more mellow about it. But when I think of the beautiful drivel that makes up most of travel advertising I wonder at the basic disregard it shows for the citizens of the countries involved. And I wonder when was the last time I got anything out of one of these ads beyond overblown generalities. By and large I think there is more reality in soap advertising.

What is wrong? At bottom it's that difference between image and identity. When you start thinking about a country in terms of its identity—its most precious asset—and project from there, some splendid things happen. A feedback mechanism is actuated. People within the country become aware of themselves, their assets, their culture. New energy is created, things do improve; and this, after all, is what everyone was shooting for in the first place.

Earlier I mentioned that a tourist program that begins with projecting involvement in effect holds up a mirror so those inside can see themselves, often for the first time. This is quite true, as you know from your own experience. The visitor to other shores will see things that the locals either don't see at all or place no value on.

It is axiomatic that no man recognizes his own environment; it's simply where he is. The extra-environmental person, the outsider, will spot it in a second. When he comments on it or admires it, then you notice it, too and do something about it. The Thai silk industry was established by Mr. Thompson in just that way. And so was Australian surfboarding, for that matter. The waves were always there, but, until Duke Kahanamoku came down and showed what else they were, nobody used them.

The word *ombudsman* has entered the language recently: an official appointed by the government to recognize problems of individuals. He gets in and tries to solve them. I think we might broaden this notion to include the cultural and environmental problems of a country and its citizens. A tourist, if given a chance to become a vistor, becomes a sort of visiting ombudsman. Being extra-environmental he sees things anyway, and you might as well have the advantage of his observation. There is also this: if he is involved he is less likely to grouse about things. He becomes a big booster and assumes a type of citizenship that continues after he gets home.

The common denominator of all these ideas is man himself. He is the measure of all things, including tourism. But would it pay? It would get my money. Any country that showed that much interest in itself and me might find it had all the business that it could handle. And, as I have suggested, it would be doing it on its own terms, in the light of its own realities; not with pancake make-up laid on to lure the bumpkins, but with the real thing. Airports might even start to look different.

Chapter 14

Culture Is a Lousy Word to Describe What Mankind Is All About

Actually, the only time culture is a good word to describe culture is when the culture is yogurt, the unflavored kind. It looks pallid, smells pallid, and tastes lousy.

The chief thing you can say for unflavored yogurt—or any other unflavored culture—is that it makes you virtuous; when you have finished you feel as though you deserve a medal. Yogurt, and other culture, manufacturers try to make the stuff more attractive, of course, but you never *really* forget that it's Good For You. Even with chunks of pineapple in it or when they have Danny Kaye conduct the symphony, there's still the feeling that you're doing a good deed; maybe not as good as getting the precious serum through to Nome, but something.

Well, a sense of cultural achievement is certainly pleasant, but I think this is the wrong sort to have, and the sponsors of our cultural activities do themselves, their art forms, and the public a great disservice in propagating this merit badge feeling.

You know what I mean; you go to an opening and you have the vague notion that unless you are nimble all the ladies in long dresses are going to come up and wring your hand in gratitude for being there.

It is even worse when it is a charity affair to boot. You just know that if you relax your face for a moment that nice woman in gold lamé will say, "God bless you, sir. The war orphans of East Flouristan will have a little sugar on their gruel this year thanks to your bounty." And all you did was come out to see the play or whatever—to enjoy yourself.

It is precisely this sort of anxiousness to reward people for what they ordinarily want to do that discourages church attendance too. Hell hath no fury like the gratitude of a parish welcoming committee.

Of course, it works the other way around as well. If you are an old hand in the community but haven't been keeping up attendance at the Actor's Playhouse or whatever, when you *do* show up someone is sure to say, "Well, we haven't seen much of you lately, have we?" No, we haven't, and that's not all. Unless you are easily intimidated into going to things you don't want to go to, the chances are that you'll find fewer and fewer things you do want to go to. Guilt is a terrible seat-emptier.

The trouble with culture as we have come to think of it is that it is something to support rather than to enjoy. By "support" I do not necessarily mean financial support, though a tin cup is certainly a deterrent to active interest, whether rattled by a beggar or a member of the finance committee.

Oftentimes, however, the things we are asked to support don't cost anything, as in "Support Your Library!" You will notice that the message here is more personal—as it should be, seeing that you, the public, own the library—but it is also more mandatory. In other words, it's not enough that you and Andrew Carnegie put the thing up and keep it stocked; you had also better get in there and start using the old Dewey decimal system if you know what's good for you.

I keep expecting that any day now I'll see one of those billboards in the public service that says: "Support Your Museum: Or Else."

There is another type of exhortation which apparently doesn't require that you do anything at all. A command like, say, "Support National Book Week!" merits *some* response; even if it's only, "OK" or "Why not?" But the ones that make me feel inadequate are those that say things like "Keep California Green." How in the world do you go about doing that? I'm really curious; what can you possibly do?

Although not in the cultural line, strictly, every year there is Advertising Recognition Week. I've never been able to figure out what its purpose is. Apparently they either want to teach people how to recognize an ad when they see it, or maybe they want us to get out and recognize *more* ads; perhaps do it in groups, like bird-watching.

I think the sign that makes me feel the least adequate to do anything about it is "Help Stamp Out VD." Public spirited as I am, I can't think where to begin. Do you go around and ask your friends if they have some? Do you stop strangers in the street? What if they say no?

Back to noncontagious cultures, I think there is little doubt that guilt is one of the major obstacles to cultural involvement. Or perhaps I should say that people will go to a great deal of trouble to avoid feeling guilty any more than they have to.

There is evidence that they will even spend a great deal of money to avoid cultural guilt. In San Francisco we have *concrete* evidence of it: the Palace of Fine Arts. It was originally built for the Panama-Pacific Exposition of 1915, and it was built of lath and plaster. The architect, Bernard Maybeck, intended that it should gradually disintegrate into a noble ruin and that would be that.

A few years ago, however, the public spirited of the community, spearheaded by an unanonymous donor with two million dollars as a spear, agitated for its restoration. A bond issue for several million dollars more was overwhelmingly voted by the citizens, who, I might say without violating a confidence, are among the stingiest, cultural-beneficencewise, in the United States, if not the world.

To understand why they would do this you must know two things: (1) that the Palace of Fine Arts is, and was, an absolutely useless building. There are not nor have there ever been any real plans to do anything in it; and even if there were, there would be no parking space unless you tore down the Golden Gate Bridge approach, which runs along right next to it. Herb Caen has suggested, in view of this, that indoor tennis courts be installed, but this plan has been hooted down as practical. Oh, one other thing of interest: to preserve this cultural monument it was necessary to tear it all down to the ground first and then rebuild it out of reinforced concrete, which makes it sound like Lafayette's sock: the very sock worn by General Lafayette—of course it had been topped three times and footed five times. (2) The second point that makes this story credible is that, until now, the most popular cultural enterprise in San Francisco has been Coit Tower, which those of you who are widely traveled have possibly noticed on top of Telegraph Hill. The notable thing about this edifice, aside from its extreme ugliness, is that it is nearly useless, and that, I think, is the reason for its popularity. I firmly believe that the Palace of Fine Arts will surpass Coit Tower in public esteem because it is even more useless. Coit Tower has an elevator that you can go up and down in; you can't do *anything* in the Palace of Fine Arts.

Now, I am not telling you all this to defame my city, but to show you how you, too, can have culture without guilt. You see, the Palace of Fine Arts is a beloved cultural establishment precisely because you can't do anything in it. If you can't do anything in it, then there is nothing you have to feel guilty about because you didn't go to it. And above all, there is nobody coming around to hustle you for tickets or to rattle the tin cup to make up the deficit at the end of an unsuccessful season. For it, every season is a . . . sellout.

This is not to suggest that we are necessarily slobs because we are more willing to invest in structures than in the activities that go on inside of them. Although there is little doubt that where cultural psychology is concerned we tend to have an edifice complex, I also think it is understandable. With a building you know where you are. It has dimensions, durability, palpable aesthetics; it can be spoken of in terms that anyone can fathom. Above all, it serves as visual evidence of a city's cultural life and heritage. One can feel a certain pride of cultural achievement without doing anything more than just pointing.

I should imagine that any resident of Pasadena, when giving out-of-towners the tour, will point with pride to the famous Pasadena Playhouse and the Huntington Museum even though he may not remember the last time he went to either of them.

What goes on inside a cultural edifice requires something more in the way of commitment. This is particularly true of the performing arts: the theater, music, opera, dance. It takes no great commitment to visit the museum, a library, or an exhibition, but a performance is something else again. The whole objective of a performance is to involve you, to make you part of the action.

Some performances will involve the audience more than others, but any performance will be more personally involving than, say, a visit to the library. If someone doesn't understand a book he doesn't tear up his library card and refuse to set foot in the place again. Conversely, if the newest bestseller is a flop it is no skin off the librarian's nose; she won't denounce the book critics if it gets an unfavorable review nor will she say that the public is ungrateful if they refuse to take the book out.

The reason there is greater involvement on both sides in attending a performance is that the performance itself is the book—a book which is published and read simultaneously. So, there is no browsing through it beforehand; you commit your time and money in advance, often for a whole season.

Any performance, therefore, is something of a pig in a poke, and not only for the audience but for the performers, too. Let's see if I can describe the process as it applies to the theater, for example. A performance works on at least three levels: its relationship to its producers, its relationship to its audience, and it also has a life of its own, quite separate. The first of these exists backstage in a mysterious, complex, ancient world, as far removed from public experience, and rightly so, as the astounding process within a pregnant woman's womb. That is a very good analogy, for the end result of this enormously complicated process is birth, the bringing forth of the complete organism, ready to live a new life in a new environment.

That is why, at the moment the curtain goes up, the play ceases to belong to its producers. It, like the baby, belongs to the world, to the audience. If it is not real to the audience it will die. The purpose of a play, as for a person, is not to pretend to be real, it is to *be* real.

This, I freely admit, is not easy to bring off, and a great many fine productions have died in childbirth in Pasadena; but nobody said the world was just. Some organisms will prove hardier than others, will overcome the original resistance, and will go on to greatness, or at least to acceptability.

The point is that beyond the moment of birth, the child, the work of art, is no longer a part of the creator; it is a separate entity, which has got to live in the world. Its existence henceforth depends on how well it is able to relate to its audience. This is true whether it is a person, a book, a play, a musical composition, a painting, or an idea.

Creators, producers, and sponsors are not always able to accept this simple fact of life. They will become angry because people do not appreciate their lovely child. In many cases the anger is understandable and even justified; little Johnny comes home with a black eye and torn clothes, Little Alice gets pallid—lousy—reviews and the audience sat on its hands.

Does this mean that the attackers are all wrong and a bunch of uncultured dopes? Yes, it could mean that. But, aside from personal satisfaction, it probably won't do you much good to tell them so. What *will* happen, if you are successful in your counterattack, is that they will feel so guilty about little Johnny, or Little Alice, or little theater—that either they won't come out to play anymore or, if they do, they won't feel easy about it.

You can make people feel guilty enough to do something, but you can't make them enjoy it. As a matter of fact, you can make them positively unenjoy it. It's like those happy family times on Sunday afternoon: if you don't go you feel guilty, if you do go, you feel awful.

I mentioned earlier that culture, instead of being something to enjoy, has become something to support—as though we were a bunch of walking trusses instead of real, live human beings who like some things and don't like others.

The trouble with presenting things as being Good For You is that you make them a duty, a virtue. Nobody really likes virtue; no one *tries* to be virtuous unless he is a stick, and self-conscious stick at that. You can turn any human activity, however enjoyable, into a wearisome chore by making it a duty, a guilt-laden virtue.

I imagine that if we were to make sexual intercourse mandatory as a cultural experience whether one felt like it or not, houses of low fame would have to apply for Ford Foundation grants simply to be able to stay off their feet.

You see, obscured somewhere in all of this to-do about culture is the idea that culture is more than esoteric art forms. It is everything that mankind does or experiences that is not absolutely necessary to his environment at any given time.

Let us say that the first man who discovered how to make a pot out of clay was producing a cultural form. He didn't know he was being cultural; he probably didn't even need it. He just did it. It became part of his life; he could cook in it, he could carry water in it, he could use it.

At some later time, some other man painted a design on a pot. He did it just because he wanted to and was able to; it was a way for him to express his own brand of truth, what he felt, what he was. It presumably caught on, and pretty soon all pots were painted or shaped and became part of ordinary life.

We do not know how show business began, but I'm sure it wasn't absolutely necessary. Perhaps Stan Freberg's hypotheis in his unpublished book, "A Funny Thing Happened on the Way to the Cave," is as valid as any. He says that a caveman was striking two rocks together while trying to invent fire when they flew out of his hands, crossed over in the air, and he caught them. Interested, he tossed the stones up once more to see whether he could do it again, and thus juggling was discovered. At the same moment, his wife, trying to keep warm, started beating her hands together. This sound was, for some reason he knew not, grateful to the caveman's ears, and he bowed. He has been bowing ever since.

In every instance, I think, the art form will at first seem quite foreign to the particular environment. Time will elapse before it becomes part of the culture, the stuff that holds civilization together and joins generation to generation. Some culture lasts, some of it doesn't. You've got to have a lot at any one time so that the best has the chance to see the light of day and be passed around and handed down.

There is another argument for variety, as well, and that is that cultural experience is a subjective thing which varies, not only from person to person, but for the same person under different circumstances and at different times. I can recall some things that I have been aware of all of my life but that at a certain moment assumed meaning and beauty of unimagined force. I remember once driving in a car and hearing Bach's "Easter Oratorio." To that moment I had never paid much attention to Bach choral music. But on this occasion it struck me. Suddenly it was so *marvelous* that I hollered at the top of my voice out of sheer delight. I was stopped at a red light, and everybody looked around at me as though I was crazy; but to hell with them.

A couple of years ago my daughter Amy, then eight, saw the magnificent BBC production of Julius Caesar on KQED, our educational TV station. Now this child, like most of her generation, was naturally a veteran at watching murder, for that is what our television has plenty of, baby. She had always taken the old slaughter-between-the-commercials without turning a hair; but when Brutus stabbed Caesar she burst into outraged howls at the injustice of it all. It was the first time she had seen killing as an unspeakable tragedy; which makes you think.

One function of culture is to just be there, ready to provide great, fitting moments. Last fall my wife and I were in London and were en route to our hotel at the height of the rush hour. As we came into Trafalgar Square I spotted the National Gallery and asked the driver to stop in front for a moment. He said, "Oh, we can't do that, we can't park here now." I said, "Can you give me four minutes?"

He said he could, so Sally and I ran up the steps, into the gallery, to the room where the Van Eycks are hung, and there on the far wall was that picture of the Italian banker and his young wife; you know the one I mean, she is all in magnificent green velvet and quite pregnant.

We were back to the car and gone in four minutes flat, and yet it was a moment of special clarity, longer than many hours I have spent—possibly because it was unexpectedly cut out of time, undoubtedly because we had just learned that Sally was pregnant.

Perhaps in the end, the best reason for culture is that it is the way we gain insights into what we were, what we are, and what we could be.

These are fine words, surely. However, at any given moment, the word *culture* is surrounded by so much hooey that it is difficult for an honest man to know what he should support and what he shouldn't bother with at all.

I think the only possible answer is to support everything and to bother only with the things that interest you. The hooey will have its day, and, if it is truly hooey, it will fall by the wayside. But there is always the chance that what one thinks is hooey is really, at bottom, worthy and durable. You should support it and give it its chance. This, however, does not mean that you need be—or pretend to be—enthusiastic about it. Enthusiasm, like love, should never become a duty.

You might ask here how one warrants supporting a cultural form that one is not involved in. It's something that we do all the time, really, and we take on more of them with the passing years. Schools, for example: two hundred years ago universal education was a novel, arty, avant-garde notion decried by sound men as, at best, unnecessary and, at worst, subversive. Did you know that today education is the single largest employment classification in this country?

Or let us consider libraries: what could be more of an art form—a repository of art forms—than a library; and yet free libraries are a relatively new thing on the American scene. Their propagation occurred within the lifetime of people yet living.

And then there are museums, parks, and other recreational areas, all of which are cultural activities, and all of which we support as a matter of course. Thus we feel no particular virtue in using them, nor do we feel any guilt if we *don't* use them.

I look forward to the time when we will feel the same way about the performing arts, but I imagine that it will only happen when we get around to supporting them in the same matter-of-fact way that we do schools, libraries, public golf courses, beaches, zoos, freeways, sewers, and other cultural activities that have become public utilities.

I think it is beyond question that culture, this lousy word, is a public utility. It is the public utility on which all other public utilities depend. It is what mankind is all about. To those who find this hard to accept we can recall Carlyle's words. A woman sitting next to him at dinner exclaimed, "Mr. Carlyle, I accept the universe," to which he replied, "By God, Madam, you'd better."

Chapter 15

The Postman Hardly Ever Rings 11,342 Times: *Dear Miss Afflerbach*

We generally figure that 1 percent of the people who think about writing in will actually do so. God knows where we get this figure, since how could anyone possibly tell? Still, it is comforting, especially when the response is small.

An Eagle Shirtmakers' advertisement containing a free, if trivial, offer ran in the *New Yorker* of March 11, 1961, and 11,342 people wrote in. Applying the formula above, we see that 1,112,858 others didn't get around to it for reasons of sloth, the lateness of the hour, or because they couldn't possibly have seen the magazine, the *New Yorker*'s circulation being in the four hundred thousands.

This slight discrepancy does not mean that we are going to discard our treasured yardstick, for it is, as suggested, a source of solace in leaner times. When, for example, only 600 respond to an ad[1] that asks the reader to send in his favorite shirt to be laundered, it is pleasant to think of 59,400 of them being mentally half-down to the buff before saying what the hell.

No, but there are apparently some elements here that deserve a little poking into. Such as: why do people bother to answer ads like this at all? Why do a few nice, solid companies run ads of this sort? And what is there about *New Yorker* advertising?

Parts of this chapter appeared in slightly different form in *Dear Miss Afflerbach,* by S. Miller Harris and Howard Luck Gossage. Copyright 1962 by Macmillan.

THE MALACHI HOGAN SCHEME

DOES anybody here recall the old Eagle Laundry gag? Maybe the only reason we do is because we are 94 years old. First Man: My sister works at the Eagle Laundry. Second Man: What does she do? First Man: She washes Eagles. ★ So much for the warm-up. Malachi Hogan, the Eagle (shirt) salesman out of Kansas City, has come up with an idea to show you how beautifully our shirts are finished. He contends that no man is *really* happy about the way his shirts are laundered; and that this is because laundries (or wives) just don't have the skill, equipment, experience, time, or love of shirts to do them up the way the ladies in Finishing do. ★ Therefore, Mr. Hogan–being a salesman and interested in such things–also contends* that we could at one time show up the competition and gain your goodwill by fixing your shirt up something like new; if we wanted to. O. K., we want to: the Eagle Laundry is in business. For the moment. ★ We can't make a regular thing of this, understand, so just send us your favorite shirt in good condition. If by some chance your favorite shirt isn't yet an Eagle, send  it anyway. Whatever it is, we'll launder it, iron it, fold it, pin it, and then put an Eagle label in it–unless it has one already. But we won't be sad if it doesn't. Many Eagle shirts have other labels put in by the fine stores that sell them.** And even if yours isn't an Eagle, the vicarious pleasure of owning a Mock Eagle*** may eventually lead you to the true joy of wearing the real thing. ★ In any case, stuff your favorite shirt in a big manila envelope and send it off to Barry Boonshaft, our Production Mgr. He'll bring it down to the Finishing Department and stand by while the ladies give it the 8-step new-shirt treatment. Better pin the coupon with your name, address and mark to the shirt so he can get it back to you as soon as it's done. Any shirts left at the end, he'll give over to charity–except maybe the 16-35's.

*He also contends that Ray Squire, our man in New England, had the idea first and that we should mention him too. All right.
**i.e. an Eagle shirt with a non-Eagle label.
***i.e. a non-Eagle shirt with an Eagle label.

Dear Barry Boonshaft, Eagle Shirtmakers, Quakertown, Pennsylvania:
I endorse the Malachi Hogan scheme which I understand expires November 15, 1961. Here's my favorite shirt. Do it up.

Name_____ Address_____ City_____ State_____

Laundry Mark_____ © 1961 EAGLE SHIRTMAKERS QUAKERTOWN, PENNSYLVANIA

Plate 10. Reprinted by permission of S. Miller Harris.

Let's start with the Eagle Shirt campaign and the first ad of the series, in which we are introduced to the legendary Miss Afflerbach.

Yes, there is a Miss Afflerbach. Revera Afflerbach is forelady in the sewing plant. She has worked there for over forty years. Her sister Alverna is also a forelady. Her sister Violet is married to Bill Underkoffler, who is Eagle's shipper. He is also marshal of West End Fire Company No. 2, Quakertown, PA.

So here is the first Eagle Shirt ad in about forty years. It ran in the February 11, 1961, issue of the *New Yorker*. Its headline read:

IS THIS YOUR SHIRT?
If so, Miss Afflerbach will send you your [Eagle] label.

More than 200 people thought it was their shirt. (Let's see, that means that 19,800 people thought about thinking so.) For instance:

New York City
February 11, 1961

Dear Miss Afflerbach:
The shirt pictured on page 51 of the *New Yorker* is my shirt.
1. How and where did you get it?
2. Send it back immediately.
3. Keep the label.
Sincerely,
Ray Izbicki

February 23, 1961

Dear Mr. Izbicki:
Thank you for your letter and this chance to get away for a moment from the Label Department. We'd send your shirt back but we're not sure which is yours. We have 7200 just like it. Thank you for writing. Write often.
Sincerely,
Revera Afflerbach

February 25, 1961

Dear Miss Afflerbach:
Get out of that Label Department! I can sympathize with you, trying to pick my shirt out of that mess of 7200. However, all is not yet lost. I know just exactly where it is. If you go over to the blues, look for the 16-1/2 neck 35-inch sleeve pile; it's the fourth shirt from the top of the pile counting the top shirt as number one. Now will you please return my shirt, and *then* get back to the L.D.!
Sincerely,
Ray Izbicki

IS THIS YOUR SHIRT?

If so, Miss Afflerbach will send you

your [] label

THIS is a two-color striped button-down shirt designed and tailored by Eagle Shirtmakers and sold everywhere by fine men's stores. Many of them admire our shirts so much they sell them under their own names. High praise indeed, and we should like to reciprocate by advertising their (our) shirts. But it's hard to know just where to start. Obviously we can't say things like "None Genuine Without This Label" when they are all quite genuine, you know. And it would be silly to say "Try An Eagle Shirt Today!" when it is likely you already have a drawerful; even though you didn't know it until just this minute. So all we can suggest is that you send in for your Eagle label. Write Eagle Shirtmakers, Quakertown, Pennsylvania; Attention Miss Afflerbach.

P.S. Thank you for the lovely label. I'm going to sew it onto the front of my shirt if I ever get it back.

March 1, 1961

Dear Mr. Izbicki:

By George, you were right. It is your shirt and you knew where it was right along. We're returning it to you today. Never would have found it without your help.

We saved you the trouble and sewed a label on the shirt front. Send us a snapshot of you wearing your (our) shirt. Back to the Label Department.

Your friend,
Revera Afflerbach

And then on March 11, 1961, the dam broke. The *New Yorker* always carried Saturday's date,[2] but hit the newsstands in the metropolitan area on Thursday. By Monday the thirteenth we had 1,354 pieces of mail, half of which included suggestions and hopefully listed a shirt size. Tuesday brought 900 more. And so it went. Two months later the rate was a steady thirty letters a day. There is still no final total; six years from now someone will pick up the March 11 issue in a witch doctor's hut in Kenya and we'll receive another request for a Shirtkerchief. (Actually this is an exaggeration; research shows that most of the busy doctors in our own country found time to fill in the coupon *themselves*. We have no reason to think the doctors in Kenya differ greatly.) But as of an arbitrarily chosen date in 1962, 11,342 coupons had come in. That year we even made a 200-page book of the ads and the correspondence.[3]

Now back to our first question: why do people write in? We aren't entirely sure, but it has something to do with them getting involved with our problems or projects. That seems a pretty simple-minded sort of answer, doesn't it? But if you'll think a minute, very few ads are involving. A good many more of them try to be involving than actually skin it. They deserve points for effort but the result often has about as much audience involvement as a man who gets a call from his wife when he has an office full of people. The message has to be repeated over and over before it penetrates. Or, with advertising, until the reader is moved to go out and buy. Actually, it is not indoctrination so much as brainwashing—eventually a zombielike reflex makes it seem the most natural thing in the world to ask for that product by name. There is evidence that when this method works well it is like shooting fish in a barrel. This is OK, outside of the petty objection that, even if people are fish, it isn't sporting to shoot them in a barrel.

An ad ideally ought to be like one end of an interesting conversation. First we say something, then you make some sort of a response. At least that is our assumption. Then, the next time, we either amplify our remarks based on your assumed response or say something new; and so on. This makes the advertising conversation more interesting for both of us. And, of course, it is not polite to be a bore. People have a much higher tolerance of boredom from advertisers than they ought. They wouldn't stand for such yawn-provoking intrusions from their children or friends, so why should they take it from any Tom, Dick, or John Cameron Swayze who happens in? But they do take it, poor souls, and it's a pity.

Most printed ads don't do much better in the boredom sweepstakes, when it comes to that. So if you can manage to turn out an ad that looks at all interesting, and is pertinent to boot, people will respond mentally and fiscally. We have spoken about actual response in the form of mail. You see, the intention of the Shirtkerchief ad, for instance, was not, as you might think, to get people to write, although that is always nice, of course. No, the intention was to make people want to write, whether they did or not, and to feel that there really was somebody there who was palpitating to hear from them; and oh, there was indeed.

There is no great mystery as to why advertisers want people to write in. A client leads a lonely life, isolated from his ultimate customers. He knows them not as men and women, but as neck sizes and sleeve lengths. For him to receive letters from them as real, live human beings and to find out that they regard him likewise, even fondly, is a delicious experience. It transforms him. He smiles at himself while shaving. He becomes unbearable around his club. He becomes an expert on advertising. He writes a book about it.

You already know the main secret—that people don't read ads; they read what interests them and sometimes it is an ad. And the rule for writing ads and other stuff—epic poems, say—is that an ad has got to grab you as you are sliding by to something more important. Ad writers know this and it makes them a humble lot; book writers, by comparison, seem stupefyingly arrogant; they are so confident as to make one's nose bleed. They are not afraid to take a chance on boring the pants off people. If any advertising writer had the effrontery to start off as slowly as Tolstoy's first sentence in *Anna Karenina,* "All happy families are alike, every unhappy family is unhappy in its own way," the intended audience would be downstairs in the kitchen making sandwiches. The first line of *Moby-Dick,* "Call me Ishmael," is no great shakes as a grabber either, nor, for that matter, is "In the beginning was the word." Not, at any rate, if you compare it with the lead that Thurber

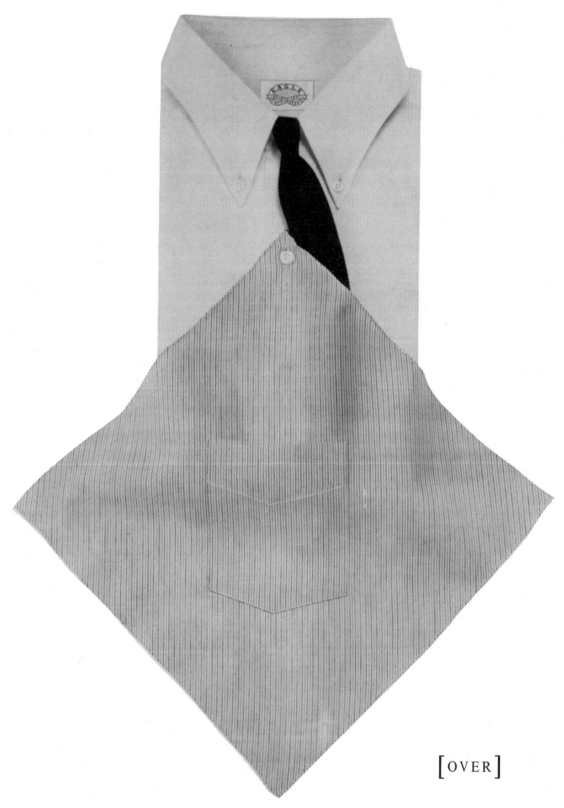

[OVER]

Plate 12. Reprinted by permission of S. Miller Harris.

SEND FOR YOUR FREE EAGLE SHIRTKERCHIEF (SHIRTKIN?) (NAPCHIEF?)

AS far as we know this is a brand new invention. Perhaps you will be able to figure out how to realize its full potential. ✷ It all started when we tried to devise something to send you—short of an actual shirt—to illustrate a few of the fine points of fine shirt making. A sample to take with you when you go shirt shopping. ✷ So first we hemmed a piece of fine shirting; *20 stitches to the inch*, just like in our shirts. At this point you could still call it a handkerchief. ✷ But it did seem a shame not to show one of our threadchecked buttonholes, so we did. It makes a pretty good shirt protector: just whip it out of your breast pocket and button it on the second from the top to avoid gravy spots. Good. And tuck your tie in behind it. ✷ But then somebody in Pockets said, "Look, if you let us sew a pocket on it, it will show how we make the pattern match right across, no matter what." ✷ So if anyone knows what you can use a pocket in a handkerchief/napkin for we will be glad to hear. We will give a half-dozen shirts for the best answer. Make it a dozen.

Eagle Shirtmakers, Quakertown, Pa.

Gentlemen :

Please send me whatever it is. (Signed)_____

Address_____City_____State_____

wrote for his college paper: "Who has seen the sores on the tops of the horses in the Agricultural Building?"

Gibbon, however, wins the first line self-confidence sweepstakes, especially when you consider that he expects you to read 1,458 pages more before the dénouement, such as it is. He starts out: "In the second century of the Christian era, the Empire of Rome comprehended the fairest part of the earth, and the most civilised portion of mankind." Nothing free, no special offers. Pretty shabby. If you wanted to know how the story comes out without wading through the whole of *The Decline and Fall of the Roman Empire,* wouldn't you be willing to fill in a handy coupon and get a quick answer?

Bertrand Russell was once asked if he thought he would have achieved his towering reputation if he hadn't started off with *Principia Mathematica,* a book so abstruse that nobody could read it. "Not at all," he replied. "At first you have got to be dull." Do you suppose that's really the theory serious writers work on? It would explain a lot.

Well, if you succeed in constructing an involving ad, the question then comes up as to where to run it. This is very important, for the nature of an advertising message is greatly influenced by where it appears—it will tend to be read differently in different magazines—and by who reads it. There is the matter of editorial content, of course, but the other advertising in the magazine is significant as well. These together with the character of readership tend to work as mutual influences, one on the other; taken together with the individual ad, they determine the results.

The *New Yorker* is the happiest blend of these ingredients to be found anywhere, which probably accounts for its success as an advertising medium.

Much has been written about the editorial side, but little about the other, the four-color half of the magazine—and why it is the way it is.

One time a woman wrote in to a *New Yorker* advertiser to protest a misspelling. She sent in the whole page with the word underlined, and in the margin she wrote: "I don't know who you are, but I'm ashamed of the *New Yorker.*"

This comes close to expressing the prevalent subscriber attitude toward what you might call the *New Yorker*'s gestalt. Anyway, there is a tendency among its readers to regard the magazine *as a whole,* and this is unusual in the periodical world. Most publications—with the exception of fashion magazines, where the editorial and advertising areas are so diffused as to be very nearly interchangeable—are neatly divided into text and ads. The *New Yorker* does this too, so there is no use looking here for the secret of its homogeneity.

As a matter of fact, the separation between God and Mammon in the *New Yorker* is more pronounced than in any other magazine you could name, not even excepting the *National Geographic* with its sharply defined advertising ghettos fore and aft, for even there some visual and contextual link connects with the glorious global technicolor center slab.

But there is little chance of ever confusing the *New Yorker*'s editorial matter with its advertising, despite their gracious tolerance in allowing advertisers to accompany the text as it uninterruptedly meanders through to the end of the book. Not only are there no editorial color pages to gull the reader into feeling that a certain community of interest with the flaming ads exists, but it works the other way around, too.

An advertiser must not covet the *New Yorker*'s format, type, column rules, nor its general appearance, nor anything else that is the *New Yorker*'s.

Nor its manservant, nor its maidservant. On one occasion an advertisement made mention of Mollie Panter-Downes (who writes "Letter from London") in a not inappropriate reference; it never ran, at least not in that form. The copywriter responsible received a person-to-person call from a man who introduced himself as the president of the *New Yorker*. The writer, much impressed (for he had never been telephoned by the president of his own company) was told courteously that he couldn't mention the names of the magazine's contributors in advertisements. "Well," the writer suggested, "we could leave Mollie Panter-Downes out without hurting things much, I suppose." No, the voice on the other end said, the whole thing would have to be changed because the ad mentioned the *New Yorker*, too. "See here," it continued, "we're pretty close to our deadline, so why don't we rewrite it? That way there'll be no question of acceptability, and then I'll call you back and read it to you. If it sounds all right to you we'll go ahead and set it in the same type and run it."

This story is not representative of the magazine's attitude toward transgressors. In fact, so far as is known, it is the only time the *New Yorker* offered to redo an ad themselves. Usually they simply reject the offender out of hand, for any number of reasons. They will not accept whole classifications, among them feminine hygiene, halitosis, hormones, and depilatories. They assume that the *New Yorker* reader knew such products were available before he or she opened this week's issue of the magazine. Nor will they publish most cigarette advertising—not because they object to smoking, but because of unsupportable medical or competitive claims.

It is quite certain that they have excluded more than a million dollars' worth of cigarette advertising on these grounds alone. The total amount of potential revenue lost is incalculable, for the tobacco companies have gotten the word and, rather than submit themselves to indignity, don't come around as much as they used to. The cause célèbre in the cigarette field occurred some years ago, when $125,000 worth of Kent advertising was thrown out of the seventeenth story of 25 W. 43rd Street. It all hinged on one word: "proof," which the Advertising Acceptance Committee[4] insisted be changed to "evidence." Kent firmly stood its ground, but it had to stand it somewhere else.

This more-sanctimonious-than-thou attitude is not due to fat-cat prosperity, even though there is no denying that the *New Yorker* is the fattest advertising cat in the country. In far slimmer times they threw out a Lucky Strike campaign, an ungrateful act on the face of it. Luckies had been with them from the early days; George Washington Hill personally placed American Tobacco's first twelve-page contract. But when Mr. Hill switched from "It's toasted" to "Reach for a Lucky instead of a sweet," he had, in the eyes of the *New Yorker,* overreached.

So it is not simply a matter of policy definable by certain rules; it is what they think the *New Yorker* reader will find interesting, pertinent, and tasteful. Apparently mere hyperbole is none of these. The magazine wages a constant battle with advertisers who seek to claim excessive supremacy. Often this does not result in blue-penciling beforehand so much as admonishments after the fact, made in the hope that the culpable will see the error of their ways and behave in future.

Occasionally the difference between acceptability and unacceptability becomes such a nice thing as to elude outsiders. In one instance an ad was rejected for saying, "The world's most popular," but accepted when it was changed to "Europe's most popular."

Well, having one's advertising rejected is a humiliating experience for advertising agencies since they, with the majority of mankind, are apt to feel pride of creation. As suggested above, some know their efforts to be beyond the pale and without hope of entering Valhalla. But others are hurt, stunned, or apoplectic when the Acceptance Committee tells them they have been weighed in the balance—not in the balance sheet—and found wanting.

Actually, it is hard to image that the *New Yorker* could be more blue-nosed today than it was under Harold Ross, its founding father, who died in 1951. In his original announcement of policy, when the magazine was first published in 1925, he said: "It will not be what is commonly called radical or highbrow. It will be what is commonly called sophisticated, in that it will assume a reasonable degree of enlightenment on the part of its readers. It will hate bunk."

Bunk covered a lot of editorial and advertising ground. Sophistication—what we are more likely nowadays to call urbanity—was and is likely to be interpreted narrowly. Let's give you some examples; here are three good ones from *Advertising Age* of February 21, 1955 (it is easier than paraphrasing. Besides, Thou Shalt Not Steal. Particularly when you know the author, James V. O'Gara):

1. "A book advertisement which proposed to sell its product by describing it as 'the story of the most fabulous madam the world has ever known,' was summarily spurned by the *New Yorker*. Reason: 'We do not want to become a publication promoting the history of bordellos.'"

2. "Another advertiser who found the *New Yorker* just not that urbane was a brassiere manufacturer. He submitted an ad showing a seated girl wearing only his product and a wedding ring. She was discreetly blacked out from the waist down, and her eyes were covered by the hands of a man standing behind her. The *New Yorker,* not taken in for a minute by the ring, rejected the ad on the ground that the man had no business in the lady's bedroom until she had some more clothes on."

3. "A bookseller . . . submitted copy that said when portions of the volume he offered had previously appeared in the *New Yorker,* 'hundreds of readers wrote in to express their delight.' This, modestly insisted the magazine, had to be changed, since only three and not hundreds of readers wrote in."

Probably the most common ground for excluding an advertisement from the magazine is that it is inimical to the reader's interest. An extensive series of four-color advertisements extolling the pleasures of tourism in the beautiful Cuban People's Republic was tossed out because the magazine couldn't see urging its readers to risk their necks by going to a patently unfriendly country. The indignant advertising agency grew more cordial toward this decision later on when Castro reneged on his bills and they had to attach his airplanes in order to collect their money, part of which was not for the $75,000 they would have paid out to the *New Yorker*.

Nor is it permitted to advertise products the *New Yorker* reader would not (or should not) be interested in. This will include a cheap line of men's shoes as well as an expensive line of women's suits and dresses which, in the Committee's opinion, are simply not up to the mark from a fashion point of view.

Certain classifications of *New Yorker* advertising are subject to quotas, depending on space demands in those particular fields. A quota is currently imposed only on alcoholic beverages.

The *New Yorker* carries more liquor advertising than any other magazine in the country, as you may have noticed. There would be much more of it but for the quota which holds it at about 16½ percent of the magazine's total advertising. It wields an enormous influence in the liquor field; any liquor campaign of note will appear there—and appear there usually before it has run anywhere else. The reasons for this are a little fuzzy. Probably the *New Yorker*'s page rate ($3,300 for a black-and-white page; $4,950 for a four-color page [at the time of this writing]), inexpensive in the face of its enormous influence, has something to do with it, but the chief reason is that it is the place to be seen.

The magazine's preeminence as an advertising medium's advertising medium is easier to explain. It is widely read by advertising men to check up on what the competition is doing. This is not due so much to the quantity of advertisements as to their quality and the catholicity of the accounts represented. The *New Yorker* also rejoices in spiritual leadership—or actual leadership in number of pages—in such varying fields as cosmetics, jewelry, travel, men's clothing (including shirts), retail and luxury items of all descriptions.

So it is easy to see why advertising men would read the book, although "read" may be a euphemism here, meaning "look at the ads." Thus other media advertise in the *New Yorker* in hopes of waylaying prospects for their advertising. The page rate is, for them, frighteningly high considering the small number of people they wish to reach; but apparently it is worth it.

Let's digress here to try to explain one theory of how advertising works, and why it seems to work better in the *New Yorker* than anywhere else.

Stephen Leacock once wrote that if he were establishing a university, the first thing he would build would be a dining hall so the students could talk about ideas with one another. Then, if he had any money left, he'd build a library. And then, if he had any money left after that, he'd hire some teachers.

A similar order of precedence exists in the establishment of an advertising concept. It is more useful to aim at influence and effect than at mere mass circulation, though if one can do both it is terribly helpful. But many mass efforts costing millions have come to nothing; they were neither much noted nor long remembered. Conversely, some efforts costing relatively small sums have accomplished their purpose and have been remembered for years afterwards. Their influence has stemmed as much from skill at placement as from adroitness of execution. It is not necessary to bruise an elephant all over to kill him.

In placing an advertisement probably the most important single audience is *other advertising men.* They are a talky lot. They will discuss it among themselves, with their rivals, and with their clients. In the outside influence groups they belong to their voices will be heard above the others, and the word will be spread there as well, and at no great cost.

The second target group, sharing certain common frontiers with the first, is one's competitors. They can be infiltrated from top to bottom ("Look at this ad those bastards ran! Put it on the routing list") right down to the sales force who—in some cases never having seen the ad—go out and talk to their customers and prospects, who are yours, too, of course. This vertical flow, as opposed to the horizontal flow above, produces salutary effects when it reaches the competitor's advertising agency *from the client*. They are already aware, as noted, but now they are on the spot, psychologically if not actually.

It works like this: the client, being a client, will want ads like it, "only different," whereupon the agency, being an agency, will either try to oblige or go in another direction altogether. They may end up by doing neither, which is just as well, since neither works. But the element of doubt has been introduced; they are playing by another man's rules whether they know it or not, and the bright ones do know it. Yes, there is nothing more rewarding than influencing the competition's advertising; and nothing will do it better than a noteworthy ad.

And then, if there is any money left over, there is the consumer. "Consumer" is an interesting word because it is so specialized. When advertisers speak of consumers they think they mean People, but they don't. A consumer is a functional being designed to use whatever it is you have to sell. He will therefore be a grotesque on the order of the creatures of Hieronymus Bosch or Artzybasheff; all mouth or belly, but with just one foot in these hydromatic days. His structure will, of course, vary considerably depending on whether one is selling toothpaste, brassieres, or toilet paper.

Consumers, because they are nonexistent except in the manufacturer's imagination, will react like people. So, if an ad appeals to the people in groups one and two (also consumers in their own right), it is likely to appeal to those in group three as well; perhaps more so, for they are not fettered by preconceived ideas. They may not know anything about advertising—America's only original art form (jazz excepted)—but they know what they like.

As a matter of fact, it turns out they possess more advertising connoisseurship than they are prepared to admit. A frightening number of them don't like advertising. Then why do they read the *New Yorker,* which is absolutely stiff with ads? What is more, they apparently read the ads too, and in about the same way they read anything else. Indeed, one readership study of the *New Yorker* (done without their knowledge by an advertising agency) showed the ads to be as well read as the general run of editorial matter.[5] The answer seems to be, to repeat, that *people don't read ads. They read what interests them, and sometimes it is an ad.*

But are ads better read in the *New Yorker* than they are elsewhere? So it appears. Recall that we have outlined a theory of the flow of advertising influence. The *New Yorker* is highly adapted to this flow; at least it seems to work better and faster there. Part of this is due to its audience's susceptibility to influence while at the same time influencing others. Perhaps it is the same thing as nobody being as open to a good sales pitch as another good salesman.

The *New Yorker* editorial offices are on the nineteenth floor of 25 W. 43rd Street; the advertising department is on the seventeenth floor. Contact between the two, while not as edgy as in the days when Ross is supposed to have thrown a man from the advertising side out of his office bodily, could not possibly be described as integrated. It is not apartheid so much as oblivious coexistence. Liaison is maintained at the top by the publisher and at the bottom by a designated official who acts as go-between and runner on such functional matters as layout. There is no true policy coordination as exists in other split-level enterprises. Nor does the Acceptance Committee count as such, for it considers only specific advertising content, never, of course, editorial.

Except for its submission to a remote, eye-on-the-sparrow censorship, the advertising department of the *New Yorker* lives in isolation to a degree unknown in any other magazine. This, paradoxically, may account for the magazine's homogeneity; lacking togetherness, it has achieved pulled-togetherness. Because of the rigid restrictions imposed upon it, the *New Yorker*'s advertising force has had to find new channels of expression. In doing so it has shaped an editorial attitude and look of its own. It is the only general consumer magazine that has one.

Just as there is a certain type of "*New Yorker* story," so there are "*New Yorker* ads," recognizable even when they appear somewhere else. There are instances where a "*New Yorker* ad" has appeared in only, let us say, *Time*. As often as not, people will recall having seen it only in the *New Yorker*.

There is another reason for this: the *New Yorker* enjoys an advertising snob value; it is somehow more uptown to have seen it there.

Advertisers work hard to mount special ads for the *New Yorker*'s pages. This may seem a small thing, but they don't do it for other general magazines, no matter how large the circulation, possibly because there are no readily identifiable *Time* ads or *Saturday Evening Post* ads. Still, it is a costly procedure, somewhat akin to a woman spending five hundred dollars for a one-time ball dress. Future wearability is the least of her worries; she has already got the good out of it. However, many of these ads do appear elsewhere, thus spreading out the production costs a bit. It costs just as much to produce an ad for one magazine as it does for a whole lot of them.

But the point is not so much that these ads are prepared for the *New Yorker* as that their attitude is influenced by the magazine's feeling beforehand so that they fit—or try to. What this attitude (or feeling) is I am not entirely prepared to say, except that it is not to be confused with pervasive technique, as in *Vogue* or *Harper's Bazaar,* for instance. Advertisements which seem to be particularly at home in the *New Yorker* (and a great many in any given issue do not) run the gamut of style, but they do share something.

This feeling (or attitude) is partially traceable to the editorial function of the *New Yorker*'s advertising department. We have mentioned this earlier in its negative or throw-the-rascals-out aspect, but it also has a positive side. They actively encourage talent they feel to be an adornment to their pages. They set great store by getting an outstanding or unusual campaign; so much so that they will grant it priority over less interesting advertising, regardless of comparative budget size or campaign extent.

(Where the category, as liquor, is subject to quota, extent may actually militate against even a highly desirable campaign: "We'd like to take it if you think you can hold it down to eighteen pages, two each month in the first and third quarters, one each month in the second and fourth; otherwise. . . .")

April, May, and June are fat months, running to an average 171 pages. October, November, and December are superfat, and average 200 pages. The top limit is 252 pages; beyond that the editors claim they cannot supply editorial matter to keep up their end. The percentage of advertising will, however, remain at around 65 percent, which does not prevent some purists among both readers and editors from mumbling to high heaven. The advertising side justifiably counters that there is more to read, too. "Read it!" the others grouse in chorus, "We can't even lift it"; which may qualify as Choruses We Doubt Ever Got Groused. Still.)

And the *New Yorker* advertising people like to get the new campaign *first,* before anybody else. Being forbidden other forms of competitive activity natural to growing boys, they are preternaturally scoop-conscious. Dad only lets them use the press on Saturday nights, and if they can't take out every girl, they aim to be the first to take out the prettiest. This goes beyond the mere greedy desire for one-time conquest; they are particularly fond of accounts that will go steady with them. There is excellent business sense in this, for if the product or service becomes established, having advertised only in the *New Yorker,* why then it is not only another notch in the old gun handle but a testimonial to the magazine's efficacy, alone, unaided, and in spite of its relatively dinky circulation.

148

The ideal *New Yorker* advertising prospect, if it is to qualify as a debutante, and an exclusive one at that, will probably also be young or small as accounts go. Otherwise it will have enough money so that the temptation will be strong to spread it around all over the place. As stated earlier (surely you remember), one of the *New Yorker*'s best selling tools is that it doesn't cost very much in comparison with other prestigious media.[6] It is possible to run a brave, lengthy campaign there for money that would buy only a short smatter in one high-circulation magazine or a one-time scatter in several. This is a strong argument, for generally speaking it is better to be outstanding somewhere than just one of the crowd everywhere, which is as pious a thought as you are likely to run into all day.

There is a natural tendency for these ideal advertisters to flow toward the *New Yorker*. But the *New Yorker,* for its part, has developed a considerable ability in ferreting out juicy prospects—particularly in the case of advertisements that promise to be truly ornamental. This consideration transcends mere selling: it is talent scouting pure and simple—the discovery and development of the people who create superior advertising.

Such talent scouting is done on the agency level because that is where the advertisements are done—by somebody. Exceptional advertisements are done by somebody; mediocre ones generally emerge from committee.

The lack of originality in most advertising can be blamed on many things, including statistical probability, there being about the same distribution of talent in advertising circles as in other fields. However, there is one factor not found in nonvenal art forms, but which advertising borrows from business: an unwarranted faith in the democratic processes as applied to creativity.

The chances of an outstanding advertisement coming from anything but a creative dictatorship are so slim as to be negligible. The best ads are almost always traceable to one man. More often than not he either owns the joint or controls it. Because it takes a great deal of effort to control everything, exceptional advertisements will usually, though not always, come from smallish, more controllable agencies. Very large, compartmentalized agencies will occasionally produce a spate of extraordinary advertising, apparently by accident. Closer examination will always show that the organizational tendency toward mediocrity has been defeated by its very size; a dictator has sneaked in and is running his own little enclave with an iron hand.

Since these rascals are the sort who produce most of the ads the magazine likes best, the *New Yorker* delights in scouting them out. Like the earthshaking discovery of Lana Turner on a stool at Schwab's Fountain. A new ad with some flair will be spotted either in their own or another publication and immediately the search is on to find the man who did it. When they do, they cultivate him, pat him on the back, encourage him in his schemes, and have indeed been known to take him out to lunch.

This, while everyday treatment for assistant account executives and junior media buyers, is heady stuff for even senior copywriters.

Good writers are always a scarcity and—except for rival advertising agencies trying to lure them away—outsiders never bother copywriters for the simple reason that they don't buy anything—neither space, art work, nor printing plates. So when the *New Yorker* shows interest in them for themselves and their work they are understandably flattered. What happens from that point depends on the man. If he is happily situated and working on an account the *New Yorker* covets they will encourage him to produce a special campaign. It is far easier to sell a client on running in the *New Yorker* if the advertising looks like the *New Yorker* to begin with. If he is unhappily situated (which is frequently the case, copywriters being an unusually malcontent lot) they will discreetly pass the news of his availability to agencies with proper *New Yorker* accounts. There is nothing even faintly reprehensible—given the mores of the advertising business—in this. A substantial part of any media representative's stock in trade is the dossier of personnel information collected on his daily rounds; and in advertising's continuing game of musical chairs, if he is not the piano player, he at least turns the pages.

But the *New Yorker*'s most fruitful work in the vineyard will be with young and struggling advertising agencies, mostly started by the people they have scouted out earlier. When these break away to start their own operations they need sage counsel, a sympathetic ear, and appropriate clients, not necessarily in that order. The magazine provides the first two as required and the last on a sort of matrimonial bureau basis, within the bounds of strict propriety. It is in a position to do this since its sales staff assiduously cultivates clients both present and potential, the better to inculcate them with the magazine's virtues.

There is another motive, of course. Clients have a delicious continuity whereas their agencies come and go. When an agency does go, another more suitable agency must be found, and it often happens that the *New Yorker* knows of just such a one and will suggest it—provided there is no hope of saving the previous match.

The preliminaries are much the same as those observed by marriage brokers the world over. Each party is delicately apprised of the availability, the character, stability, prospects, and financial status of the other. What follows will either be an exchange of tentative correspondence or—if both are in the same city—a meeting, sometimes lunch with the *New Yorker* go-between as host. The conversation will be cordial, general, and wary unless, as sometimes happens, the principals hit if off famously and start courting on the spot. However, in the ordinary course of things they will part with vague promises of getting together again. Whereupon, provided the meeting approached anything like success, the two parties will retire, mull it over, and draw Dun and Bradstreets on one another. At this point the *New Yorker* slips unobtrusively away, leaving the happy couple on their own. In a surprising number of cases betrothals are subsequently announced; all has been handled with such delicacy that the happy pair is aware only faintly that theirs has been a marriage of convenience.

After this last it would be apropos to say that the joining of our agency with Eagle Shirtmakers was such an arranged marriage. No, the way it happened was this:

> EAGLE SHIRTMAKERS
> Quakertown, PA.
> May 16, 1960

Mr. Howard Gossage
Weiner & Gossage, Inc.
451 Pacific
San Francisco, California

Dear Mr. Gossage:

We sell men's shirts in what has come to be known as traditional styling to the better men's stores and department stores across the country. Many of our shirts carry only the store label. During the past few of our ninety-three years we find that our volume has doubled—not that it is any great surprise to us after all the work we have put in to make it so.

However, should the market we serve shrink in the next few years (famine, pestilence, the return of the dickey) we should very much like to remain in these stores as the line with the best consumer acceptance. This we hope to do by continuing to lead the field in styling, quality, and performance in delivery. But it might also help if we let the public know that many of the shirts bearing such labels as Saks Fifth Avenue, Robert Kirk, Neiman-Marcus, and Marshall Field were made by Eagle Shirtmakers.

Well, there is our problem. We have had no planned advertising program in many, many years. (Our last campaign ran in the *Saturday Evening Post* forty years ago.) Now that we have decided to begin again we plan to begin modestly. Modestly here does not mean behind drawn curtains; it means we would like to keep some of the profits ourselves. I, for one, have my eye on a Rolls Royce converted to run on Irish Whiskey.

Please fill in the coupon:

COUPON

(   ) I am interested in continuing this discussion.

(   ) The thought of pouring Irish Whiskey into a petrol tank repels me. Go away.

Very truly yours,
S. Miller Harris
Executive Vice-President

It was answered so:

May 18, 1960

PROSPECTIVE AGENCY RESPONSE COUPON

Mr. S. Miller Harris

Eagle Shirtmakers

Quakertown, PA.

Dear Mr. Harris:

(x) We are interested in continuing the discussion.

(x) If we made shirts as well as you write letters we'd run you out of business.

Yours very truly
Howard Gossage

It worked out all right. Joe Weiner, the agency's other president (a circumstance he explained by saying, "We're too small to have vice presidents") went East to settle the financial arrangements.

NOTES

1. "The Malachi Hogan Scheme," *New Yorker,* 7 October 1961. See Plate 10 for complete text.

2. Now it carries Monday's date. –ED.

3. S. Miller Harris and Howard Luck Gossage, *Dear Miss Afflerbach.* New York: Macmillan, 1962.

4. The Advertising Acceptance Committee is comprised of three members of the Advertising Department. Surprisingly, there are no editorial members.

5. Once, during an otherwise social moment with a *New Yorker* editor, an advertising friend suggested blithely that it was entirely possible that some ads were *better* read than some features. The editor turned away with a dark shudder and did not cause his face to shine on him again.

6. Usually the cost for producing an advertisement will be figured at 10 to 20 percent of the space cost, and there is great concern at maintaining this ratio among the business people who comprise most of what are called advertising men. More paper is exchanged, shuffled around, passed on, and fired back — all with accompanying memos — on this sore point than on any other in a chronically aching business. The balance works out beautifully to fair enough if the magazine is *Life* ($50,140 for a four-color page [at the time of this writing]), the *Saturday Evening Post* ($44,250), *Time* ($23,050), or *Holiday* ($10,185). Moreover, the printing plates — which may themselves, exclusive of the art, photography, and type, cost a couple of thousand — are "bicycled" around; that is to say printed in more than one magazine, so the ratio improves with repetition — 9 percent, 8 percent, 7 percent. How fine! But the *New Yorker* ($4,950 four-color) blows all the percentages to hell. Production costs, therefore, will frequently run over 100 percent of the space cost. And sometimes not a bicycle in sight.

Chapter 16

The Shade Tree Memorandum:
Personal and Professional Matters

Nobody who has read this far will attribute to modesty my putting this chapter near the end of the book.

The reason is quite different. I think it's insufferably dull to talk about things instead of ideas. And I've already set before you the things that have enriched me and in some cases my bank account. So let me keep the autobiography short.

I was born in Chicago in 1917. I grew up in New York, New Orleans, and Kansas City.

One Sunday morning in 1936 I was reading *Huckleberry Finn* in bed. I came to the part where Huck feigns his death. You know, he smeared blood all over an ax and made a chance getaway. Oh, it was a fearsome thing. I got up and went right out and bought a canoe that very afternoon. And my friend George Mathews and I left.

Oh, it was all right, I was a Sea Scout. We made it 45 days later. I remember it didn't rain for 44 days. We got to New Orleans on my birthday, August 30. It rained that day. There are lots of clippings about it. I was even on the radio in St. Louis.

In case you were wondering how anybody knew about me, I've always been a ham. A publicity hound. As soon as we'd stop at a town, I'd go see the newspaper editor. The river was three below zero on the markers at Cairo that year, and the lower Mississippi was green all the way to the delta.

In 1938 and 1939 I was publisher of the *Kangaroo*, the Kansas City

University newspaper. I know how venal advertising salesmen can be; I resorted to blackmail, bribery, and threats just to sell a five-dollar ad. But that wasn't how I got into advertising.

I didn't get out of the navy until I was 30; I was a flier and a professional navy officer until then. Then I worked for a couple of years at a radio station as promotion manager. Then I went to Europe with a food shipment and stayed a month or two. Then I came back and worked for CBS and others for two and a half years; then I went to Europe and studied at the Universities of Paris (where I pursued a doctorate in sociology but didn't get it; I am a P.U. drop-out) and Geneva.

When I came back I had my first agency job, with Brisacher, Wheeler & Staff in San Francisco. I started out as a junior copywriter and was a vice president in a year. Cunningham & Walsh bought the agency; I quit shortly after, which was a pity because my ads were the principal reason John Cunningham bought the place (or at least so John Orr Young said in a *New York Times* interview).

All of the jobs I have had since the navy (and three before) have either resulted in firing or in leaving in dudgeon, save two, I think. That is why I am in business for myself. I am not a very good boss, but a damn sight better than any other, for me.

I got into advertising, actually, because there wasn't anything else I knew how to do. (In fact I don't know of a good mind in the business that has any respect for it.) I think a successful ad man has to have something missing in his character, the way an actor does. My mother's family was riddled with actors. Great-Uncle Sam Wheeler was a famous showboat performer on the Mississippi. My mother was in vaudeville.

During my time at Brisacher Wheeler, I got Stan Freberg into advertising; this was just before I started the Weiner & Gossage agency with Joe Weiner.

The other day I was looking through the files on the insistence of a friend, and I found a radio commercial Freberg and I did once, but never produced, as I recall. I guess I like it best of anything we did:

First Man: Hey, I got that jingle worked out for Pictsweet Frozen Foods.
Second Man: Good.
First Man: Do you want to hear it?
Second Man: Sure.
First Man: (sings) Pictsweet, Pictsweet, something something something something, something; Pictsweet, Pictsweet, something something something something, something; lah dah dah dah dah dah dah you and me; Pictsweet, Pictsweet, where the mountains meet the sea.

First Man: Well, how did you like it?
Second Man: Fine, but I'd tighten up those lyrics a little.

I met Freberg when I was trying to get somebody to do a jingle in a simple, direct, childlike fashion. It's very hard to find that sort of thinking. I remember running through all the first returns in the Qantas contest to name a Super-Constellation and despairing of finding a decent entry; you'll see in a moment what happened.

Well, then we started Weiner & Gossage. In 1963 I bought Joe out, and Robert Freeman, an art director I've known since the end of the war, went on the masthead.

Our agency opened up in a second-hand firehouse, where it still is.

People in the business probably feel we haven't made much progress in all that time; we started with ten people, and in ten years we've grown 20 percent, to 12. We aren't even the biggest agency on our block, as I told *Time* when they were doing an advertising story.

We only have three or four accounts at a time in the actual ad agency—at the moment Rover Motor Company, Eagle Shirtmakers, the Random House dictionary, and the Sierra Club. I fired my original client, Paul Masson Vineyards, after ten years (we're still the best of friends), because I told them I didn't like their advertising. "But you do it," they said. "That's just it," I wound up.

We've resigned two beers (very skitterish, beers), and one gasoline, Fina, for which see below.

Irish whiskey, which I'll talk about in a moment, we handle on a consultant basis, the initial aim to get Irish whiskey introduced to this country having been accomplished.

It's tough to say what our billings would be, because the way I operate it doesn't mean anything. We are a rather profitable—or at least efficient—enterprise, though.

I have never spent much money on advertising campaigns. It's not only that the sort of clients who come to me have impossible problems, though interesting; they also don't have a great deal of money.

But that's not the chief thing. Even if they did have a great deal of money there is not much sense in spending it, because there is only so much effective audience for some techniques or messages. Size has absolutely nothing to do with it. If, for instance, I had run the Irish whiskey ads in *Life* instead of the *New Yorker*, they wouldn't have reached the right audience even though they reached one ten times the size.

Besides, I don't know how to speak to everybody, only to somebody.

TWA SUPER-G Constellation

QANTAS SUPER-? Constellation

BE THE FIRST ONE IN YOUR BLOCK TO WIN A KANGAROO!

WE ARE pleased as Punch with TWA, and we are sure that Henry Dreyfuss is, too. For TWA have chosen for their domestic service the same splendid *super* Super Constellation that Qantas flies across the world to 26 countries on 5 continents. Dreyfuss designed interior and all.

And we admire the special name TWA have chosen for their version of this ultra Super Constellation. Super-G just, well, *fits* as a designation. We wouldn't mind using it ourselves, seeing they've done such a bang-up job of advertising it, but would that be playing the game?

What we really want is a name of our *own,* neat, evocative, alluring; a name calculated to send hordes of tourists to their Travel Agents. Tourists brandishing fistfuls of large notes and demanding to be sent via Qantas Super Constellation to Sydney, London, Johannesburg, Tokyo, or wherever. Wallowing in Henry Dreyfuss luxury at several hundred miles an hour. We need a name, and *your help.*

So we will be much obliged if you will fill out the attached entry blank and send it to us. Neatness and legibility will count for next to nothing, but please try to spell Qantas without a "u". You pronounce it* but you don't write it.

First prize is a real, live Kangaroo; second prize is a stuffed Koala Bear (*live* koala bears are very picky eaters—you wouldn't want one); and 98 prizes of one boomerang each. In addition, *every entrant* will receive, absolutely free, an explanation of why there is no "u" in Qantas. All set?

NEXT WEEK . . . *an idyllic domestic scene!*

*As in Qality.

QANTAS

AUSTRALIA'S OVERSEAS AIRLINE

OFFICIAL ENTRY BLANK

QANTAS
Union Square, San Francisco, California

MENIIII

I think it is a shame that your speedy, sybaritic Super Constellations do not have as nice a name as TWA's. In an effort to correct all this, I suggest that they be called: ·

_____

NAME_____

ADDRESS_____

Plate 13. Reprinted by permission of Qantas Airways Limited.

What we do is charge an annual fee of $50,000 minimum. Some clients give us a percentage of their sales above a certain figure corresponding roughly to the client's wildest dreams. In one case we got paid for stopping the decline in share of market.

The fee usually runs between 20 percent and 50 percent of the budget, if that tells you anything. As you know, we credit the client with the agency commissions. Sometimes we'll advise a client not to advertise at all; then the fee is 100 percent of the budget.

One hedge I have to keep my sanity; I will do no point-of-sale, merchandising, trade ads, or any of the other things that advertising agencies do. I just do ads, and as few of them as I can. My notion is that it is an organic thing; you do one ad and see what happens, then you do another.

Unfortunately, this, like other pat systems, breaks down eventually. Once you have got a client through what I call the propagation stage, you settle down to turning out a series once a year. This is something that someone else can do as well as I can, or even better. But the hooker is that it is possible to turn out the occasional blockbuster amid all the nice cultivation ads. So I allow them to stay on.

Also, I am getting tired. One time I asked Jim Young how he happened to get out of advertising, and he said, "One morning I woke up and I didn't give a damn whether they sold more Quaker Oats than I did Cream of Wheat."

I guess what has exhausted me subconsciously is the struggle to keep the clients from spending more money. Rare indeed is the client who can bear to think that he is not reaching everybody. I get very tired of fighting that battle, and find more and more that I don't care, really. Let them follow their dumb media patterns because some salesman has complained that not everyone reads the *New Yorker,* or whatever.

Never pay any attention to salesmen, although I do like to talk to them; they understand if you aren't afraid to give it to them in el groino. I went back once to Quakertown, PA., to Eagle's national sales meeting, and when it was my turn, one of the salesmen said, "How come we don't have ads, interesting stuff, like at first . . . you know, the Shirtkerchief."

And I said, "It's like copulation: you don't have to keep doing it nine months to have a baby. You do it right the first time, and after that it's tender loving care."

Somebody else said: "How come we don't have the label showing in the ads?"

And I said, "The label is something that is only of interest to salesmen, not human beings. Consider, nearly everyone can read. We have the name

Eagle there where people can see. That leaves the retailer. Does he care? No. And there you are. Why screw up a nice ad so you will feel better?"

As an example of how antsy clients get when there is money left in the till at the end of the year that you haven't spent, one man with $50,000 left over insisted on running three ads in *Time*. I told him it was a simply terrible idea, but nothing else would do. Results just what I expected, a goose egg.

I do still enjoy writing most of the ads. I find thinking up and working out an ad will usually take about forty-eight hours' effort (six days, that is, not two).

Over the years I suppose that I have had the top ten coupon-drawing ads in the *New Yorker*. The top one was the Shirtkerchief; the second was one titled "Keep Times Square Green"; the third was, I think, the Qantas Kangaroo contest, at perhaps 7,500; the fourth (I guess) the first Irish whiskey ad; the fifth . . . ah hell, I don't remember any more . . . don't nag.

As I say, there were thousands of entries for Qantas. I had just about given up, and I said to my wife, "You'd think that some donkey would be direct enough to think of calling it Joe, or Charley." At that moment she unearthed one that said, "Sam." Now, mind you, a direct mail house had gone through all of them and had never spotted this at all; it was clipped to another entry.

The winner was seven months old at the time. Her father was a copywriter for an airline at J. Walter Thompson. The *New York Times* ran a big picture of baby and kangaroo.

For the modest expenditure of $15,000, these ads made Qantas an important factor in the travel business overnight. Until then Australia had been a place everyone had heard of but nobody went to. From then on they thought, "Australia—oh, yes, Qantas."

I have been criticized, as you might gather, for trying to build up myself in my ads. I have never denied it, though I put it a different way that is possibly stronger than they would dare.

The first thing the creator of an ad should do is make himself look good. Because if he does, then he is sticking his neck out; he is responsible and identifiable. If it lays an egg he is the culprit, no one else. And the chances are that if it makes him look good it will make the client look good, too. (Besides it is tough enough for me to know what *I* like.)

I guess old Claude Hopkins was the first to say an ad shouldn't be admired. He may have been right for his kind of advertising. But look, there is a type of advertising that Claude Hopkins never thought of. And neither, to my knowledge, has anyone else aside from myself. This is possibly why they don't execute it more often except accidentally. It is something a step beyond

NEW YORK CHILD WINS KANGAROO, HER FIRST!

THE gigantic Qantas Super Constellation naming contest is history and things just couldn't have worked out better, about the winning name we mean. It's got everything: class, verve, brevity! Especially brevity and class. And when you come right down to it, there's too much verve in the world today anyway, we say.

We won't keep you on tenterhooks any longer, the name is SAM! Not "Super Sam Constellation," just plain old Sam. And don't try to read any hidden meaning into the letters S-A-M, for it's no use. Sam. Oh, there's consternation at TWA tonight you can wager.

Of course there *may* be a little difficulty working this gracefully into our advertising. (Fly Qantas to the South Seas, Australia, the Far East, South Africa; or conversely from London to Rome, Cairo, Singapore, and around that way. All by Sam, splendid, speedy, Henry Dreyfuss-decorated Sam.) We'll think of something. If you think of something first please feel free to write. We insist on it, if it comes to that.

So, to you, Dena Walker Seibert, small daughter of Mr. and Mrs. Wilson Seibert, 17 Stuyvesant Oval, New York 9, N. Y., our Grand Prize Kangaroo and gratitude. Good show.

Now, in the travel trade category Norma Davis of the San Jose (Calif.) Travel Service wins a kangaroo as well. There'll be hopping in the streets of San Jose, one feels sure. And a kangaroo to Mr. Warren Lee Pearson, Chairman of the Board of TWA, so they can start their own contest. We personally feel that they're stuck with "Super G," though. After we started our contest, they were nice enough to say we could use "Super G" if we wanted to. Well, maybe we will from time to time, if it just happens to fit. And they can use Sam.

If you're wondering why all the kangaroos, the fact is we got carried away. And after all, it's that first kangaroo that's tough; the ones after that come easy. Winners of didjireedoos, stuffed koala bears, Qantas ties, and boomerangs will be told by mail. Congratulations, all!

Well, there are probably some die-hards around who think that Sam is an absolutely terrible name. Although we're a big corporation (ltd., but not very) we're willing to listen. We're not querulous*, so if you want to toss in your two bob's worth, pro or con, even at this late date, go on ahead. A simple "Sam!" or "Sam?" scrawled on a post card will do nicely. Qantas, Union Square, Sam Francisco.

*Pronounce the Q as in Qantas.

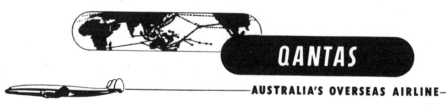

QANTAS
──────AUSTRALIA'S OVERSEAS AIRLINE──────

institutional advertising. It is a form of identity projection, and I think we shall see more and more of this sort of advertising; especially since, as you know, I believe advertising as a marketing instrument is outworn.

Identity is a huge problem in this age, both for individuals and for corporations (who, after all, are legal persons and subject to the same ills). To engage the people out there is to engage themselves. There is nothing nicer for morale or sales volume than for a salesman—or the president—to feel he is the salt of the earth. It affects the office workers and the stockholders, too.

For Hopkins to argue that an ad should not be admired is to say that the company should not be admired. What is an ad except the projection of a company?

Now let's turn it around: if you ask what is the projection of a company except an ad, the boys answer with one voice, "Nothing at all." You as an attentive reader, however, will have gathered from the chapter on creativity that I think otherwise. Some years ago the Volkswagen people came to me; I told them not to bother about advertising, the car would sell itself. I hear they went ahead anyway.

The more I weary in advertising, the more related fields interest me. Along with the Freeman & Gossage agency we now have several other units.

One is Intrinsics, Inc., which makes and designs things. It started when we had our enormous success with Beethoven, Brahms, Bach, and Wolfgang sweatshirts (a brewer's idea of culture, I said at the time) and now has a magnificent catalog of stuff we sell to the trade—cardboard suitcases and stools, French cutout sheets, I don't know what.

And then I was fed up with not getting money for telling people not to advertise. So I took a partner, Gerald Feigen, M.D., who is, among his other accomplishments, one of the top proctologists in the world, a psychiatrist, one of the two or three best ventriloquists in the country, the leading columnist in American Negro newspapers (he writes from the white man's point of view; it is tough for us to integrate, you know), and doubts that he will learn enough from the next ten thousand operations to make it worth his full time. As you know by now, the company is called Generalists, Inc.

We have as open clients *Scientific American, Ramparts,* Squaw Valley, and Neiman-Marcus; our covert clients include corporations and various ad hoc groups.

If this seems to you of limited general interest, here are some excerpts from a document that looks at us extra-environmentally:

The Shade Tree Memorandum

Date: 11 February 1966

From: Howard Gossage

To: All employees, co-owners, and advisers of the below listed organizations . . . and others to whom this may pertain, now or in the future.

Subject: An explanation of Shade Tree Corporation: the reasons for its existence; an outline of its formal organization and that of its wholly-owned subsidiaries and sheltered divisions; and some rough, but precise and immediate suggestions as to how to put them into effect as of 1 February 1966.

1. Everybody knows about Shade Tree, but nobody knows very much about it, including myself. At least it has never been all put down in one place before.

It is hoped, therefore, that this memorandum will be comprehensive enough, and understandable enough, so that it will explain what Shade Tree is all about and serve as a basis for the formal organizational work which must follow. This does not pretend to be substitute for any of that.

The meeting at which this is being read is preliminary and informative. Its purpose is to acquaint you with what, in many ways, is a unique concept; to discuss it, and to answer your questions. It is entirely possible that it will have profound and beneficial effects on our work, our future, our collective and personal security, and our individual ambitions. That is its intention.

2. All of the people involved here are exceptionally individualistic. (Perhaps all people are if given a chance.) It is interesting that each of you is, to my certain knowledge, a maverick in one way or another. Maybe that is why you are here. Even the outside advisers—our accountant, our attorney, our banker—all have this quality, and maybe that is why they are here, too. It is a quality which, though innate, improves with practice; and practice is what we have been able to offer plenty of.

Whatever the faults of our organization over the years past—the well-nigh calculated financial brinkmanship, the flouting of conventional business procedures, the unconcealed groping where business usually finds it prudent to attect infallibility—have produced, amazingly enough, a certain surety which is hard to explain or describe. It attracts a certain type of person and something within him flourishes. What he finds is not all he seeks, but the test is this; it is not to be found anywhere else at all.

3. The result has been a new sort of organizational structure. As we have developed individually, we have tended to arrange ourselves horizontally, rather than vertically as is the customary thing. That is to say, that as new individual talents and enterprises are developed they tend to tack

themselves onto the end, like a new motel unit, rather than finding a place somewhere in an organizational pyramid. And this is true of outsiders who come along, too. It happens this way partly because their talents or functions are unique and non-competitive, and partly because our organizational pyramid has never been all that easy to find. If it exists at all it must be about five miles wide and four inches high.

4. Before we get into this further let us explore why it exists at all. I have been asked many times over the years why we have not let the advertising agency simply grow, the way other God-fearing enterprises do.

I can't remember that it was ever intended to. Right from the beginning it started out as a limited concept. We would do what we could well, and what we could do better than anyone else. This meant that we had to remain small. Why?

It is theoretically possible to have a large, expanding advertising agency and still do everything superlatively. However, in practice it doesn't work that way. I am speaking now about a singular product, with a distinctive quality of thought behind each item. This sort of thing must be made by one person—made by hand, so to speak. It will be unique. If you wish to expand production you must get other people who are able to work in this fashion. But the result will not be expanded production in the accepted sense, for the item that the second person, for instance, puts out will not be the same. He is, in effect, in a different business. Doctors understand this and so do lawyers, and so do artists. Their associations, therefore, will be in the form of partnerships or cooperative arrangements where each may do his own work.

But advertising is presumed to be different. In my experience it isn't. What happens in advertising is that a unique talent will, to foster production, establish a pattern which its subordinates will then work within. Since these subordinates, even if very talented, will all be different in their capabilities and approaches, it is necessary to find a least common denominator which all can fulfill. This results, at best, in a certain sameness; at worst, in a slick mediocrity. The other alternative occurs when the unique talent at the head is strong enough and a good enough organizer so that all the work comes out bearing his stamp; to all practical purposes it is his. I know of no exceptions to this rule.

In the beginning I will admit that I thought I could beat the system. The way I proposed to do it was to start out small, as I said, and expand as I was able to understand more. This day never came, for the more I understood most advertising and the processes which I have described, the less feasible expansion into a large agency became.

From the beginning we settled for a policy of national accounts only, and those of a limited size. That was because they were the most likely to require—indeed be able to use—exceptional advertising that would gain both them, and us, reputation. We charged them fees commensurate with the work.

It so happened that we, and they, did achieve adequate recognition right from the start. The catch to this, what might have been a highly profitable arrangement—and aside from the fact that expansion proved impossible—was that it required the very best people possible to do it at all. Which brings us to an interesting point; it is precisely the people who do the best work in advertising who are the least likely to be content with it. The reason is that advertising is by nature a very limited art form. But like any other form, it requires superlative talent, if the results are to be superlative. The upshot is, that a large talent will have to settle for a small, if precise, outlet. It is like making Steinways which will only be used for playing Chopsticks. We have some of the best Chopsticks players in the world right here in this room. It is fun to play Chopsticks and do it very well; but there is more to music and life than Chopsticks.

"What did you play during your career as a concert pianist, Dad?"

"Chopsticks."

Aside from that, there is no future in it. It costs a lot of money to keep a stable of concert Chopsticks players and the money only comes in as long as you are playing Chopsticks like crazy. The moment you stop, there you are on the Poverty Program. For this reason alone we have had to diversify. I will admit that we didn't start out to do it on purpose, but it happened that we started making things and designing things, that other people wanted to buy. Also, there was the heady revelation that people were willing to pay us for advice, for just talking to them. Up till then, we had been doing that for nothing. Indeed, if put to the test, I would probably pay people to listen to me, I enjoy talking so much.

5. The upshot has been that four distinct functions began to emerge, starting perhaps three or four years ago. These are: Designing, Consulting, Advertising, and Public Relations.

There is also another function which we might call collective security.

A couple or three years ago we formed a corporation then called "Intercorp." Intercorp was owned jointly by people in the firm and was, in turn, supposed to own things so that in our old age we would have something to treasure besides fond memories.

But first, a word about the name "Shade Tree." Alice Lowe thought it up when we first organized Intercorp. I can't remember why we chose Intercorp except maybe it sounded dirty. Alice's reasoning was that it would be "a shade tree for our old age." When we started our present reorganization, we asked Frank Boydstun whether he liked "Shade Tree" better than "Intercorp," and he said, "Yes" in his usual gabby fashion. I said, "Why?" and he said, "Because it sounds rich."

The exact makeup of the group is not particularly fascinating to non-participants. Along with the three direct subsidiaries, Freeman & Gossage, Intrinsics, and Generalists, it consists of two "sheltered" studios, that of artist Marget Larsen and press and public relations specialist Jerry Mander. All five pay a percentage of their gross receipts to the parent company. The parent holds all stock in the three subsidiaries. The five pay their salaries, the subsidiaries their share of office rent and overhead. The parent company writes all bills, credits the income to the appropriate unit, and makes all payments on their behalf; it also keeps the books of the entire concern.

About a year and a half after Shade Tree began, a name suddenly occurred to me that would pull together my various attempts to undermine the commission system. The result was [an] ad, which *Advertising Age* refused as the *New Yorker* refuses deodorant ads (i.e., with nose-holding). Word got around, of course, even so; though I don't what the upshot will be.

In conclusion, I would like to quote something one of the founding fathers of our republic said on the eve of the First Constitutional Convention, also an adventure into new structure: "Experience must be our only guide, reason may mislead us."

So much for the Shade Tree Memorandum. On the logically unfounded assumption that your curiosity extends to the ultimate details of the agency proper, here are a few.

The agency, c'est moi. More or less. We have about four people who work full time on ads, though we fudge a bit even there.

Our impeccable type and layout is due to Marget Larsen, who is brilliant, and Robert Freeman and George Dipple, who think so, too; I mean that Marget is. They are merely excellent. We do all our own finishes, photography, and everything except the typesetting itself on the premises.

Somebody once asked me incredulously how I could ever hire a copywriter. Well, I can't really. Rather, I do have one person at any given time who is nominally a copywriter. What happens is they usually drift off to better jobs in time. I take a half-hearted try at training them, but I expect I am pretty good competition. As you remember, we have no trivial ads for them to learn on, even if I could teach them.

All I can offer for that purpose are some procedural rules, such as: (1) never mistake the thing promoted (the involving idea) for the thing itself; (2) only use enough string to go around the package; sometimes it take quite a lot; (3) never put raisins in the matzos; and, as we've said before, (4) it is a good thing for a writer to have a built-in crap detector.

People who make interesting advertising are always being asked, "Yes, but does it sell anything?" When other advertising men ask this question it

Starting today a new agency, Kick-Back Corporation* at 451 Pacific, San Francisco, 415-YUkon 1-0800 will place advertising, prepared by the advertiser, other agency, or creative group. The charge will be 5% of the medium's quoted rates. The remaining 10% will be returned to the originator of the advertising.

Howard Gossage
Freeman & Gossage, Inc.*

*wholly owned subsidiaries of Shade Tree Corporation

Plate 15. Reprinted by permission of Sally Kemp.

usually gives me the feeling that they really think I have found a way of stealing the client's money without actually knocking him over the head. Also, the implication is strong that they are too honest to resort to such knavish tricks themselves. Since I am a kind-hearted man it saddens me to have to tell them that interesting advertisements do indeed sell things. I hate to tell them this because I know it must make them feel bad and that there is no justice in the world.

Why do many people distrust interesting or humorous or beautiful advertisements and feel that they are not sound? Possibly because they do not know how to do them themselves. Moreover, there is a prevailing notion that it is probably sinful to be interesting, and that there is a virtue in being boring—it is the sort of thing *nice* people do. Also, dullness is believed to be the sort of thing rich people do. This may be true for people or companies that are *already* big and rich, but that is not the way they *got* rich; they got rich by being interesting.

I should mention here that there are two sorts of clients: those who are already big and rich and those who would dearly love to be big and rich. Those who are already rich will, on the whole, put out duller advertising than those who merely want to be rich—or richer. The reason is this: the first group will have more to lose than they have to gain, therefore they won't care to take chances. The second group—the ambitious ones—will have more to gain than they have to lose, so they have to be interesting.

As a result they will look around for somebody who can do interesting ads. This, as we know, is not an easy job because not very many advertising agencies will do interesting work. Many people think this is because most agencies—especially in what we call Big Advertising—can't do stimulating work. This may be partly true, but the reason is more profound, I think. Most Big Advertising is unstimulating because that's what Big Clients want. They don't want anything that will rock the boat and disturb the organization too much. Therefore, big advertising agencies will tend to be rather ordinary after they become successful. And most little agencies, mistaking dullness for success, will do ordinary work, too. So, at any given time the greater part of the advertising business will be solidly committed to being as inconspicuous as possible. "You can't argue with success" is apparently the motto. So, with what appears to be an unending demand for boredom, it is small wonder that trainee programs in advertising usually stress orderliness, predictability, and limited goals—with all sorts of rules to cover any situation.

In spite of this some interesting advertising will come out from time to time. The one thing against it from the point of view of advertising economics is that it doesn't cost as much to run, therefore agencies won't make as much money because they can't run it over and over again: people would notice. The advantage to a very dull ad is you can make a whole campaign out of it, run it over and over again, and nobody will mind because they never saw it in the first place—or the ninth place. I know some advertising theorists say it is the very unobtrusiveness of often-repeated ads that give them their success—that it's *better* if they aren't noticed because then they creep into your subconscious. I find this a very safe theory—like the good, old, reliable Five-Year-Result Plan. You know: "We can't promise results immediately, we are sound people, but just see what happens over five years." These are very practical approaches, and I recommend them to all advertising men who want to be successful but are too nervous to steal.

The fact is that interesting advertising has *got* to produce results—and immediately—or the agency that does it will go right out of business. When you do a very interesting ad you stick your neck out; and if the ad doesn't work your neck gets chopped off. It is like playing golf for a hole-in-one every time. Most advertising is content to play for par; and maybe they make it— it's hard to remember when the score isn't totalled up for five years. Playing for a hole-in-one isn't as difficult as it sounds. You have to be a pretty good golfer, of course, but there's one other thing to remember: always try to start out about two inches from the cup if you can—by dividing up your objectives into reasonable goals and suiting your techniques to what you want to accomplish.

I have never really figured out the advertising business in any way I could tolerate—so that I could perpetuate a system. So I have settled for dinkiness and making a mild splash every now and then. If someone came along who could take it over I would let him have it gladly. But anyone good enough to do that would also have too much ego to allow him to do it properly, so what the hell. It worries me, because there is no prospect at all except Chopsticks; which is why I am diversifying.

Chapter 17

Sample Portfolio
(or "Experience Experience")

I've more or less lost my taste for prognostication; so let's take a look backward. I can stand it so long as I don't have to look up coupon returns.

Take for instance Irish whiskey.

To start at the beginning, a friend said to me, "All of David Ogilvy's rules may be nonsense, but one is sure as hell dead right: 'If you aspire to produce great advertising, never take associations as clients.' How did you manage to do that campaign?"

About David Ogilvy's rules, one time I ran an ad for a snuff company (which we own), and I showed it to him and pointed out that it followed his notion that the coupon should be at the top. He said, "Oh, I'm sorry, I have evidence that would suggest that this isn't true." (It wasn't.)

I'll still allow him his rule about associations. I didn't handle the Whiskey Distillers of Ireland. The client was the Irish Export Board and the money the government's. William Walsh, the general manager of the board, had final word, and that was that. The way he hired us: he had seen our ads, flew to San Francisco, and hired us. The only trouble I ever had with him was that in one case he wanted to spend more money than I thought made sense. The total outlay for space and production was less than $250,000 in two and a half years. The first ad to appear was in the *New Yorker* of September 13, 1958. The second ran on September 29. Ad number 7 closed with the prediction, "The next issue but one, that of 6th December will announce an outing. We have taken to announcing coming attractions because a nice woman

HAS IRELAND BEEN LED FALSE
BY A BAKED BRAZILIAN BERRY?

[NUMBER 1]

We'll not pretend that we 〖The Whiskey Distillers of Ireland〗 weren't the pleased ones when Irish Coffee became the darling of the Western World. We still are. There are few things more enjoyable than standing on the quay seeing the great ships off to America with golden cargoes of matchless Irish Whiskey. And yet, have we sold our birthright for a mess of coffee pottage? And money? It may well be. For while Irish Coffee is admittedly a luscious drink the fact remains that the Whiskey is somewhat *obscured* by the coffee, frothy cream, and the sugar cube. ℬ Do you begin to see the shape of this bittersweet quandary? There's much, much to be said. You will fathom how much when you recall that Joyce's *Ulysses* took over three-hundred-thousand words to deal with just twenty-four hours in a tiny corner of Dublin and not one of the very best tiny corners of Dublin at that. ℬ Our subject covers several years and a hundred and twenty degrees of longitude. So it's not likely this one page will do it justice. Still, advertising costs the earth and when we reach the bottom we'll just have to stop wherever we are and continue over to next week. ℬ Back to Irish Coffee and its popularity. The upshot is that thousands upon thousands of Americans have taken the Irish Whiskey without ever having fully known the goodness of it. 〖Its emphatic, burnished flavor must (fortunately) be tasted to be appreciated〗. Otherwise they'd be drinking it all the time; in other ways less darksome and exotic, to be sure, but equally satisfying. There's no need to tell *you* what these other ways of drinking fine whiskey are. It'd be like teaching your grandmother to

Plate 16. Reprinted by permission of Irish Distillers International Ltd.

OH, IT'S A HORRID THING TO BE TORN BETWEEN PRIDE & PROFIT

[NUMBER II]

suck eggs. ⟨ What we were saying when we (The Whiskey Distillers of Ireland) ran out of space last week is that it would be presumptuous of us to tell *you* how to drink fine whiskey. It'd be like teaching your grandmother to suck eggs, as they say. Whatever that means.⟩ ⟨ Still, there's no denying that, thanks to Irish Coffee, any number of the Americans have taken Irish Whiskey without having *truly* tasted of it and that's a fact. What happens is the fragrant coffee and the sugar cube and the cool, frothy cream on top all but drown out the principal ingredient! At no *monetary* loss to us, mind. It has been a real treat to watch the dear sales curve soaring. ⟨ But Profit is not all in all; Pride has its innings. We are an enormously Prideful lot when it comes to the elegant, burnished, *emphatic* flavor of our whiskies. This is why we should like you to buy them, to drink them, to cherish them for themselves alone. ⟨ "Ah! but there are nine grand brands of Irish Whiskey," you say, "Which to choose?" You've stated the problem well, we think, if floridly. Look, why don't you ask the man at the whiskey store for *his* recommendation. He will be overjoyed at your humility. ⟨ Now you've grasped our dilemma you'll no doubt be wishing to take your stand for Pride or Profit as the case may be. You'll appreciate that we must remain neutral ourselves, can't afford to do otherwise. But don't let our shilly-shallying prevent *you* from being forthright. ⟨ To this end we are issuing badges which we trust you will wear openly and diligently. They are quite attractive and are sure to draw admiring glances from one and all. You may obtain either the Pride Badge or the Profit Badge at no cost to yourself, that is to say, absolutely free for the asking. Address your requests to: Pride, P. O. Box 186, Dublin, Ireland, or to Profit, P. O. Box 207, Dublin, Ireland, as the case may be. Air Mail is fifteen cents; surface mail, is eight cents; post cards, four cents. ⟨ The lovely stamp you'll get on the return envelope is alone worth the effort, not to mention the brave badge. Perhaps you'd better write us via the air mail. It's speedier for one thing, more flamboyant, and be-

Plate 17. Reprinted by permission of Irish Distillers International Ltd.

A NEW & INGENIOUS
SHOWING OF IRISH WHISKEYS

[NUMBER VII]

And don't we know the better part of a month has past since we have shown you pictures of themselves to feast your eyes on? ☞ It's not so much that we ⟦The Whiskey Distillers of Ireland⟧ are thoughtless as that we too often become engrossed in "the hard sell" and fill up the page with words. ☞ But this week we have portrayed the bottles again the better to help you browse at the whiskey store. Bearing in mind that while there are splendid differences between Irish Whiskeys, all share an emphatic, *burnished* flavour. It was no easy task rearranging the lot to present a startlingly different but still attractive "lay-

COMPLIMENTS
OF
A FRIEND

out". Moreover, a pyramid is sticky to build when you have but *nine* grand brands. In the end it worked out beautifully because none of us would allow any of the others to be on top anyway. Time was too short to sub-let the space.

☞ The next issue but one, that of 6th December, will announce an outing. We have taken to announcing coming attractions because a nice woman in Plainfield, New Jersey, we think it was, wrote asking "Where was your page this week?". Well, bless her heart, if we published every week it would have us out in the street, advertising is that dear. But thoughtfulness costs nothing at all.

POWER'S GOLD LABEL

DUNPHY'S ORIGINAL IRISH

PADDY

GILBEY'S CROCK O' GOLD

OLD BUSHMILLS

MURPHY'S

JOHN JAMESON

JOHN LOCKE

TULLAMORE DEW

© 1958, THE WHISKEY DISTILLERS OF IRELAND (*Box 186, Dublin, Ireland. Air mail is 15c; by boat 8c; postcards 5c*)

Plate 18. Reprinted by permission of the Irish Distillers International Ltd.

in Plainfield, New Jersey, we think it was, wrote asking "Where was your page this week?" Well, bless her heart, if we published every week it would have us out in the street, advertising is that dear. But thoughtfulness costs nothing at all."

An interesting aspect was that people tended to act on some of our suggestions. They organized a Boston Coffee Party (advertising people there-cum-Harvards) and held it for three years.

And another ad, which appeared in the summer, had no offer at all beyond the privilege of sending in the coupon, yet over 2,000 people did, pre-marked, by air mail.

Possibly we made good the lack of content in the next installment, which dealt with the Irish Geophysical Year. The bit about the handful of intrepid explorers was not just a joke, at least so far as we were concerned; we actually got seven letters from the South Pole.

Incidentally, *Scientific American* does not accept liquor advertising; but they had a meeting of the board to accept the ad for the Irish Geophysical Year. I believe some of the scientists are still carrying their IGY ID cards.

Perhaps the most dazzling bit was when we brought the whiskey distillers to New York and ran two sixth-pages in the *New Yorker* at one time. Oh, maybe 3,000 people submitted their names to Dublin for a drawing. On the day appointed (having drawn the names and sent out engraved invitations) these 200 people showed up together with the mayor, the governor, the president of the United Nations, Cardinal Spellman, and a few other worthies. The remarkable thing was that if I had gone over a list of my best friends I couldn't have got a more fitting group of people.

You may be casually interested in what happened to the campaign as against what had originally been intended.

In the beginning the Irish government wanted to help move the oceans of Irish whiskey that were in bond, so as to collect the taxes. And as a matter of fact whiskey exports to America went up, though nothing sensational because they never built up real distribution. (By the way, the Irish government quietly got the Ulster distillers into the act, although there was no financial advantage to Eire.)

But other Irish exports went up like a rocket. And the series of ads, with their severely classical (and enormously expensive) topography and the eighteenth-century illustrations accomplished something more. They replaced the old picture of Ireland as bog-trotters and lace curtains current in America and to some extent in Ireland, with the conservative elegance that you can actually see in Dublin.

SHALL IT BE THE
BOSTON
COFFEE PARTY?

[NUMBER VIII]

As we know, Irish Whiskey drinkers are divided into two more-or-less militant factions: 1. Those who take it in the Irish Coffee and 2. Those who relish its burnished emphatic flavor unadorned save for the usual additives, or "Upon The Rocks," as you say. Please appreciate that we [The Whiskey Distillers of Ireland] are loathe even to *hint* that there is any strife between you. And yet, across the water have come reports of the harsh word, the bitter jest. Perhaps as a result of your being cooped up during the hard weather. It's neither natural nor desirable for people to stay indoors all the time and have no fun. So what we should like to propose is the first of what we hope will become annual outings in which both parties may participate, mingle, vent high spirits, and mend differences. Tuesday, December 16th, seems as good a day as any, coming as it does in the middle of the week when hearts need lifting. We find, interestingly enough, that this is also the 185th anniversary of the Boston Tea Party! Let ours be the Boston Coffee Party, then. ⌘ While we shall have to leave the actual arranging of the affair up to those of you who are natural-born leaders, we can outline something of an agenda. The following is one which might be followed in Boston itself though we expect that celebrations in other cities could be arranged around whatever body of water is at hand.

AGENDA FOR BOSTON COFFEE PARTY.

Tuesday, December 16, 1958

HIGH NOON:	Assemble peaceably at Scollay Square wearing Pride, Profit or other identifying Badges. Hotheads may carry banners with appropriate inscriptions. Everyone bring a token quantity of coffee, say a spoonful, in a paper bag.
12:01:	Listen well to exhortations by leaders.
12:02:	Form ranks and march on Harbor. Allow ample time for stragglers, last-minute speeches, and for such side excursions as the occasion demands.
12:30:	Irish Whiskey purists dump their coffee into Harbor as gesture of protest.
12:31:	Irish Coffee buffs *cast* their coffee upon the waters in the hopes that it will return to them ten-fold.
12:32:	All adjourn. The rest of the day will be devoted to unsupervised activity.

Now then, synchronize your watches.

© 1958, THE WHISKEY DISTILLERS OF IRELAND (*we will publish next on 10th January*)

Plate 19. Reprinted by permission of Irish Distillers International Ltd.

IS IT WORTHWHILE TO ADVERTISE IN THE SUMMERTIME?

[VOL. II №º IV]

After the many times that we ⟦The Whiskey Distillers of Ireland⟧ have been told by them ⟦Those In The Know⟧ that we simply must do or must not do such-and-such we decided this once to disregard them altogether, oh entirely, and perhaps we made a mistake. ℘ This time it was about the advisability of advertising in Dead of Summer: we were never to do that ⟦they said⟧ unless we wished to throw our money out into the street; not that there would be anyone to pick it up with everybody away on holiday and all. ℘ Well this made no sense to us. For even if you *are* gone away surely you will return one day soon and when you do you'll find a stack of journals there and this one among them and presently you will open it and eventually arrive at this very page and it being a hot day you'll make yourself a tall glass of something with burnished, emphatic Irish Whiskey in it ⟦and the ice cubes clinking merrily away⟧ and you'll settle down to read what we have to say here and nothing will be lost after all. ℘ So we believe. Still, we would feel easier if we could confront Them with the evidence that you had indeed seen this piece. The report form below is so simple as to seem simple-minded, we'll grant, but how else to put it? ℘ Before we go we'd like to recommend Iced Irish Coffee. But please to omit the whipped cream; that is to say it is plain iced coffee with a noggin of old Burnished Emphatic. Delicious.

> ### SUMMER READING REPORT FORM
> *Whiskey Distillers of Ireland, Box 186, Dublin*
> *(Postage: Air Mail 15c; Surface 8c; Post Cards 5c)*
> X I read it.
>
> *Name*_____
> *Address*_____
> *City*_____*State*_____*Country*_____

© 1959, THE WHISKEY DISTILLERS OF IRELAND (*On 18th July, an Announcement of Scientific Importance*)

Plate 20. Reprinted by permission of Irish Distillers International Ltd.

PROPOSING:
THE IRISH
GEOPHYSICAL
YEAR

[VOL. II № V]

It's the old story: man's eternal thirst for truth. Since our problem defies the laboratory there's nothing for it but we ⟦The Whiskey Distillers of Ireland⟧ must go to the field. Pure research. Even if we don't make a penny out of it the first three months. ⬩ Our problem has nought to do with the whiskey itself, understand. Perfection there was arrived at long ago; progress is perhaps our least important product. And even if we *did* achieve unthinkable advances you'd wait with your tongues hanging out for some time; the burnished, emphatic Irish Whiskeys you so enjoy today were laid down years and years and years ago. ⬩ No, we pursue another enigma: Yourself ⟦The Irish Whiskey Drinker⟧. What are the solid innate qualities that turned you to Irish Whiskey? And how to encourage these traits in others? ⬩ What is needed is geographical isolation from the distractions of competitive drink. Yes, and a scientific Control Group of *non*-Irish Whiskey drinkers. All under the aegis of the Irish Geophysical Year Expedition. ⬩ Well, you'll appreciate that appropriate base camp sites are not to be found on every street corner. Only one seems to fill the prime requisites of cleanliness, vigorous climate, and unspoiled countryside: McMurdo Sound. ⬩ Now, as to organization and indoctrination of the Expeditionary Party:

[1] Irish Whiskey drinkers should A) Send in for their I.G.Y. Expedition I.D. Cards; B) Immediately get in touch with other Irish Whiskey drinkers and arrange among yourselves about transport, projects, mittens, spending money, and so forth. Yes, and partake of a drop as you ponder; maintaining mood is important in the planning stage.

[2] *Non*-Irish Whiskey drinkers who wish to join the Control Group will please do nothing at all beyond sending in the form below. Instructions will be forthcoming from Dublin with your I.D. Card.

IRISH GEOPHYSICAL YEAR
EXPEDITION RECRUITMENT FORM
Whiskey Distillers of Ireland
Box A186, Dublin (Air Mail 15c; Ship 8c; Post Cards 5c)
I am interested in doing my part for the advancement of science and the propagation of Irish Whiskey. Please send me my I.D. Card and inscribe my name on The I.G.Y. Honour Roll which you will publish later.
____ I am an Irish Whiskey drinker
____ I am a *non*-Irish Whiskey drinker *check one*

Name_____
Address_____
City_____ State_____ Country_____

Ah, were we free to join you on this great adventure! Alas, someone must stay behind here at G.H.Q. to guard the sales curve. Watch this space: from time to time there will be bulletins of significance.

Plate 21. Reprinted by permission of the Irish Distillers International Ltd.

WANTED TO RENT
FOR JUST THE ONE WEEK:
A NEW YORK TOWN HOUSE
SUITABLE FOR SEVEN
IRISH WHISKEY DISTILLERS

YES, we [The Whiskey Distillers of Ireland] shall be in New York the week 24th April through 1st May and have thought to rent a suitable house, suitably furnished, in a suitable neighborhood to accommodate our goodwill mission of seven. And with reception rooms spacious enough for quite big cocktail parties.* The picture above will give you some idea of the character we have in mind. ❧ If you have such a house and wish to rent it to us please send a note around to Miss Colette Kilmartin, Ireland House, 33 East 50th St., New York. How much do you suppose it will cost?

*See advert below

NOW: IF YOU WOULD
LIKE TO BE INVITED
TO A PARTY AT OUR
NEW YORK TOWN HOUSE...

WE must assume we shall have a house when the day of the cocktail party arrives. (We ourselves shall arrive from Dublin on the 24th and it will be one evening that week.) We should like to invite all of you but unfortunately the house, roomy though it may be, will not even hold the 31,794 people who have written to us. ❧ So what we propose is a sort of Irish Whiskey Sweepstakes. If you would like to come and are willing to take a sporting chance please fill in the form below and airmail it for there isn't much time. Then on the 6th April we shall draw names blindfold and the invitees will receive their invitations shortly thereafter. Husband and wife may use the same coupon but please specify. Good luck and thank you for asking to be invited.

IRISH WHISKEY SWEEPSTAKES
[INVITATIONAL] FORM

The Whiskey Distillers of Ireland
P.O. Box 186, Dublin, Ireland. (*Airmail 15¢*)

Name _____

Address _____

City _____ State _____

Plate 22. Reprinted by permission of the Irish Distillers International Ltd.

The campaign ended eight years ago. But lots of people don't realize; they still have this picture of Ireland.

Oh, and one other thing. If I have any "the-man-who" trademark in the ad business, I suppose it's the idea of breaking off in the middle of an Irish whiskey ad and picking up in the next where I left off. To show you how this kind of revolutionary invention comes about: I'd simply written too much copy for the first ad. So I said, "Hell, let's stop here and continue next time." What we ultimately got was one ad consisting of four chapters that ran for four weeks. Originally I wasn't even trying to be cute. And people actually read the serial. The key was the bland assumption that people would be interested enough in an ad to follow it from week to week.

In this connection perhaps I should confess something that is an affront against all that is good and decent. I have always got tons of publicity because I just let my news leak out. I don't care for press releases because I have never found them necessary. The alternative is to do something and leave it around where some sharp-nosed chap will find it and run up asking what it is.

I have only sent out one press release in all these years. It was against my best judgment then, but everyone else thought it would be nice, so what the hell. Even then my original principle had already proved itself. Have you got a moment? Thank you.

As you climb to our fourth floor, formerly the hose tower, you will pass a large, slightly worn American flag hanging high on the wall of the wood paneled stairwell. A small plaque underneath says, "In Memory. This flag was flying over the firehouse November 22, 1963. It was lowered to half-mast at 11:45 a.m., PST."

On March 24, 1964, four months after the assassination of John F. Kennedy, *Look* magazine ran "Memo from a Dallas citizen" by J. M. Shea, Jr. The article criticized Dallas civic leaders for not opposing extremist organizations. "When the hate throwers came along, they simply stood back and let the stones fly." He also reported that acquaintances had said, "I'm glad the son of a bitch is dead. But why did it have to happen here?"

Shea also blamed himself for not having spoken out enough. He mentioned in passing that he had been helping build an oil business, but did not give the name. It was plain from the whole article that he was speaking only for himself and his own conscience.

The result, as he had foreseen, was a tidal wave of indignation in Dallas— part of which (in organized form) touched the company. Seventeen credit-card holders returned their cards, torn up, to the company. (When Shea gave a talk before a women's club, the ladies wanted to retort by applying en masse for cards; but he asked them not to try to influence his employer even in this way.)

A campaign by the *Dallas Morning News* against Shea finally led the management and directors of Fina to demand that Shea promise not to write anything again without submitting it for approval. Just afterward Shea and I were together in the Lombardy Hotel in New York. He decided to quit.

I picked up the phone and called Peter Bart, who was then advertising columnist for the *New York Times,* and told him that I was resigning the American Petrofina account. (It was by far our biggest at the time.) He, being a newspaperman, asked why; and I said one of the few things you could do in this business was decide whose money you wished to take.

He, of course, started inquiring around, and so did the news side of the paper, and then the wire services, and before long the whole story was out. It wasn't too hard for them, since the *Look* thing had already made some waves.

To let his company know he had left, I sent a wire from San Francisco (arranged by telephone) to whom it may concern, American Petrofina Dallas, announcing our resignation. Thus it rattled around the entire system on teletypes through seventeen states, piquing curiosity all the way. The reason I did it was that Jack was the operating head of the company and there *was* nobody to resign to.

In August *Look* ran a "Memo About a Dallas citizen," describing the whole case. "His career in the oil industry is 'finished'," said a competitor. "Forget him."

In November we made him chairman of the agency, which then became Freeman, Gossage & Shea. (Since Jack's name is gone from the masthead again, I might mention that he set up for himself in the real estate business early in 1966. So his career outside the oil business is a long way from finished; after all, he was only forty-one at the time of the row.)

Thus far no other oil company has clamored for the help of Freeman & Gossage. But that is popularity like the Beatles's compared to my standing at times with the leading groups in our own industry. As you know by now, David Ogilvy and I are notorious throughout advertising as the reprobates who don't hesitate to slander outdoor, putting innocent colleagues out of work. But I have one client who encourages all my outrages (with reason, I may say; the ads have sold a lot of cars).

The client is Rover Motors, and the stink began with a billboard ad, which, incidentally, was an idea of the client's, not mine. Subsequently the board of directors of the Advertising Association of the West, at its sixtieth anniversary convention in June 1963 at Los Angeles, resolved that "this ad-

HOW DO YOU FEEL ABOUT BILLBOARDS?

FOR reasons which will surely keep until next time we have not been as aggressive as we might at advertising our Rover cars and Land-Rovers to you. But that is in the past, and now we are prepared to be as aggressive as you please. And we really mean "as you please"; you should not allow yourself to be imposed upon if you can avoid it.

Usually you can avoid it: if a salesman is officious or over-zealous you can, and ought to, walk out on him. (If a Rover salesman should ever prove rude or pushy—or you simply can't stand him—please let us know immediately and we will take steps and inform you of them by return post.)

If an advertisement displeases you, you can, so to speak walk out on it, too. Unless it is a billboard; it is very difficult to walk out on a billboard. Which is probably why they continue to enjoy the favour of advertisers—despite the fact that many people apparently don't care for them at all.

How many people? Well, there must be quite a lot, to judge from the enormous amount of anti-billboard legislation and other activity one reads about.

In view of this flood of public opinion it is strange that no advertiser has thought to ask the people to whom he hopes to sell his goods how they feel. It seems to us a prudent and legitimate question to ask, so we shall ask it.

You will note that the wording of the reply form is more explicit than that of the headline above. For this reason: many people who profess to dislike billboards may not, by the same token, dislike the advertising on them. They may even *like* the advertising, or some of it, very much indeed. And some people may not care a fig one way or the other. Hence the three questions.

However, we would not have you think for a minute that this effort at fairness conceals even the slightest impartiality. We don't mind saying that we personally loathe billboards, and for a highly personal reason: they tend to diminish our value to you.

We make motor cars, and make them with a great deal of care so that they will please you in every possible way. The Land-Rover is unquestionably the finest four-wheel-drive vehicle—and the most versatile vehicle—in the world. Of the Mark II Rover (Sedan and Coupe) let us say that the only car even comparable to it in engineering or comfort costs thrice the price.

However, the single best feature about a Rover —or any car, for that matter—is the world as you drive through it from one place to another. So, it is to our interest that the world and its views be as attractive as possible; for, to the degree that they are not the car's value to you decreases. Therefore, it does not seem shrewd for a motor car manufacturer to purposely make the world *less* attractive by publicly sponsoring eyesores.

In passing, however, it would be churlish of us not to admit that the most engaging and clever automobile advertising campaign in the country looks wonderful on billboards; but then, it looks wonderful in magazines and newspapers, too.

Well, we'd appreciate your filling in the form and sending it to us. One other thing: we haven't allowed room for pictures of our cars or much other information, but if you'd like them just check the appropriate boxes in the postscript. Thank you.

The Rover Motor Company
405 Lexington Avenue, New York 17, N. Y.

☐ I'd just as soon you didn't advertise on billboards.
☐ I have no feeling one way or the other.
☐ I'd like to see you advertise on billboards.

Name_____

Address_____

City_____State_____

P.S. I would like some information on ☐ The Land-Rover; ☐ The Mark II Rover; ☐ Your Overseas Delivery Plan

Plate 23. Rover Motor Company.

Special Report:

"THE LAND-ROVER AND CRIME"

◆

PREFERRED BY THE POLICE OF 37 COUNTRIES
AND THE BANDITS OF AT LEAST 1

Dᵁᴱ ᵀᴼ ᵀᴴᴱ ᴳᴿᴼᵂᴵᴺᴳ ᴾᴼᴾᵁᴸᴬᴿᴵᵀʸ of the Land-Rover in the commission of grand theft, an interim report seems in order. Apparently our 4-wheel drive vehicle has latent virtues which may be of interest to the prospective owner.

It is not our intent here to point out raffish ways for one to pick up a great deal of extra money in one's spare time. Rather the opposite: to abet law and order by useful suggestion.

For instance: in two recent major crimes Land-Rovers were most helpful in hauling away £2,500,000 ($7,000,-000) and £90,000 ($252,000), respectively. Now, although it is well-known that the police of the United Kingdom also employ Land-Rovers, *nowhere is it reported that they employed them on these occasions for hot pursuit of the brigands.* Perhaps that was their mistake.

NEAR LEIGHTON BUZZARD, BEDS.

The first theft, widely if grudgingly admired for its sheer bulk of loot, was, of course, the Great Train Robbery which brought the title back to England.

This Olympics of knavery took place, you recall, at Cheddington, just five miles out of Leighton Buzzard, Bedfordshire, on August 8 last, a Thursday.

Nearly a week passed before any clues turned up. Then, on Tuesday, August 13, a Times of London article datelined Brill, Buckinghamshire, reported:

"A lonely farmhouse near here, twelve miles from Oxford, was the hideout for the mail train gang and their haul of £2,500,000 in bank notes. Mailbags in three abandoned vehicles—an Army type truck and two Land-Rovers—have been found but no money."

NOT LIKE DARTS

Dismissing the Army lorry, one surmises that the Land-Rovers were given the arduous getaway assignment not only for their rugged dependability, but for their capacious rear doors, as well.

Bank notes in excess of so many tend to be cumbersome. When you are trying to on-load literally bags and bags of the stuff you simply haven't got the time to aim nicely; it's not like darts.

No, robbing a train is a very near thing at best and one has got to have the tools to do the job.

FOUND BY MUSHROOMER

Paradoxically, another Land-Rover feature, its outstanding over-all height, caused the thieves to flee the farm, it is thought. According to The Times:

Left Profile   Rear View

"On Sunday afternoon a local man went mushrooming near the farm and noticed the top of a Land-Rover sticking out of a dilapidated outhouse among the trees." This he duly reported.

The Times account continues: "Police believe that the gang fled in haste. In the garden, near a row of runner beans, was a partly dug hole about 3 ft. deep, a spade still standing in a mound of clay.

"Detective Superintendent Fewtrell,

head of Buckinghamshire's C.I.D., surveyed the hole and commented: 'Presumably they intended burying the evidence. We know they got out before they intended...they must have got the wind up'."

Naturally we are pleased that, having been an accessory to the crime, the Land-Rover was also helpful in its solution.

LAND-ROVER STRIKES AGAIN

Though piddling by comparison, the latest Land-Rover effort—the Longfield, Kent, job of September 27—was respectable by county competition standards. It also illustrated an entirely different aspect of the Land-Rover's amazing versatility.

Under the headlines "£90,000 Stolen In Bank Van Ambush" and "Getaway By 8 Masked Men: Guard Felled By Cosh", The London Times describes how the armoured car was high jacked. The bandits lay in wait with their vehicles along a hedgelined road at the T-junction leading off to Horton Kirby and South Darenth. And then:

"A brick was hurled through the windscreen of the bank van, forcing the driver to stop. The bank van was hemmed in by the Land-Rover and the lorry." Whereupon the bandits leaped from the ambush vehicles armed with pick-axe handles, enveloped the bank van, carried the day, and drove off towards Horton Kirby.

To our knowledge this is the first time the Land-Rover has been used in the actual *commission* of a stick-up of this magnitude. While this dubious demonstration of its versatility would seem conclusive, one wonders: what would the

(cont. on next page)

outcome have been had the victim-vehicle *also* been a Land-Rover (Model 109 Bank Van)? An interesting conjecture.

LAW-FEARERS ASK

"Why," decent, law-fearing people may ask, "do you sell Land-Rovers to chaps who are going to use them to rob trains and banks?"

Actually, we can't always tell.

We've sold Land-Rovers to all sorts of customers in over 160 countries, including the armed services of 26, the police forces of 37, veritable legions of country squires, desert chieftains, titled persons, oil and gold prospectors, light and heavy sportsmen; and to multitudes of nice families for skiing, beach buggying and other pleasant things. With this limitless range we often don't know precisely how a buyer intends to use his Land-Rover.

NEW OWNER OFTEN CLUELESS

More often than not the new owner doesn't know himself until he's tested its enormous virtuosity. For all we know, the recent bandits were ordinary citizens who only turned to lives of crime *after* they found their Land-Rovers were just the thing for sticking up trains.

As a matter of fact, we can give you what appears to be a character reference on one of our customers; this one also from The London Times of August 13. A member of the Mail Train Mob got the key to the farmhouse hideout from a neighboring housewife (he said he was the new owner).

She describes him thus: "He was a well dressed, well spoken, and charming man. I have not seen him since."

Neither have we; we do hope he's keeping it serviced.

▬▬▬▬▬▬▬▬▬▬▬▬

BORED WITH YOUR
PRESENT LIFE?

IF YOU STILL TRUST THE MAILS,
MAIL THIS COUPON TODAY!

Rover Motor Co. of N. America Ltd.
Section 009
405 Lexington Ave., N. Y. 17.

My name is:

_____

Address_____

City_____State_____

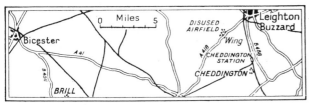

Plate 24. Rover Motor Company.   (Plate 24A.)

Land-Rover 109 Station Wagon with Heat Shield Roof.

"At 60 miles an hour the loudest noise in this new Land-Rover comes from the roar of the engine"

What <u>makes</u> Land-Rover the most conspicuous car in the world? "There is really no secret," says an eminent Land-Rover enthusiast.

1. "Except for rattles, I am against silence in a car," writes John Steinbeck, a Land-Rover enthusiast, "and I don't know a driver who doesn't want to hear his engine."

2. If this is so, then you may like the Land-Rover very much indeed.

3. Our 4-wheel drive (8 speeds forward, 2 in reverse) masterpiece is not mousey. Its throaty authority is assuring in times of stress; which nowadays is usually.

4. Nor is this claim true only at 60 miles an hour. A Land-Rover is more conspicuous even when it is standing still. With the ignition off.

5. The Land-Rover stands nearly seven feet tall. All its features tend to heroic proportion.

6. Therefore, when driving, you will simply loom over traffic which previously had scared the devil out of you.

7. This is not only safe and enjoyable, but you will exult to observe how other

drivers, awe-inspired by the Land-Rover's casual might, yield in deference.

8. (Small wonder that women are enormously fond of driving Land-Rovers. The easy command of such massive, maneuverable masculinity is heady stuff.)

9. You may have read of tests where "imported cars" fared badly in collisions? It's a pity we weren't in there to help out the side. The Land-Rover is built to resist the charge of a bull rhinoceros; or a bull Lincoln for that matter.

10. The Land-Rover's sturdiness of construction (the under-frame resembles a reinforced section of railway track) makes it ideal for trackless wastes, car pools of small children, wretched ordeals, et cetera.

11. There are perhaps 14 Land-Rover hardy perennials ranging from safari cars and campers to police vans and getaway cars. Our most popular passenger models are the 7-seater Model 88 and the 10-seater Model 109 Station Wagons.

11-A. An attractive feature of the '66 Land-Rover is that it is precisely as attractive as the '65.

12. Both of these have capacious rear doors for unloading bulk or people. The unathletic may use the fold-down step.

13. The after compartment has facing seats. This arrangement, although somewhat reminiscent of riding in a paddy-wagon, is extremely sociable. Late at night, it is hilarious.

LAND-ROVER WITH & WITHOUT TIRE ON HOOD

14. The Land-Rover is available with a spare tire either mounted on the rear door or on top of the hood. The tires are identical in every respect save that it costs $7.40 more to have one on the hood.

15. People who feel diffident about driving a Land-Rover with the spare tire on the hood can buy the conventional Land-Rover and save $7.40.

PRICE: The Model 109 Station Wagon illustrated in this advertisement costs **$3,906** on the Atlantic Coast, **$4,092** on the Pacific Coast; at places in between, it costs in between. The Model 88 Station Wagon (shorter by 1 door) costs about **$600** less.

If you would like to listen to the Land-Rover, or to the embarrassingly quiet Mark II Rover Sedan, or to the Rover 2000 Sports Sedan (which has "a little panty mutter when idling that rises to a whispering roar in the lower gears," according to Mr. Steinbeck), please ask any dealer here listed. (LR) signifies a Land-Rover dealer; (R), a Rover dealer; (R & LR), both.

Thank you.

Plate 25. Rover Motor Company.

vertising is not a fair consideration of the merit of this respected form of advertising, and that the Advertising Association of the West, through its Board of Directors, unanimously agrees that this advertisement is not in good taste and also fails in its presumed purpose of influencing public opinion due to the obviously prejudiced position taken by the advertiser."

But the worst was yet to come. "Be it resolved, therefore, that copies of this Resolution be sent to all member advertising clubs; the Rover Motor Car Company, and its advertising agency, and to the publishers or advertising directors of the above listed publications, and that member organizations of the Advertising Association of the West are urged to individually voice their disapproval of this method of advertising, and call particular attention of this action to the media which has [*sic*] carried it."

What a fiendish retribution! (And a hanger-on of mine adds, "Just because they were mad with you I don't see why they had to blackball the English language.") *Advertising Age* was also against the ad. And yet Rover allowed me to go on defying all decency.

To wind up this chapter, there's another Rover ad that callously flouted all the rules, as several authorities pointed out. I wrote to David Ogilvy and told him I wanted to parody his famous Rolls-Royce ad about the electric clock. He sent me a proof, signed. I copied everything except his writing style and content (feeling my own had merit). David invited me to dinner the night it came out, and I gave him a copy. He was so delighted, as well he should have been, that he insisted on reading it aloud to me. I inscribed it: "To David; Imitation is the sincerest form of larceny."

Printers' Ink complained editorially that it was an in-joke and didn't do justice to the client.

It sold cars like crazy, though.

Chapter 18

Two More Rules Gone to Hell

Just as David Ogilvy says "no associations," so I used to declare righteously "no political advertising." And I also said a chapter or two back, "I can't teach anybody to write copy."

Both of these rules went down at one fell swoop when the Sierra Club, whose beautiful books we had been advertising, asked what I proposed to do about some conservation things.

The trouble with conservation, like a lot of other things that do good in the world, is that people who are interested in good causes will oftentimes be so intense about it that you feel absolutely guilty all the time, you know, because you're not doing something. So you'll shun them because a person doesn't like to feel guilty, about redwood trees, for instance. There aren't very many redwood trees left, and every time I read about something about redwood trees—some group trying to protect the redwood trees—these enormous trees, 3,000 years old—I felt guilty because I was sure they expected me to fling my naked body up against the trunk to keep them from sawing them down. You know I can't do that with every tree. So when they came to us for counsel, I happened to mention this to them and said, "What you've got to do is to give people recourse. You've got to give them something they can do so they don't feel guilty and therefore, hate you for making them feel guilty."

So what we did was start with the proposed damming of the Grand Canyon and put coupons up at the top there addressed to the president of

(If they can turn Grand Canyon into a "cash register"
is any national park safe? You know the answer.)

Now Only You Can Save Grand Canyon From Being Flooded…For Profit

Yes, that's right, *Grand Canyon!* The facts are these:

1. Bill H.R. 4671 is now before Rep. Wayne Aspinall's (Colo.) House Committee on Interior and Insular Affairs. This bill provides for two dams—Bridge Canyon and Marble Gorge—which would stop the Colorado River and flood water back into the canyon.

2. Should the bill pass, two standing lakes will fill what is presently 130 miles of canyon gorge. As for the wild, running Colorado River, the canyon's sculptor for 25,000,000 years, it will become dead water.

3. In some places the canyon will be submerged five hundred feet deep. "The most revealing single page of the earth's history," as Joseph Wood Krutch has described the fantastic canyon walls, will be drowned.

The new artificial shoreline will fluctuate on hydroelectric demand. Some days there will only be acres of mud where the flowing river and living canyon now are.

4. Why are these dams being built, then? For commercial power. They are dams of the sort which their sponsor, the Bureau of Reclamation of the Department of the Interior, calls "cash registers."

In other words, these dams aren't even to store water for people and farms, but to provide *auxiliary* power for industry. Arizona power politics in your Grand Canyon.

Moreover, Arizona doesn't need the dams to carry out its water development. Actually, it would have more water without the dams.

5. For, the most remarkable fact is that, as Congressional hearings have confirmed, seepage and evaporation at these remote damsites would annually *lose* enough water to supply both Phoenix and Tucson.

As for the remainder, far more efficient power sources are available right now, and at lower net cost. For the truth is, that the Grand Canyon dams will cost far more than they can earn.

6. Recognizing the threat to Grand Canyon, the Bureau of the Budget (which speaks for the President on such matters) has already suggested a moratorium on one of the dams and proposed a commission consider alternatives.

This suggestion has been steadily resisted by Mr. Aspinall's House Committee, which continues to proceed with H.R. 4671. It has been actively fought by the Bureau of Reclamation.

7. At the same time, interestingly, other Bureaus within Secretary Udall's domain (notably National Parks, Fish and Wildlife, Indian Affairs, Mines, Outdoor Recreation, Geological Survey) have been discouraged from presenting their findings, obtained at public expense. Only the Reclamation Bureau has been heard.

8. Meanwhile, in a matter of days the bill will be on the floor of Congress and—let us make the shocking fact completely clear—it will probably pass.

The only thing that can stop it is your prompt action.

The Grand Canyon: How man plans to improve it. *(Newsweek, May 30, 1966)*

U.S. Bureau of Reclamation

9. What to do? Letters and wires are effective, and so are the forms at right once you have signed them and mailed them. (You will notice that there is also one in the box below to the Sierra Club; that's us.)

10. Remember, with all the complexities of Washington politics and Arizona politics, and the ins and outs of committees and procedures, there is only one simple, incredible issue here: This time it's the Grand Canyon they want to flood. *The Grand Canyon.*

WHAT THE SIERRA CLUB IS FOR

The Sierra Club, founded in 1892 by John Muir, is nonprofit, supported by people who sense what Thoreau sensed when he wrote, "In wildness is the preservation of the world." The club's program is nationwide, includes wilderness trips, books, and films—and a major effort to protect the remnant of wilderness in the Americas.

There are now twenty chapters, branch offices in New York, Washington, Albuquerque, Seattle, and Los Angeles, and a main office in San Francisco.

This advertisement has been made possible by individual contributions, particularly from our Atlantic, Rocky Mountain, Rio Grande, Southern California and Grand Canyon chapter members, and by buyers of Sierra Club books everywhere, especially the twelve in the highly praised Exhibit Format Series, which includes books on Grand Canyon, Glen Canyon, the Redwoods, the Northern Cascades, Mount Everest, and the Sierra.

Sierra Club
Mills Tower
San Francisco, California

☐ Please send me more of the details of the battle to save Grand Canyon.

☐ I know how much this sort of constructive protest costs. Here is my donation of $_____ to help you continue your work.

☐ Please send me a copy of "Time and the River Flowing," the famous four-color book by Philip Hyde and François Leydet which tells the whole story of Grand Canyon and the battle to save it. I am enclosing $25.00.

☐ I would like to be a member of the Sierra Club. Enclosed is $14.00 for entrance fee and first year's dues.

Name_____

Address_____

City_____State_____Zip_____

Note: All contributions and membership dues are deductible.

Plate 26. Reprinted by permission of the Sierra Club.

the United States, the secretary of the Interior, the head of the Interior Committee of the House of Representatives, and both senators and the congressmen representing the district. And down below we put one to the Sierra Club in case you wanted to buy some of their books—which are magnificent books selling for about $25. They have a huge library of some of the best books on natural photography that I've ever seen. Or if you'd like to join.

Well, everything was a great smash. The issue here was that the government wanted to put up two hydroelectric dams on the bottom of Grand Canyon, effectively making it a dead river. You see, it would move the water level up 600 feet. Now this wasn't to accumulate water, it was simply for auxiliary electric power for the Phoenix, Arizona area at peak hours. But they thought these two dams were necessary. All it would do is make this river that had been working for 2 or 3 billion years, or however long making this huge canyon, which I believe belongs to the world and is not for somebody to dam up if they so please, it would have made it dead water. Three billion years more and it still wouldn't be any deeper than it is now. That would be a terrible thing, you know to wait around that long and not have it any deeper.

But even people who couldn't feel very strongly about that—you know, you couldn't see it from the top, it's way, way down there over a mile deep— did feel strongly the next morning when the Internal Revenue Service (IRS) delivered a registered letter to the Sierra Club depriving them of their tax exempt status. That meant that any contributions you gave to the Sierra Club, could no longer be taken off of your income taxes.

Well, did that ever make noise. It was the noisiest thing I've been connected with, except that I'm also the editor of a magazine called *Ramparts* and we exposed the Central Intelligence Agency. *That* made a lot of noise on the front page of the *New York Times,* too. But this, what it effectively did was to say the IRS is against the Sierra Club, and this ad—therefore, all right-minded grabbed hands and were for it. The bill was defeated in Congress the next week. It never even got to the floor. It was one of the greatest propaganda victories I ever saw, because it happened so suddenly.

But then, you can't count on the IRS attacking you every time. But what also happened was the membership of this club increased. When this started, they had about 35,000 members and at the end of six months after these ads ran they had 50,000 members and had made a great deal of money.

Now the unfortunate thing about it was they were very happy to just have their initial goal of stopping the Congress from putting dams in the bottom of the Grand Canyon. But when they found out there was money in it, too, they turned into regular clients. Now everything that we run has to make money for them.

I didn't write these ads, or the paper airplane ones I'll tell you about. A fellow in our company called Jerry Mander did. (Perhaps I had the wrong rule anyway. How about, "I can't teach anybody, just somebody." And of course, I didn't teach him how to write. Possibly how to think like a generalist.) Secretary Udall, the Secretary of the Interior of the U.S., had said at some odd moment that if they raised the water level it would be better for tourists in boats down there because they could see the walls of the canyon better. So Jerry wrote the headline, "Should We Also Flood the Sistine Chapel so Tourists Can Get Nearer the Ceiling?"

Now, about the redwoods. We ran an ad showing all the redwoods there ever were on the top line and on the second line all there were 100 years ago. The third line is what is left, and the fourth. . . . The headline, "History Will Think it Most Strange that America Could Afford the Moon and 4 Billion Dollar Airplanes, While a Patch of Primeval Redwoods, Not Too Big for a Man to Walk Through in a Day was Considered Beyond Its Means," tries to put it in perspective. I think that's worked. We still have to see.

In another one it was easier to attack the president; it was easier to approach him than anybody else. So we said, "Mr. President, There Is One Great Forest of Redwoods Left on Earth, but the One You're Trying to Save Isn't It. Meanwhile, They Are Cutting Down Both of Them." The lumber companies agreed not to, and then went in and cut them down anyway. Terrible thing.

Now I suppose I need to tell you about something that didn't work at all. And I think it would have been a very good protest thing because it's got a good idea. But unfortunately, we ran it in the *New York Times* the day that the Israeli-Egyptian war started. Now, New York was about as inclined to read an ad or read anything—you know there must be about 2 million Jews in New York and they were enormously interested in their way—but they weren't enormously interested in this angle here. So an ad expressing protest, although it had to do with personal responsibility, personal expression, simply didn't work. I wrote it, and it had a very limited success. You see, there was a young man came to me and wanted to run an ad, so I wrote it for him. And it cost about seven thousand dollars and we ended paying for four of it, but that's what's happened at times. It was a good ad, but it simply didn't work. Not everything does. (I got a check from a man a few months ago for $250. He says, I find I have a spare $250 which I'd be happy to give to you if you could figure out a way to stop the war in Viet Nam. I haven't thought of how to do it yet, but when I do I think maybe the headline of

SHOULD WE ALSO FLOOD THE SISTINE CHAPEL SO TOURISTS CAN GET NEARER THE CEILING?

EARTH began four billion years ago and Man two million. The Age of Technology, on the other hand, is hardly a hundred years old, and on our time chart we have been generous to give it even the little line we have.

It seems to us hasty, therefore, during this blip of time, for Man to think of directing his fascinating new tools toward altering irrevocably the forces which made him. Nonetheless, in these few brief years among four billion, wilderness has all but disappeared. And now these:

1) There is a bill in Congress to "improve" Grand Canyon. Two dams will back up artificial lakes into 148 miles of canyon gorge. This will benefit tourists in power boats, it is argued, who will enjoy viewing the canyon wall more closely. (See headline). Submerged underneath the tourists will be part of the most revealing single page of earth's history. The lakes will be as deep as 600 feet (deeper for example, than all but a handful of New York buildings are high) but in a century, silting will have replaced the water with that much mud, wall to wall.

There is no part of the wild Colorado River, the Grand Canyon's sculptor, that will not be maimed.

Tourist recreation, as a reason for the dams, is in fact an afterthought. The Bureau of Reclamation, which backs them, prefers to call the dams "cash registers." They are expected to make money by sale of commercial power. *They will not provide anyone with water.*

2) In Northern California, four lumber companies are about to complete logging the private virgin redwood forests, an operation which to give you an idea of its size, has taken fifty years.

Soon, where nature's tallest living things have stood silently since the age of the dinosaurs, the extent of the cutting will make creation of a redwood national park absurd.

The companies have said tourists want only enough roadside trees for the snapping of photos. They offer to spare trees for this purpose, and not much more. The result will remind you of the places on your face you missed while you were shaving.

3) And up the Hudson, there are plans for a power complex —a plant, transmission lines, and a reservoir on top of Storm King Mountain—destroying one of the last wild and high and beautiful spots near New York City.

4) A proposal to flood a region in Alaska as large as Lake Erie would eliminate at once the breeding grounds of more wildlife than conservationists have preserved in history.

5) In San Francisco, real estate developers are day by day filling a bay that made the city famous, putting tract houses over the fill; and now there's a new idea—still more fill, enough for an air cargo terminal as big as Manhattan.

There exists today a mentality which can conceive such destruction, giving commerce as ample reason. For 74 years, the 40,000 member Sierra Club has opposed that mentality. But now, when even Grand Canyon can be threatened, we are at a critical moment in time.

This generation will decide if something untrammelled and free remains, as testimony we had love for those who follow.

We have been taking ads, therefore, asking people to write their Congressmen and Senators; Secretary of the Interior Stewart Udall; The President; and to send us funds to continue the battle. Thousands *have* written, but meanwhile, the Grand Canyon legislation has advanced out of committee and is at a crucial stage in Congress. More letters are needed and more money, to help fight a mentality that may decide Man no longer needs nature.*

David Brower, Executive Director
Sierra Club
Mills Tower, San Francisco

☐ Please send me more details on how I may help.

☐ Here is a donation of $_____ to continue your effort to keep the public informed.

☐ Send me "Time and the River Flowing," famous four color book which tells the complete story of Grand Canyon, and why T. Roosevelt said, "leave it as it is." ($25.00)

☐ Send me "The Last Redwoods" which tells the complete story of the opportunity as well as the destruction in the redwoods. ($17.50)

☐ I would like to be a member of the Sierra Club. Enclosed is $14.00 for entrance and first year's dues.

Name_____

Address_____

City_____State_____Zip____

*The previous ads, urging that readers exercise a constitutional right of petition, to save Grand Canyon, produced an unprecedented reaction by the Internal Revenue Service threatening our tax deductible status. IRS says the ads may be a "substantial" effort to "influence legislation." Undefined, these terms leave organizations like ours at the mercy of administrative whim. (The question has not been raised with any organizations that favor Grand Canyon dams.) So we cannot now promise that contributions you send us are deductible—pending results of what may be a long legal battle.

The Sierra Club, founded in 1892 by John Muir, is nonprofit, supported by people who, like Thoreau, believe "In wildness is the preservation of the world." The club's program is nationwide, includes wilderness trips, books and films — as well as such efforts as this to protect the remnant of wilderness in the Americas. There are now twenty chapters, branch offices in New York (Biltmore Hotel), Washington (Dupont Circle Building), Los Angeles (Auditorium Building), Albuquerque, Seattle, and main office in San Francisco.

AGE OF TECHNOLOGY ↓
↑ FIRST MAN
2 MILLION YRS. AGO

FIRST ELEPHANTS
60 MILLION YRS. AGO

FIRST REDWOODS
130 MILLION YRS. AGO

FIRST MAMMALS
160 MILLION YRS. AGO

FIRST DINOSAURS
180 MILLION YRS. AGO

FIRST TREES
250 MILLION YRS. AGO

FIRST REPTILES
275 MILLION YRS. AGO

FIRST FISHES
400 MILLION YRS. AGO

GRAND CANYON
550 MILLION YRS. AGO

FIRST CORALS
575 MILLION YRS. AGO

FIRST SPONGES
650 MILLION YRS. AGO

BIRTH OF THE EARTH
4 BILLION YRS. AGO

Plate 27. Reprinted by permission of Sierra Club.

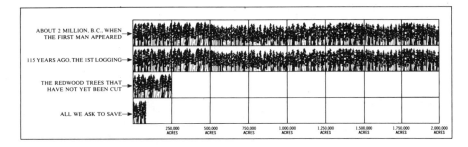

ABOUT 2 MILLION, B.C., WHEN THE FIRST MAN APPEARED →								
115 YEARS AGO, THE 1ST LOGGING →								
THE REDWOOD TREES THAT HAVE NOT YET BEEN CUT →								
ALL WE ASK TO SAVE →	250,000 ACRES	500,000 ACRES	750,000 ACRES	1,000,000 ACRES	1,250,000 ACRES	1,500,000 ACRES	1,750,000 ACRES	2,000,000 ACRES

"History will think it most strange that America could afford the Moon and $4 billion airplanes, while a patch of primeval redwoods—not too big for a man to walk through in a day—was considered beyond its means."

EARTH BEGAN four billion years ago, and Man two million. The Age of Technology on the other hand is hardly two hundred years old, and to give you an idea of just how little relative time *that* is, imagine a line an inch long, and then one mile from New York to Japan.

Yet, during this inch of time, Man has become so impressed with his brand new power as to alter his world irrevocably.

For instance:

1) By the time Man appeared on this planet a forest of giant redwood trees already covered about two million acres of Northern California. (See chart.)

2) They were there in the age of the dinosaurs and when Rome was built. They were there when Christ was alive, and when Columbus discovered America. They were still there during the Gold Rush just a hundred fifteen years ago; a reminder, to those who've walked through them, of how we all started.

3) But in the last 115 years (a half-inch on your mental chart) nearly all of the forest has been logged.

4) Of that which remains a few are in small state parks. The rest is scheduled for cutting.

5) A national park has been proposed for Redwood Creek which could, at any rate, save 2% more of the old trees.

6) But lumber interests, having cut so much and taken the rest for granted, are eager to get on with business. They see little reason why they should not.

7) Tourists, they point out, want only enough old trees for the snapping of photos, and they have offered to leave "enough." (The result would remind you of the places on your face you missed while you were shaving.)

8) The companies add that redwood forests are dark and gloomy, and furthermore clearing out old-growth trees is *good* for the forest. "Overmature" timber they like to call it.

It's hard to say how the forest grew so well before the loggers were there to protect it.*

9) The real heart of the matter is simply this: A logger will resist his job being changed from logging to running a park; a local businessman will fear a decline for a time, and the companies believe they've an inalienable right to cut down trees for money.

But this planet is all we non-loggers have, and any other will forever feel strange.

It seems to us, therefore, we should not be so hasty about removing all our natural environment: the element which makes Earth feel like home.

Deciding what is *too much* destruction in the name of commerce is not always easy, but in the case of the redwoods it is.

By default, the world has given up the rights to 97% of what has been growing for 2 million years. That is surely more than enough. Buying 2% back ought hardly be thought much to ask, on behalf of our children's children.**

History will think it most strange that America could afford the Moon and $4 billion airplanes while a patch of primeval redwoods—not too big for a man to walk through in a day—was considered beyond its means.***

This generation will decide this question and hundreds of others just like it; questions that will determine whether or not something untrammelled and free will remain to prove we had love for those who follow. To impress people with that, and to suggest they *do* have some say in what happens, the Sierra Club (now with 47,000 members), has been taking ads such as this.

We have been asking that people write letters, mail coupons and that they send us funds to continue our efforts.

Thousands *have* written, but meanwhile, in this session of Congress, a bill which will propose a park at Redwood Creek —the only possible location for a meaningful, varied redwood park—will face its greatest and probably its last test.

More letters expressing your view are needed, and more dollars to help fight the notion that man no longer needs nature.

*Lumber companies who own the redwood forests have spent tremendous sums to suggest that even when the land is cut completely clear of trees, as is often the case, no permanent harm is done the forest; as the cut-over area is immediately reseeded, and is then designated a "tree farm." However, because the special growing conditions that redwoods require are often impaired by modern tractor logging, the "tree farms" are most often not seeded with redwoods, but douglas fir, spruce and Monterey pine.

**The arithmetic on the acreage goes this way: At present, 85% of the two million virgin acres has been cut. 3% of the original virgin acreage is held in tiny museum-like California state parks, while the other 12% that's left is scheduled for cutting; which would make a total of 97% of the redwoods given over to that purpose. A Redwood National Park at Redwood Creek would save, in one forest, an additional 2% of the virgin growth as well as a lovely, remote beach area, a number of spectacular wooded hills where redwoods are displayed in the variety of growth conditions in which they thrive, and a navigable river which includes The Emerald Mile, a stretch of huge redwoods running along both sides of the stream. The net effect, then, would be that instead of 97% of the original redwoods going to cutting, only 95% would be gone and we would then have a real sweep of forest large enough for people to walk in without it seeming like a parking lot outside a baseball game.

***A redwood national park of 90,000 acres in the Redwood Creek area would cost $150 million. That is, about 75 cents per American. Or, if amortized into the future, a few pennies from our children as well. Considering it will last their lifetime, and THEIR children's and grandchildren's and so on, it would seem to qualify, in economic jargon, as a "steal."

The Sierra Club, founded in 1892 by John Muir, is nonprofit, supported by people who, like Thoreau, believe "In wildness is the preservation of the world." The club's program is nationwide, includes wilderness trips, books and films—as well as such efforts as this to protect the remnant of wilderness of the Americas. There are now twenty chapters, branch offices in New York (Biltmore Hotel), Washington (Dupont Circle Building), Los Angeles (Auditorium Building), Albuquerque, Seattle, and main office in San Francisco.

(Our previous ads, urging that readers exercise a constitutional right of petition to save Grand Canyon from two dams which would have flooded it, produced an unprecedented reaction by the Internal Revenue Service threatening our tax deductible status. IRS called the ads a "substantial" effort to "influence legislation." Undefined, these terms leave organizations like ours at the mercy of administrative whim. [The question has not been raised with organizations that favor Grand Canyon dams.] So we cannot now promise that contributions you send us are deductible—pending results of what may be a long legal battle.)

EDGAR WAYBURN
Vice President, Sierra Club
Mills Tower, San Francisco

☐ Please send me more details on how I may help.

☐ Here is a donation of $_____ to continue efforts such as this to keep the public informed.

☐ Send me "The Last Redwoods" which tells the complete story of the opportunity as well as the destruction in the redwoods. ($17.50.)

☐ I would like to be a member of the Sierra Club. Enclosed is $14.00 for entrance and first year's dues.

Name_____

Address_____

City_____State_____Zip_____

HERE ARE SOME STEPS YOU CAN TAKE:

HON. RONALD REAGAN
Governor, State of California
Sacramento, California

Dear Governor Reagan,

I urge that you join in support of a meaningful redwood national park in your state: 90,000 acres at Redwood Creek, saving but 2% more of what once grew.

It is an accident of geography that the redwoods are in California. They are the property of every American; even of every person in the world, and of future generations as well. And you are the steward of this inheritance.

I ask that you do your utmost to assure that they are preserved not only as isolated museum-like groves, but in their original magnificent sweep; so that walking through them will remain among Man's most moving experiences.

Yours sincerely,

Name_____

Address_____

City_____State_____Zip_____

MR. C. DAVIS WEYERHAEUSER
Chairman of the Board
Arcata Redwood Company
Tacoma Building, 1015 "A" St., Tacoma, Washington 98402

Dear Mr. Weyerhaeuser,

Yours is one of the two companies that presently own almost all the virgin redwood forests within the proposed Redwood Creek Park.

Therefore, you are in a rare position to singlehandedly assure that one of Mankind's great heritages will be preserved.

Considering that, 1) a meaningful redwood park would return to public hands only 2% of the forest that once grew, and 2) the government would then reimburse your shareholders more than amply, I urge that you join in supporting a 90,000 acre park at Redwood Creek.

Future generations will thank you even more than I do today.

Yours sincerely,

Name_____

Address_____

City_____State_____Zip_____

MR. OWEN CHEATHAM
Chairman of the Board
Georgia-Pacific Corporation
Executive Offices, 375 Park Avenue, New York, N.Y. 10022

Dear Mr. Cheatham,

Yours is one of the two companies that presently own almost all the virgin redwood forests within the proposed Redwood Creek Park.

Therefore, you are in a rare position to singlehandedly assure that one of Mankind's great heritages will be preserved.

Considering that, 1) a meaningful redwood park would return to public hands only 2% of the forest that once grew, and 2) the government would then reimburse your shareholders more than amply, I urge that you join in supporting a 90,000 acre park at Redwood Creek.

Future generations will thank you even more than I do today.

Yours sincerely,

Name_____

Address_____

City_____State_____Zip_____

Also, write:

The President, Secretary of the Interior Stewart Udall, Your Senators and Congressman.

Urge them to support a 90,000 acre national park at Redwood Creek, in *this* session of Congress.

Plate 28. Reprinted by permission of the Sierra Club.

The President
The White House
Washington 25, D.C.

Mr. President: There is one great forest of redwoods left on earth; but the one you are trying to save isn't it.

...Meanwhile they are cutting down both of them.

THE lumber industry has already cut nearly two million acres of redwoods down to two possible sites for our much-talked-of Redwood National Park.

One of them—Redwood Creek—is magnificent still. The other—Mill Creek? Well, it is less unacceptable to the lumber companies.

Soon Congress will decide which of these to save from the saws—which in the meantime buzz on, despite a so-called moratorium on cutting.

It's an old story, Mr. President. In the 1920's there were four great forests left: 1) that along the Eel River and on the Bull Creek and the Dyerville Flats, 2) along the Klamath River, 3) along Redwood Creek, and 4) on the Smith River at Mill Creek.

Considering these as possible sites for *that* year's Redwood National Park, Madison Grant, a founder of the Save-the-Redwoods League, said: *"Each has its peculiar beauty and it is difficult to choose among them."* And so they didn't.

The lumber companies did, however:

I have just seen the rip-rapped banks of the Eel, and its slash- and gravel-choked side streams. I saw the high, steep slopes pitifully scarred and eroded by logging. I drove through the great groves left along the Eel—on a high-speed freeway that has effectively and forever ruined the integrity and peaceful beauty of this place.

I walked in the Rockefeller Forest, among the sky-scraping giants, and then saw the glacier of gravel up Bull Creek—the product of catastrophic logging and floods—moving inexorably and lethally toward them.

There is no longer a chance for a great Redwood National Park on the Eel River.

I have just seen the final throes in the destruction of a superlative landscape on the Klamath.

The waters of this river—only a short time ago among the most gorgeous in the northwest—are muddy and roiled and swollen with silt. The high hillsides through which they travel, once clothed in dark, magnificent forests, are now shorn and scraped bare. They are shucking off huge fans of topsoil in a classical display of erosion.

Side streams, long beloved of fishermen, are now gutted and filled with slash—their bright fish gone.

No one talks about a National Park on the Klamath any more.

A few exquisite fragments of the Smith River groves at Mill Creek still remain. They are already protected in California's Jedediah Smith and Del Norte Coast State Parks.

I walked through these in a few hours.

Outside these state parks less than 1,100 acres of superior old-growth redwoods remain in Mill Creek. More than half its forests have been logged.

The proposed park is girdled along the Smith River by summer homes, motels, gas stations and grocery stores. The heart of it has been completely cut out, and now boasts a splendid multi-million dollar industrial complex.

Hardly the stuff a great National Park is made of. Yet Mill Creek would cost us an estimated 60 million dollars.

Much of that would go to buy developed private property. The rest would add only 7,500 acres of virgin redwoods to the existing state parks. (Consider Olympic National Park: nearly 900,000 acres. That, indeed, is preserving the marvelous Douglas Fir forests of Washington for the enjoyment of people for all time. Can we seriously be talking about adding *only 7,500 virgin acres* to our present state parks to preserve the incomparable redwoods? And this for $60,000,000?)

Yet this is the site that the Secretary of the Interior has espoused on behalf of the Administration, because he "wanted to pick a park, not a fight." Not a fight with the lumber industry, anyway.

One last chance remains: Redwood Creek.

In 1920 Madison Grant called it "peculiarly adapted for a national park." In 1964, after fifteen months of study, National Park Service planners called it the finest large block of redwoods left, in terms of park values.

This was confirmed, at one time or another, by conservation groups throughout America. And it was re-confirmed *this year* by the Hammon, Jensen and Wallen report to the Secretary of the Interior.

I was four days exploring Redwood Creek and its drainages this trip. Even then I saw only a fraction of the area I and other Sierra Club members have been looking into for four years. For there are great reaches of it not yet penetrated by logging roads—a unique circumstance in what is left of the redwood country.

The last long stretches of virgin acres in all the redwood region are at Redwood Creek: 20 miles and 34,000 acres of them. And there are more than 10,000 acres of superior old-growth stands. *Ten times what is left at Mill Creek.*

The last virgin forests on both sides of a river are at Redwood Creek: over four miles of them, including the magnificent Emerald Mile.

In short, the last chance to preserve the entire ecological variety of the redwood species—from the ocean shore at Gold Bluffs Beach through inland stands of near rain-forest luxuriance to 3,000 foot high mountain ridges, is at Redwood Creek.

And it is here that the National Geographic Society discovered the tallest tree on earth—and where the second, third, fourth, sixth, eighth, ninth, and tenth tallest trees were subsequently discovered.

Clearly then the $60,000,000 mentioned us the price of a park at Mill Creek would buy far more at Redwood Creek. If indeed $60,000,000—the equivalent of but 2 days' work on federal highway construction projects—is all the money available.

$140,000,000—*but 3 more days of highway building*—would give us the great national park we ought to have.

Meanwhile they are cutting it down. The area the National Park Service recommended for preservation *in 1964*; that named at Senate hearings as the best possible Redwood National Park by 94% of those who favor any park at all; the subject of Senate and House Redwood National Park bills sponsored by 17 Senators° (S. 514) and 41 Congressmen°° (H.R. 2849, for example) is being cut down.

Mr. President, the Sierra Club and most of its 53,000 members, the 58 Congressmen listed below—and we believe *all* conservationists, were some of them not afraid that lumber interests had ruled it out already—are convinced that Redwood Creek is the only national park this wealthiest nation in history can *afford* to establish.

Speaking for them, and for future generations with every interest in the creation of the park—but no voice in it—I urge you to reconsider the site of the Administration's proposed Redwood National Park, while there is still time.

Yours sincerely,

Edgar Wayburn, President
Sierra Club, Mills Tower, San Francisco

P.S. to other readers. *Your* letters, giving the President and the following Congressmen your opinion in the Redwood National Park crisis, could just do it.

Senator Henry M. Jackson, Chairman
Committee on Interior and Insular Affairs
Senate Office Building, Washington 25, D.C.

Members:
Clinton P. Anderson, New Mexico
Alan Bible, Nevada
Frank Church, Idaho
Ernest Gruening, Alaska
Frank E. Moss, Utah
Quentin N. Burdick, North Dakota
Carl Hayden, Arizona
George S. McGovern, South Dakota
Gaylord Nelson, Wisconsin
Lee Metcalf, Montana
Thomas H. Kuchel, California

Gordon Allott, Colorado
Len B. Jordan, Idaho
Paul J. Fannin, Arizona
Clifford P. Hansen, Wyoming
Mark O. Hatfield, Oregon

Representative Wayne Aspinall, Chairman
House Committee on Interior and Insular Affairs
House Office Building, Washington 25, D.C.

Members:
John P. Saylor, Pennsylvania
James A. Haley, Florida
Ed Edmondson, Oklahoma

Walter S. Baring, Nevada
Roy A. Taylor, North Carolina
Harold T. Johnson, California
Hugh L. Carey, New York
Morris K. Udall, Arizona
Phillip Burton, California
John V. Tunney, California
Thomas S. Foley, Washington
Richard C. White, Texas
Robert W. Kastenmeier, Wisconsin
James G. O'Hara, Michigan
William F. Ryan, New York
Patsy T. Mink, Hawaii
James Kee, West Virginia
Lloyd Meeds, Washington
Abraham Kazen, Texas

Santiago Polanco-Abreu, Puerto Rico
E. Y. Berry, South Dakota
Craig Hosmer, California
Joe Skubitz, Kansas
Laurence J. Burton, Utah
Rogers C. B. Morton, Maryland
Wendell Wyatt, Oregon
George V. Hansen, Idaho
Ed Reinecke, California
Theodore R. Kupferman, New York
John H. Kyl, Iowa
Sam Steiger, Arizona
Howard W. Pollock, Alaska
James A. McClure, Idaho

°Senators Lee Metcalf, Montana; Mike Mansfield, Montana; Quentin Burdick, North Dakota; Joseph S. Clark, Pennsylvania; Thomas J. Dodd, Connecticut; Ernest Gruening, Alaska; Daniel Inouye, Hawaii; Robert Kennedy, New York; Eugene McCarthy, Minnesota; Gale McGee, Wyoming; Walter Mondale, Minnesota; Gaylord Nelson, Wisconsin; Claiborne Pell, Rhode Island; Abraham Ribicoff, Connecticut; Joseph D. Tydings, Maryland; Ralph Yarborough, Texas; and Stephen Young, Ohio.
°°Messrs. Jeffrey Cohelan, California; John P. Saylor, Pennsylvania; William R. Anderson, Tennessee; Jonathan B. Bingham, New York; George E. Brown, Jr., California; John Conyers, Jr., Michigan; John G. Dow, New York; Don Edwards, California; Donald M. Fraser, Minnesota; Richard Fulton, Tennessee; Cornelius E. Gallagher, New Jersey; Henry Helstoski, New Jersey; Chet Holifield, California; Joseph E. Karth, Minnesota; Richard D. McCarthy, New York; Joseph G. Minish, New Jersey; William S. Moorhead, Pennsylvania; John E. Moss, California; Lucien N. Nedzi, Michigan; Barratt O'Hara, Illinois; James G. O'Hara, Michigan; Arnold Olsen, Montana; Richard L. Ottinger, New York; Claude Pepper, Florida; Joseph Y. Resnick, New York; Henry S. Reuss, Wisconsin; Peter W. Rodino, Jr., New Jersey; James H. Scheuer, New York; Frank Thompson, Jr., New Jersey; John V. Tunney, California; Lionel Van Deerlin, California; Jerome R. Waldie, California; Charles H. Wilson, California; Phillip Burton, California; Ogden Reid, New York; Thomas P. O'Neill, Jr., Massachusetts; Edward Boland, Massachusetts; Philip Philbin, Massachusetts; William D. Ford, Michigan; Dominick V. Daniels, New Jersey; and John D. Dingell, Michigan.

The Sierra Club, founded in 1892 by John Muir, is nonprofit, supported by people who, like Thoreau, believe "In wildness is the preservation of the world." The club's program is nationwide, includes wilderness trips, books and films—as well as such efforts as this to protect the remnant of wilderness of the Americas. There are now twenty chapters, branch offices in New York (Biltmore Hotel), Washington (Dupont Circle Building), Los Angeles (Auditorium Building), Albuquerque, Seattle, and main office in San Francisco.

Edgar Wayburn, President
Sierra Club, Mills Tower, San Francisco

☐ I have sent the letters.

☐ Please tell me what else I can do.

☐ Here is a donation of $_____ to continue your effort to keep the public informed. (I understand that you can't promise this will be tax-deductible.)

☐ Send me "The Last Redwoods," which tells the complete story of the opportunity as well as the destruction in the Redwoods. ($17.50)

☐ I would like to be a member of the Sierra Club. Enclosed is $14.00 for entrance and first year's dues.

Name _____

Address _____

City _____ State _____ Zip _____

Plate 29. Reprinted by permission of the Sierra Club.

Why I am going to: 1) Wear a black tie; 2) Drive with my lights on in broad daylight; & 3) Keep it up until this war is stopped.

I AM FED UP with feeling hog-tied.

It is a year and a half until the next election. I cannot and will not wait that long to stand up and be counted. Also, this time I want my vote to be unmistakable. I thought I was voting against this war the last time. I won by a landslide; but so did the war.

I am not the sort of person who is comfortable about marching in demonstrations, carrying banners, or burning things. Still, I have got to do something, now.

So I am going to vote "No" today and each day from now on.

The way I am going to do it is this:

1) Every morning I am going to put on a black necktie.

2) Every time I drive in the daytime I am going to turn on my headlights.

Why these actions? Because they are the nearest thing to a vote that I can do now. They are personal commitments that only I can make; and they require conscious decision each time. ("Am I going to wear the black tie?" I am. "Shall I flick on the lights?" Yes.)

And they are visible actions. I stick my neck out when I do them. That's very important, for otherwise I'll just be muttering to myself the way I have been until today. This is assuming that other people will know what I am doing, and why. That's the reason for this ad; so *you'll* know. If you turn on your lights or wear a black tie then we'll both know. We may even get rid of that frustrated, all-alone feeling which may be our greatest enemy at the moment.

There is also this: a vote of this sort ought to be something anyone can do, once he decides. And it ought to be simple enough so that he *will* do it. And it should be decisive enough so that he feels it counts, but not so spectacular that he feels like a damn fool; because if he does he won't keep it up. (I mean, an orange tie with a blazing slogan, or a fluorescent sandwich board are all well and good, but they don't have much staying power. The Black Tie and Lights-On feel about right to me. The only way I can tell is that I can do them comfortably.)

I hope that others—the more the better, obviously—will take up the idea, but as individuals. I want to see the war stopped, but I think—I *know*—it's got to start with each man: Me. You. Him.

Can one man do such an enormous thing? One man always has. It is apparently hard for people to accept this simple fact.

Test: If you say to someone, "You can't fight City Hall," he'll nod in sage agreement even though the statement is poppycock. If there is any central fact in American history it is that one man *can* fight City Hall, or the State House—or the White House. That's what City Hall is there for, and how it got there in the first place. One man's action, one man's vote, one man's commitment.

Even so, will *commitment* stop the war?

Yes it will. Commitment is the first step. Until we take it we'll be like a man who has been in bed too long and lies there stewing about the problems he'll have to face once he is on his feet.

The solution is quite simple: First we've got to stand up.

———

Well, that's it. The only snag I can foresee is your forgetting to turn *off* the lights when you park in the daytime. (Slogan: "Lights On For Peace; Lights Off For Parking.")

I'm sorry that there doesn't seem to be a black tie equivalent for women. Maybe they can think of something else. Lysistrata did.

———

Something good will happen immediately: We'll start to shake off the bleakness that comes from not being able to do anything except feel mute horror. Maybe we'll even be able to read the whole newspaper again; statistics, pictures, and all.

Kent Bach
16 Irving Avenue
Atherton, California

P.S. *When I ran this last week in the New York Times, a lot of people asked about reprints to mail out; some wanted to run the ad elsewhere over their own names and asked for newspaper printing mats. Good, but since I'm only one man I hope you won't mind if I charge you my cost: $2.50 per hundred for reprints (9" x 12"); $2.50 each for the mats. (If you would like to contribute something to help pay for the ads, thank you.) K.B.*

Plate 30. Reprinted by permission of Sally Kemp.

the thing will be "We Have Been Offered $250 to Stop the War in Viet Nam."
It would be a rather interesting headline.)

On the somewhat lighter side there was *Scientific American.* They came
to us to find some new approach to promoting themselves as an advertising
medium. We concluded that the most fertile field in which to establish an
identity was in air travel, because that is the readiest access most people have
to the scientific age. Yet most people have never ridden in a plane. One area
in which they have had common experience, however, is plane design—making
paper airplanes. Everybody does it, but nobody knows how the others do it.
As a matter of fact, it was apparent to us that modern plane design, in the
revolutionary lines of the supersonic transport, is just now catching up with
the paper airplanes we used to make forty years ago.

Well now, one thing led to another, and Jerry Mander wrote a wonderful
ad announcing the whole thing. By the way, we ran a total of three ads for
them—in the *New York Times, New Yorker,* and *Travel Weekly*—and, oh
my, did they ever get things going.

Remember that story a few chapters back about the chap with acres of
hollyhocks? Well, once you get the idea for a paper airplane contest, you just
need to follow through, the way our hollyhock farmer did. Distinguished
judges. Four distinct competitive categories—duration aloft, distance flown,
aerobatics, and Origami—and appropriate prizes—a silver Leonardo for the
amateurs and a titanium one for the pros.

Well, there were over 11,000 entries from 28 countries. The *New York
Times* found it all entrancing, as did the *LA Times, Der Spiegel, Time, Newsweek,* our own dear *San Francisco Chronicle,* and the radio and TV networks.
American Airlines even supplied their passengers with entry blanks and paper
for creating designs in flight—the right environment and all that.

We ran a follow-up ad to kind of add a sense of closure, and, as you
probably know, the whole thing ended up as a best-selling book. Lest you
think we were overindulging ourselves, you'll also notice reference to *Scientific
American* readers' flying habits. Well, there's no doubt the airlines got *that*
message; which was, after all, the reason for the whole thing.

Another time, this little island of Anguilla, with about 6,000 people on
it, withdrew from a confederation in the Carribean with three islands. Now
Anguilla is called the ugly duckling of the Carribean. It's not a very pretty
place. There's nothing anybody wants there. So for 300, 400 years, nobody's
paid any attention to it. Because there's no way to make money out of it.
There's not enough water to grow big crops with, so what they've done is
to live on a subsistence level by fishing, doing a little truck gardening, making
ships, and working on other nearby islands. But the thing is, because of this,

[Scientific American Calls For Entries: Can It Be There's A Paper Plane Which Makes The SST 30 Years Obsolete?]

1st International Paper Airplane Competition

SCIENTIFIC AMERICAN primarily concerns itself with what Man is up to these days, and our readership is known for travelling more than that of any other magazine. So it is little wonder we have spent considerable time studying the two designs for the supersonic SST airplane recently announced by Boeing and Lockheed. (See Fig. 1 and Fig. 2.)

Soon we'll all be flying around in thin air at Mach 2.7, i.e., from New York to London in 150 minutes. Quite a prospect!

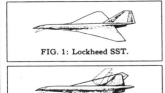

FIG. 1: Lockheed SST.

FIG. 2: Boeing SST.

Still, at the close of our inquiry there remained this nagging thought: Hadn't we seen these designs somewhere before?

Of course. Paper airplanes. Fig. 3 and Fig. 4 illustrate only the more classical paper plane designs, in use since the 1920's or so, having a minimum performance capability of 15 feet and four seconds.* (See over)

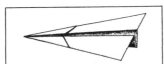

FIG. 3: Paper plane circa 1920, the classic paper plane. Smoothness of flight, grace.

FIG. 4: First developed among paper airplane designers in the 1930's. Known for spectacular darting motions. Note hooked nose.

We do not mean to question the men at Boeing and Lockheed, or their use of traditional forms. But it seems to us unjust that several million paper plane designers around the world are not also given their due, a credit which if it had been extended some years ago would have saved the pros quite some straining at the drawing boards.

Well anyway, with design having caught up with itself, we can now postulate that there is, right now, flying down some hallway or out of some moviehouse balcony in Brooklyn, the aircraft which will make the SST 30 years obsolete. No?

Consider this: Never since Leonardo da Vinci, the Patron Saint of paper airplanes, has such a wealth of flight research and experimentation remained untouched by cross-disciplinary study and publication. Paper airplane design has become one of those secret pleasures performed behind closed doors. Everybody does it, but nobody knows what anyone else has learned.

Many's the time we've spied a virtuoso paper plane turn the corner of the office hallway, or suddenly rise up over

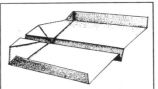

FIG. 5: Drawn from memory, this plane was last seen in 12th floor stairwell at 415 Madison Avenue. Do you know its designer? Where is he?

the desk, or on one occasion we'll never forget, veer first down the stairs to the left, and suddenly to the right, staying aloft 12 seconds in all. (See Fig. 5.)

But who is its designer? Is he a Board Chairman or a stock boy? And what has he done lately?

All right then. In the interests of filling this information gap, and in light of the possibility that the future of aeronautics may now be flying in a paper plane, we are hereby calling for entries to the 1st International Paper Airplane Competition.

RULES

1. Scientific American has created The Leonardo (see Fig. 6) to be winner's trophy in each of these four categories: a) duration aloft, b) distance flown, c) aerobatics, and d) Origami.

2. A silver Leonardo will go to winners not involved professionally in air travel, and a titanium Leonardo (the metal being used in the SST) to professional entrants, that is,

FIG. 6: The Leonardo.

people employed in the air travel business, people who build non-paper airplanes, and people who subscribe to Scientific American, because they fly so much.

3. We have left the page nearly blank so you would rip it out and fold at will. If this paper is not suitable to your particular design, feel at liberty to use your own paper of any size or description. (Rag content and water marks will not, however, have any bearing on the final decision.) Or, send for your free Official Entry Form Pad — reprints of this ad, padded, which you can stand on your desk, or hang near it, and with which you and your associates can make literally dozens of Official Entries.

4. You may enter as often as you like, being sure to include your *name, address, employer*, if any, and the *classes* in which you would like your entry to qualify.

5. Send your entry to us, somehow, at this address: Scientific American, Airplane Design Dept., 415 Madison Ave., New York 10017, postmarked by January 16, 1967. On January 21 all entries will be test-flown down our hallways by a panel of distinguished judges whose identity we'll announce at a later date (so as not to influence anyone's design).

6. Except that we will publish scale drawings of the winning designs, all other rights to same remain reserved to the designer. We, however, will do our bit towards assuring immediate production. Thank you.

---

*(In paper plane circles, of course, a *better* time is a *longer* time. If a plane can stay aloft, floating on the air as it were, for 15 seconds, *that* is a virtue, as indeed it was for the Bros. Wright. One would assume that today's commercial designers, who seek planes to get from here to there and *down* as quickly as possible, would not have been much interested in the study of paper planes, or the Bros. Wright. In light of the illustrations, our assumption appears to be wrong.)

Plate 31. Reprinted by permission of *Scientific American.*

(ad continued on back.)

1st International Paper Airplane Competition; A Last Backward Glance

Fig. 1. Six members of the Panel of Jurors at the 1st International Paper Airplane Competition shown during Final Flyoffs observing one of 43 finalists launched for their study and the press. The particular entry they are watching was entered in the distance category, and flew some 87 feet before crashing into a CBS camera, at one foot three inches above ground. It was reflown.

By now, most of you are acquainted with the names, performances and other details of the Final Flyoffs held Washington's Birthday Eve at the New York Hall of Science. (As one news account put it, the event "drew international press coverage not seen since the visit of Pope Paul.")

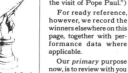

Fig. 2. The Leonardo. Proud possession of 7 winners whose paper planes were judged best of 11,851 entries.

For ready reference, however, we record the winners elsewhere on this page, together with performance data where applicable.

Our *primary* purpose now, is to review with you what we have learned from this experiment.

This much *is* certain. At long last the hitherto uncelebrated and uncatalogued achievements of aircraft design's "underground" have had their day in the sky.

And, there's this: A mere eight weeks after our competition was formally announced the long lost notebooks of Leonardo da Vinci, the Patron

Fig. 3. Two pages of drawings by Leonardo da Vinci, Patron Saint of Paper Airplanes, discovered eight weeks after competition was announced. This development alone is said to have made the entire project worthwhile.

Saint of Paper Airplanes, whose name graces our winner's trophy (see Fig. 2 and Fig. 3), were suddenly discovered.

If no further benefit accrued to science during this project, would not this discovery be ample?

But, going on....

One of our distinguished panel of jurors, Prof.

David Hazen of Princeton's Aeronautics Dept., when asked if indeed we *had* found the key to the SST of the year 2000 flying about in a paper airplane, stated categorically, "No, we have learned nothing new at all."

Berkeley Protest

Not wishing to excite controversy within academia, we must yet observe that another juror, Prof. Edmund Laitone of Berkeley protested, believing Prof. Hazen may have spoken hastily.

Fig. 4. Entry from Mr. P. W. Swift of Xerox Corp., considered by Prof. Edmund Laitone, Chairman of the Aeronautics Dept. at the Univ. of California, Berkeley, so interesting aerodynamically, as to warrant "serious additional study."

Several of the entries need further study, Prof. Laitone indicated, particularly one dart-like object distinguished by flight-perpendicular ring air foils (hoops) both forward and aft. (See Fig. 4.) Prof. Laitone felt "it raises important questions concerning an aspect of aerodynamics that has had virtually no study."

"I would like to know," he added, "exactly what the optimum diameter-length ratio for cylindrical lifting surfaces would be at various Mach and Reynolds numbers? We may find it demonstrates lift characteristics and stability potentials applicable to *both* supersonic and subsonic speeds."

An exciting prospect to be sure.

And now on to the statistical data.

U. S. Government

In all, 5,144 people entered 11,851 airplanes. They came from 28 countries including Liberia and Switzerland, though the largest number of foreign entries were from Japan (some 750), mostly in origami categories. The U. S. government, while not admitting that it considered the winning of this competition vital to national interests, was represented by entries from 18 of its agencies.

Fig. 5. Actual size study of smallest entry. Entered in the distance category with instructions to drop straight down from upstretched hand. It was decided, however, that distance would be judged on horizontal rather than downward vertical, as that measure would be limited by the inherent size of the individual dropping it. Furthermore, entry was discovered to be made from foil, not paper.

The smallest entry received measured .08 x .00003 inches (see Fig. 5) submitted by the Space Particles and Field Dept. of Aerospace Corp. The largest entry was 11 feet. Entered in the distance flown category, it flew two times its length.

Dr. Sakoda

The most interesting statistic, we believe, is that against an estimated 5,000 entries from children, the seven winners were all grownups and between them have devoted 314 years to paper airplane design and experimentation. All seven are engaged in science and engineering, even the ori-

gami winner, Dr. James Sakoda, a professor of anthropology who specializes in computer programming.

Frederick Hooven, of Ford, whose flying wing (see Fig. 6) won in duration aloft, learned his aerodynamics as a student of Orville Wright's, using Mr. Wright's own wind tunnel for early testing.

And Capt. R. S. Barnaby, an aerobatics winner, was founder of the N. Y. Model Aero Club back in 1909.

England, 1934

Captain Barnaby presented us with the startling news that the very model that won him first place in our competition won him second place in a paper plane competition in England, 1934.

Does this suggest that aerodynamics has retrogressed over the years? It is hard to say since who knows *what* won first place in '34?

Fig. 6. Flying wing which won duration aloft category. It is shown here in stroboscopic illumination taken at 17 images per second.

You see, without continuously available data, we have merely our imaginations to guide us, which brings us to this special good news:

Commander Richard Schreder, another of our jury who is also national Soaring Champion, has suggested that the American Soaring Society will be pleased to keep our effort aloft, as it were, by sponsoring the 2nd International Paper Airplane Competition, a suggestion we heartily endorse.

For, even as a magazine whose readership is devoted to technological advance and for whom air travel is a way of daily life, we still remain convinced that there is a world of discovery, pleasure and satisfaction in all manner of subsonic activity, from the walking through forests to the flying of paper airplanes. Or as Capt. Lee Cermak, still another of our judges and pilot of the Goodyear blimp Mayflower put it:

"I don't care how much you fly, you won't ever see a jet stop, just to take a better look at the sharks."

Winners of the Leonardo

Duration aloft Nonprofessional*	Jerry A. Brinkman Assistant Sales Manager Globe Industries, Dayton, Ohio	9.9 seconds aloft	
Duration aloft Professional**	Frederick Hooven, Special Consultant to the General Manager, Ford Motor Co., Detroit	10.2 seconds aloft	
Distance flown Nonprofessional	Louis W. Schultz, Engineering Group Manager, Stewart Warner Corp., Oak Brook, Illinois	58 feet, 2 inches	
Distance flown Professional	Robert B. Meuser, Lawrence Radiation Lab., Univ. of California, Berkeley	91 feet, 6 inches (At this point, while still aloft entry hit rear wall of Hall of Science.)	
Aerobatics Nonprofessional	Edward L. Ralston, University of Illinois, (and Clark, Dietz & Associates, Consulting Engineers) Urbana, Illinois		
Aerobatics Professional	Capt. R. S. Barnaby, USN (Ret.), Exhibits Consultant to the Director, Science Museum, Franklin Institute, Philadelphia, Penn.		
Origami Nonprofessional	Prof. James Sakoda, Professor of Sociology and Anthropology, Brown University, Providence, Rhode Island		
Origami Professional	The judges did not consider that any entry in this category was worthy of The Leonardo.		

*"Nonprofessionals" were defined in our rules as those not involved professionally in air travel.

**"Professionals" were defined as "people employed in the air travel business, people who build non-paper airplanes, and people who subscribe to Scientific American, because they fly so much."

NOTE: All entries were pre-tested by students of the NASA Goddard Inst. of Space Studies who reported that entries performed considerably better in preliminary testing than in the finals. The reason for this was not nervousness before the judges, but rather that the TV lights created severe thermals invariably hazardous to paper plane flight.

Plate 32. Reprinted by permission of *Scientific American*.

because they don't have anything anybody wants—not enough to make other people greedy—they're one of the few self-sufficient places in the world. You can't starve them out.

Now these other two islands in this confederation are right next to one another, and they have a sugar cane economy. Anguilla is maybe fifty or sixty miles away, and it has nothing in common with them whatsoever. But the British Commonwealth just put them all together because they were the last bits they had left in that area.

Well, when they withdrew from this confederation, they said we're going to set up our own country and everybody said well of course, you can't do that. Nobody with 6,000 people can do it. But, of course, there was no reason why they couldn't. They were getting along and they were trading with people, and they had boats, schooners, sloops, sailing boats they made themselves, some of them very big—one of them is ninety feet long. But the British were very unhappy about this because they figured if this one island can get away with it, then they're going to have trouble all over the Carribean. Well, the fact was they already were having trouble all over the Carribean.

At that point I got involved. I don't know how I get into some of the things I get into. I do in this case, it was a friend of Barrows Mussey's. A professor Leopold Kohr at the University of Puerto Rico got interested in this island, so he asked me to come down. So I had a meeting in Puerto Rico with the president of the island, with an assistant to Vice President Humphrey of the United States and a couple of other people. And I said let's see what we can figure out. Well, we did an ad, probably the best I've ever written, we designed their currency, we stamped 10,000 coins for them, we made their stamps, letterheads, passports, flags, the lot. I hope I make a lot of money out of the advertising business next year to pay for all that. They had had a plebiscite two days before I had that meeting and the vote of the adults was something like 1,843 to 8 for independence.

I didn't do anything else for two months—it's very hard to make a country when you've never made one before. Right now I have my upstairs neighbor and his wife down there for three weeks. He's taking his vacation there. He's a television announcer. He's also an engineer putting up a radio station and just answering the mail that came out of this. We collected $25,000, but the interesting thing was that the ad ran in the *New York Times,* I think in the middle of August. At that time the British had a frigate off shore and were going to land a force of Royal Marines. After this ad appeared in the *New York Times* on a Monday morning we got a report from, I think it was, the editor of the *Daily Mail* in London, all of the opposition had taken up the cause. I told him we were wondering whether to run the ad also in the

(The Anguilla White Paper)

Is it "silly" that Anguilla does not want to become a nation of bus boys?

THE NEW YORK TIMES, in its editorial of August 7, described the Republic of Anguilla's desperate efforts to remain independent as "touching and silly."

With a pat on the head, the Times advised us to return to the awkward Federation of St. Kitts-Nevis-Anguilla, itself newly formed, from which we had withdrawn shortly after its arbitrary inception on February 27.

We say "arbitrary" because, as you can see from the map, Anguilla does not, even geographically, have much in common with the other two islands. St. Kitts and Nevis are right next door to one another and share a common one-crop, sugar cane, economy dominated by huge, foreign land holdings. Anguilla's land is owned by the islanders themselves; each family has its own little plot and lives off it. Why, then, did Britain lump us in with the other two islands? Because we were their last odd-parcel of real estate in the Caribbean; it's probably that simple. (The Times disregarded these basics, if it ever knew them.)

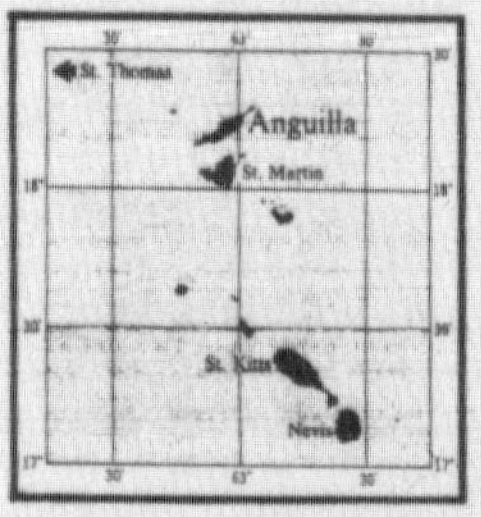

The Times then dismissed our aspirations to independence by pointing out that, "Anguilla has an area of only 35 square miles and a population of 6000. Its people subsist on agriculture and fishing and *lack such modern amenities as telephones*." (Italics ours.)

This is a terrible indictment in New York eyes, we suppose, but do you know what one Anguillian does when he wants to telephone another Anguillian? He walks up the road and talks to him. Primitive as this arrangement is, it is hardly grounds for justifying the Times' conclusion that Anguilla cannot hope to go it alone.

The fact is that we *have* gone it alone economically, socially, and politically for centuries. The British have neither bothered us, nor bothered about us. We have never been exploited, possibly because there has been nothing much to exploit.

UGLY DUCKLING

To understand this, you must know that Anguilla is referred to in guidebooks as "the ugly duckling of the Caribbean." Objectively that may be so, though to us Anguilla is beautiful because it is our homeland.

There is not enough water on the island for major crop cultivation, nor is it a "tropical paradise"; it is not the prettiest island in the West Indies. The highest point on Anguilla is but 200-and-some-odd feet. There used to be a lot of trees we are told, but these were burned for charcoal long ago. So we must bring in wood to build Anguilla's famous knife-like schooners and sloops.

OLDER THAN U.S.

Anguilla has been left to herself, with generations of the same people, since the 17th century. We are, therefore, a very old nation by any standards. It can even be argued that, as a distinct nation with a stable people, we are older than the United States.

Anguilla is only "new" in the sense that the New York Times had never heard of us before, nor have we had to assert ourselves recently. The last time we were threatened was 250 years ago when the French attempted an invasion with 600 men. They were thrown back by 60 of us, men whose names nearly all Anguillians still bear in direct descent.

There is also this, and it is all-important: Anguilla has proved its self-reliance. It can feed itself, and does. How else do you suppose it could have withstood a blockade—the impounding of our funds, and even our mail—plus the threat of siege by the St. Kitts Government for more than three months now?

"ERRATIC PROCEDURE"

Back to the Times editorial, there is more than a suggestion that Anguillians, though enthusiastic for freedom, are also undisciplined, unrealistic, and given to "erratic procedure." In a word: natives.

We would point out that, whatever the British failed to do on Anguilla, they did give us 300 years of grounding in democratic institutions; and they did establish schools. Anguilla's literacy rate is over 70%, by far the highest in these islands.

Which brings us to the Times's unfounded assertion that "there is no truly representative government to speak for the island." That is quite untrue. Anguilla is ruled by a duly elected Council. The premise for this statement was the supposition that Mr. Peter Adams, who has served as a member of the Council, "had a mandate to negotiate for Anguilla" with the British. This is not true either.

Mr. Adams was in the United States seeking help and recognition for us when he, already at the point of exhaustion, enplaned in the middle of the night for Barbados to meet with Great Britain's Minister for Commonwealth Affairs, Lord Shepherd. He flew there from San Francisco arriving after 15 hours of hard travel, with no luggage—only the clothes on his back.

UNREMITTING PRESSURE

It is impossible to know the pressures that were subsequently exerted on this man whom we know to be ordinarily unswerving and extraordinarily dedicated. But after a week, virtually incommunicado toward the end, he submitted to the following demand (in writing) by Lord Shepherd:

> "If you now reject the settlement which we regard as being very reasonable, I must say, in all seriousness, that the British Government cannot continue to countenance the present situation in Anguilla, which constitutes a threat to the stability of the whole Caribbean.
>
> "I shall therefore have to consult with the other Caribbean Governments as to the steps which shall have to be taken to deal with this serious situation."

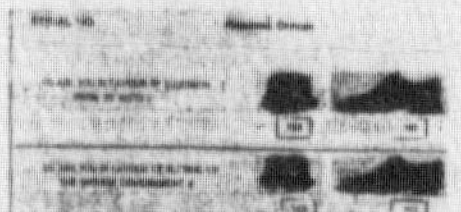

This "serious situation" was simply that Anguilla, after withdrawing from the embryo Federation in May, had, on July 11, held a plebiscite by secret ballot (above) to confirm its independence beyond question. To insure complete accuracy and believability to the world, this election was supervised, and the ballot count confirmed, by outsiders; correspondents, chiefly.

The returns were embarrassingly lopsided: 1813 For independence, 5 Against. It is therefore utterly impossible that Mr. Adams carried with him what the Times calls "a mandate to negotiate"; i.e., to give up.

BRITISH THREAT NOT EMPTY

Why did he succumb? Well, the British threat of force has seldom been an empty one. Also recall that the St. Kitts government's Prime Minister Bradshaw had, in addition to blocking our mail and our money, threatened—and continues to threaten—our small island with armed force; with no success thus far, though it has meant manning our beaches all night every night for months.

Meanwhile, a British frigate with a force of Royal Marines aboard, lies off our shores. One imagines that the least civil disturbance on Anguilla would serve as a pretext for landing these imposing troops. There is small likelihood of an *internally* induced incident of any kind.

To resume, the Barbados Agreement was immediately declared invalid by the Island Council and by the people themselves in mass meeting. A provisional head of state, Mr. Ronald Webster, was immediately acclaimed pending regular election.

One last insight into why the unfortunate and unauthorized Barbados Agreement calling for Anguilla's return to the St. Kitts-Nevis Federation was signed at all: We do not mean to suggest that melancholy measures were applied to gain assent, but the might and authority of Great Britain especially when embodied in one who is a high British official *and* a Lord—is not easily ignored after centuries of respect.

WHY WANT US NOW?

It occurs to us that one question may remain in American minds. If Anguilla is as we say it is, why would St. Kitts-Nevis, or the British for that matter, wish to bother with us now? Well, we *are* somewhat of an affront to what they would regard as fitting and proper; and we are a maddening challenge to Prime Minister Bradshaw's authority over his own troubled domain. The fact that unreachable Anguilla is not troubled by St. Kitts's inherited economic and political ills likely does nothing to allay his discontent; that is only human nature.

But there is another reason, quite new, for finding Anguilla desirable. Anguilla, though unassuming, does have an extremely pleasant climate, cool and dry...and magnificent, untouched beaches. We are "developable."

We could settle our financial distress today were we willing to sign any of the numerous offers we have received from land and resort developers. One company dangled $1,000,000 cash for gambling concessions. We turned it down flatly, despite the anguished realization that this amount of money would underwrite our development for years.

EVEN ONE GREAT HOTEL

Why did we turn these offers down? Because even one magnificent, Hiltonesque hotel on an island of 6000 people, *4000 of whom are youngsters*, would turn us into a nation of bus boys, waiters, and servants.

There is nothing wrong with service or hard physical work, you understand, but a whole *nation* of servants is unthinkable. In five years—or perhaps less—Anguillians would become as sullen, malcontent, and rootless as the rest of the Caribbean; or Harlem, as far as that goes.

Though we haven't mentioned it before, we are a nation of what you would call "Negroes." To us, we are simply Anguillians, because nobody has ever brought the subject up, and that's the way we intend to keep it. But you do see what we mean, don't you? Even one fine hotel and we would become "natives."

HOW LONG CAN WE RESIST?

That brings us up to now. As of this writing the British have not landed troops nor are we given to despair. We still hope for recognition from the United States, from the United Nations, from Great Britain, or from anyone. But if no one chooses to recognize us we shall continue, as we always have, to go it alone.

How long can we hold out? Indefinitely—even without recognition—but we can use temporary financial aid in the meantime.

Our needs are ridiculously small by any standards but our own. For example: our entire island budget—including schools (for those 4000 children)—comes to only $25,000 per month. All our island funds to the amount of $250,000 U.S. are impounded in St. Kitts, yet we have managed.

We have eased the currency shortage somewhat by the issuance of emergency coinage. These "Anguilla Liberty Dollars" are overstamped South American silver dollars, for the most part (see next column).

These coins are being redeemed by friends of Anguilla abroad, and we are putting into circulation the money they fetch.

...TO SURVIVE NOW

It is a little embarrassing for our government to ask you for financial aid on the basis of the unique collateral we have presented here. However, we have no doubt that we will survive this crisis—and do it without selling ourselves out—if we have enough money to survive *now*. We must seek assistance from individuals.

To show our gratitude, we should like to give you something in return, if only to prove that Anguilla is really here and thinking of you even as you think of us.

First off (to disprove the Times's allegation that we don't really have a "representative government"), we had better send you an autographed picture of the Island Council, a facsimile of the original handwritten version of our national anthem, and a small Anguillian flag (a replica of the one now flying over the airstrip). If you wish to help us with as much as $25.00, we'll also send you one of the Anguilla Liberty Dollars.

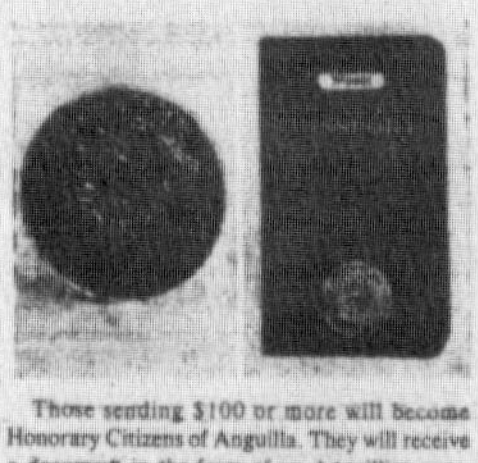

Those sending $100 or more will become Honorary Citizens of Anguilla. They will receive a document in the form of an Anguillian passport, identical to that which we are issuing to Anguillians, except that it will have an Anguillian Dollar inlaid as shown in the picture. While Americans should not expect to use this passport for foreign travel, it will be good for entering Anguilla. In fact, *only* holders of this passport will be able to visit Anguilla as guests. Why?

In the first place, we have only 30 guest rooms on the entire island at the moment, with no plans to expand. We would not think it either good or polite that so many visitors should be on the island at once that they couldn't at least have lunch with the President. (Besides, since we have such a small population, any more than a very few guests would automatically become "tourists"; we wouldn't want that, and neither would you.)

> **HOW TO SEND CONTRIBUTIONS TO ANGUILLA**
>
> *Since we are cut off from direct postal service—and to give you assurance that your money is safe—an account is being established at the Chase Manhattan Bank on nearby St. Thomas, U.S. Virgin Islands. So please make out your check to: THE ANGUILLA TRUST FUND. And address the letter to: The Anguilla Trust Fund, Chase Manhattan Bank, St. Thomas, U.S. Virgin Islands.*

Thank you for your kind attention during all these troubled weeks, and for hearing us out now, and for your generosity. We won't forget it, or you.

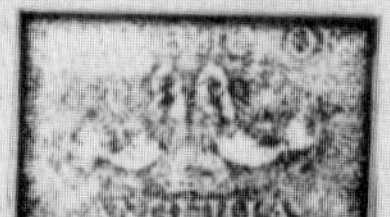

Ronald Webster
Chairman, The Anguilla Island Council

Plate 33. Anguilla Island.

London *Times* and he said don't worry about it, the government wouldn't even try to land a canoe on Anguilla now.

So what happened was that we somehow or other, with a single ad, I think, were very instrumental in obtaining their de facto independence. And although neither Great Britain or the United States is recognizing them, they have been given a de facto recognition to their postage—although they're not a member of the international postal union, you can mail letters out of there now. And both the United States and Great Britain gave approval to establishment of a trust fund in the U.S. Virgin Islands. And so in effect they have recognized them and that's all the recognition they need.

I mention this because I think that we don't realize what a powerful weapon we have in advertising and how much you can do with very little money. This ad in the *New York Times* and in the *Herald Tribune* in Europe together cost $10,000. Well, to do that much with just one ad, and really to do it that inexpensively, is something. I think it's a very good thing for an advertising man to do this type of thing and to do it within his own skill. I rather object to leading a split life. Life is too short to keep two sets of books. And I think it's very good to be able to exercise our political, our public sentiments in this fashion by our own skills. I know it works, and that's why I'm pleased to show you some of the things we've done.

Chapter 19

"Tell Me, Doctor, Will I Be Active Right Up to the Last?"

Our society views dying as being in questionable taste despite the fact that ten out of ten still do it. Perhaps it is part of our emphasis on eternal youthfulness as opposed to maturity. The life-span expands, and we have chosen to put the stretch on the early part. We apparently like to think of ourselves as being young or youngish right up to the moment when we proceed with bouncy step to retirement communities, there to live on forever in spry clusters of ranch-style death houses.

The word "death" is almost never employed nowadays except as a legal term or for intentional shock. I note the increasing use of "passed on," a usage confined until recently to Christian Scientists and others who deny death categorically.

It is therefore not surprising that our funerals are no longer scenes of terrible public grief, nor are there purging wakes, celebrated from the dawn of history, to confirm that we are still alive. Overt performance of death rituals is not considered good form unless televised nationwide. But this, too, has diminished returns. Over the years from J. F. Kennedy to Eisenhower we have seen that a TV formula can turn even death into a bore.

This refusal to recognize a threatening phenomenon, or even to utter its name lest it gain power over you, is magical thinking of a primitive order. One of the choicer recent examples is the substitution in many newspaper

Originally appeared in the *Atlantic Monthly*, September 1969, pp. 55–57.

horoscopes of "Moon Children" for the zodiac sign Cancer. A sardonic friend of mine was recently cornered at a cocktail party by one of those horoscope-spouting sibyls. He was asked, "How did your mother go?" He replied, "She was taken by Moon Children"; thus passing on two birds with one stone.

The price we pay for this pastel-washed denial of the only inevitable experience of life may be higher than we know. Our abnegation, as a people, of death may be the chief reason we seem to get so little genuine joy out of everyday life. For when life stretches out indefinitely, world without end, there is no yardstick for momentary pleasures, and passing pains are blown up out of all proportion.

One might say that this never-never thinking is a natural evolution of the Greco-Judeo-Christian ethic, but this is not supportable. The ancient Greeks did not hold with a personal, defined afterlife, nor does Judaism even now. Christianity, since it does believe in a hereafter, necessarily recognizes life as a prerequisite. However, it is notable that the more specific a given religious society's acceptance of death as a finality, at least of life as we know it, the more importance its members are likely to assign both to funerals and to day-to-day living. Whatever else may be said of this mode of thought, it is apparently not boring. A modern Greek, a Spaniard, an Irishman-in-Ireland will still put on a funeral worth going to. At the same time their countries have the lowest suicide rates in the world and an enviable relish of dinky temporal joys.

As an aside, the ancient Egyptians, because of their notable death rituals, elaborate preparation of bodies, and staggering devotion to necropolises, are popularly supposed to have had a morbid preoccupation with dying, so that it hung over their entire lives like an immense pall.[1] I think, however, just the opposite must have been true: that the Egyptians, because they had death so well sorted out, must have led vigorous, rewarding, and even sunny lives. It is hard to imagine how a civilization could have lasted for all those thousands of years—much longer than anyone else's—unless life itself had been purposeful and worth the living.

In spite of my citing these national and cultural examples, I don't think that dying is or ever has been a mass phenomenon; it is something that each man ought to do for himself, without assigning a proxy. What a society can do is grant him permission to die so that he need think no more about it, but can go ahead and live until the time comes—staving it off as long as possible, of course. In America, we seem to walk around this subject entirely, so that with the passing of old-time religious sureties—and the stretching-out of life so that three score and ten is no longer a goal, but a mere norm—we simply do not know how to think about death at all. Nobody has given us permission to die, or to live, for that matter. So what we do is sort of happen until one day we sort of stop happening.

In our culture dying has a vocabulary, surely, but it is mostly expressed in figurative terms and by euphemistic rituals derived from popular art forms. Nature imitating art is no new thing but, thanks to mass communication, it is probably more pervasive today than at any other time in man's history. It extends to acts so commonplace that one would suppose they had always existed as they are. The matter of closing one's eyes when kissing, for example. I understand that it became social convention only with the birth of motion pictures. Some early director must have noticed that his actors looked funny kissing while staring at one another, so he told them to close their eyes. If you find this hard to believe, observe how small children as yet unimpressed by movie love scenes will kiss eyeball-to-eyeball. Seventy years ago presumably everybody did; at any rate, it was not considered bad manners to do so.

I had graphic proof of this conditioning-by-media one time when I was informed that I had contracted a fatal disease. "Contracted" seems a strange word to use in this connection; it sounds as though you have to sign up for it, with codicils, and all. Well, codicils is what I had, all right, terminal codicils, with maybe six months to live.

On the basis of this one experience I found out where doctors acquire their graveside manner. There were two of them in there to break the news, and from the first clearing of the throat it was pure *déjà vu*. It was uncanny. I knew exactly the words they were going to say, and I made the responses automatically.

Then it dawned on me why. They had picked it up the same place I had, at the knee of old Auntie Procter & Gamble. What we were enacting was an amberized sequence from an antique episode of Helen Trent or Young Dr. Kildare. Honest to God, I found myself saying at one point, "Tell me, Doctor, will I be active right up to the last?"

Not to keep you on tenterhooks, the deal was stalled off before the deadline. On that day, however, neither I nor the doctors suspected that the cavalry was going to gallop up waving a reprieve. I believed it was a moment cast in bronze; it still is: there is nothing like it.

I believed it, but had no intention of abiding by it, and began thinking how I could turn this disaster to an advantage. This quick reaction (the soap opera dialogue was still going on) was due to life-long conditioning, I suspect, for I have made a career out of the notion that if you are stuck with a lemon, make lemonade. Still, I recall that the part of one's brain that observes such things was surprised and even pleased at this unexpected burst of objective activity. It may have illustrated Bertrand Russell's thesis that "all unusual

200

energy is inspired by an unusual degree of vanity." But the line that passed through my thoughts just then was Samuel Johnson's, "Depend upon it, Sir, when a man knows he is to be hanged in a fortnight, it concentrates his mind wonderfully."

None of this prevented me from feeling perfectly happy. Bertrand Russell describes this sensation, though it sprang from an obverse experience, as I shall try to explain. He had been given up for dead (at about the age I was, fifty), but was making an unexpected recovery. He says: "Lying in my bed feeling that I was not going to die was surprisingly delightful. I had always imagined till then that I was fundamentally pessimistic and did not greatly value being alive. I discovered that in this I had been completely mistaken, and that life was infinitely sweet to me. . . . I have known ever since that at bottom I am glad to be alive. Most people, no doubt, always know this, but I did not."

I question the long-term endurance of this gladness-to-be-alive unless it is preceded and accompanied by an equally poignant revelation that one will die; whether soon or sometime is academic. I have found that the gratitude for life that follows mere escape from death, however vivid and narrow, is not likely to stick to one's ribs. I am sure you can confirm this from your own experience: in the glorious, shaken aftermath you swear never to worry about anything trivial again; you do, of course, usually within hours. On the other hand, it is possible to acquire and retain this bone-deep feeling of life *because* there is no reprieve, for one is alive now. Lord Russell, no doubt, has always known this; I did not.

Let me try to clarify this uncomplicated awareness by separating it from two other types of life-before-death recognition which, unlike the other, are familiar even to those who haven't experienced them personally—possibly because they are not usually private, but involve other people. Also, both are perversions of real life and are therefore more recognizable. The first occurs when the doctor assigns what John Steinbeck calls "one of those carefully named difficulties which are the whispers of approaching age," and with it a lecture that ends, "slow down." You know that you're going to die, but it doesn't make you feel more alive. You do cut down, but these diminutions of activity are not limitations which concentrate energy, but are truncations of manhood. It is, in fact, a reversion to babyhood, and is encouraged by others, especially wives. It is all extremely comfortable, for "who," Steinbeck asks, "doesn't like to be a center for concern? A kind of second childhood falls on so many men. They trade their violence for the promise of a small increase of life span."

The above is from *Travels With Charley,* and was the reason he took the trip. "I did not want to surrender fierceness for a small gain in yardage. My wife married a man; I saw no reason why she should inherit a baby. And in my own life I am not willing to trade quality for quantity." This was no mere retroactive dress-up. And he was complimentary enough to assume the same attitude in others. When I told him of my own prognosis, he looked at me gravely and said, "If you tell your friends you're going to die in six months you'd better do it or they'll be pissed off at you."

The second variety of death recognition to be sorted out from the above is, in fact, a ghastly parody of it. Flat acceptance that one is going to die does constitute a proof of one's own uniqueness as a man distinct from others; is not unpleasant, even heady; and lends immediacy and importance to matters that were routine before. But what I am talking about is a perversion, a monstrous contained exultation. It is manifested in certain daredevils, paranoid psychopaths who, after nebbish lives, suddenly feel themselves invulnerable in the certain wooing of sweet death; or it can be the Götterdämmerung complex that gripped the Nazi mind. Such a delusion may arise because life appears so meaningless that some significance must be assigned to it, even if it is only death. In turn, death must be justified to remove it from nothingness and give it certain worth. The commonest of the resulting delusions is called martyrdom, for whatever cause. If this seems an unusually harsh judgment, recall that it is invariably on a volunteer basis. A drafted martyr is not a martyr, but a victim. Gibbon recounts that one of the more exhausting aspects of Roman soldiering was a shooing off of hordes of early Christian volunteers. I'm not sure that being men of goodwill had much to do with it at bottom. People to a man regard themselves as men of goodwill; even a Hitler, especially a Hitler, for how otherwise could he have justified such dreadful acts? And he, in the end, showed martyrdom, the only glorious form of suicide.

The key notion here, and the common thread in the two examples of death anticipation I have just cited, seems to be the scampering after certainty. In each instance the scamperer is metamorphosed into a subnormal or abnormal creature. The trick, it seems to me, lies in the opposite direction. Bertrand Russell, again, states it well: "Uncertainty, in the presence of vivid hopes and fears, is painful, but must be endured if we wish to live without the support of comforting fairy tales." He proposes as an ideal, "to live without certainty, and yet without being paralyzed by hesitation," and suggests that this admirable state may be attained through the study of philosophy. When I first read these words many years ago, I thought them the noblest view of man I had ever seen, but thought it probably unrealizable except through the toughest self-discipline. I have since found, to my surprise, that it is attainable and that whatever portion one gets through discipline or logic is subject to backslide without notice, for it is a very fugitive state of mind. It is something like an account I once read of a game Tolstoy and his little chums used to play at Yasna Polyana: they would sit around the nursery trying not to think about the Great Bear who sits on top of the North Pole. They found this difficult.

If there is any doubt that to learn to live without certainty is a worthwhile aim, it's not as though we had any choice about it: it's another of those ten-out-of-ten things. And the problem is fiercer in our age than in any which has preceded it. The basic reasons for this, I think, are neither as confused nor hopeless as we are led to believe. They are really quite simple, but, nevertheless, have never existed before in the history of man. I shall get around to them in a minute. . . .

In a postscript, the *Atlantic* editor wrote:

Howard Gossage, an advertising and propaganda genius and an irrepressible wit, died on July 9, 1969, a few days after having written this essay for the *Atlantic*. Stricken with leukemia, he was given six months to live, and was reprieved for a while when the disease appeared to be arrested. A man of warm friendships and good causes, he devoted himself to both until the day of his death. Said one of his closest friends, Dr. Gerald Feigen: "He mitigated our discomfort in having to face the finality of death; he did not for an instant reveal an envy of the living; he did not bemoan his fate. . . . Just as he believed it possible to live, he showed us it is possible to die."

NOTE

1. As I write this it occurs to me that "pall" cannot possibly mean coffin, as in "pallbearer." Checking the dictionary, I find this to be so: the pall is a cloth, usually black, purple, or white velvet, lofted over the coffin by six attendants. So, whatever those men carrying the box are, they are not pallbearers.

Bibliography

WORKS BY HOWARD LUCK GOSSAGE

1959   "Is Advertising a Dinosaur?" Speech to the San Francisco Junior Advertising Club, January 8.

1959   "Where Are You When the Paper Is Blank?" Speech to the San Francisco Magazine Representatives Club, February 17.

1960   "The Easy Chair—How to Look at Billboards," *Harper's Magazine* (February).

1961   "The Golden Twig—Black, White, and Pango Peach Magic in Advertising," *Harper's Magazine* (March).

1963   "How to Want to Do Better at Advertising," *Penn State Journalist* (January).

1965   "The Fictitious Freedom of the Press," *Ramparts* (August).

1966   "Understanding Marshall McLuhan," *Ramparts* (April).

1967   "Creativity Comes Best from 'Extra-Environmental Man,' Not Stuck with Past, Says Gossage," *Advertising Age* (March 6).

1969   "If You're Stuck with a Lemon, Make Lemonade," *Advertising Age* (February 3).

1969   "Advertising Has Tremendous (Unwanted) Economic Power and Here Are Things It Should Do About It," *Advertising Age* (May 5).

1969   "Freedom of the Press . . . Is There Such a Thing?" *Media/Scope* (May).

1969 "Tell Me, Doctor, Will I Be Active Right Up to the Last?" *Atlantic Monthly* (September).

WORKS ABOUT HOWARD LUCK GOSSAGE

1959 "Advertising—The Kooksters," *Time* (October 26).

1960 "They Write Ad Conversations," *Printers Ink* (August 5).

1963 "Mavericks on Madison Avenue," *Saturday Review* (December 14).

1965 "8 Great Tomatoes Man to Speak on Advertising," *PSU Daily Collegian* (May 27).

1965 Mathe, J. "Gossage Sees Life Through Pop Ads," *PSU Daily Collegian* (May 28).

1966 "Who 'Understands Media'? Gossage Does; Explains All," *Advertising Age* (May 9).

1966 "Scientific American Paper Plane Contest Lampoons Super-Jet," *Advertising Age* (December 19).

1967 "The Adman Who Plays with Paper Airplanes," *Business Week* (February 11).

1967 "Gossage Forms New Agency for Placement of Ads," *Advertising Age* (July 10).

1968 Cundall, A. W. "The Medium Is the Gossage," *Western Advertising* (January 10).

1969 "Advertisers Are Killing or Altering Media, Heedless of Public: Gossage," *Advertising Age* (February 3).

1969 "Ach! Gossagism Blitzes Germans," *Advertising Age* (March 24).

1969 "Gossage on Media," *Media/Scope* (May).

1969 Caen, Herb. "A Singular Man," *San Francisco Chronicle* (July 10).

1969 "Howard Gossage, Top Ad Man, Dies," *New York Times* (July 10).

1969 "Howard Gossage, Maverick of Ad World, Dies at 51," *Advertising Age* (July 14).

1969 "Gossagisms: Sometimes Funny, Sometimes Poignant—Always Disturbingly Trenchant," *Advertising Age* (July 14).

1969 "Howard Luck Gossage," Transition, *Newsweek* (July 21).

1969 Stermer, Dugald. "Advertising Is No Business for a Grown Man," *Ramparts* (September).

Is There Any Hope for Advertising?

1970   "Gossage Memory Honored in Copy Hall of Fame," *Advertising Age* (March 30).

1973   Hinckle, Warren. *If You Have a Lemon, Make Lemonade* (New York: G. P. Putnam's Sons).

1974   Hinckle, Warren. "The Adman Who Hated Advertising," *Atlantic Monthly* (March).

Index

A PROLOGUE...

ONLY ONCE IN A WHILE, a great talent appears on the scene, someone who creates original, beautiful, classic, joyful and wonderful things. Marget Larsen was one of those people.

The small sampling of her work, shown in the following article, speaks more eloquently than anything I might say.

The article was written by Bob Freeman. Actually, it is an abridgement from three major chapters of a book he is writing about his life and career. It is a colorful one, and almost thirty years were spent as a partner in life as well as creative enterprises with Marget.

Frequently mentioned here, and the subject of another chapter in Freeman's book, is an extraordinary man who figured prominently in both of their careers, Howard Luck Gossage. Howard was an original thinker who also worked in advertising, writing some of the most unusual but effective copy I have ever read. And, under Marget's deft touch, it was presented with beautiful, often classic typography.

They functioned under several agency names, Weiner & Gossage, Freeman & Gossage, and Freeman, Mander & Gossage. All of the principals carried the title of president, for the simple reason the firm was too small to have vice presidents.

Freeman's position was art director/creative director, but *Examiner* columnist Cyra McFadden described the role as "genius keeper, without whom it would never have worked."

Once, Howard defined the operation as "A bunch of loners, huddled together for warmth."

They were selective in the accounts and projects they took on, and it had little to do with budget. Of importance was the nature of the product, or cause, and the media audience the advertising would be directed toward.

One year, they placed more advertising in *The New Yorker* than any other agency west of the Mississippi. Because of their high profile, the agency's size was consistently overestimated, even though the body count was only thirteen at its peak. One ad, written by Gossage and designed by Marget, in an image campaign for Eagle Shirtmakers, set an all-time record for coupon response to an ad in *The New Yorker*. Howard and Miller Harris wrote a best-selling book about the campaign, *Dear Miss Afflerbach* (the recipient of the coupons) with a subtitle of "The Postman Hardly Ever Rings 11,342 Times."

Luncheons at the agency were almost legendary. Among the many creative guests that often appeared there were John Steinbeck, Buckminster Fuller, Dr. Benjamin Spock, Tom Wolfe, Herb Caen, and Marshall McLuhan.

The Firehouse, referred to on a number of occasions in the article, housed this unique agency. It was a former firehouse. Marget located it and visualized it as a perfect location for their operation. She also found the city was going to put it up for bids. The agency got it, and converted the building into offices that were the last word in modern elegance.

—*Dick Coyne*

MARGET LARSEN

PHOTOGRAPH BY LEWIS LOWE

*The following article says there were no good
photographs of Marget. Until now. ❧ Lewis
Lowe took this slide during one of the agency's
"Strength Through Joy" journeys to Mexico. ❧
We are pleased to share it with you.*

MARGET LARSEN

BY ROBERT BREWSTER FREEMAN

BY CHANCE ONE DAY IN 1954, the art director of Joseph Magnin dropped in at the studio of Gordon Brusstar, the artist I'd commissioned to illustrate the Bank of Italy's (now America's) 50th Anniversary booklet. The main illustration was A.P. Giannini in 1904, banging his fist on the table and shouting to a fellow director of a little bank in the Flatiron Building on Columbus, "All right, I'll start a bank of my own!" Just for the hell of it Gordon had blown up the illustration and stuck it up on the wall. And he'd put my head where Giannini's was supposed to be.

His visitor just happened to spot it. "Who's *that?*"

Gordon told her.

Her curiosity aroused, she visited my studio on the pretext of borrowing a book. I had my feet up on the desk, and was talking into the squawk-box. When I finished, I turned around to see my visitor, took one look, a very long and searching look, and then literally slid to the floor. That one look determined the direction of the rest of my life!

Marget-Aagot Larsen was one of a rare species of humans that had been actually born in San Francisco; in fact she was second generation. Her mother Ragna (Norwegian) and her father George (Danish) were also San Francisco born. Her grandmother Aagot was born in Norway, but she gave birth to a son, Marget's Uncle Art, in a tent in Golden Gate Park. Guess when.

From an early age, Marget wanted to be an artist. Her art education was quite limited, fortunately. She didn't learn a lot of rules telling you what you can't do. She studied with Bob Howard, the sculptor, who was married to Adeline Kent, also a sculptor. And with a very creative and politically progressive jewelry designer named Margaret de Patta. And she learned a lot from Paul Klee, her idol, from his books.

After getting her first job, at I. Magnin, she took night courses at the California School of Fine Arts, and set such a killer schedule for herself that she contracted tuberculosis and spent the next couple of years recuperating in a sanitarium.

The series of promotional boxes that Marget designed for Christmas each year (her idea) had a major impact on Joseph Magnin sales. The group below was based on building blocks. When they were put together in the correct sequence, they formed a cube. At right is a series based on games. Many people made purchases just to get the gift boxes.

Her "For Sale" ad wound up on art directors' bulletin boards all over the country.

Marget pioneered in the development of clean color on newsprint with the first really successful color newspaper ads ever run. She also posed for this cosmetics ad.

Photograph by Lars Speyer

Meanwhile, Cyril Magnin had a good idea; to do the exact opposite of what the rest of his family had always done, namely to cater to the "old" wealthy establishment families. Cyril's idea was to go after the new post-war generation with smart and youthful styling at his store, Joseph Magnin. The rest of the family told him he was crazy, "They don't have any money. They can't afford quality merchandise!"

When smart, youthful and talented Marget Larsen showed up looking for a job, Cyril was smart enough, and lucky enough, to hire her on the spot as his art director, along with talented advertising manager Toni Harley and talented artist Betty Brader. The first thing the new art director did was to dream up, with Toni's help, a great promotional device. Every year she designed a series of Christmas boxes, each with a different theme (such as clocks you could wind up, musical instruments you could practically play, building blocks you could build things with and even games you could gamble with.) They were right on the money, having great appeal for the clientele Cyril was trying to reach.

"C," as they called him, was quick to see their promotional value. Although they cost much more to produce than any previous packaging, he readily allocated the money.

One year there was a Christmas slump. Bay Area department store sales were way down, all except Joseph Magnin's. Naturally the other merchants were eager to discover Cyril's secret weapon. At a meeting of department store heads, he gave full credit to the boxes. Then he told them about his very talented advertising department, and that his secret was to leave them alone and let them do their thing.

I was lucky enough to watch the advertising department in action on several occasions. It was really something to behold. About 10 a.m. the buyer would bring down the day's "merch." All three ladies would grab it and start kicking around ideas for an ad. Marget might have a hunch about a headline. Toni might suggest an illustration to Betty. Very soon Marget would start making a layout which she'd send over, along with Toni's copy, to their typographer, Bill Hoshiyama, who was standing by at Reardon & Krebs. (Marget had made sure J. Magnin ads took precedence over everything else in the shop.) When it came back she quickly made, with Betty's drawings, the camera-ready art for the ad and it went to the engraver who was also standing by. (Everything was letterpress and hot metal in those days.) The first time Cyril saw the miracle they'd wrought was when he opened up his *San Francisco Chronicle* the next morning.

Cyril was rewarded for this management style in 1955. I'd been made president of the San Francisco art director's club and commissioned a young designer, Walter Landor, newly arrived in town, to design a suitable medal for the outstanding client. Most really creative ads are controversial, and somebody had to stick his neck out to defend them and put up the money.

The first year it was awarded to Cyril Magnin, for hiring the very best people possible and for letting them have complete freedom.

About that time, Jim Hastings came out from Detroit looking for an art supervisor for Campbell-Ewald. I took the job, which entailed being in charge of a pride of art directors. I went around to meet my charges and over half of them had proofs of Marget's ads on their bulletin boards.

While in Detroit, I had Marget do some ads, not just for Chevrolet, but other accounts too. Not having modems then, we used AP and UPI to send roughs back and forth.

It didn't take me long to discover I couldn't stand the place. It escaped me how to escape, until a young account exec named Carl Ally suggested I could simply get myself canned, stuff my gear in the little DKW and freilauff west. So I did.

Back in San Francisco and driving up Montgomery Street, I happened to spot Howard Gossage, whom I'd worked with after WW2. I gave him a lift down to his office, and he offered me the use of a spare desk temporarily. After I'd made a few phone calls, he came in and told me I'd better keep using the desk. A fellow named Bill Walsh had arrived the night before to propose that Howard do an advertising campaign for Irish Whiskey.

The connection was Sean Lemass, newly elected Premier of Ireland, who'd just discovered that exporting whiskey had been prohibited after the war, supposedly to provide a lot of revenue locally from the sales tax. Lemass called his export expert, Walsh, then general manager of Coras Trachtala Teoranta (the Irish Export Board), and told him: "Get yourself

LEASING

Marget pushed design as far as it could go. Here's "US" simplified to the ultimate.

Right: Number 3 in the 1958 ad campaign for the Whiskey Distillers of Ireland, in which the agency's belief that an entertaining and interesting ad would be read allowed them to continue the copy from one week's ad in *The New Yorker* to an ad appearing the following week. The Pride and Profit badges had to be reprinted several times to meet the demand.

STAND UP & BE COUNTED!

ARE YOU PRIDE OR PROFIT?

[NUMBER III]

sides you'll probably be terribly anxious to receive your Pride Badge or your Profit Badge, one. For the benefit of you latecomers we 〔The Whiskey Distillers of Ireland〕 are referring to the very nice badges we are sending out from Dublin to all who write us here.

We unfortunately ran off the page last week and had to continue over. No harm done, we suppose. ✍ The badges, then, are as illustrated. "Profit" to be worn by those who glory in Irish Coffee and the money it sends flowing to Ireland. And a pretty thing it is, too, watching the dear sales curve course upwards thanks to the Profit Party's interesting taste. If bizarre. Not that we condemn, no, no, no. ✍ It's just that there are the others: the Prides; proud of the taste, proud of the altogether distinctive, burnished, but emphatic flavor of Irish Whiskey. They claim the subtlety is *quite drowned out* in Irish Coffee. Strong words! Strong feelings! Before we run out of space again perhaps we'd better get our coupon in. We are given to un-

Now this isn't to say that you must already be an all-outer for Irish Coffee or a practicing Irish Whiskey drinker to qualify as a Profit or Pride respectively. All we require is a willing heart and an open mind. Choose the side that appeals to you; state your allegiance and then justify it by deeds. If you change your mind

later write in and we'll send you the badge of whichever side you defected to. No recriminations, no sidelong glances, just understanding smiles is what you'll get from us. ✍ If you're a novice, though, this great, brilliant world of Irish Whiskey is likely to set you quite agog with its variousness. There are nine grand brands. It'll do no harm to list them 〔if you'll excuse us for a moment while we draw lots to see whose name shall go first〕: Murphy's, John Power, Old Bushmills, Tullamore Dew, Paddy, John Jameson, Gilbey's Crock O' Gold, John Locke, and Dunphy's Original Irish. Now . . .

P.O. Box 186
Dublin, Ireland   **[COUPON]**

Pride [ ] Profit [ ] *(indicate one)*

Please send me a badge so that all may say
"There goes a (PRIDE), (PROFIT) man."

Name_____

Address_____

City_____State_____Country_____

---

derstand by those who know that a coupon 〔rather than just saying to write in〕 boosts the response tremendously. We hope this is true; so much advice nowadays is simply terrible.

at once to America and publicize our excellent whiskey!"

Walsh had met an attractive redhead from San Francisco named Janet Livingstone. Before leaving Dublin he asked her whom he should get to do some ads. She remembered seeing an ad headlined "Be The First One On Your Block To Own A Kangaroo" with which a mad genius named Howard Gossage had put a little airline that nobody'd ever heard of (Qantas) on the map.

Walsh boarded the first plane for San Francisco, stopping in New York only long enough to have Hank Lucking, the New York liquor man, confirm his choice of agencies. Which he did, despite the fact that several big New York agencies had prepared very elaborate presentations to pitch for the account.

So I went to work for what was then Weiner & Gossage, and immediately involved Marget Larsen. Howard told us what his feelings were about Dublin, "An 18th Century Georgian city with a 19th Century population," and that these were to be long copy ads. He set up some limitations within which Marget could probably function better than anyone else. And surely Centaur, her favorite of all typefaces, was the best one she could have used for the classic ads we produced.

It seemed advisable for Howard to work in Ireland for a while. Marget and I decided we'd like to see Ireland, too. So we conned Walsh into bringing

---

I think these were the first sweatshirts ever to have portraits silk-screened on them. We'd unwittingly started what would soon be a major industry. The ad (reproduced here from a 35mm slide) for Rainier Ale, but really to sell the sweatshirts, ran in *The New Yorker*. Once, the entire Boston Symphony Orchestra pulled on the sweatshirts for Beethoven's birthday.

Later, Marget designed a full line of Picasso sportswear and a line of Picasso draperies.

[*Rainier Ale Strikes a Blow for Culture; a Public Service Advertisement*]

BE THE FIRST HIGHBROW IN YOUR NEIGHBORHOOD TO OWN A BEETHOVEN, BRAHMS, OR BACH SWEATSHIRT

BEETHOVEN BRAHMS J. S. BACH

us over to do a report on what was wrong with Shannon Airport, not too difficult an assignment then. Walsh had made arrangements for us to drive a tiny Hillman Minx to Dublin after we'd given Shannon the once-over. But he hadn't figured on the tidy little town of Ennis, hard by the airport. Marget took just one look at the place, plunked her drawing pad down on the sidewalk, stopping traffic. Three days later he phoned us from Dublin. He thought we'd been kidnapped. What would anyone do for three days in *Ennis?* So I told him, and I think he approved of her artistic endeavors.

After we finally made it to Dublin, we went to visit a ceramics works and a food processing plant. Also the famous Waterford plant, the only place to which Marget gave brownie points for design. Gossage had made a career out of never going through the plants. He didn't want his subjective impression of something to be distorted by the facts, so that chore was invariably left to Marget and me, and she adored doing it.

We were working on one of the series, "Behind The Green Curtain," for Premier Lemass: "You May Be The Missing Hereditary Chieftain of One of Ireland's Ancient Families." There were six million Irish in Ireland and over 22 million in America; and 229 Chieftains had "quite vanished." We paid a visit to Gerald Slevin, Chief Herald of Ireland, at Dublin Castle and he said he'd be glad to help. At his suggestion we went to Trinity College and arranged for the geneology students to handle the replies that came in, which would have been voluminous if the whole ad series hadn't been abruptly cancelled.

A black & white photograph of the Shandigaff restaurant. Marget and Barbara Stauffacher were the earliest designers of supergraphics.

Shandigaff menu. On the other side, the menu items were presented in beautiful typography.

SHANDYGAFF

Shandygaff is a Good Food Restaurant specializing in vegetarian dishes. Natural and organic restaurants were common 40 years ago, but it was not necessary to label them such. All food was fresh and raised naturally, and proprietors were concerned with the quality of the products served and the welfare of the customer. Unfortunately, this has changed, and many feel this philosophy is no longer economically feasible. We believe differently. Shandygaff is not a health food restaurant commonly thought of as preparing bland and tasteless products for sickly patrons. We are a natural foods restaurant — one that is concerned with serving our healthy, robust and vital friends the highest of taste experiences and sensual pleasure comparable to the finest gourmet restaurants. We hope to satisfy the most devoted hedonist. Since the terms "natural" and "organic" are ambiguous, we will use them to refer to (1) produce grown in fertile soil that is not treated with harmful chemicals and not sprayed with artificial pesticides; and (2) food products that have not been supplemented with chemicals, preservatives, artificial flavoring, or coloring agents. Thus they are nutritionally superior and let one taste the true flavor of food. Fruits and vegetables are fresh and prepared to order. Produce is organic whenever available. Breads are baked fresh daily from 100% natural ingredients. No chemicals, preservatives or artificial flavorings taint the natural whole wheat, honey and nuts used in the preparation. Honey is nature's oldest, purest sweetener, and a major source of energy, far superior to artificial and refined sugars (including the brown varieties). Our honey is strained (not filtered or boiled) to retain the grains, yeasts and enzymes so vital to its nutritional value. We serve homemade soy butter with bread. The soy bean is freshly ground and small amounts of garlic, onions, and lemons are added to provide vegetarian customers with one of the best sources of protein available. Fertile or natural eggs are utilized exclusively. The term "fertile" refers to the method by which the producing hen is fed and raised, i.e., fed with natural products and permitted the freedom of the yard to live and reproduce. The supermarket or commercial egg is produced from a hen that is fed with synthetics and hormones, and is bred in an artificial environment. All eggs contain cholesterol, but fertile eggs also contain lecithin, which is a natural emulsifier and counteracts cholesterol. Aside from the nutritional advantages, this natural farm egg has true flavor that is no longer commercially available. Certified raw milk and goat's milk are served and used exclusively in the preparation of every item on the Shandygaff menu. Tamari soy sauce is provided to enhance the flavor of vegetables, grains, etc. It is made from whole soy beans, aged in cedar kegs and all ingredients are organic. Certain grains are organic, and vary depending upon their availability and the cook's choice. Cracked and bulgar wheat, Chico San brown rice, oats and barley are some of the choices. Most desserts are baked on the premises, and we use only natural ingredients, such as fertile eggs, raw milk, organic honey, yogurt and natural cheese. We serve fish for non-vegetarian friends, delivered fresh daily in small quantities. The selection will depend upon the season and weather. Bottled spring water, free of polluted substances and chemicals, is used in our tea and coffee and is available for drinking. The house salad dressing consists of chives, parsley, safflower oil, white wine, vinegar and lemon. We ask you not to smoke in the dining room. The majority of our friends appreciate fresh air. We agree wholeheartedly. If you must smoke, and this is certainly your privilege, please do so behind the green door marked "ROOMS," where smoking facilities are provided. Our friend Fred Rohe of New Age Natural Food Store supplies us with many of our natural and organic products. If you like what you taste, feel and see, visit either of his stores, at 1326 9th Ave., San Francisco, or at 260 California Ave., Palo Alto. We feature steam beer. This product is naturally carbonated, stored in barrels, and is made with barley malts and hops, using no artificial ingredients.

Get High on the Beautiful Food and Eat According to the Seasons.

© 1971 Shandygaff (but never you mind; take the menu home if you like.) Design Marget Larsen / Photography George Dippel

But at least we got a brief stay at the Brown's in London out of it. We were fortunate in being able to get Diogenes (pen name used by the editor of *The Spectator*) to search diligently and find a rare reference book *Display of Heraldry* for us, dated 1660, which proved to be very helpful in picking up the trails of some of the vanished Irish Chieftains. While we were in London, Diogenes took us on a tour of Fleet Street, the literary and publishing part of the city. At St. Bride's Library, we found that they'd already added some of our Irish Whiskey ads to their permanent collection of the best typography from every part of the world. For Marget, a great tribute to her talent with type!

Back in Ireland, we discovered that our friend Mr. Walsh, without saying a word to us, had scheduled an evening for the newly formed Dublin Packaging Council. The announcements stated Marget Larsen, a packaging designer from America, would talk to them about packaging. Knowing that Marget was a very shy person who'd rather die than get up in front of a bunch of people and talk, I told her and Walsh that I'd do all the talking.

The publicity had brought out over 200 designers, complete with packages. After we were introduced I took the podium and started dishing out some blarney or other. At one point I started praising one of the packages. Marget couldn't stand it any longer. She walked over, took it from me, and ripped it asunder, design-wise. I quietly sneaked back to my seat. For the next two hours, she analyzed every one of the packages, telling them how she would have done them, praising some and damning others, even

Newspaper ad featuring her handsome wrapper design for Parisian sourdough French bread.

They offered to fly Marget to Detroit to pick up the National Truck Painting first prize award. She thanked them but said, "No thanks."

including several being done for our dear clients. At the end she got a proper Irish ovation.

Years later I ran into Bill Walsh. The first thing he said after "Hello" was: "Bob, they're still talking about that terrific dog and pony show Marget put on for the Packaging Council when you were in Ireland!"

Marget had an uncanny knack, developed more in her than in anyone I've ever known, of taking one quick look at a thing, anything, and with not a single moment's hesitation or meditation, disclosing what was wrong or right, with the design. Practically always, her answer was right on. She also had the "what if" instinct, the real nub of creativity in my opinion, to a greater degree than anyone I've ever known. To borrow from a *Vanity Fair* article dealing with Peggy Guggenheim "…she was free from dogmatic assumptions."

Here's an example: Once she was asked to do the graphics for the Cecil H. Green Graduate Library at Stanford. Our office was right across the street from the interiors architect. One day when she was very busy, one of the architects walked across the street to weep on her shoulder about a problem he'd been fighting for weeks: what to do with the card catalogue files (which were certainly one of the more essential parts of a library, to say the least).

This fellow moaned and groaned until she finally dropped what she was doing for exactly 14 seconds, drew four lines which intersected at the center making an eight pointed star. "What if you did *that?*"

The guy flipped out, raced back

She practically invented the fireplace taper packaging for Ted Van Dorn's Vandor Imports; also the long, skinny telephone number book.

DuPont chose several top designers for this promotion series, "Color on Colored Stock." She screened on both sides of colored tissue.

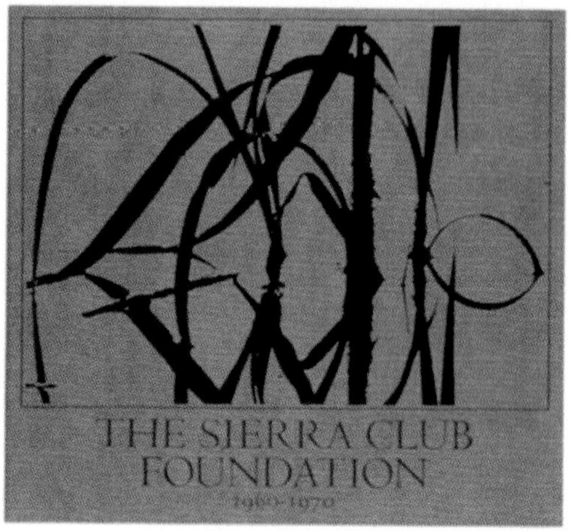

I think it's safe to say that Marget was the first to print an entire annual report on manilla wrapping paper.

Federal reaction to the "lobbying" in this newspaper ad, written by Jerry Mander and designed by Marget, forced David Brower to leave his position as executive secretary of the Sierra Club, but membership almost tripled due to widespread anger at the IRS position. Brower formed a new conservation organization, Friends of the Earth.

Right: She and Mander created this anti-war ad during the Vietnam war. Friends of the Earth has recently run a revised version of this ad to help avoid another war.

New Sierra Club publications advance this urgent idea: An international program, before it is too late, to preserve Earth as a "conservation district" within the Universe; a sort of...

"EARTH NATIONAL PARK"

I. The Moon, Mars, Saturn...nice places to visit, but you wouldn't want to live there.

ANY MOMENT NOW, Man will find himself hurtling around in an Outer Space so enormous that descriptions of its size only boggle the mind. (One attempt has put it this way: The size of the Earth is to the size of the known Universe as a germ is to our entire solar system.)

Yet, we already hear excited talk of locating, out there, a planet that duplicates the natural environment on Earth, i.e., trees, flowers, water, air, people; you get our meaning.

The fact is that if we do find such a duplicate Earth out there, it may be some thousands of years from today. Until then, the only place in the Universe that will feel like home is Earth, unless *your* idea of home life could include setting up house on space platforms, or the Moon or taking your evening walk with oxygen helmet and space suit.

We haven't got used to thinking about it this way yet, but, as Astronaut Borman pointed out—for us people, Earth is a kind of inhabitable oasis in an unimaginably vast desert.

Also, Earth is a strange sort of oasis, in that quite apart from providing us what we need to live—water, air, sustenance, companionship—this oasis actually *grew* us and every other life form. We are all related.

Darwin, during his famous Galapagos journey, found all life on Earth—from plankton to people—to be part of an incredibly complex interwoven and interdependent blanket spread around the globe. There is no loosening one thread in the blanket without changing the stresses on every other thread, or worse, unraveling it.

So then, if it is life on Earth that most of us are stuck with for the next little while, we had better consider the consequences of what has recently been going on here.

II. Toward a more Moon-like Earth.

There was not always enough oxygen to support the existence of Man. It wasn't until green plants and certain ocean plankton had evolved that the natural process was begun by which oxygen is maintained in the atmosphere: photosynthesis.

Man, one would think, has a stake in assuring that this process continues. Consider then, these bits of news:

—*In the U.S. alone, oxygen-producing greenery is being paved over at a rate of one million acres per year and the rate is increasing. Also, paving is contagious. Other countries are following suit.*

The oceans have become the dumping ground for as many as a half million substances, few of which are tested to see if the plankton we need can survive them.

—*New factories, autos, homes, and jet airplanes have incredibly increased the rate at which combustion takes place—i.e., at which oxygen is used and replaced in our atmosphere by carbon dioxide and carbon monoxide.*

The result is a kind of Russian roulette with the oxygen supply. Dr. Lamont C. Cole, ecologist, Cornell University, New York, has said this:

"When and if we reach the point where the rate of combustion exceeds the rate of photosynthesis, the oxygen content of the atmosphere will decrease. Indeed there is evidence that it may already have begun to decline around our largest cities."

There is a bright side: If we should continue what we're doing, overpopulation will cease to be a problem.

Sterile

In only 25 years, traces of DDT have found their way into the average American to the extent of eleven parts per million. They are also found in animals, birds, fish and recently, in notable quantity, in the fatty tissues of Antarctic penguins. (If you wonder about the consequences, similar pesticides have already made sterile a species of hawk and owl in England. Here is the way it works: insects eat sprayed plants, small birds eat them, and then big birds eat *them*. By that time, the insecticide has been concentrated many-fold and the big birds are in big trouble. Now, if we humans were in the habit of eating owls and hawks...)

Aside from the toxic effects on Man and other animals, pesticides like DDT and newer more voguish chemicals eliminate whole populations of certain bacteria and pest organisms.

However, and here is the shocker, *no one in the world knows, when we aim at a particular pest, which other organisms may be eliminated by ricochet*. Someone had better find out.

If some pesticide, herbicide, or defoliant should by inadvertence kill too many of the "nitrogen-fixing" organisms—those organisms that enable living things *to make use of* the nitrogen in the atmosphere—*then life on Earth could end.*

It is that dependent and fragile.

Rampant Technology

The Aswan High Dam was dreamed up to prevent the Nile from overflowing its banks as it had yearly throughout history. (It was thought such a great idea that countries vied for the honor of helping build it; the U.S. foremost among them.) The goals were electricity and year-round irrigation, thus greater productivity. No one, including the U.S., thought much about certain *side* effects, which may ultimately prove the most important:

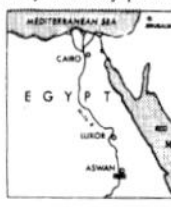

—Since the natural floods have been halted, life-giving nutrients that were formerly delivered to the land and the Mediterranean sea are now piling up in a reservoir above the dam, unusable.

As a result the Eastern Mediterranean sardine fishery is already doomed.

As for the land, the lack of nutrients, plus the waterlogging caused by old irrigation, plus salinization, *may actually decrease productivity*. Newly irrigated lands have the same fate in store.

—A particular snail has begun to thrive in the warm irrigation canals. The snail hosts a worm which causes schistosomiasis, a debilitating, often fatal disease. In one region around the dam, the incidence of this disease used to be 2%. It has now risen to 75%.

—At Aswan, we may also see repeated the awful developments at Kariba Dam, East Africa. At Kariba, rafts of hyacinths and reeds have spread over much of the reservoir's surface. It has been estimated that if this growth should cover just 10% of the reservoir at Aswan, the plants could actually transpire into the desert air enough water to stop *all* flow into the lower Nile.

Looking at the bright side again: In a few centuries, the dam will fill up with silt, and end its useful life. Then, the river will flow right over it, creating a huge, perhaps lovely, waterfall. Tourists will enjoy the view.

More Improvements

Engineers are improving things everywhere:

In Alaska, a $2 billion dam is proposed—to bring power to non-existent industry—which would flood a wilderness and nesting region the size of Lake Erie.

—In Brazil, engineers propose an Amazon dam that would flood a green area as big as Italy.

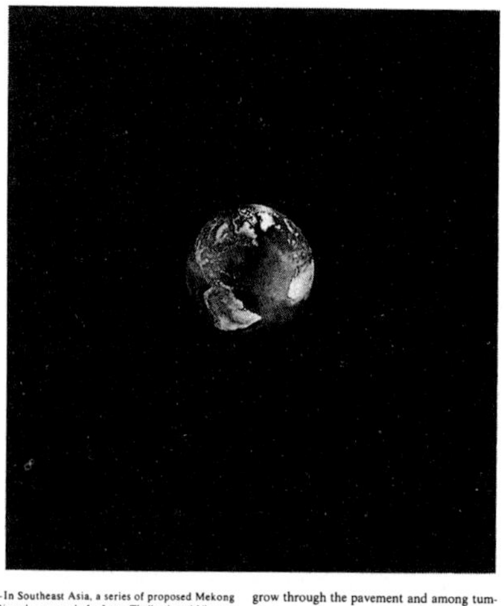

—In Southeast Asia, a series of proposed Mekong River dams may do for Laos, Thailand, and Vietnam what Aswan is doing for Egypt. *Every* country should be spared such improvements.

III. A wildlife preserve where *we* are the wildlife.

The speed with which our world is being altered is so rapid that there is no cataloguing it; it is everywhere... forests are gone, hillsides eroded and bulldozed, waters filled, and air and water polluted. The implicit assumption is that Man is the Master of Nature, and that losing a wild place or species or plant is of no great importance to us, and never mind the esthetics. But as we have shown, tinkering with the natural order of things can be a dangerous business, *for there is a need to think of the organic wholeness of nature, not man apart from that*. Man's vanity notwithstanding, he is irretrievably intertwined with everything on his planet and therefore must proceed with a degree of caution, until, at last, he has the option of actually leaving Earth.

If, before then, we should so alter our environment that we rid it of ingredients we need for life, then *we* will merely pass the way of other life forms that have become extinct for one reason or another. And, as humbling a thought as it may be, Nature might scarcely miss the people. Things might eventually get back into their own pattern, the natural order reviving. Plankton might evolve; oxygen might re-form in the atmosphere; grass might grow through the pavement and among tumbled columns as it has before.

With all this in mind, you may see that we, the 70,000 member Sierra Club, the groups we work with, and the critical publishing project you see outlined at right, are not so much proselytizing on behalf of Nature. In due course, Nature will take care of itself.

Our motives are more selfish, in fact. They are on behalf of our very own lives and the lives of our children who, we feel, have not only the right to live but also the right to live in a world that maintains the natural order enough to continue to feel like home.

We find therefore, that it is not tenable to confine our activities to local crises in the United States. The problems are everywhere and are doubling by the decade.

And so, we have embarked upon an antidotal new international publishing program to export the view that it is now the entire planet that must be viewed as a kind of conservation district within the Universe; a wildlife preserve of a sort, except we are the wildlife, together with all other life and environmental conditions that are necessary constituents of our survival and happiness.

If you wish to participate and support this approach, general means to do so are suggested at the right.

Thank you.

—David Brower, *Executive Director*
Sierra Club, Mills Tower
San Francisco, Calif. 94104
or
15 E. 53rd St., New York City

How You Can Further the Idea of "EARTH NATIONAL PARK"

1. Write Mr. Nixon.

A new administration is coming to Washington, and with it the greatest opportunity in history for, on the one hand, far-ranging conservation programs, or, on the other hand, incredible, irreversible, and perhaps disastrous destruction of the environment. We urge you therefore to write Mr. Nixon or forward this coupon to him.

MR. RICHARD M. NIXON, President Elect
The White House, Washington, D.C. 20020

Dear Mr. Nixon:

I respectfully urge that you publicly commit yourself and your administration to a program of world leadership in conservation thinking, to wit:

a) Considering the state of things, and the imminent dangers, issues relating to world conservation should no longer be relegated to afterthought status, but should rather be publicly cited as among the critical issues of our time, perhaps the most critical.

b) Nations should place high priority on the development of blueprints for the economics of peaceful stability. Exhortations for a "vigorous, growing economy" by international leaders must be placed in the context of an Earth of fixed size. Only so much growth is possible before the natural balance is destroyed and *all* growth with it.

c) Nations should each establish centers for the advanced study of ecosystems—looking into the science of how everything fits together.

d) Nations should have a "Plan for the Reinterpretation of Nature"... an educational program to help remind people about *natural* law and order.

e) Nations should cooperate in an immediate program for preserving the last of the Earth's irreplaceable wild areas within a sane kind of world heritage trust. They should also cooperate in *reclaiming* as many as possible of the places not *irretrievably* mauled. The science, technology, and genius of all countries will be needed, as will your leadership.

Thank you.

Name__________
Address__________
City_____ State_____ Zip_____

2. Write your congressmen.

The most effective way to present your views is in your own words by personal letter. Or in lieu of that, send your senators and representatives the following message. It is vital that we all be heard from in some fashion:

Dear Sir: I urge you to support the view that if our environment is to be preserved in anything like its natural state, then all development projects—national and international—must be studied for ecological implications, not merely engineering and economic implications. The dangers to the environment and to all life on Earth—from plants to people—are now too great to ignore. (Your name and address.)

3. Support those few organizations that are working toward the international goals stated herein.

There are many organizations working constantly to stop the degradation of the Earth's environment. *All* are important. We urge you to write them and involve yourself in their programs. For a list of these national and international organizations, with details on their aims, mark the appropriate box in the coupon at right.

The Sierra Club itself has both national and international programs. We are a non-profit, primarily volunteer organization, founded in 1892 by John Muir and devoted to Thoreau's thesis that "In wildness is the preservation of the world."

The Club currently has 70,000 members around the world, and has offices in San Francisco, Albuquerque, Seattle, Washington, D.C., Los Angeles, New York, and now, London. In addition to such efforts as this, promoting conservation causes through advertisements, publications and films, the club has an extensive program of outdoor activities and wilderness trips.

If you wish to join the club, learn more about activities, purchase books (a major means of conservation support), or make a donation, kindly use the coupon at right.

The Sierra Club Foundation (see coupon below) is a separate organization devoted solely to scientific, literary, and educational work. Contributions to the foundation are tax-deductible.

To: Edgar Wayburn, Treasurer
Sierra Club Foundation
Mills Tower, San Francisco, California 94104

Dear Sir:

I realize that a publishing project of the magnitude of the Earth's Wild Places (see right, above) will require a heavy capital investment if it is to serve its good purpose. I enclose, as a tax-deductible gift for this purpose, the sum of $_____.

Name__________
Address__________
City_____ State_____ Zip_____

SIERRA CLUB BOOKS

Sierra Club Exhibit Format publications have been called "the most beautiful books in the world" by several distinguished reviewers. They have received frequent honors for design and graphics, and also the 1964 Carey-Thomas Award, as "The outstanding achievement in creative publishing in the United States." (All the series is 10¼" by 13½", printed on high gloss paper, in gravure or full color lithography.)

International Series

The prologue publication in our anticipated international series on the Earth's Wild Places is called *Galapagos: The Flow of Wildness*. It is about the islands off the coast of Ecuador that revealed to Darwin, for the first time, an understanding of the flow of life.

Some one hundred books are planned in this series, all of them concerning Earth's still untouched places where there remains the possibility of learning about organic diversity, the genetic pool, the Earth's thin, miraculous biosphere—to learn enough about natural systems so that we may ultimately be able to educate even some benighted engineer friends and send them off to *good* works without fearing that they'll do us all in while they work.

Several organizations are cooperating in this series. The board of editors consists of representatives of four organizations in England, Switzerland and the United States, including the Sierra Club.

To: William Siri, Treasurer
Sierra Club
Mills Tower, San Francisco, Calif. 94104

☐ I would like to join the Sierra Club. Here is $14 to cover first year's admission and dues.

☐ Please send further information about the club's conservation activities and wilderness programs, as well as including a complete book catalog.

☐ Please forward a list of other organizations working toward similar goals.

☐ Here is my contribution of $_____ to help the work of the club. (As the IRS has ruled that the club's conservation program involves substantial legislative activity, dues and contributions are not deductible—unless the court or the Congress clarifies the law, or you make your check out to the Sierra Club Foundation, which does not involve itself in legislative activities. See lower coupon at left.)

☐ Please send the books I have checked, for which I remit $_____. (Note: Purchase and distribution of books is of major assistance to the club's conservation effort. Members or applicants are eligible for cash discounts if payment accompanies order: under $20, 15%; $21-100, 25%; $101-500, 33%; $501 and over, 40%.)

RECENT EXHIBIT FORMAT BOOKS

☐ *Galapagos: The Flow of Wildness.* Eliot Porter, Loren Eiseley, John Milton, Kenneth Brower, and others. Two-volume prologue to the international series, revealing the importance to man of the diversity of the earth's wild places. $45.

☐ *Central Park Country: A Tune Within Us.* By Mireille, Nancy, and Retta Johnston. $25.

☐ *Baja California and the Geography of Hope.* Eliot Porter and Joseph Wood Krutch. $25.

☐ *Everest: The West Ridge**. Thomas Hornbein, and photographs by American Everesters. $25.

☐ *Navajo Wildlands. "As Long as the Rivers Shall Run."* Philip Hyde, Stephen Jett. $25.

☐ *Kauai and the Parklands of Hawaii.* By Robert Wenkam. $25.

☐ *Glacier Bay: The Land and the Silence.* By Dave Bohn. $25.

☐ *"In Wildness Is the Preservation of the World."** By Eliot Porter. $25.

☐ *Gentle Wilderness: The Sierra Nevada**. Photographs by Richard Kauffman; text by John Muir. $25.

☐ *This Is the American Earth**, by Ansel Adams and Nancy Newhall. The first Exhibit Format book. "One of the great statements in the history of conservation." —Justice William O. Douglas. $15.

☐ *The Place No One Knew: Glen Canyon of the Colorado**. By Eliot Porter. $25.

☐ *Summer Island: Penobscot Country**. By Eliot Porter. $25.

☐ *Time and the River Flowing: Grand Canyon**. François Leydet, Philip Hyde, and others. $25.

☐ *Not Man Apart: Photographs of the Big Sur Coast.* Lines from Robinson Jeffers. $25.

AMONG 35 OTHER TITLES:

☐ *The Population Bomb**. By Paul Ehrlich. Every cause is a lost cause, Professor Ehrlich points out, unless we defuse this bomb. $5.95.

☐ *On the Loose.* Photographs and hand-lettered text by Terry and Renny Russell. Homage to the unadorned grandeur of the land—and to the spirit of freedom that loves it. The club's bestseller. Slip-cased. $6.95.

**All the books are available at book stores and those marked with an asterisk are available as Sierra Club-Ballantine paperbacks.*

Name__________
Address__________
City_____ State_____ Zip_____

across the street and put together one of the best card catalogue files ever devised for a library.

Gossage had a friend, Al Leavitt, who owned KSFR, a small, then classical, FM station. (Howard was a real music buff, by the way.) Leavitt was having financial problems and came over to see Howard late one Saturday. He said he was about to lose the station.

"Suppose I give you a check for thirteen weeks of commercials for Rainier Ale, bud-d-d-dy," (Howard had a slight speech impediment), "and I'll tell the client about it Monday. Will that d-do-o-o it?" That did it. After Al left, Howard got to thinking: "What the hell do you do on KSFR for a brewery?"

Let me mention here that Howard Gossage was a person with total recall.

I mean total. Remembering a *Peanuts* strip he'd seen a couple of years back in which Schroeder had said something about having a Beethoven sweatshirt, a light bulb lit up!

Over the weekend he saw his friend Herb Caen. On Monday morning, in Marin, I opened the *Chronicle* and read in Caen's column that Weiner & Gossage were about to issue Beethoven, Brahms and Bach sweatshirts. Sweatshirts? Beethoven? What kind of a crazy idea was this?

Marget and I blasted across the Golden Gate Bridge, stopping off at Mechanics Library long enough to find some engravings. Brahms was tough. He came along later and photographs of him were plentiful, but engravings were vary scarce.

Where do you buy sweatshirts in bulk? And what kind of ink or paint will stand being laundered? Who in the hell prints sweatshirts anyway? This was virgin territory no one had ever invaded!

Marget did a masterful job of the design and typography. And if you were to drive to the end of New Montgomery and turn up the alley past Taylor & Ng, you could see sweatshirts hanging out to dry at the Emerson Flag Company. With a few announcements on the air, we sold all of the original 600 we'd printed. So, consistent with our fat, dumb and happy methods, we decided to run one ad in the *Chronicle* and in *The New Yorker*. How many should we print this time? We were up in the hose tower trying to decide. Weiner wanted to print 10,000; but brother Howard insisted: "What in hell's the difference, let's go for broke and make it 20,000!"

I listened for a while, then quietly went downstairs and called GET (Government Employees Together) out on Sloat Boulevard, where I'd discovered an inexpensive source, and ordered 15,000 "athaletic greys" (as Howard called them), half "L"

for ladies, half "XL" for men. I hit the jackpot. It turned out to be the exact number the ad sold for $4 each, including postage.

It was obvious they were a real hot item, and that somebody'd peddle them retail, so why not us? We had a client with a national rag-biz sales organization, Eagle Shirtmakers of Quakertown, PA. So we formed a separate company called The Three B's, 50/50 with their CEO, S. Miller Harris. I sent him the screens, which he sent to some mill in the deep south. This time around we went first class and produced every size that anybody might ask for.

Ten thousand dozen sweatshirts later, some donkey knocked us off. I went back to Philadelphia to testify in court. Judge Luongo, after issuing a cease and desist order, was unable to impound the inventory because the guy's lawyer had somehow gotten hold of one of the original 600 that nobody had thought about copyrighting because it was such a nutty idea. The judge issued a ruling I'm not likely to forget. "If you publish one of anything without notice of copyright, it's in the public domain."

So we're all back in the Firehouse trying to figure how we can foil the future knocker-offers.

"Who's the world's greatest living artist?" asked Howard. Marget and I both said Picasso right away.

Howard's friend, Barnaby Conrad,

Symbol for the Stanford Graduate Library was developed from a design for the readers carrel.

For the Stanford Shopping Center, Marget overcame a problem of making a basically round mark work on long, narrow banners by having the emblem "continued on next flag."

Marget designed, and engineered, the locally famous Bagel Bag boxes for David's Deli.

was about to make a trip to the south of France. He was instructed to see Picasso and ask him about the possibility of our using some of his artwork.

Conrad, of course, never got within fifty miles of the old man, but he did find out that Picasso had an agent in this country, a French government agency with the initials SPADEM, that owned the rights of all French artists except Matisse and a couple of others. Don't ask me why. We quickly located the SPADEM man, who was in Montreal. With help from silk-screen expert Peter Girolami, Marget made up some super items using Pablo's artwork.

In Montreal we were armed with a contract written by Ed Huddleson. The highest royalty ever paid in the rag business up to that time was 5% (to Grandma Moses). After some haggling, and one call to Ed in San Francisco, we made the deal for 15%!

Somewhat elated, we prepared to proceed as we had with The Three B's; but Joe Weiner suggested going to see an old magazine rep buddy from San Francisco, Bob Lapham (recently retired as president of Conde Nast) who at that time was advertising manager of *Vogue*. He arranged for us to meet with the legendary Lady of the Hats, Jessica Daves, *Vogue's* editor, who flipped over the stuff Marget showed her.

"You pick the store you like, any store in New York, and I'll arrange to have the buyer see it. He or she will suggest a manufacturer. If they suggest it, the manufacturer will do it, believe me. And I think you also ought to do some draperies."

Marget promptly picked her favorite NY department store, Lord & Taylor. They picked White Stag in Portland for sweatshirts etc., and Bloomcraft in NY for the drapery line. Under

Marget's supervision, we produced a full line of apres-ski sportswear, later also a spring line, and a full line of draperies. They were certainly successful, and would have been much more so if the White Stag salesmen had ever heard of Picasso, which most of them hadn't.

A couple of other design triumphs of Marget's ought to be mentioned before we run out of space. For instance, the one she achieved for our little agency's chairman of the board, Henry Schoenfeld. Henry'd been a flat-mate of Howard's out on Green Street, and had started U.S. Leasing. He had also bought the Parisian Bakery, so we did some ads and Marget did a spectacular package (at cost) for Henry. The bread wrapper won practically every award going. Even so, a few days before it came out, Aldo Fontana, president of Parisian, called us to say we'd better forget the whole thing. His drivers had asked all of their customers whether they preferred the new package or the old one, the design of which had been thrown in with the purchase order by Zellerbach. He insisted that the majority of them liked the old bag better.

"Have faith, Aldo," said I.

Marget and I used to have lunch quite often at Frank Alioto's sidewalk crab stand down on the wharf. We had shown Frank the new bag and asked him how he liked it. "Leave it alone. Parisian's got the best bag in the business so why change it?" The day

She convinced the developers to alter a whole outside wall to accommodate her Cannery Star inspired by the old building's tie-rod washers.

A refreshingly original and friendly parking lot sign designed for the Cannery's parking.

One of the many wine labels and packages she designed for a number of California wineries.

the new one came out we went to see if Frank was still in the French bread business. There he was, in the middle of the street, waving the new bag in the air. "The tourists are buying it just to get the bag for Chrisesakes!"

Another design triumph was a much admired and much imitated format Marget worked out for a series of ecology ads for David Brower and Alvin Duskin. Dave, aided by Ed and Peggy Wayburn of the Sierra Club, Jerry Mander and Marget, really invented ecology during the sixties, with an assist from Stewart Udall in Washington.

If there's any person who should be called the John Muir of this generation, it would have to be David R. Brower. Uncompromising, energetic, ornery, he's done more than anyone else to stave off the vandalizing of our fragile planet.

Marget really *believed* in the ads she made for Dave.

Jerry Mander was one of the only two copywriters Howard ever allowed to stick around the Firehouse for any length of time. Jerry and Marget worked together like gangbusters. He wrote most of the ecology ads. Richard Stearns was the other writer and he wrote the other ecology ads.

In handling her various design projects, Marget was well aware of Gossage's Law Number X3J and one half: "Never take on a client unless it is one person only, and that person is in charge." At her first graphics meeting for the Stanford Shopping Center, she was confronted by sixteen people sitting around a table. She gritted her teeth: "All right, who's in charge here?" After some loud whispering, Jim Nelson replied, "I guess I am." Then she went around the table and asked each one what he was doing there. One guy piped up, "If this meeting's about color, I don't know why in hell I'm here. I'm color blind," and left.

Marget loved to design stuff, all sorts of innovative and intriguing stuff, and we frankly didn't know what to do with it. One day, we showed one of her items to Brentano's. This was a large "Calendrier" made with Pellerin prints from Epinal that she had collected, perforated and scored so you could build twelve buildings. They snapped it up and sold them very briskly at Christmastime.

A giftbiz agent asked, "What'll you have in your line this year?"

Line? Quick like a mouse we gathered up some of her left over Magnin giftwraps which Cyril was happy to donate, and a number of her other designs and formed a Freeman & Gossage division which Howard named "Intrinsics." After all, it made no sense for an agency to have an inventory of Saratoga Trunks. In the first year of Intrinsics, we grossed over $100 thousand.

I'm suddenly aware that I'm in the same predicament Howard was in with the Irish Whisky ad number 4. "We're almost out of page again; still, if we go to smaller type we may make it yet" (Marget's ploy). Rather

Packages Marget designed for Roger Horchow when he was sales manager for Neiman-Marcus.

Hyatt utilized her favorite fabric design for the interior decor of a hotel, walls and all.

Marget's beautifully designed snuff packages and snuffboxes are still selling very well.

Right: Intrinsics, a division of Freeman & Gossage, was formed to market some of the things Marget was constantly designing. The first item in the line was a "Calendrier" made with Pellerin prints from Epinal. You could assemble twelve different buildings. The "Phonet Chair," made of corrugated board, was shipped flat and, once assembled, could hold the weight of several people. Two of many desk calendars and books she designed. Gift papers and the detail of one titled "…and kisses." The picnic hamper, made of corrugated board, unfolds to make a circular picnic table top. The "Saratoga Trunk" design, made from a simple file box, was one of Intrinsics best sellers, reprinted seven times at 5,000 each rerun.

than go to smaller type, I'm going to list in condensed form some subjects which deserve more attention, but must be mentioned.

She'd never fooled around with fabrics until Peter Rocchia encouraged her and started Aagot/Rocchia Fabrics. He sprang for a splendiferous trip to Italy for us since the fabrics were printed near Lake Como.

Her finest work, in my opinion, was never seen by the public. This was her fine art drawings and paintings. I've thought about donating them to Art Center College for reference use. The Marget-Aagot Larsen Fund scholarship is there.

Her demise was caused by an MD, after removal of a colon tumor, allowing her to go unchecked for a year and a half. We almost saved her, but were too late. She was resigned to her fate, actually happy. Her sister Eleanor, a trained nurse, came up from Orange County to take care of her.

On November 11, 1984, she said, "El, do me a favor. Go upstairs and propose to Bob for me." We'd never bothered to get married. El made her look like a million and a Justice of the Peace performed a stunning ceremony in the cellar rock room we'd converted into a hospital. A week later she was gone.

Soon after buying the Marin house in 1959, we'd buried a small offering to Paul Klee on the very top of Mount Tamalpais, which we could see clearly in the beautiful view from our windows. That's where she wanted to be, and is, too. On November 11, 1986, I was hit by what they call "anniversary syndrome" and was completely dehydrated for seven days (I'm told the limit's eight) and spent four months in the hospital. I feel fine now, and more healthy and capable at 79½ than before.

Marget was camera shy. The only photo opportunity she'd allowed was by the fern trees in Golden Gate Park. Look right and see she was also muy simpatico to sunflowers.

So on our third anniversary I had Ponciano Chavez plant, from one gallon cans, seven (her favorite number) fern trees on the north side of a fifteen foot stone wall. Fern trees take several years to reach tree height. This A.M., I took their measure, 3½ feet tall in one month. Do you think Marget is making them grow faster?

In these few pages, I've tried to convey what it was like to live and work with this truly remarkable woman over a period of quite a few years. She was responsible for so many innovations, and was the very embodiment of "What if?" She, probably as much as any other, changed the look of advertising and graphics in the last generation. As a human being, she was, to me, without equal. Why her career had to be ended so soon is hard to understand. But isn't it great that she happened at all!

HOWARD

by Alice Lowe

He had a quality which the Irish call *Flaithiulach* (pronounced "Flahoolick"), a marvelous Gaelic word meaning *"princely exuberance, a generosity or lavishness of spirit,"* a term particularly apropos of advertising's flamboyant wizard.

Wizard? He was called *"The Socrates of San Francisco,"* but it wasn't just his philosophy – it was his *magic.* § For he not only conjured up quietly spectacular advertising campaigns with magical ease, but he had a dramatic appearance which fit the part perfectly.

How can I describe it?

A Perpetual Spotlight

It began with a mass of unruly gray hair that shot erratically in all directions as if cunningly miscombed by a witchy hairdresser. § Then there were those eyes – cavernous, gray-green – they'd glow with a fierce, smoky intensity when he became excited, or they'd instantly dim with listlessness when he was bored. The change occurred as easily as the flicking of a light switch.

A wide, expressive mouth, ready to break into a broad conspiratorial grin at the slightest provocation, betrayed an innate puckishness. § His laughter had a wild, joyous, ear-bursting ring about it, guaranteed to penetrate the uppermost reaches of any theater balcony.

An exceptionally pale, luminous complexion added a suggestion of mystery; it lit his lined, craggy face with a faint pearly sheen, as if some omnipotent Stage Manager provided Howard with a perpetual spotlight of his own.

Loose Won-Ton

He never thought of himself as handsome, though most people considered him strikingly so. § He would pull at the washboard fold of his cheek and say in a deprecatory manner, *"Look, this fits like a loose won-ton."* § Yet he was not ignorant of his effect upon others.

When his attention was called to a lock of hair which had tumbled over his forehead just as he was about to give a speech, he made no attempt to brush it back. § With beguiling roguishness, he confided in a whispered stammer, *"It's o-o-o. k., the ladies think it r-r-ro-man-tic."* Finally, in the middle of that face, was the nose – imperious, but saved from disdainful hauteur by an unexpectedly bashed-in tip. § His presence was startling.

Sally Kemp Gossage recalled the first time she saw him as he entered a fancy New York restaurant. *"Looking as though he was considering whether or not to buy it."*

A WIZARD, NOT A SAINT

Gossage was not without fault. He was, after all, merely a wizard, not a Saint. § He was obstinate. He had an explosive temper. He did as he pleased. § He behaved paradoxically: courtly in manner, he freely indulged in profanity; an autocrat, he continually urged others to speak up for themselves. § But this was overwhelmed by his redeeming qualities: a pungent wit, tremendously creative mind, delicious sense of humor, and most of all, an embracing love of mankind. § Maybe that was why we all loved Howard. § He loved us.

STATE OF TURMOIL

He was an Irish revolutionary who spent his life *"stirring up the mush."* He embroiled himself and others in a constant state of turmoil. § If he saw something which needed improvement, he pounced upon it, calling the attention of one and all to this less than perfect state of affairs, and urging immediate action. § Polite entreaty would not do; he had to rally everyone to the cause, berating those who were reluctant to get involved with a matter likely to upset the orderly pattern of their lives. § Whatever was done was carried off with gusto and abandon. § A favorite maxim was: *If it's worth doing, it's worth overdoing.*

He was a perfectionist who revised his copy endlessly, driving his production staff to desperation with last-minute changes. § It was a standing joke that someday Howard would take the ultimate step and change an ad *after* it ran. § He ignored their comments, laboring over every word with loving care, like a jeweler polishing and repolishing each gem.

His campaigns generated hundreds, sometimes thousands, of reader responses. § Howard would riffle through them eagerly. *"Listen to this,"* he would cry and read one aloud as he adjusted his wire-rimmed reading glasses. § His normally pale face flushed with unaccustomed pink and he would interrupt himself from time to time with a great burst of laughter.

Is this Bob Freeman asking Howard (seated at Bob's desk) whether he will really change the copy on an ad <u>after</u> it runs? Howard seems to be considering it.

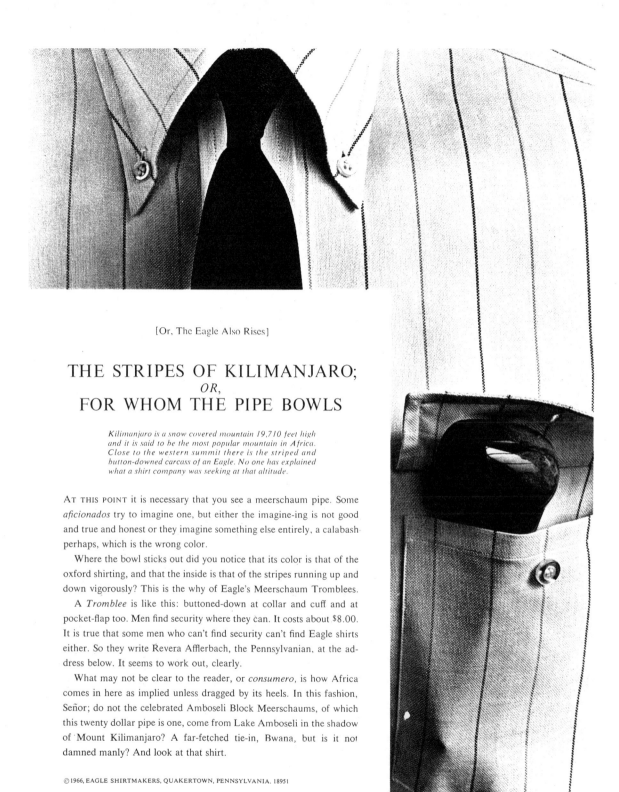

[Or, The Eagle Also Rises]

THE STRIPES OF KILIMANJARO;
OR,
FOR WHOM THE PIPE BOWLS

Kilimanjaro is a snow covered mountain 19,710 feet high and it is said to be the most popular mountain in Africa. Close to the western summit there is the striped and button-downed carcass of an Eagle. No one has explained what a shirt company was seeking at that altitude.

AT THIS POINT it is necessary that you see a meerschaum pipe. Some *aficionados* try to imagine one, but either the imagine-ing is not good and true and honest or they imagine something else entirely, a calabash perhaps, which is the wrong color.

Where the bowl sticks out did you notice that its color is that of the oxford shirting, and that the inside is that of the stripes running up and down vigorously? This is the why of Eagle's Meerschaum Tromblees.

A *Tromblee* is like this: buttoned-down at collar and cuff and at pocket-flap too. Men find security where they can. It costs about $8.00. It is true that some men who can't find security can't find Eagle shirts either. So they write Revera Afflerbach, the Pennsylvanian, at the address below. It seems to work out, clearly.

What may not be clear to the reader, or *consumero,* is how Africa comes in here as implied unless dragged by its heels. In this fashion, Señor; do not the celebrated Amboseli Block Meerschaums, of which this twenty dollar pipe is one, come from Lake Amboseli in the shadow of Mount Kilimanjaro? A far-fetched tie-in, Bwana, but is it not damned manly? And look at that shirt.

©1966, EAGLE SHIRTMAKERS, QUAKERTOWN, PENNSYLVANIA. 18951

Here's some of Howard's copy — by way of Hemingway.

233

His undisguised pleasure at his own cleverness had an innocence about it which made it impossible to resist sharing his jubilation.

HOWARD AT HOME

He liked to work at home in an all-red study – its walls, high ceiling, and black-figured carpet completely done in deep, rich burgundy – an overwhelming flood of ruby color relieved only by a black leather swivel chair, oak desk, and a deep purple leather couch extended along one side, facing a fireplace wall solidly lined with books. § The dominance of that single, pulsating, life-giving color girdling the room gave it a peculiarly sensual unity, a womb-like quality. § Gossage submerged himself in its ease and warmth, completely relaxed in a fire-engine red shirt which made him part of his carmine surroundings, even as the shirt, by some subtle magic, transformed the room into an extension of his private self.

He was an omnivorous reader. § He possessed insatiable intellectual curiosity and whenever he came across a writer with an unusual idea, or one who entertained thoughts similar to some of his own offbeat notions, he became ecstatic over this serendipitous discovery. § He could hardly wait to contact the author, if a contemporary, to discuss these fascinating matters directly. § It was this attitude which led him to contact an obscure Canadian professor, Marshall McLuhan, and introduce him to New York's publishing elite.

Howard provides performance tips for Mr. and Mrs. McLuhan

Howard as a Friend

Gossage was a truly compassionate man. § Almost anyone he knew could call him at any hour of the day or night about a personal matter and be confident of receiving his sympathetic attention. He immediately put aside whatever he was doing to listen, even if the request came at a terribly inconvenient time. § Often, the matter was of a disturbing or delicate nature, such as an impending divorce or the possible need for psychiatric care. § Sometimes it just struck his fancy.

One day a young friend of his nephews, Rick and Steve Bowerman, asked Howard if he would think up a song for the newly-built school she was attending, Stanislaus State College. § He smilingly agreed to try, and proudly wore the sweatshirt which the school gave him in gratitude for their new song: *Stanislaus Is Coming To Town!*

Howard the Critic

Despite his personal success in the advertising profession, he was its most caustic critic, lashing out at it relentlessly. *"What are grown men like us doing in the play world of advertising?"* he thundered to his audience, during many speeches to advertising groups.

He fearlessly accused advertising of infantile or worse, unethical behavior, and fervently urged the adoption of major reforms. § Although he unhesitatingly attacked the industry savagely as a whole, he rarely singled out any individual for his harsh words. He was immediately contrite when he learned he had offended someone.

Joe Weiner, photogenic friend, and Howard modeling Beethoven sweatshirts.

When that happened, he customarily sent a dozen long-stemmed red roses as an apology, whether the presumed victim was man or woman. The size of his florist bill was staggering. When pressed for his opinion about someone who vituperatively opposed him, he would admit with a slight reversion to a childhood stutter, *"Well, I can t-take him or l-leave him, not necessarily in that order."*

THE LEMONADE THEORY

Challenge stimulated him. Whatever the problem, and the more cataclysmic the better, he approached it confidently with his Lemonade Theory. § This was, in essence: *When you're stuck with a lemon, make lemonade.* § It provided him with a magic formula for converting a supposed obstacle into an asset.

His technique was to grapple tirelessly with a problem until he found its root, and then come up with an ingenious solution which capitalized on the dilemma. § He applied this process to personal and business matters alike and urged it upon everyone in the firm belief that it would work equally well for anyone. To Gossage, there was no such thing as an unsolvable problem.

He even facetiously claimed at times, that his Lemonade Theory was so successful, *"When there wasn't a lemon handy, I'd find myself rummaging around in the fruit bowl just so I'd have something to work with. Life – and clients – being what they are, I generally didn't have too far to look."*

Will it fly?

236

The Lemonade Theory at Work.
The Scientific-American Paper
Airplane Contest takes off.

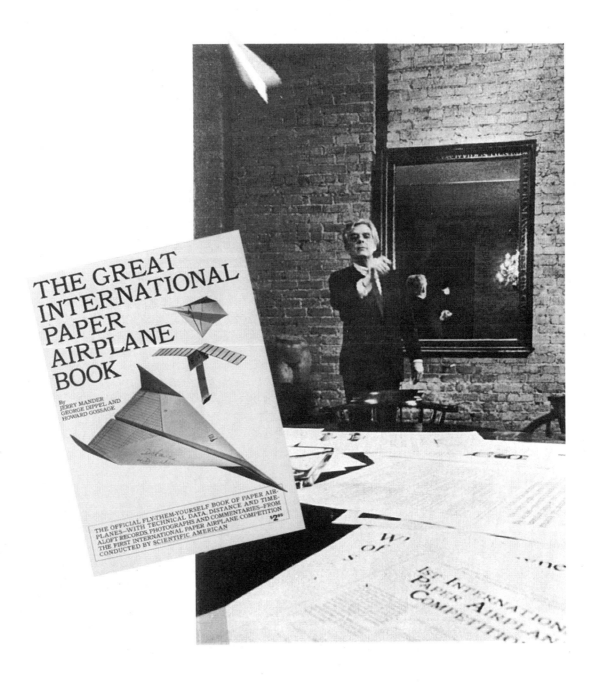

238

HOWARD'S FIREHOUSE

★ ★ ★ ★ ★ ★ ★ ★ ★ ★ ★ ★

"I am convinced," an advertising journalist wrote, *"that Howard Gossage's Firehouse has been publicized more than any other building in the world, with the possible exception of the Sistine Chapel."*

ORIGINAL FIREHOUSE #1

The old Firehouse at 451 Pacific Avenue became so closely identified with Howard that many people find it difficult to think of him in other surroundings. ★ Built in 1869 as Original Firehouse No. 1 and rebuilt after the disastrous 1906 earthquake and fire which leveled most of San Francisco, the building remained in continual use as a Firehouse. ★ By late 1958, the city found it more feasible to sell the building at auction than to remodel it.

We had been looking for new quarters and were intrigued by the thought of working in an old firehouse. ★ This one was in a particularly choice location, a colorful area formerly known as the Barbary Coast. Professional decorators had in recent years turned it into the most elegant showroom section of the city – a Mecca for window shoppers, tourists and San Franciscans alike. ★ Our chief competitor was the Chinese fortune cookie factory across the street from the Firehouse. The owners wanted to expand, and the Firehouse was a convenient site for them. ★ As the bidding inched up tortuously by the hundred: $39,600; $39,700; $39,800; Howard and his partner, Joe Weiner, could barely restrain themselves from shouting out additional bids. At a strategic moment, our broker stepped up the pace, calmly increasing the bidding by $500 per bid.

Dismayed by his professional coolness and apparently limitless backing, the Chinese cookie makers, after a few counter-offers, reluctantly yielded. The building was ours! Howard and Joe let out a happy whoop, hugged each other ecstatically, and rushed back to our California Street offices to break the good news.

FIREHOUSE PARTY #1

A gala remodeling party was held on a sunny April afternoon, with seven hundred guests of all ages. § Bouquets of lilacs were tied around the brass pole down which countless firefighters had slid on their way to innumerable fires. § Additional flowers festooned the steps of the cast iron, circular stairway which led to the upper floors. § A lavish buffet lunch was set out, highlighted by a three foot cake and an ice sculpture, both in the shape of a fire truck. § The first floor walls were covered with murals depicting fire-fighting scenes, especially painted for the occasion by members of the San Francisco Artists and Art Directors Club. § A peppy combo, The Firehouse Five Plus Two, provided live music.

The center of attention was a big, shiny, bright red fire engine attended by an official fireman. Adults and children alike, wearing red fire helmets provided for the occasion, clambered excitedly all over the fire truck, ringing its bell vigorously as their imaginations took them on a hair-raising, pell mell drive to the scene of a blazing fire.

Those who were lucky enough to be there at the end of the party had an unexpected treat – an actual ride on the fire truck, bells ringing, siren blowing as it wound its way back to its own firehouse through the deserted San Francisco streets on that Sunday afternoon. § It was an auspicious prelude to the many Firehouse parties to follow.

MARGET'S MAGIC

Designer Marget Larsen had *carte blanche* in planning the decor. § A small brick building on a typically narrow San Francisco lot, it was a structure of beautiful proportions, with a facade suggestive of an elegant town house. § As much of the original architectural feeling as possible was retained. § Throughout the building, brick walls were left as they were. § Floors were all of gleaming random plank dark wood; ceilings were covered with the same hammered leaf gold paper in square tile pattern used for the entrance halls; all the window ledges and display areas were finished with Italian marble in muted shades of orange.

The large, gracefully arched doors in the front room were converted to a huge show window using the original door frames. § A narrow door to the right became the building's main entrance. § The ancient spiral stairway was retained for aesthetic purposes and a flight of conventional stairs added for more practical access to the upper stories. § A fragile, sparkling, multi-tiered crystal chandelier

"…Marget Larsen had carte blanche in planning the decor. …The ancient spiral stairway was retained for aesthetic purposes."

241

was hung in the same room as the old cast iron stairway to offset its rugged handsomeness.

THE GARDEN

The handball court became a high-walled, intimate Italian garden designed by Thomas Church, one of the city's best-known landscape architects. The garden floor was a stone mosaic set in a single huge star-shaped design and graced with a large olive tree in the center. § A winsome stone cherub frolicked above a small bubbling fountain on the west wall. § Tucked discreetly beneath flowering bushes of pink and red camellias, white rhododendrons, and a profusion of ferns, were a few unobtrusive, curved stone benches.

The Dynamite Shack, where Fire Department explosives had been stored, was formed into an open portico with columns supported by Etruscan caryatids. § Visitors were invariably transfixed by the unexpected sight of this exquisite garden glimpsed through the glass panels of the rear room. § A small mezzanine was added between the first and second floors, with rear windows looking towards the garden.

THE OFFICES

The second floor housed the agency's main offices: a large art and production department facing Pacific Avenue; a smaller central section which served as reception and general office area; and the spacious rear conference room, which was, at various times, Joe Weiner's, Howard's or my office.

The impressive conference room, with its floor-to-ceiling black-shuttered windows, and slim, black-framed French doors leading to a balcony which overlooked the garden, had a distinctive character of its own. § It was eclectically furnished. A highly polished, nineteenth-century, three-tier brass chandelier bearing candle-shaped lights, shone above an antique oval table, around which clustered a group of English walnut armchairs fitted with purple seat cushions. § A well-worn Oriental rug with mellowed orange and blue geometric design covered most of the highly-polished oak floor. § Along the left wall, stood a fourteen-foot high, custom-built armoire, its upper border inlaid with blue and green semi-precious stones from Thailand. § Against that same wall, was a handsome antique Spanish desk, its wooden writing surface unevenly grooved by the pressure of generations of users.

Directly opposite hung a massive sixteenth-century Spanish mirror. A Latin inscription painted in gilt circled the mirror's wide wooden frame. Translated, its message seemed directed to the new Firehouse denizens: *"Do not look in this mirror to see yourself as you are, but as you would like to be, and you shall become that desired image."*

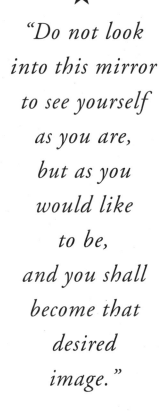

★

"Do not look into this mirror to see yourself as you are, but as you would like to be, and you shall become that desired image."

THE ART OF GRAFFITI

In contrast to the formality of some of the furnishings in the conference room, the large wall immediately to the left of the entrance was covered with graffiti scrawled by famous visitors. § Among them: architect Moshe Safdi's sketch of the cubicle habitat houses he designed for Montreal Expo '67 and a huge, writhing dragon belching fire from its nostrils – rendered by writer Tom Wolfe. § Below Marshall

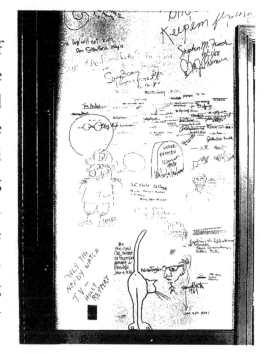

McLuhan's name, and his well-known theme, "The Medium is the Message," a disbeliever had crossed out the "M" in "Medium" and substituted a "T."

THE TOWER

Above the second floor, there were two additional levels, comprising a small tower which the firemen used to store their hoses. § The central portion of each of these floors was only about ten feet square, but the tower as a whole suited Howard perfectly. § It was far enough removed from the general office din to give him privacy and, he liked the feeling of being an eagle alone in his aerie. § The lower portion of the tower became his office while the rest of the space was converted to a small apartment with kitchenette, shower, and bed. For a while, it served as Howard's bachelor quarters.

In that tiny office with its black-shuttered windows and orange wall-to-wall carpeting, Gossage had a small teak desk covered with the same rust-colored marble used so lavishly throughout the Firehouse. § Above it hung an inverted, tulip-shaped Tiffany lamp. Against the wall directly facing him was a down-filled black and white tweed sofa extending the full width of the room except for a small marble-topped table flanking each side. § On one of these end tables he placed his favorite sculpture, a magnificent white marble torso of a Hellenic female figure. § On the wall beneath the narrow stairs leading to the upper tower, hung a red and gold carved wooden *garuda,* a fierce-faced half-man, half-bird creature of Hindu mythology. § The over-all effect was one of comfort, ease and intimacy.

THE CONFERENCE ROOM

The focal point of the Firehouse was the conference room. § It exuded an aura of graciousness and warmth which made it a welcome retreat from the frenzied pace of the business world.

"This place is a stage set and all you people came directly from Central Casting to fill your roles. None of this is real."

It was ideal for luncheons. There was an ineffable pleasure about dining leisurely in that high-ceilinged room, with sunlight peeking in through the half-shuttered windows, streaking the rug with bold rays of light which vied with the brilliant blaze of the chandelier. § Every gesture of the diners was captured in the antique mirror, which seemed to make people look and act their best, as if every move was being recorded by history's camera.

Actress Sally Kemp recalls her first impression of the Firehouse and its occupants when they assembled in the conference room to meet her: *"This place is a stage set and all you people came directly from Central Casting to fill your roles. None of this is real."* § But it was.

HOW TO "DO LUNCH"

"Lunch at Howard Gossage's Firehouse" became something of a San Francisco institution. For large groups, there was a generous buffet of beautifully arranged cold cuts, cheeses, salads, and rich desserts. § Howard's favorite comment about this menu was, *"Now I know how Jesus fed the masses. He ordered lunch for four from a Kosher delicatessen."*

A stream of illustrious visitors, many of them writers, were luncheon guests at one time or another: John Steinbeck, Tom Wolfe, Marshall McLuhan, Dr. Benjamin Spock, Jessica Mitford, Buckminster Fuller, economist Leopold Kohr, anthropologist Ashley Montagu, and *Harper's* publisher Bill Blair, as well as local luminaries such as environmentalist David Brower, designer Walter Landor and columnist Herb Caen. § There were also visitors from the world of show business: glamorous opera star Mary Costa, a stunningly beautiful guest of honor at an evening party; actress June Lockhart; comedian Stan Freberg, who sometimes entertained us extemporaneously for an hour, non-stop; and Alan Alch, television writer and producer and surely one of the world's great storytellers.

Under Weiner & Gossage's ownership, the rejuvenated Firehouse assumed a glittering new life. § It became the scene of all kinds of festive and intellectual gatherings: fashion shows, weddings, christenings, art previews, seminars, and innumerable parties. § There was even an after-hours exercise class conducted by Janet Sassoon, a former prima ballerina of the Berlin Opera.

Howard was a gracious and hospitable host. He reveled in the laughter, the crowds, the merry mingling. § When it was time for a party to end, he simply went about saying smilingly, "Out! Out!" The guests always left reluctantly but with good grace. § Interestingly, Howard rarely attended other people's parties. He preferred small intimate dinners with a few good friends rather than elaborate affairs.

MARCHING MARIACHIS

Howard's favorite parties were those with mariachis. § At five o'clock, Señor Salvador Padilla's Mexican mariachis magically appeared in their silver-trimmed, powder-blue boleros and tight-fitting, wide-flared pants, huge broad-brimmed sombreros, and carrying their shining brass instruments. § They formed a circle in the first-floor lobby, where they sang and played with verve. § Spirited numbers alternated with Latin songs of romantic tenderness. § The sound of their music floated down the long entrance hall to the street where the door was left open for the convenience of arriving guests.

Inside, the foyer was crammed with musicians, guests, and staff members. The listeners, enthralled, kept time with clapping hands and cheered the musicians on with cries of *"¡Olè!"* after each number. § Some of the audience sat on the stairs, some leaned against the wall, some simply stood where they were, all of them happily absorbed in the joyous sounds.

When it got too crowded for new arrivals to squeeze through, the party moved upstairs. The mariachis continued playing as they marched up the stairs, until they reached the conference room, newly cleared of rug and furniture. § There, some of the partygoers, in an excess of *joie-de-vivre,* staged what can only be described as never-before-seen-and-never-again-seen dance steps. § No stance was too bizarre. § Each innovation was wildly cheered by applauding onlookers. A few exhibited near-professional form...among them, black-haired Eleanor Piel, in an elegant flutter of peach chiffon, twirling confidently with husband, publisher Gerard Piel. § The dancers continued until exhausted, pausing only briefly for a drink or an *hors d'oeuvre.*

Firehouse guests were typically a melange of socialites, artists, writers, publishers, suppliers, visiting celebrities, friends of the staff, and a few clients – the latter invited for their own sake rather than for any hoped-for business advantage.

THE INSTANT PARTY PLAN

Perhaps, of all the titles bestowed on me during my long association with the agency, the most truly descriptive was "Ring Mistress of Howard Gossage's Circus." At times, the Firehouse bore a remarkable similarity to the confusion of activities going on simultaneously under the Big Top. § It was my responsibility to create order out of chaos and to see that everything got done on time and in keeping with our self-imposed Firehouse standards.

Howard's inordinate enthusiasm for parties and the pressure this put upon the rest of us to get necessary business matters taken care of before the guests arrived, led to the creation of our Instant Party Plan. § Everyone knew just what to do. § All desks were cleared, covered with specially designed decorative paper, and lined up against the walls. Overhead hanging lights were temporarily removed and the rooms lit by the glow of dozens of candles; masses of cut flowers added fresh beauty and fragrance everywhere. § The two largest desks were set up as bars. § Huge, brightly-colored paper flowers decorated the stairway. § Hastily cleared tables in the art department served to hold coats and bags.

We were a marvel of efficiency on those occasions; we had to be. We were too small a group to stand on ceremony and none of us wanted to be neatly categorized anyway. As Howard put it, *"We are all chiefs, with no Indians."* This wasn't strictly so, for, at times, someone had to cater to his lordly whims, but it was mostly true.

SMALL IS BEAUTIFUL

Because of its size, the Firehouse automatically limited the size of the staff it could harbor. § There was a natural order imposed by the physical structure of the building, which Howard found enormously appealing. § He was certain that a large share of the agency's creative vigor was due to the sense of freedom made possible by its compact quarters. § Here, there was no bureaucratic tangle. § For a person of Howard's temperament, it was clearly the most satisfactory way to work.

The Firehouse was a miniature world which thrived, limited yet abetted by its physical boundaries. § Expansion beyond a certain point was not possible, the certain knowledge of which comforted Gossage tremendously.

He much preferred to work within limitations and by so doing, develop special strengths and expertise. § Activities which required a lot of bodies or a lot of space were simply not considered. § The old brick building which was so much a part of the Gossage mystique served as both a stage and the embodiment of some cherished beliefs. A living example of how apparent limitations can be turned into assets.

Gossage made the Firehouse a symbol of independence and creative vigor. § At the same time, he was inescapably shaped by the conditions inherent in living within it. § He was, as we all were, both its Creator and its Offspring.

PRESIDENT ALICE LOWE

As President, Media Director, Office Manager and Ring Mistress of Howard Gossage's Firehouse Circus, Alice Lowe worked with Howard from the establishment of Weiner & Gossage in 1957 until his death in 1969. She is the former Chairman of the Asian Art Museum of San Francisco. The preceeding two sections were excerpted from Mrs. Lowe's memoirs, "The Wizard of Ads."

WHAT HOWARD GOSSAGE TAUGHT ME ABOUT ADVERTISING

by Jay Conrad Levinson

Howard Gossage gave me a first glimpse of a world that even now, few professionals truly understand. § And he gave me a view of a way that life can be lived that surprised me, that dazzled and enlightened me. § He showed me, in my first job ever, how much *fun* it is to work in advertising.

He hired me in 1958, fresh out of the Army, because I proved, with sample ads for his clients, how much I wanted to be a copywriter. Not only that, I could also type 120 words a minute, was willing to wash floors and windows, and even agreed to go to shorthand school.

For six magic months, I was Howard's secretary. § Before starting, I had no idea that the man was a legend, a character, a genius, a comedian, an iconoclast, a literary lion, and a god-in-training. § After one week, I began to realize that my boss was no ordinary adman. After 38 years, I now know that nobody is an ordinary adman, but that Howard was more extraordinary than most.

Along the way, I saw first hand the sheer joy that could be achieved by taking on a marketing challenge and surmounting it with a style and *pizazz* that generated profits.

251

How to empty a bottle of Paul Masson Champagne

NO. 1—THE BOTTLE (OR 5th)

First buy your champagne. Let's make this act meaningful for both of us. Buy a bottle of our superb Paul Masson California Champagne.

This isn't as simple an act as you might think. Actually there are ten standard champagne bottles: the Nebuchadnez-zar, the Balthazar, the Salmanasar, the Methuselah, the Rehoboam, the Jero-boam, the Magnum, the Bottle, the Half-Bottle and the Split. Let's start with the most familiar: The Bottle.

The Bottle (as we call it) is a fifth; it holds 1/5 gallon of champagne. It is made of heavy green glass, has a long slim neck and an inverted bottom. It is never with-out these features because they are all necessary to the perfection and fermenta-tion of champagne.

Very well. Now to emptying it: First remove the cork. There is a whole eti-quette on this. Some say you shouldn't let fly but should *ease* it off; what *we* say is, "It's your champagne". Just be careful where you point it, that's all.

The Bottle pours about eight glasses of champagne; perfect for four people. Un-less you are exceptionally thirsty or have

Continued on page 5

Whatever his concerns about advertising, he knew how to make money for his clients.

CONTINUED ON NEXT PAGE...

I remember Paul Masson Wine ads in the *Wall Street Journal* that began on one page, said "continued on page 5" at the bottom, and then continued on page 5, just as the *WSJ* articles do.

MARKETING AT WORK

Howard's creativity was manifested not only in his wit and words, but also in his marketing savvy. § Much of the success of these strategies came from Howard's unique understanding of media and his utilization of an advertising medium.

He also understood the importance of national distribution as an advertising goal. § For Irish Whiskey, his research showed that almost every liquor store everywhere had at least one bottle of Irish Whiskey in stock. If he could get them to carry two bottles, he could double Irish Whiskey sales in America. § With long copy ads in *The New Yorker* aimed at taste influencers, he pulled it off.

GUERRILLA AT WORK

Not taking himself seriously was an art form with Howard. But he did take his job seriously. § Let me tell you what I saw when Howard worked:

First, he would meet with Joe Weiner, his partner; Bob Freeman, his art director/production manager; Alice Lowe, his media director/office manager; and the client. § This was followed by a second meeting that excluded the client, but included me – so I could put my shorthand to work and write up a conference report. § Then, Howard would disappear into his office, the big, bright one with the black and white tiled floors, the Knoll pedestal table with a marble top, the one black chair and the Dictaphone. § No typewriter.

Hot Chocolate

He would spend a week in that office, coming out infrequently to ask for hot chocolate, which I would fetch immediately from the coffee shop beneath us at 149 California Street. This was my major contribution to his work.

At the end of the week, he would come out with one ad – one wonderful ad that encapsulated an entire marketing campaign: strategy, theme, art, copy, signs, brochures, distribution, PR – everything needed to launch a full-scale marketing attack. § A lot of it was what I've come to call Guerrilla Marketing.

Today, I implore wannabe guerrillas in my *Guerrilla Marketing* books to integrate a full 100 different marketing weapons. I wonder if Howard was my muse.

"Only Enough String to Wrap the Package"

It was the first time I saw Guerrilla Marketing at work. § Howard had the astonishing talent to distill a guerrilla marketing attack down to a single ad. § He called it using, *"only enough string to wrap the package."*

This talent was matched by his ability to turn it all into action. § In his head, he would have the follow-up details for media, creative, research, production, distribution, the whole works. § Yet, at the first, to breathe the spark of life into an aggressive integrated marketing campaign, one ad was created. In one week. Sometimes longer.

Secretary at Work

Meanwhile, I was doing more than practicing my shorthand and transcribing Howard's copy on my own Dictaphone.

Each evening, after 5:00, I'd take a stab at the ad that Howard was working on and leave the results on Howard's desk. § Each morning, I'd arrive to find my ad blue-penciled to a horrible death. § I realize now, that Howard was trying to give me the gift of his skill and taste. I also realize now what a privilege it was for me to have Howard Gossage take the time from his schedule to give me the help I needed. But at that time, my pain and agony at the mega-editing distorted my view.

Then, one day, he presented to me for typing a Dictaphone belt with headline and copy for a full-page *New Yorker* ad for Paul Masson champagne. § The marketing idea was to switch people from Christmas holiday egg nog to Christmas holiday champagne. Howard's headline was *"No Nog is Good Nog."* § As usual, I did my own version. The headline was *"Don't Put All Your Eggs in One Nog."* I placed the copy on Howard's marble table.

I didn't realize it then, but my apprenticeship was over.

The next morning, Howard asked me to come into his office. He had the ad on his desk. § No blue pencil marks.

Howard told me that my headline was better than his and since my copy was on target, too, he would run the ad exactly as it had been written and that I was fired. § He said, *"You're too g-oo-ooood a copywriter to be a secretary,"* I didn't know whether to feel depressed or elated.

He said I should get the feeling of seeing my own work in print and that I should now become a writer. § He told me there was no more room for writers at Howard's small shop. He was right. § Virginia Mannon, a killer copywriter, also worked at the agency. She and Howard were all the writers they needed.

But Howard did give me a choice. § He said I could stay with Weiner & Gossage as executive secretary at double the salary, a window office and business cards. (Business cards were very important to me, never having had any.) Or, he'd call some people he knew and help get me a job as a copywriter at a standard ad agency. § I took the second option.

I realized the first day at my new job, when I was asked to come up with 12 one-minute radio spots before I went home that night, that my life would never be the same. § I also realized that taking one week to work on one ad was one more thing that made Gossage special.

The pace didn't let up much after that. § I went from San Francisco to Chicago – which included a stint at JWT as a Sr. VP and Creative Director; and five magic years at Leo Burnett in Chicago and London. § Leo joined Howard as the other advertising mentor in my life.

SAN FRANCISCO MEMORIES...

Still, no other agency had the enchantment of Weiner & Gossage. Being visited by Stan Freberg, Herb Caen, and other personages of the time made my days there very memorable.

I remember Howard leaping onto a desk and hollering, *"You're all fired!"* then grinning and hopping down – that kept me on my toes. I didn't know bosses did such things.

Said Howard, *"We're too small to have a lot of vice presidents."* So Howard and Joe both took on the title of president.

Once, when preparing to live in Ireland for a summer, he placed an ad in the *Chronicle* listing his Pacific Heights Victorian mansion as being available at *"$650 without children, $600 with children."*

Howard was truly one of the landmark advertising people, the kind who can move the entire industry up one step on the evolutionary scale. § His contribution to our evolution came in the form of helping us to see advertising in its proper perspective.

In his words, *"People do not read ads. They only read what interests them."* § And often it was one of Howard's ads. He had the knack with ideas, with words, with media. § I was lucky to have him as a mentor. We all are.

THE GOSSAGE SPIRIT AT WORK

Everything I say and write has been elevated by what I learned working for Howard Gossage. § Many of my words are his words expressed in my voice. § I learned principles that today's agencies and clients can lean upon. The Guerrilla Marketing principles and twelve-word foundation* were spawned by ideas passed on by Howard.

I saw that spirit in his agency while it was growing up. § Now that I'm grown up, I have my fun in the three days a week that I work (and have been since 1971) and the four days I play. § Today, I write two books a year, give three talks a month, write a newsletter once every two months, write monthly columns that are syndicated in magazines, newspapers, and two online Internet services, and I consult. § It's a pretty good balance, but sometimes I think Howard had an even better idea. § Sometimes it seemed Howard managed to have his fun every single day he worked. With Howard, work and play were inseparable.

THE ORIGINAL GUERRILLA

Was Howard the Original Guerrilla? There's an easy answer to that question and it's a resounding "YES!" § Guerrillas employ the non-traditional and unconventional to accomplish their goals. Sounds a lot like Howard to me. § Guerrillas rarely go by the book and make up rules as they go along to provide extra flexibility. That sure is Howard all the way. § Guerrillas rely on the brute forces of time, energy, and imagination to substitute for the brute force of a bottomless bank account. Once again, it proves that Howard was Adam in the Guerrilla Bible.

Looking through his files one day, I noticed that he'd had a ton of jobs before his name appeared upon any door. *"Why did you switch jobs so much?"* I asked. § Howard answered, *"Before I settled down, I had to know what to settle for."* § He never lost sight of that line at the bottom. He would never change his focus from a prime selling idea to a jazzy special effect. § He would never abandon a new marketing concept because he didn't have the courage to run with it. Or stay with it.

And he would never work in advertising unless it was *fun.*

Jay Conrad Levinson is the author of 18 books, including the Guerrilla Marketing *series (Houghton Mifflin) now the best-selling marketing books in the world, available in 30 languages. (Jay says this means he doesn't understand 29 editions of his books.) His book,* Guerrilla Marketing Excellence, *is dedicated, in part, to Howard Gossage. And here, free of charge, is…*
The Guerrilla Marketing Twelve-Word Foundation: *Commitment, investment, consistent, confident, patient, assortment, subsequent, convenient, amazement, measurement, involvement, and dependent. If you want to know what it all means, well, we guess you'll just have to buy his books.*

[This article was written by the "discoverer" of Marshall McLuhan – it is perhaps the most readable presentation of McLuhan's thinking in the history of the world.]

UNDERSTANDING MARSHALL McLUHAN

by Howard Luck Gossage

During the past few months, Marshall McLuhan of the University of Toronto has become that phenomenon of our times, the In intellectual celebrity. § That is to say that suddenly Everybody – the press, the vanguard of business, the new youth – discovered him in the curious way that these things happen: at a certain moment all elements grab hands, and there you are.

This after years of relative anonymity. He has taught; he has published to wide and, for the most part, complimentary reviews; he has been recognized, if grudgingly, by his ivy-walled colleagues. § At a high-level academic conference on mass communications in Washington, references to McLuhan's theories were accorded that profound non-response usually reserved for unfortunate noises in chapel. This was only a year ago; things have changed.

ISOLATED HUDDLES OF MCLUHANITES

What has happened? Obviously the clamor has followed on the publication of his newest and most readable book, *Understanding Media: The Extensions of Man.* But at best this is a partial answer, for the book came out in 1964, and until recently, it had been largely unavailable despite the undoubted capacity of its publisher, McGraw-Hill, to swamp the market if it so chose. § Perhaps one reason it didn't so choose was that the demand pattern must have been puzzlingly

258

random/intense in the early days – say to the end of last year – as isolated huddles of McLuhanites back-ordered their holy writ in quantity.

This suggests that at least some of McLuhan's currency at the moment must be either in second-hand catch phrases or simply in that he is a "celebrity"; one who is well-known because he is well-known. § The former is understandable; how many ever read Great Books? The latter is deplorable, not only because such fame passes as quickly as it came, but because it tends, through over-exposure, to *amberize* a man; to encase him, like a fly in amber, so that he is seen but not heard. § This is very easily done, and very hard on men who still have much to say. § Let us start with what McLuhan has said already:

UNDERSTANDING UNDERSTANDING MEDIA

Marshall McLuhan's *Understanding Media* has possibly the least catchy title for an important book since *Principia Mathematica;* however, it is somewhat easier to read once you have got the hang of it. The hard part is getting into it. § One school of thought says that you should start at page 77, or wherever, and then sit through it again the way you do when you come in on the middle of a movie. § Another holds that you should skim through it once, saving your thunderstruck (or indignant) marginal notations for the second time around.

The trouble with this is that skimming McLuhan is like trying to fill a tea cup from a firehose; there is likely to be no second time.

It is quite possible, I think, to start cheerfully at the beginning, provided one has some notions going in of what McLuhan is up to. § To begin with, what Professor McLuhan means by a "medium" is any extension of man – whether it be a book, an automobile, an electric light bulb, television, or clothes. § His theory is that the media a man

"...any medium will tend to amputate the function which it extends. You can test this very easily by walking into a warm house on a cold day. The first thing you do is take off your overcoat."

uses to extend his senses and his faculties will determine what he is, rather than the other way around. § To give a simple example: a car is certainly an extension of a man's legs. Moreover, when he drives a car he has in a sense amputated his legs. He is an amputee just as surely as though he had lost his legs first and then looked for a way to get around.

UNDERSTANDING EXTENSIONS

Similarly, by wearing clothes a man eliminates a good many of the functions that his body would have to perform were he naked. § Let us consider this proposition in its most extreme form: a native living at the Equator and an Eskimo. § The tropical native, because he is naked, has no means of retaining body heat; therefore he must eat constantly or die. He can starve to death in a day or two. § The Eskimo, heavily furred, keeps his body heat and can go without food for weeks if necessary.

This is not, of course, to suggest that the Indians of the Upper Amazon would be better off with long johns and fur coats, or that Eskimos would be better supermarket customers if they ran around in the buff, but that the media a society uses or is forced to use will determine what it is and how it behaves.

Incidentally, we are used to thinking of clothes as something we wear next to our bodies. Objectively, however, clothes are an extension of our skins. § For a naked tribesman, the jungle is his clothes. When one of us runs around naked in a heated room, the room itself is clothes, an extension of our skin, a medium. § You recall that earlier I said that any medium will tend to amputate the function which it extends? § You can test this very easily by walking into a warm house on a cold day.

The first thing you do is take off your overcoat.

LITERATE VS. PRE-LITERATE

Now, to carry this one step further, any new medium or extension of man constitutes a new environment which controls what people who live within it do, the way they think, and the way they act. § If you wonder why the Russians behave and react differently from us, part of the answer is probably that until quite recently they lived in a pre-literate society, whereas ours has been literate for a very long time. § They are historically ear-oriented whereas we are eye-oriented.

There is a great difference. § A man who cannot read will pick up all information about what has gone on before and what is happening outside his field of vision by hearing about it. His world will, therefore, be more diffused and kaleidoscopic than that of the literate, eye-oriented man because the ear cannot be focused and the eye can.

The process of reading – which I suppose we could define as using our eyes to learn about things we cannot see – is dependent on this unique ability of the eye to focus and follow sequentially. § Few people have been able to read at any given time during the past few thousand years since writing was invented. § It is only recently, since Gutenberg, that literacy has become the general environment for even a small part of the world. Latin America, Eastern and Southern Europe, Asia, and Africa are still either pre-literate or Johnny-come-latelies to reading;

"They are historically ear-oriented   *whereas we are eye-oriented."*

their environmental structures arc still ear-oriented.

The differences between literate and pre-literate societies are enormous. § Not the least of these differences is technological. Mass production did not begin with the industrial revolution, but with the first printed page that Gutenberg pulled off his press. § For the first time, items could be mass produced so that one was indistinguishable from another and all of the same value. This was quite a breakthrough after millennia of making one object at a time and each somehow different from the other.

But more important was the environment imposed by the medium of print itself: one word after the other, one sentence after another; one thing at a time in a logical, connected line. § The effects of this linear thinking are deep and influence every facet of a literate society such as our own.

Understanding the Electric Teenager

An ear-oriented society, on the other hand, will neither act nor react in this one-thing-at-a-time fashion, but will tend to receive and express many experiences simultaneously. § It is the difference between our baseball, which is their soccer which is everything happening at once. Perhaps it is why most of the best chess players – and chess is surely everything happening at once, with millions and millions of simultaneous possibilities – come from pre-literate countries. Or why so many atomic physicists are either Hungarians or Americans in their early twenties. § Or why teenagers can listen to the radio full blast, study, and put their hair up in curlers at the same time.

I mention teenagers because it is becoming abundantly apparent that they are not, as we previously thought, going through a phase. They are a different breed of cat entirely. § All sorts of reasons have been given for their emergence as a distinct group, among them prosperity and lack of discipline. And what the hell, I was young once myself. I *was* – but not like that. § For one thing, I wasn't as smart as that. Also, this teenage revolution has been going on for quite a few years now and the early crop is getting up in its late twenties. And I wasn't like them when I was 26 either.

Well, what has happened? McLuhan's theory is that this is the first generation of the electronic age. § He says they are different because the medium that controls their environment is not print – one thing at a time, one thing after another – as it has been for 500 years.

It is television, which is everything happening at once, instantaneously, and enveloping. § A child who gets its environmental training on television – and very few nowadays do not – learns the same way any member of a pre-literate society learns: from the direct experience of his eyes and ears, without Gutenberg for a middle man. § Of course, they do learn how to read too, but it is a secondary discipline, not primary as it is with their elders. § When it comes to shaping sensory perceptions, I'm afraid that Master Gutenberg just isn't in the same class with General Sarnoff or Doctor Stanton.

Despite the uproar over inferior or inept television fare, McLuhan does not think that the program content of television has anything to do with the real changes TV has produced; no more than whether a book is trashy or a classic has anything to do with the process of reading it. § The basic message of television is television itself, the process, just as the basic message of a book is print. As McLuhan says, *"The medium is the message."*

FROM LOGICAL LINKS TO "INSTANT SPEED"

This new view of our environment is much more realistic in the light of what has happened since the advent of McLuhan's "Electric Age." § The Gutenberg Age, which preceded it, was one thing after another in orderly sequence from cause to effect. It reached its finest flower with the development of mechanical linkages: A acts on B which acts on C which acts on D on down to the end of the line and the finished product. § The whole process was thus fragmented into a series of functions, and for each function there was a specialist.

This methodology was not confined to making things; it pervaded our entire economic and social system. It still does, though we are at an age when cause and effect are becoming so nearly simultaneous as to make obsolete all our accustomed notions of chronological sequence and mechanical linkage. § With the dawn of the Electric Age, time and speed themselves have become of negligible importance; just flip the switch: *Instant speed.*

UNDERSTANDING "THE PROBE"

If you are one of those who read McLuhan and find that your independently arrived-at theories not only are confirmed by, but fit neatly into his far broader structure, it is very heady stuff indeed.

It can also be maddening. For right there, in the middle of a paragraph, you are likely to find an apparently extraneous thought of the kind he calls a *"probe."* § The "probe" is apt to be a flat and final pronouncement about a subject on which the reader just happens to be the World's Greatest Authority. § How could McLuhan possibly have known? And as long as he was at it, why didn't he amplify it into the 5,000 words it deserved?*

McLuhan's defense of his random "probes" is that if he stopped to develop them he'd never get on with the main body of his work. They occur to him there so he puts them in there. § Perhaps he, as an old teacher, also feels the pupils ought to have something to do besides register his conclusions. If so, he is roaringly successful. He is the only author I know who writes a paragraph that one can read for two hours profoundly.

The probe technique does not always work out orally, particularly with small groups. § A World's Greatest Expert is liable to grab the probe and run like hell for his own goal leaving the rest of the group – and the ball – upfield somewhere. § Also, when he is in exceptionally fine probing fettle, he has probes sticking out of him like a porcupine, which is somewhat baffling to the uninitiated.

At such times, a lot of Marshall goes a little way.

*

[Note on Marshall McLuhan as a conversationalist: when you expound one of your own abstract ideas, he is all rapt attention; it is possible that he also listens. If he wore a hearing aid you would wonder whether he had turned it off. As a non-listener, he is excelled only by Buckminster Fuller, who does wear a hearing aid and does turn it off. Fuller is the champ: one time he interrupted me in the middle of a question with, "Do you want an answer or don't you? Very well..." He then answered the question; I only wished it had been mine!]

Speaking of Richard Schickel...

Richard Schickel categorized those who balked at McLuhan's theories in *Harper's* (*"Marshall McLuhan, Canada's International Intellectual Comet"* November 1965) as the "compulsively liberal" and the "compulsively academic." I will grant these, but I would like to add another major grouping which cannot be characterized so invidiously. They are bright and flexible enough, but they long ago made their commitments elsewhere. § We might call them the Gutenberg-oriented (McLuhan admits to being one himself by inclination). Their attitude is epitomized by something that Barrows Mussey, an American author living in Germany, wrote me, more as explanation than justification: *"The difference between McLuhan and me is that, by temperament — and by experience too — I am the sort who says the Wright brothers will never get it off the ground. He is the one who says that every family in America will have a private plane by 1950."*

Speaking of James Joyce...

A major key to McLuhan's probe style and his outlook is to be found in his undoubted stature as a Joyce scholar, which is where he started out while working on his doctorate at Cambridge. § He regards *Finnegan's Wake* as the most important book of our era and the one that has done the most to chart his own explorations. § His immense Joycean joy at snuffing and roiling about in the double-bed of language is evident throughout his work; as is his delight in elaborate puns, some of which are pointed and pregnant (which is to say I get them), while others are so obscurantist as to demand a "Key to McLuhan's Wake."

Mosaicked, Empyrean, Richly Larded...

The avalanche of referential material, probes, and indicators within his work is so vast and diverse as to keep his interpreters busy for some time. § Since he isn't much given to going back and clarifying, and at any rate isn't terribly good at it, we can also expect a spate of articles with titles like "Understanding Marshall McLuhan," and "Mechanical Brideshead Revisited."

The Mechanical Bride, published in 1951, was his first book on media and his most bizarre. I will not dwell on it more than to say it is a collector's item fetching upward of $50 in mint condition. § His second, *The Gutenberg Galaxy,* is what is called an Important Book. It is mosaicked, empyrean, richly larded with magnificent literary substantiations. (McLuhan has total recall of his own and everybody else's material.) § While it is not a book I would volunteer to write jacket blurbs for, its basic premise alone is enough to justify it. § It is something like Norbert Wiener's *The Human Use of Human Beings;* if you only get the notion of the title you are miles ahead.

A UNIFIED FIELD THEORY . . . A NEW LAYER OF HELL

I believe McLuhan will endure, for the reason that there is an observable pattern in his work building towards a unified field theory. § It is reasonable that he should try, for to account for creation is the proper goal of those who are able to envision it at all; it is the name of the game.

Understanding Media: the Extensions of Man is the first book of what McLuhan intends to be a trilogy. § The second will be called *Cliché to Archetype,* and I hope it will be subtitled "The Environment of Man," because that is what it is about. § We all know what scorn is reserved for the man who hasn't read the book, only the review, and discusses it anyway? And what really poor form it is for a writer to review a book he hasn't actually read? § Here, I am going to excavate a new layer of Hell for myself: I am going to do both to a book which hasn't yet been written. I haven't even seen one page of McLuhan's unfinished manuscript, but he has talked enough about it so that I think I can wing it, chancy though it is:

CLICHÉ TO ARCHETYPE TO CHANCE

Everybody talks about environment but nobody does anything about it. This is because, McLuhan says, *"The moment a man recognizes his environment it becomes something else, his 'old environment,' and as such is the content of his new, or true, environment; which, of course, again is unseen."*

Has he lost you already? Let's set out the bread crumbs: by "environment," he means that accustomed, unnoticed set of conditions which limits an organism's world at any given moment. In the ordinary course of events, we are not aware of our environment any more than a fish is aware of his. § As Father John Culkin of Fordham, a leading McLuhanite, says, *"We don't know who it was discovered water, but we're pretty sure it wasn't a fish."* [Editor's Note: Here we see another example of Howard quoting himself and attributing it to others.]

EXTERNAL ENVIRONMENTS & INTERIOR DECOR

Imagine a series of clear plastic domes, one within another. You can only see them from the outside; from the inside they are invisible. You become aware of an environment – one of these domes that surrounds you – only when you get outside of it. § At that point you can see it. But you can't see the one which is *now* above you. § To put it another way, let us suppose that an ant has lived all his young life inside an anthill. He is not really aware that the anthill is his world; it simply *is* his world. § So one day they send him off on his first important assignment, to drag back a dead beetle, say. He goes outside the anthill. Two things happen: 1) He sees the anthill for the first time; 2) He becomes aware that the world is a very big place.

Does this mean that he is aware of his environment? No, because what he doesn't know is that his anthill is inside a greenhouse. The only way he'll become aware of the greenhouse is if he goes outside it. § And even then it won't do him much good, because, you see, the greenhouse is inside the Houston Stadium, and so on. § In each instance, you will notice that the old environment becomes content for the newer one, never the other way around. § McLuhan, in one of his random conversational probes, notes that this seems to work out even in decor. Victorian furniture fits into a modern room, but a modern piece looks simply awful in a Victorian room.

CONSCIOUSNESS & TEN MARTINIS

So, awareness is becoming conscious that there is something higher controlling us than we had thought. The catch is that we can never catch up; we are always one step behind, for everything is contained by something bigger. § McLuhan will not, I think, take us on this route, at least not in this book. Perhaps he will in the third leg of his trilogy, but it is hard to say. § Although he is a convert to Roman Catholicism, he is chary of airing his religious speculations. § His concern at this time is not so much with goals as with process.

There are many sorts of environments besides the simple one of physical space which I mentioned: business, political, social, cultural, communications, etc. But for the moment let's just call it all environment. § Two things will make us aware of an environment: either it changes or we do. A man who has lost a leg will become aware of steps. A man who has had five martinis may see things he has never seen before. § A man who has had ten martinis may see things *nobody* has seen before.

THE EXTRA-ENVIRONMENTAL VIEW

There is another variety of environmental recognition reserved for those viewing it as outsiders. There are several varieties of what McLuhan calls "anti-environmentals," though I think "extra-environmental" is more descriptive. § An "extra-environmental" can be a person within a society whose perceptions have not been conditioned to obliviousness of the structure of a given environment.

ILLUSTRATIVE STORY

The story of the Emperor's new clothes is a good example. The child, because he was not yet committed to the environmental power set-up, was not committed to see the Emperor's clothes, so he didn't. § It was only when the extra-environmental child pointed out that he was naked that the others were able to see it too. § Similarly, a teenager with his other-conditioned perceptions will be extra-environmental in our Gutenberg-ish society. [Editor's Note: As good an explanation of "Generation X" as we are likely to read. Is the "X" short for "extra-environmental?"]

A SECOND ILLUSTRATIVE STORY

A second type of extra-environmental is apparently due to an innate deficiency. That is to say that some people are unable to see things in a normal fashion. On the other hand, they will see things that normal people can't. § During the Second War, I understand that some aerial observers were recruited because they were colorblind. Their colorblindness made them unable to distinguish things designed for normal eyes, such as camouflage. § They'd look down at a quite ordinary stretch of landscape and say, *"Hey, there's a gun emplacement!"* Because of their disability, their impairment of vision, their eyes were not taken in by the camouflage; all they could see was the thing itself. § The extra-environmental thus has a great advantage, assuming he has anything else going for him. His mind isn't cluttered up with a lot of rules, policy, and other environmental impedimenta that often pass for experience. § The more experience you have the less able you are to look at a given environment, especially your own, with fresh eyes.

UNDERSTANDING TERMINOLOGY

I said earlier that one of the ways that we can become aware of environment is for it to change. However, sometimes an environment can change without our really noticing what has happened. § Part of this is due to a lag in terminology, part to our Mechanical Age commitment to specialists.

Travel, as an example, has changed drastically, and I don't mean that it's just faster. § Travel, for the most part, is no longer travel; it is a process which has a beginning and an end but virtually no middle. § Travel is not an experience so much as a suspension of experience. Flying in a plane from San Francisco to New York is nothing more nowadays than a horizontal elevator ride. § One imagines that if we had buildings 3000 miles high, there would be a young woman on the elevators offering us coffee, tea or milk.

Is terminology all that important? § Yes, because to name things is to recognize them; it is the way we learn about our environment.

WHICH BRINGS US TO SPECIALISM...

The specialist is by nature environmental. § He is committed to what McLuhan calls a fragmented function within a given process linkage. § If his environment changes he will not necessarily become extra-environmental. § It is more likely that he will carry his tendency to specialism with him the way a snail does his shell. § A born specialist will tend to interpret all experience in the light of his own expertise.

Still Another Illustrative Story:

One time a cloak and suit manufacturer went to Rome and while he was there managed to get an audience with His Holiness. Upon his return a friend asked him, *"What did the Pope look like?"* The tailor answered, *"A 41 Regular."*

...And the Need for Generalists

If specialism epitomizes the environmental stance, then "generalism" probably covers the extra-environmental. § A generalist starts from the outside of a given environment; a specialist works on the inside. § McLuhan has a special aversion to specialism; a sign in his office proclaims, *"No specialist need apply."* § This does not mean that he is against professional expertise in the solution of problems, only against its built-in blinkers. [Yet Another Editor's Note: At about this time, Gossage formed a consulting company called *Generalists, Inc.* with his good friend Dr. Gerald Feigen.]

Once you take a problem to a specialist you are wired in to a specialist's solution. However well executed it is, the odds are against its being a real answer.

Let us say that your company is having growing pains, and is uncomfortable in its present quarters. So you go to an architect. § Let us also suppose that he is a very good architect, broad-thinking, one dedicated solidly to the proposition that form follows function. So he inquires after your needs, your ambitions, your hopes, your fears, what manner of people you are, etc. Do you know what you are going to end up with? A building. § Now, a building, however nice, may not be the answer to your problem at all. § Perhaps the real answer is to stop expanding, or fire the traffic manager, or everyone stay home and do cottage work connected by closed-circuit TV. But these are generalist solutions, not the sort of thing you expect an architect to come up with. If he did, you'd probably think he was a busybody.

GENERALISM DIAGRAMMED

Those who find McLuhan most compatible are those who have already figured out a structure and wonder where it fits in the larger scheme of things. The generalist area looks like this, a circle.

The dot in the middle is you.

The area within the circle is your field of specialization; therefore any problem solution (save one by a greater specialist) which fits inside will be unacceptable because you already know all about it, and have probably tried it, and it doesn't work. § On the other hand, anything outside the circle is incomprehensible; any solution placed there will simply be inapplicable. § The generalist problem-solving area has got to be right on the circumference itself; close enough in so that you get it, far enough out so that you can't pick it to pieces.

HOW TO SOLVE PROBLEMS

McLuhan's terminology accommodates this concept and improves it by expanding it into a process. He would call the inside of the circle "environment," and the outside "anti-environment." § You can't really recognize things inside your environment, and you can't really see things outside it; so there we are sitting on the circumference again.

The thing that is added by this change in terms is this: you solve problems by expanding the environmental area, by moving the circumference out.

273

ANOTHER EXPLANATON

"Cliché to Archetype," McLuhan's main title, deserves an explanation here too. "Cliché" means any environmental element, omnipresent, unnoticed. It becomes noticed when the environment changes. § At this point, as it becomes "content" of the new environment, it also becomes an art form. If you live in a room that has cabbage rose patterned wallpaper, you will notice it at first but after awhile, it will become just wallpaper. What was once fresh and new turns into a cliché and assumes its role as part of the environment. § Now let us suppose that when you repaper the room, you decide to save a square of the old stuff and have it framed. As a picture it is no longer wallpaper, but content for the new environment.

Something else has happened too: it has become an art form. If it is successful as an art form and is admired and copied- or at any rate persists so that eventually it becomes the one and only from which all others emanate- it constitutes an archetype. § Today's archetype was yesterday's art form, day before yesterday's cliché, and the day before that it was the last word.

"WHAT IF HE IS RIGHT?"

It is hard to tell how much of the above will turn out to be McLuhan and how much McGuesswork when the book finally comes out. One thing is sure; it covers only a tiny bit of the material therein. § Tom Wolfe titled his jaunty, perspective piece on McLuhan in the *Sunday Herald Tribune Magazine* (Nov. 21, 1965), "Marshall McLuhan. Supposing He Is What He Sounds Like, The Most Important Thinker Since Newton, Darwin, Freud, Einstein and Pavlov – *What If He Is Right?*"

That's it, of course; the reason why he is attended by attentive, if mystified, communications and other business executives: what if he is right? § McLuhan's most powerful appeal, in the end, is to those who have thought themselves into a sort of intellectual isolation, who lie awake and groan, *"Doesn't anyone else think in the same patterns I do?"* For some of these McLuhan does.

Reprinted from <u>Ramparts</u> magazine, 4/66.
Illustrations by Dugald Stermer

The Famous "Gathering of Communicators" aboard the Ferryboat Klamath in 1965:
First Row: Walter Landor, Howard Gossage, Tom Wolfe. Top Row: Alice Lowe, Herb Caen, Justin Herman (city planner), Dr. Gerald Feigen (Gossage's partner in Generalists, Inc.), Mr. & Mrs. Marshall McLuhan. *Photograph courtesy Landor Associates*

"ADVERTISING IS NO BUSINESS FOR A GROWN MAN"

—Howard Gossage

He also said, "Freedom Of The Press must imply the public interest, otherwise why bother to guarantee it?" And, "It seems wrong to me that a newspaper (magazine) should go under while its readers still want it." In fact, he said a great deal about advertising's economic stranglehold on all forms of public communication and about the resulting loss regarding the public's rights and considerations—and he was in advertising.

On July 9, he died.

["STEALS YOUR WATCH"]

Gossage was really in the business of inventing people. He consistently maintained that his only genius was the ability to recognize and identify the talent of others and then to create an environment in which they could exercise it comfortably—"A rare ability indeed."

Nicholas Samstag, also recently deceased, once defined a consultant as one who "steals your watch and then tells you what time it is." It's been a bad year for good people.

[KICKBACK]

The advertising industry has long been operating under the illusion that its real business is purchasing space in the various mass media. Agencies make their money by buying the space from the publishers at a lower rate than you or I can, and then charging their clients the full tariff, pocketing the difference (20 per cent). The actual ads are produced almost as a sideline, as if an artist charged for the frame and threw in the painting as a bonus.

In the simplest terms, this means that the agency which is able to produce ads at the lowest cost, and can then con its clients into running them (often in the most expensive magazine pages or at prime time on television) makes the most money. Not only is this method inefficient, misleading and insulting, it is also probably illegal.

When he entered the ad game (at

about age 35), Gossage was called the "enfant terrible" of the industry, because he operated his agency on the principle that he should get paid for actually making ads for clients and products he liked—not for calling up some magazine to get a right-hand page up front. He even gave his clients back their 20 per cent, the premise being that everyone should pay the same price for the same space whether he called himself an agency or not, and that the only criterion for acceptability should be the question of taste—the editor's analysis of the tolerance level of his readers. (The same applies to television.)

[ORIGINAL SIN]

"Newspapers (magazines) ought to belong to their readers." Gossage felt that once the reader paid less for a publication than it cost to produce, he had traded away his power to keep it alive—much less to voice his opinion of its policies—and that this practice is patently wrong and probably ultimately disastrous to any notions we may still have regarding a free press.

It's pretty difficult for an editor to keep his readers in mind when he is losing money on every copy he sells. Most magazines that go belly-up do so with their readership on the increase,

simply because there aren't enough pages of advertising to pay for the difference in production costs.

And this is original sin: a publication loses its independence and its readers surrender their right to complain about that loss the moment those readers do not pay enough themselves to keep it alive. Make no mistake about it, the advertising industry is a most demanding mistress.

Gossage spent his life trying to reverse this trend. He felt that an advertisement appears only by permission of the editor and reader, that it should not insult, offend, or even interrupt the editorial flow; that it should be entertaining, informative, and never misleading. Advertising people called this approach "off-beat." (They are nothing if not trite—a weird bunch.)

["GROWN MAN"]

Some time ago RAMPARTS hired Gossage as a consultant and put him on the Board of Directors. One of the first things he did in this capacity was to drag me out of advertising to be RAMPARTS' Art Director, telling me at the time that I would have to take a pay cut, and that the magazine had about enough money to last four more months.

This issue marks the fourth *year* since then, and our survival is largely due to Gossage's efforts: raising investment capital, reorganizing the structure, and generally being a busy-body. (He was graceful when wrong, like the time he told us that the key to RAMPARTS' success was the retention of its Catholic origins—"Fortunately they ignored me.")

On the following pages appears part of a series of advertisements Howard wrote and designed for the Irish Whiskey Distillers. To my mind they are still some of the handsomest, best written, and most entertaining pages ever to appear anywhere in any publication.

Howard Gossage finally got out of advertising. —DUGALD STERMER

THE ADMAN WHO HATED ADVERTISING

by Warren Hinckle

"WHAT GOOD IS FREEDOM OF THE PRESS IF THERE ISN'T ONE?"

The sixties was the decade when the frightened cry of "Timber!" was everywhere in the unclean air of publishing. § The flow of competitive daily newspapers dried up, and magazines great and small fell like the trees chopped down for the paper to print them.

Now that the flagship *Life* has joined its lessers in the Sargasso Sea of bestilled publications, some conventional wisdom prevails as to how American publishing became trapped in such an economic rathole; spiraling production costs, quadrupling postage rates, blood-sucking competition for advertising dollars from television, the general malaise of the economy, mass circulations sustained at uneconomical cut rates, the decline of print, etcetera. § None of these reasons, to my way of thinking, explains the big picture. The man of thinking, explains the big picture. The man who, Cassandra-like, doped out what was going to happen, long before the casualty lists began to mount, was Howard

The man who, Cassandra-like, doped out what was going to happen, long before the casualty lists began to mount, was Howard Gossage.

Gossage. § Hardly anyone listened to him when he was alive and telling why so many papers were going to die. Now he is dead, and has the small epitaph of having been proved right.

Howard began to formulate his stone heresies, centering on the proposition that the reliance of publishing upon advertising was umbilic, transitory and fraught with peril, in the early sixties. § He kept it up, and kept increasing the ante, until he died in 1969; the decade previous, he had occupied himself throwing wooden chips in the porridge bowl of the advertising industry – here a deserved kick below the belt at the commission system, there a broadside at the billboard industry, here again a swipe at Smokey the Bear.

Smokey was the American advertising industry's gift to the nation, the symbol of the industry's vaunted "public service" campaign, which had the stated purpose of reducing forest fires. § Howard was aghast at the very idea that the advertising industry, which was responsible for so much of the glut and waste of consumerism and which had made of the country one giant depository for throwaway products including the automobile, so piously purported to be lending a helping hand to Old Mother Nature.

In fact, Howard said, Smokey the Bear was inept and potentially disastrous in his job; Gossage had amassed considerable statistics to argue that the forests were better off when people weren't breaking their matches, as Smokey so often told them, because numerous small forest fires were part of the state of nature, and the "improvement" rendered by the anti-forest fire campaign had produced a situation where the forests were imperiled by larger and more ruinous "blockbuster" forest fires.

"It's a simple matter of kicking sleeping dogs awake," Howard would say, when asked the obvious by those among the incredulous who could not savvy why an advertising man would so consistently bite the hand that fed him.

Gossage was a demanding man with a chalky, bony face, sunken eyeballs resting cheerily in charcoal gray pouches of skin, a magnificently busted nose and wild-demon white hair, who chainsmoked Gauloises like a Pittsburgh chimney. § He was the Socrates of San Francisco. The visiting gauntlet from Tom Wolfe to Terry Thomas came to call on him in the magnificently restored old firehouse on Pacific Street that was his place of work.

Gossage operated the Firehouse as if it were a French court, and he the captive king. He did everything first class – he ate, flew, wrote, talked, traveled first class. He believed every man should be comfortable while engaging in the necessary business of rescuing the world. He was at the time as open and innocent as a doe-eyed calf and as crafty as a raunchy old owl.

Howard was, nominally, in the advertising business. That at least was how he made his living, but he did it wholly on his own terms – first class – and with an originality of purpose and imagination that staggered the redundant minds of his profession. He was the inventor of Beethoven sweatshirts, the popularizer of Irish whiskey in America (he lived for a year in County Wicklow to get the taste of his task), and sky admiral of the Great Paper Airplane Contest of 1967. § His commercial outputs gained the rank of legend and a raft of copiers because of the strength of his stubborn originality. But Gossage was forever stirring up the waters that his bread was cast upon. He had little use for the advertising industry and felt very uncomfortable and apologetic about doing what he was so damn good at.

I owe some dues to the tradition of oral history, or the memory of Boswell, since although Howard talked almost constantly about his media theories – at least, he did to me – he rarely got around to writing them down, except in bits and pieces, and then usually in the self-defeating format of speeches to the advertising fraternity, those pearls who came to hear Gossage tell them what swine they were in much the same way that white liberals, in the halcyon days of the civil rights movement, would crowd into some Greenwich Village arena for the soul-cleansing experience of hearing LeRoi Jones tell them they were no good white motherfuckers.

It is accordingly in the nature of things that, although Howard Gossage was, within his profession, perhaps the most famous maverick of recent decades, he is known, in Daniel Boorstin's phrase, "for his well-knowness." Very few souls, except those of us who lived the hurricane experience of being close to him, know what he really thought. That wealth should, I think, be shared.

Gossage's postulate was based, as with so many things he did, on a great line: "What good is freedom of the press if there isn't one?"- a quotation Gossage made up, but laid the authorship on A. J. Liebling. § The quotation has a no doubt unprecedented use in the threnody of dead publications, or those about to die. Whenever Gossage employed those words, usually on the occasion of a publication's passing, he attributed them to the late Liebling, long *The New Yorker's* resident bird dog of the press. Although Liebling never said that, it sounded like something he *might* have said, and that was good enough for Howard. *"Otherwise, I'd be in the position of quoting myself,"* he said once, when I asked him why. (The attributing of bright things they were supposed to have said to people who had not in face said them was one of his favorite pastimes. The definition of a consultant as a man who borrows your watch to tell you what time it is, and then charges you for it – I have heard him credit, on separate occasions, to three different friends, advertising man Carl Ally, Gerry Feigen, and Nick Samstag, a valued co-conspirator.)

Howard believed that publishers had become quite piggish about Freedom of the Press, which they interpreted wholly as the freedom to publish. § But, he argued, there was also such a thing as Freedom of the Press for the Reader. Nobody thought much about that, especially the readers, who were largely unaware that their Freedom of the Press had been taken from them by the clubbish and ill-starred reliance of almost all publishers upon advertising revenues to sustain life, or, conversely, bring on death.

"In this century we have seen effective control of our press shift from the public, for whom it presumably exists, to the advertiser, who merely uses it to sell wares to the public."

"Vell, Herr Doktor Gossage, ist dot not apparantk?" I once heard a German advertising man (West Germany, of course) ask the Master. *"No!"* said Gossage, leaping to his feet, eyes flashing, arms waving, his shock of white hair flowing back like an unraveling turban. *"No!"* he said in his magnificent stammer, the words coming out hyphenated, slowly, as in water torture. *"No, bu-uu-buddy, it's not ap-par-ent- it's <u>ob-vi-ous,</u> and that's one hell of a big difference!"*

What was obvious to Howard had aspects of a sacred mushroom. He had an uncanny ability to see the obvious before anyone else, although not in the usual fashion of the self-deprecatory clap on the head: *"Mon Dieu!* All this time the letter was *here* on the sideboard!"* Gossage didn't merely see some pedestrian fact, such as the emperor having no clothes on, but rather some cosmic truth, a sudden blinding wisdom about the way things were that made everything else, related and interrelated, make some sort of grand, organic sense.

So it was with what Gossage saw as *obvious* about advertising, which was not just the truth about advertising but about communications, which was more than about communications; it had really to do with man's plight and man's fate, linked in so many ways to the definition and exchange and clash of ideas that was communications before the tinkerers and landlords and polluters of the media had at it...

The German advertising man said he did not understand. No wonder, said Gossage, explaining the man's own incomprehensions to him. "Loo-oook at it this way, bu-buu-buddy, *we don't know who discovered water, but we're pretty sure it wasn't a fish.*" That was another of Gossage's favorite quotations, a line of absolutely Delphic ambiguity. It came from his McLuhan Period, when he was schlepping McLuhan around the country, introducing him as Mohammed to his friends ruling the media mountains. Gossage was always kind of translating for the potty prophet. "What Marshall means by all this is that..." But a lot was added in the translation, and McLuhan would look at Gossage like the Mad Hatter peering over the tea cup and say, in a voice that was part confused innocence, part modest genius, "Gee, Howard, that's exactly what I meant when I wasn't saying it."

The fish-didn't-discover-water line Gossage, after his fashion, occasionally credited to McLuhan, when the great man was in need of explanation, but the more frequent quotee was Father John Culkin, then a Jesuit and a McLuhanite, Culkin may even have said that, but primary authorship was as difficult to trace in quotations favored by Gossage as the authorship of the Dead Sea Scrolls. At any rate, what Gossage told the German, courtesy of the Jesuit, was that it was no wonder he knew zilch about what advertising really was, since he was

Gossage told the German… it was no wonder he knew zilch about what advertising really was, since he was in it: "You become aware of your environment only when you, somehow, get outside of it."

in it: *"You become aware of your environment only when you, somehow, get outside of it."* he maintained.

The process, or posture, by which one could see one's own environment, or profession, or country, for what it really was – the fish looking in from outside the fish bowl – Howard called "extra-environmental" perception. § That is, the person oblivious to, or not conditioned by, his surroundings would see things. This intuitive capacity he explained by analogy to the color-blind aerial observers recruited during World War II because their color blindness enabled them to see things which were camouflaged to normally sighted eyes; Gossage thought it marvelous that these guys would look down at a quite ordinary stretch of landscape and say, *"Hey, there's a gun emplacement!"*

My faith in the obvious was never quite as strong as Howard's, so I saved these notes, taken from the Gossage, for a syllabus of errors, suitable for tacking on the front door of the cathedral of Madison Avenue.

Although most of us accept advertising as some sort of providential clock, taking its tick-tock from whatever deity governs the market economy, the fact is that advertising is relatively a Johnny-come-lately. It did not exist in the mass-market form that we know much before World War I, and did not exist in any form at all before the late 19th century.

But before advertising, there were newspapers and magazines. They were very much as we know them today, except of course that the pages were filled with news instead of paid hustle. Since they had almost no other source of revenue, the publications of that time lived or died by the reader's penny spent, and charged an honest price; if a publication cost five cents to produce, you can bet a publisher charged at least five cents for it, and hoped like hell that what his paper had to say was interesting enough to get enough people to pony up their nickels. It is no coincidence that the great muckraking magazines of American legend flourished under these game conditions; he who pays the piper calls the tune, and the only paymaster was their readers, who apparently liked what the muckrakers were playing.

If this was publishing's state of nature, advertising was its original sin. With the growth of consumer advertising early in this century, publishers found themselves in the sudden happy situation of getting income from both ends; and they enjoyed that mightily, as one will gravy.

Although most of us accept advertising as some sort of providential clock, taking its tick-tock from whatever deity governs the market economy, the fact is that advertising is relatively a Johnny-come-lately.

With the growth of consumer advertising early in this century, publishers found themselves in the sudden happy situation of getting income from both ends; and they enjoyed that mightily, as one will gravy.

At a point uncertain in time but no later than the flapper days of the post-World War I period, publishers took the fatal bite from the apple. Faced with rising costs, most publishers decided not to risk losing circulation by raising the price per copy accordingly. This decision was dictated by elemental greed, not charity toward the penny-pinching reader; the way publishers figured it, they could get more money from advertisers the more readers they had, so what the hell, why antagonize the customers when the advertisers were footing the bill?

"Well," said Gossage, "that tore it." The day a reader paid five cents for a publication that cost six cents to produce was the day, by Gossage's calculation, that he lost his economic Freedom of the Press.

Publishers soon became so hooked on the gravy of advertising that they could not do without it and, the first junkies, took to junk mail, discovering that they could "buy" readers, that is, build up circulation, simply by lowering the subscription price, making it a loss leader while getting a handsome return from the advertisers – while it lasted.

The reader has paid dearly for all this. For one thing, he suffered the ultimate indignity that Western society can bestow upon its members: he became a consumer. The word "consumer" is another cigarette burn in the tablecloth of the English language that we can trace to the chain smokers of Madison Avenue. When advertisers speak of consumers they think they mean people, but they don't. What they call a consumer is, by Gossage's definition, *"an anthropomorphic being designed to use whatever it is you have to sell – it will therefore be a grotesque on the order of the monsters of Hieronymous Bosch or Artzybasheff: all mouth or belly, but, in these days of automatic drive, just one foot."*

For a second thing, the cheaper that publications were priced, the fewer of them there were. Publications died right and left without regard to the fact that their subscribers were loyally paying their bills, or that their readers actually *liked* them. A newspaper reader who pays a dime for a paper that actually costs thirty-five cents to produce is being subsidized, and has as much to say about whether his favorite paper will live or die as he did about ending the war in Vietnam. Gossage's favorite illustration of the utter madness of publishing economics was that a newspaper or magazine was the only consumer product from bubble gum to bras, where the selling price had no relation to the actual cost

The word "consumer" is another cigarette burn in the tablecloth of the English language that we can trace to the chain smokers of Madison Avenue.

of production. It costs less, for instance, to have a magazine delivered at home than it does to buy it in the store; try that with milk.

Naturally, advertisers want to reach as many people as possible, but not necessarily in as many publications as possible. That can be rather expensive in, say, a town with six daily newspapers. Both wasteful duplication and angst about making the right choices among the six papers would be eliminated if there were only, say, two daily newspapers. The advertisers could reach everybody who read the papers in those two, saving the expense and bother of the other four.

Since Gossage began preaching his Apocalypse in the early sixties, a veritable armada of newspapers and magazines has gone down with circulations intact, so there is demonstrably something to what he said.

The way Gossage figured it, *"People don't read ads; they read what interests them, and sometimes it is an ad."* Similarly, there is only one process of the flow of ideas and exchange of information – "communications," which includes billboards, and whatever – and it is that entire process of information and mass education that advertising, in Gossage's phrase, has firmly by the sweetbreads.

Whether advertising doesn't want or shouldn't have such power over the press is immaterial. The fact is that it has it, and Gossage's singular contribution to the pole-axed discussions of the narcoleptic state of the mass media was to raise original questions about the responsibility that is implicit in such enormous power. It is a question that is largely ducked in the more popular critiques of the media; when Spiro Agnew opened fire at the Eastern Establishment types conducting the press according to their own tunes, it is doubtful that he was thinking of the media buyers of Madison Avenue, who not only pay for the orchestra and the sheet music, but also subsidize the audience.

Advertising is generally assumed, even by its critics, to be necessary to the economy. Howard Gossage found that a highly questionable and undifferentiated assumption. *"That's a crock of sour owl shit."* was how he put it, with uncharacteristic brevity. Although apologists for advertising say it makes the wheels go 'round, Gossage maintained that most advertising merely makes some wheels go 'round, and pretty dinky wheels at that. The way he totted it up, over half of national advertising goes for items which account for barely five percent

Since Gossage began preaching his Apocalypse in the early sixties, a veritable armada of newspapers and magazines has gone down with circulations intact, so there is demonstrably something to what he said.

of the Gross National Product, and perhaps 2 percent of the labor market; bulwarks of a strong and free economy such as breakfast cereals, soaps, cosmetics, hair oils, toothpastes, deodorants, smokes, and booze. Taking television by itself, the figures are even more striking; fully two-thirds of television advertising is in those and kindred categories of fee-fo-fum.

"Viewed in its entirety, advertising is a seventeen-billion-dollar sledgehammer to drive a forty-nine-cent thumbtack," said Gossage.

The constitutional guarantee of Freedom of the Press from government control tends to obscure other incursions that can equally limit the citizen's plurality of choice and content, and are therefore just as dangerous. That these incursions are economic rather than political makes them much harder to recognize, Gossage said, since politics is a *bad* word, but economics is a *nice* word. § But *Star Trek* fans and other bereaved deprived of their favorite programs know there is an unseen Evil Hand at work. It is hard to conceive of television being such a mishmash if programs were not designed primarily to be attractive advertising "buys" geared to reach the largest gluttonous mass of unblinking consumers.

Howard believed in the power of analogy as a talisman which would ward off any lack of comprehension of his theories. He was constantly building elaborate analogy-castles in the sky, and none was more elaborate than his ultimate analogy of the process by which advertising shapes the content of the media it controls.

What has happened to television, he said, is what would happen to football if the hot dog vendors took over the game.

Gossage insisted that a good analogy should be capable of "being engraved on the head of a ten milligram Dexamyl tablet." This one is a little longer than that.

THE HOT DOG ANALOGY

by Howard Luck Gossage

[As told, at least 100 times, to Hinckle]

Hot dogs are nice, but they are not the reason people go to the stadium. They go to see the game, but as long as they are there, why not have a hot dog?

That is also, somewhat, the operating principle of commercial television. Once the crowd is there to see the show, you also sell them something.

However, to get the big picture about television, you have to reverse the analogy.

The constitutional guarantee of freedom of the press from government control tends to obscure other incursions that can equally limit the citizen's plurality of choice and content, and are therefore just as dangerous.

291

*What has
happened to
television, he
said, is what
would happen
to football if the
hot dog vendors
took over
the game.*

Suppose that the proceeds from hot dog sales were greater than ticket receipts. § Moreover, hot dog-wise it is more profitable to have a full stadium, even if you have to let spectators in for nothing, or at greatly reduced admission, than to charge full admission to a smaller crowd of die-hard fans, who are the only ones who regularly show up when the home team is on a losing streak, anyway.

This would shortly affect the complexion of the audience, and eventually the game, because it's never quite the same thing when you get it free, and the type of people who are willing to pay for their pleasure expect a different quality of show than those who get it on the cheap. But as we are now only interested in numbers, things would be going along famously; the stadium is packed and the bleachers happy, even though by getting in for free the spectators have been demoted from fans to potential hot dog consumers.

Now, along comes that old spoilsport, economics. High football production costs make it necessary to bring in more money, and, as it is impractical to call in the Pinkertons to bust up the players' union, increased volume is the only answer to the profits to which you have become accustomed.

However, once the spectators have become accustomed to seeing games for nothing, you certainly can't expect them to pay. The only thing to do is to sell more hot dogs.

The simplest marketing solution is to create ten-minute intermissions between quarters, on top of the traditional half-time break, so the fans can better stretch their pocketbooks and hear their stomachs growling. But, so as not to extend the game so much that it runs over into the game which immediately follows in the same stadium- the late game – five minutes are chopped off each period.

So spectators wander in and out the open gates with varying degrees of interest; and sometimes hardly anybody is interested, even for free; attendance dwindles. To cope with that, the games that pull the biggest and most enthusiastic crowds are studied for their successful formats. Soon, all games are alike – including a mandatory five interceptions, one bloody field free-for-all, and an upset victory in the last ten seconds by a forty-yard pass or seventy-yard run, interchangeable so the suspense does not become monotonous.

Thus, football would be a sort of open-air television; the analogy wasn't perfect, Howard admitted, because if you wanted to escape the hot dog vendor during intermissions, you had to walk a half-mile to the bathroom.

PROFESSOR GOSSAGE

Gossage developed this thought while lecturing as a visiting professor at Penn State in 1962. When he expounded at his usual length about it, he inevitably got into a discussion of the "rights" of advertisers versus those of the spectators. One insistent coed, like the dreadful little girl who recited to a captive Lewis Carroll during a long carriage ride the entire text of *The Hunting of the Snark,* kept arguing that advertisers had the right to control what was on television, because, after all, they paid for it. Howard asked if she thought that hot dog vendors had the right to control the university's football games. *"Of course,"* she said, *"if they paid my way in."*

When Gossage got annoyed his stammers came on like jackhammers, his spectacles would perch up on the edge of his nose – an epic, beat-up nose that suggested the bumps and grinds and contours of a freeway interchange collapsed in an earthquake.

"But what right have they got to pay your way in?" he fumed. *"Whose football game is it? Whose stadium is it? Whose university is it? It's yours. It doesn't belong to the hot dog vendors, it belongs to you; and so do our communications media."*

Broadcasting is most arguably a public utility, using as it does the public air for private profit; but Howard was upset that the FCC, while accepting this proposition to the extent of regulating broadcasting license applications, shied from the even more basic issue of regulating the advertising industry that had more control over the content of broadcasting than the station owners or the networks themselves, since Madison Avenue was paying everybody's way.

To the insistent coed who argued that advertisers who pay the piper have the right to call the tunes Lawrence Welk plays, Gossage's reply was: Baloney – advertising got itself into that position by default, and it was a default that had become self-perpetuating. It had been that way for so long that people just didn't realize it could be any other way. Yet the day was long past when anyone would argue that any private industry, such as electricity or transportation or telephones, could do what it wanted with a public necessity, or necessary public convenience, that it wholly controlled; but only Gossage thought of communications, and advertising, in the same way.

Gossage had the sauce to tell the advertising industry that it had the responsibility to inform the public just what terrible shape the mass media were in because of their dependence on, and connivance with, advertising. Instead of running all those "public service" ads in favor of US Savings Bonds, or coming out four-square against forest fires, Howard wanted the ad boys to mount a massive campaign to get the price of newspapers and magazines up to a realistic, fair figure (and to get overinflated circulations, accordingly, down). Gossage even invented a catchy, advertising-type name for it: Pay Reading. *"We have to put over the idea that a newspaper is worth at least as much as a package of cigarettes,"* he often said.

Throughout the sixties, when advertisers were flocking to the happy land of television at the expense of the mass magazines they had helped create. Gossage told them they were little better than murderers, and not even mercy killers; in league with greedy publishers, ad men had gotten the reading public hooked on cheap magazines, which meant there were fewer magazines, with less difference between them — and now they were killing the publications that they had artificially kept alive, pulling the plug from

"We have to put over the idea that a newspaper is worth at least as much as a package of cigarettes."

295

*He tried
to explain
to the lords
of advertising
that reform was
in their own
self-interest,
that so many
lousy ads
cluttering up
the tube was
counter-produc-
tive for their
clients, that
people were
turned off by
advertising
domination...*

the kidney machine, without so much as a tip of the hat to the widowed reading public. The least the advertising industry could do, Howard said, was to tidy up the graveyard and attempt to put American publishing back in the more or less healthy state it was in before Madison Avenue subverted it.

Gossage had harsher readjustments to suggest for the nation's favorite whipping boy, television, which ill-used the same air space. Since the television channels were owned by the citizens, and the owners were merely licensed to operate them in the public interest, who was it who said the stations ever had the right to interrupt programs with commercial announcements, which could just as well be bunched between programs while people went to the bathroom? It was only that the considerable profits of the stations were even more considerable that way, and they did it only because they got away with it — more precisely because the FCC let them get away with it.

As it was inconceivable that a good newspaper or magazine would allow an advertiser to sponsor its articles, so, Gossage argued, it should be with television — advertisers would take pot luck as to when and where their TV spots ran, somewhat along the lines of the system operative on the English commercial channels, where ads are grouped on a rotating basis between programs and there is no such animal as commercial "sponsorship" of a show.

That was the type of thing Gossage used to tell advertising men; it is little wonder they didn't listen. § He tried to explain to the lords of advertising that reform was in their own self-interest, that so many lousy ads cluttering up the tube was counter-productive for their clients, that people were turned off by advertising domination, that Madison Avenue should renew itself by strangling the golden calf; but his fellow hot dog vendors didn't listen to that either.

At times, when he would get discouraged, Gossage would look out the window at a gray San Francisco day, his eagle face wrinkled up in a frown, and say, *"To explain responsibility to advertising men is like trying to convince an eight-year-old that sexual intercourse is more fun than a chocolate ice cream cone."*

❧

"To explain responsibility to advertising men is like trying to convince an eight-year-old that sexual intercourse is more fun than a chocolate ice cream cone."

❧

"Journalist-activist/renegade and Jesuit trouble-maker" Warren Hinckle *is the former muckraking editor of* Ramparts Magazine *and author of* If You've Got a Lemon Make Lemonade *(from which this article was excerpted),* The Agnos Years, Deadly Secrets: The CIA War Against Castro and the Assassination of JFK, The Fourth Reich: The Menace of the New Germany, The Mitchell Brothers, New York Without Jews, Rediscovering American Resources *and others.*

> *"Jerry Mander is not a political district finagling system, but the only person who has ever understood what I am up to."*
>
> *Howard Gossage*

"THE RALPH NADER OF ADVERTISING"

Howard's last partner was a young mover and shaker from New York, Jerry Mander. He has carried on another part of Howard's legacy – as the founder and now senior fellow of the first non-profit ad agency, The Center for Public Media. § He has been called (by the *Wall Street Journal*) "The Ralph Nader of Advertising." Mr. Mander is the co-author (with Howard Gossage) of *The Great International Paper Airplane Book,* and, more importantly, author of *Four Arguments for the Elimination of Television* and *In The Absence of The Sacred. The Failure of Technology and the Survival of the Indian Nations.* § The following is excerpted from the introduction to *Four Arguments...*

It begins like this...

> ❧   ❧   ❧

MY FATHER RAN A CLOTHING BUSINESS.

I had always planned something flashier for myself, something with greater glamour. It was snobbery, I suppose. § When I thought about my career - always a hot topic around our house - certain images would fly through my mind. Since so many of the images were from the ads of the period, the world of advertising seemed appropriate. There was something about that lifestyle, those big cars, ... the polished people... the life of leisure and pleasure - The Dream.

IN 1966 MY DREAM WAS REALIZED.

Following a successful career as head of a theatrical publicity agency, I joined the celebrated San Francisco ad agency of Freeman & Gossage. Later it became Freeman, Mander & Gossage. § It was the most elegant office in town. I was commuting coast to coast weekly, taking five-day vacations in Tahiti, eating only in French restaurants, jetting to Europe for a few days' skiing.

We concentrated on so-called class clients. Triumph, Land Rover and Rover cars. Eagle shirts. Paul Masson wines. KLH audio equipment. *Scientific American.* Random House publishing.

While I was showing clients through my

PANELED OFFICES,

a lot of people only slightly younger than I were lying about on the floors of San Francisco auto showrooms, restaurants and hotels, demanding that these places hire blacks.

Across the Bay in Berkeley, students were stopping classes to insist upon participation in university policies. Thousands of others were standing in front of trains carrying war materials for Vietnam or blocking entryways to draft induction centers.

Living in the Bay Area in those years, one could scarcely avoid reflection and even involvement in these goings-on. In my own case, the involvement soon became direct.

Since I had been a publicist, I knew many reporters and had a feeling for the nuances of influencing media. Because of that, and through friendship with a number of politically inclined actors in a satirical comedy group called The Committee, I began to meet many protest leaders and found myself serving as a part-time media advisor for some of the demonstrations. § Like many young lawyers, I was part of what was called "the liberal support group."

...GOSSAGE KNEW THAT THERE WAS MORE

to the problem of advertising than the way it emphasizes trivia. He would rage about the function itself, speaking of it as an invasion of privacy on an order far more extreme than the merely rude telephone solicitation, the door-to-door salesperson or even the computer file on your credit. § *Because advertising was an invasion of the mind, which altered behavior, altered people.*

"Advertising expresses a power relationship," Gossage said. § One person, the advertiser, invades; millions absorb. And to what end? So that people will buy something! A deep, profound and disturbing act by the few against the many for a trivial purpose.

THE ECOLOGY MOVEMENT PUSHED ME OVER THE EDGE.

Our agency was hired first by the Sierra Club and then by Friends of the Earth and other organizations. § Unlike most other do-good groups, these had a little money to buy an occasional one-shot ad on some critical issue. § I found myself writing ads about keeping dams out of Grand Canyon. We wrote ads about halting the overdevelopment of cities, stopping the development of SST's, and urging people to stop buying and wearing furs.

The ads attacked the prevailing lifestyle of the country, which certainly included my own. § They spoke of an inevitable conflict between corporate growth and the health of the planet. They encouraged a habit of mind which could grasp the inter-relationships between all natural systems, including humans. § They described a growing environmental destruction which reflected itself in individual lives as well as in economic policies.

As I thought about these ads, it got harder and harder to separate my new perspective from an awareness that it was in conflict with our corporate work. § On Tuesday, I was writing about the impact cars and other technologies had upon the environment, and on Thursday I was promoting the sale of cars.

THE CRUNCH CAME ONE DAY IN 1969

when a young *Wall Street Journal* reporter called about doing a story on our agency's public-service work. § By that time we had gained public attention for having invented a new style of advocacy advertising. § Our ads were characterized by coupons urging changes in policy. The coupons could be torn out by readers and sent to corporations and government agencies. § They produced enormous volumes of mail on conservation issues that until then had been considered the province of bird watchers and little old ladies in tennis shoes.

THE ADS HAD NOT ONLY AFFECTED POLICY,

they catalyzed and organized the public, because they allowed a new level of involvement. § By mailing them, people became more committed to the issue. For once they were doing something more than feeling bad. A number of senators and congressmen publicly gave the ads credit for determining the outcome of several issues, and Robert Glatzer in *The New Advertising* went so far as to credit them with *"starting the whole ecology boom."*

The reporter told us that the *Journal* was interested in the way we had developed this technique. However, while the story that appeared on the front page praised our work, the reporter went to considerable lengths to reveal our misgivings about our conflicting roles. § The article cited my own anxiety at doing ads for an auto account, British Leyland Motors (Rover, Land Rover, Triumph), at a time that I was making speeches that said automobiles were at the heart of so many problems.§ Leyland didn't like this. Within two hours of the story's appearance we were fired.

The next day's *Journal* carried the headline: AD MAN NEED WORRY NO MORE ABOUT AUTO ACCOUNT.

I could describe fifty less spectacular incidents similar to this one. § We began to feel that our balancing act was draining us personally. Maintaining commercial accounts in the hope of using the income from them to finance other projects about which we cared more deeply was not going to work out. [Editor's Note: At about this time, Howard passed away.]

...FOR YEARS BEFORE HE DIED in 1969, Howard agonized about the absurdity of working in such a profession. § He loved to tell the story of the retired ad man who once said to him: *"I got out of this business when I woke up one day and didn't give a damn whether they sold more Quaker Oats than I sold Cream of Wheat."* [Note: This quote was attributed – by Howard – to James Webb Young.] He also said, *"I'd hate to go to my grave and be remembered as the man who invented Beethoven sweatshirts or competitions for paper airplanes."*

I began to work with a number of other people to establish a foundation-funded, non-profit advertising and public relations office.

THE FIRST IN THE COUNTRY,
it was called Public Interest Communications
and it was devoted solely to working for
community organizations which are largely
excluded from media.

The project was launched in 1972 with a
grant we used for ecologists and farm workers,
consumer groups, Indian rights activists and
peace groups…

> ॐ   ॐ   ॐ

That project continues to this day.

Today, Mr. Mander is senior fellow at
The Center for Public Media. At the
conclusion of *Four Arguments for the Elimination of Television,* he writes…

*"Howard Gossage exposed me to a way of
thinking about media, its power and its
absurdities, which probably affected my own
perceptions more than any other single person
or source.*

*Often while working on this project, I
found myself mentally checking with the way he
would have seen them, his mind remains that
alive for me."*

Excerpted with permission of the author from
"Four Arguments for the Elimination of Television"
© 1977, 1978 by Jerry Mander.
Published by Quill. New York

ॐ

*"Howard
Gossage
exposed me
to a way
of thinking
about media,
its power and
its absurdities,
which probably
affected my
own perceptions
more than any
other single
person or
source."*

ॐ

FOUR ARGUMENTS FOR THE ELIMINATION OF ADVERTISING:

1) All advertising is a gross invasion of privacy;

2) All advertising is political propaganda representing only the rich to the detriment of everyone else;

3) All advertising is dependent upon economic growth, which further concentrates wealth and power while destroying the planet;

4) All advertising encourages the centralization of feeling, destroys diversity of experience, and corrupts human interaction.

MAIL TO: Public Media Center • 466 Green St. • San Francisco, CA 94133 • 415-434-1403
Dear Mr. Mander,
I'd like to know more about your organization.
Name: _____
Company: _____
Address: _____
City: _____ State: ___ Zip: _____
Phone: _____ Fax: _____
❐ Enclosed is my check for $_____.
❐ Please send me more information.

MAIL TO: The Copy Workshop • 2144 N. Hudson • Chicago, IL 60614 • 312-871-1179
Dear Copy Workshop,
I'd like to know more about your organization.
Name: _____
Company: _____
Address: _____
City: _____ State: ___ Zip: _____
Phone: _____ Fax: _____
❐ I can handle it. Send the complete text of "Four Arguments for the Elimination of Advertising."

Whatever became of back yard fallout shelters? Remember? They were *the* topic for years. It was big business, remember the ads? Banks offered E-Z credit. IBM gave employees interest-free loans. Companies were formed with names like Surviv-All. Clergymen argued the morality of shooting your neighbor if he tried to get in, and TV was filled with dramas on the theme. Remember them? "Life" published details on How to Build Your Own Survival Shelter. And every one of us, for at least a moment, thought maybe it *was* a good idea. Remember? What happened? It was only seven years ago. How many of those back yard shelters still exist, stocked with condensed milk, stale water, and army cots? Are they playrooms now? When did we stop believing we could ever be "safe" in fallout shelters? We were all taken in, for an

Howard's last ad. This dramatic two-page ad features the "Gossage spread" (cont.)

305

instant anyway. It was a mass delusion, but we wanted to believe we could still do *something*. Remember? Well, now, what do you think about the ABM?

Please fill in and mail to Cass Canfield, Harper & Row, Publishers, 49 East 33d Street, N.Y., N.Y. 10016. We will tally the results and forward them to Congress.

I REALLY BELIEVE MY FAMILY AND I WILL BE SAFE ONCE WE PROCEED WITH THE "SAFEGUARD" ABM

YES ☐   NO ☐

Just published, and in your bookstore now:

"ABM: An Evaluation of the Decision to Deploy an Anti-Ballistic Missile System"

BACK IN THE DAYS of back-yard fallout shelters, seven years ago, there remained the delusion that each one of us could do something individually to protect our families and ourselves.

Never mind that most of us didn't actually build a shelter, we *considered* it. That showed our vulnerability to "security" appeals right there. And ever since then, whenever the Pentagon announced some new multi-billion dollar "safety" system we tended to go for the "experts'" word that it was just the thing.

It is certainly understandable. A man has got to believe in something. And in this, the nuclear-computer age, the forces that control a man's life or death have been pretty much removed from his *own* decision-making power. The data is *so* complicated and so much of it is classified, how are we to know what to think about it, one way or the other? Most of us laymen haven't yet figured out if it's a good idea to get into airplanes, or how they ever manage to stay up in the air.

With no way even to start thinking intelligently about today's "security" problems, we tend simply not to think about them at all. The result is that our safety is truly in the lap of the gods, or, to put it more accurately, in the lap of the Pentagon.

Experts in high places "with greater access to information" tell us that for our safety we need this or that. And we implicitly give our go-ahead and wind up paying for it besides. Like putting quarters into the insurance machine before getting onto an airplane. It won't keep the plane up, but at least it's doing something.

Which brings us to ABM.

"An anti-missile defense is foolproof. It will give us a seamless garment of security in an age of acute danger."
    —AP quote from pro-ABM presentation, May 7, 1969

The ABM (Sentinel-Safeguard) is probably the most complicated electronic system ever attempted.

Each of its elements—missiles, computers, radars—is at the extreme of sophistication for its type. The computer programming alone, for example, presents problems not yet solved even on the theoretical level.

The computers will be asked simultaneously to steer the radars, identify potential targets, predict trajectories, distinguish between warheads and the thousands of possible decoys, eliminate false targets, reject signals from earlier explosions (some of which may be deliberately diversionary), correct for blackout effects, allocate and guide interceptor missiles, and *automatically arm and fire them* if an enemy missile is interpreted as being in range.

All of this must be done continuously and with 100% precision between the time attacking missiles first appear and their moment of impact. That time may be as little as 10 minutes.

The whole operation, in other words, is just too rapid and complex even to allow for human checking or more than a last second okay by the President.

The computer will do the checking itself.

Well. If everyone knew for sure that Safeguard would work, then there might be some (shaky) confidence about turning our lives over to it. But a look at the chart shows the gap between expected performance and actual performance in the case of systems many times less complex than this one. Performance is nearly always below promise, even when there is plenty of time and the possibility for testing.

There is no such margin of error with Safeguard. It must work first time out. There is no reason to believe it will.

The possible consequences of its not working just so may be illustrated by this Newsweek note, December 19, 1960, concerning the Pentagon's previous "security" creation, Ballistic Missile Early Warning System:

"The Air Force disclosed last week that the giant radar picked up a [hostile] signal, and the 'missile's' position [30 minutes from a U.S. target] was instantly flashed on a screen at the underground SAC headquarters in Omaha."

Fortunately for the world, the reflex to counterstrike, which was supposed to be nearly instantaneous upon sighting of such an enemy missile heading our way, did not operate on this day, simply because the scientists who worked on BMEWS radar, and who supervised and knew its real capabilities had in their hearts no confidence that it had yet been made to work with any reliability. They realized the much too frequent fallibilities of such inventions as these. It is a good thing they did. For as Newsweek concluded:

"The 'missile' that had reflected the radar signal turned out to be the moon."

MODERN WEAPONS SYSTEMS—PERFORMANCE MEASURED AGAINST ORIGINAL EXPECTATIONS

The chart compares actual performance achievement against Pentagon promises for systems not nearly as complex as Safeguard. The study from which it was extracted also shows that on the average these systems—even if they didn't work at all—cost from 200-300% more than was budgeted for them, and whichever ones were created in a hurry, like Safeguard will be, cost the most and failed the most. Included among the "disappointments" are the BMEWS system, the SAGE system, and the DEW line system, which have been the backbone of our "defense" over the last years. This news raises indelible questions concerning how "safe" complex technology has ever made us. Of course, even if they "work," anything less than destruction of *every* warhead aimed at our cities would result in millions of deaths. And there simply is no way to calculate for every contingency of an attack. As Professor Herbert York, writing in Scientific American, said: "Such calculations always involve predictions about the form of the attack. But since the form is unknowable the calculations are nonsensical."

Malfunction of such new equipment as BMEWS is more the rule than the exception. And yet now, some scientists at the Pentagon say we should proceed with a far more difficult project, and, what's worse, one that does not allow for ultimate human analysis and control.

At a certain point it is necessary for the people in whose names these creations are introduced to remind government that we do not wish to abdicate our rights of control and approval merely because we don't understand the technology right off. We do understand the consequences.

And simply taking the experts' word, while it may relieve the anxiety (as with back yard fallout shelters), all too often leaves us with the feeling that we've just had one more turn around the track after the rabbit we can never catch.

It is the ultimate conclusion of the authors of "ABM: An Evaluation of the Decision to Deploy an Antiballistic Missile System" that Safeguard, for all its tens of billions of dollars, will produce at best a *false* sense of security, and at worst, an increased prospect for nuclear war.

They explain why, point by point, cutting through the technological rhetoric, demonstrating the distinctions between Pentagon fantasy and simple fact.

The book is, therefore, the first full scale attempt to provide, in lay terms, and while the Congressional debate still rages, the non-Pentagon side of this issue.

You will find it in bookstores now. *(Harper & Row cloth-bound edition, $5.95; New American Library paperback, $.95.)*

Abridged Table of Contents from

"ABM: AN EVALUATION OF THE DECISION TO DEPLOY AN ANTIBALLISTIC MISSILE SYSTEM"

The book also contains extensive notes, a glossary, basic documents, and a summary of the full case against ABM deployment at this time.

...utilizing both sides of the same page. Gossage felt this created more involvement.

FROM OUR ARCHIVES…

Here are some more pieces of Howard's work that caught our eye. § In this cartoon, he expresses thanks for having divined an almost divine idea, only to have it, like the light bulb, broken. § From *Sometimes It's Advertising,* an un-published work by Robert Brewster Freeman.

A
Valentine
For Marget
(you gotta use
special techniques
to snag the
brainy ones)

Howard Dean

A VALENTINE

from Howard Gossage to Marget Larsen

When Marget first came to work with Howard, she was wearing very pointed shoes. By chance, a client from Portland, Freddy Wessinger of Blitz-Weinhard, and the market research man, the later famous Lou Harris, were in town. After introducing them, Howard asked. *"Tell me, Marget... where do you get your shoes sharpened?"*

From Sometimes It's Advertising.

Mr. and Mrs. Howard Luck Gossage
Pension Les Bastions
18 Rue de Candolle
Geneva, Switzerland

Gossage report

Vol. 1, No. 11

LETTER FROM HOME, or The Duck Who Made Good

When the diplomatic pouch was delivered to our hand this morning at Ten Hundred Hours by the help, a well-muscled fraulein of perhaps 14 stone, we found a lone letter from San Francisco. The writer, one Dean Moxley, is an old expense account item dating from those happy and distant days when I entertained the toffs of the advertising world in the diamond encrusted purlieus of the Palace Hotel with only a casual glance at the staggering total of the bill before I tacked on a little something for the waiter to buy another polo pony with.

Moxley, a keen observer of the sub-human, recounted an experience so poignant that I must pass it on. He was in New York last summer and all this happened on the day that the American Legion marched for 12 hours as a fitting climax to its national convention....

"I met a friend of mine at the Plaza about 5:30. The bar was filled with New Yorkers huddling together within sound of drums and bugles. The men were dressed in their tight-shouldered Brooks Brothers shantung suits and their hats placed squarely on their heads so they looked to me like a group of Godless Amish. At a nearby table there was a most beautiful and worldly looking doll, a sort of aging Za Za Gabor, with three oldish men who could have been international munitions magnates. They were talking French. Then what happened was amazing. A drunken World War I Legionnaire came in with the most extroverted duck I ever saw, on a leash. The duck was quacking, quacking loudly, and was dirty as hell from walking around New York all day with his buddy. The ZaZa went out of her mind at the sight of the bird. She reached down and petted it, offered it a canape, which it gobbled, and gave it a sip of her martini to wash it down. The old soldier, aware of a chance to do himself some good, asked the woman if she'd like to buy the duck. The price was set at $10.00, at which the three men with her brought out those fat pouches that will hold bonds as well as cash and there were three bills at her disposal. She took the first one she could reach and the transaction was completed. The Legionnaire moved up to the bar while the excited blonde called for a bell-boy whom she told to take the duck to her suite and give him a bath so he could go to dinner with his new mistress at 8:00. Still quacking like mad, the duck was borne away to a life that could only be filled with glamour with such a woman. My friend and I contemplated all this and decided that we had just witnessed one of those miracles called the lucky break. Here was an upstate duck, well up in years, a bird who could only hope to survive another few hours on the crowded streets of New York with a drunken master. He would be trampled to death by the revelling throngs before midnight. But just because his master led him into the Plaza Bar at an instant when a munitions makers darling was perhaps feeling lonely for something that could really be hers, this duck made a deal that transformed his entire life. Now he will live out his years amid diamonds and candlelight and gay conversation in all languages but English. And all he'll ever have to do is just look happy and say quack quack once in a while."

I think there is a message in this for all of us.

The Tale of The Lucky Duck. From The Gossage Report, "a publication which was published every so often," telling about the adventures of the Gossages in Europe. This one was posted from Europe and then Bob Freeman printed it in the US (with illustrations from Lowell Herrero) and mailed to Howard's friends. A charming example of Howard's writing.

WOMEN ARE DIFFERENT FROM MEN !

by ANONYMOUS

(The 19th amendment, as we know, became law on August 26, 1920 and gave the vote to women. This was a poor idea, according to some authorities. They feel that, as a result, masculine and feminine roles have become so confused that everything else has become confused too. Things don't even taste the same any more. We are not confused, our ale is male, just the way it always has been; it has a male flavor and a male color. We feel that the whole subject deserves a good deal of thought, so today we have a guest contributor who asks that his name be withheld.)

"Many people believe that it used to be a man's world and now it is a woman's world. This is not so.

"The truth is that it used to be a man's *and* a woman's world. Why? Because in those days even idiots knew that men and women were different from each other, they liked different things. Some things were for men and some for women.

"She felt womanly and he felt manly—not that either one of them felt there was a choice.

"And then one day (August 26, 1920) everything started to change. The idea got around that women were not really so different from men after all. So a lot of things that used to be made to please men *or* women are now made to please both. And *nobody* is very pleased.

"Automobiles, for example. It used to be that a woman could enter a car gracefully. She stepped on the running board (after the man had opened the door for her, remember?) and *walked* in, like a lady. Nowadays, no running boards, and a girl has to sort of skootch in, especially in a tight skirt. It's the most pitiful thing you ever saw.

"Not that men get much out of it either; the roof is so low they can't even wear hats any more. All because some well meaning mfr. got a thoughtful idea one day and said, 'Hey, let's ask women what *they* like.'

"You can imagine the answers he got.

"The fact is that women hate to be asked questions about things that are none of their business. Still, in spite of all they have endured, they are quite anxious to please men. So, a woman will tell a man what she thinks he wants to hear, whether it makes any sense to her or not. The very least we can do is quit bothering them with foolish questions.

"Like: 'Who do you want to vote for?'.

"So here we are, at the very heart of the matter: should we repeal the 19th amendment? I say yes, because it is the only way to rectify the injury men did women by inflicting suffrage upon them.

"And men *did* inflict it on women; not one woman sat in the 66th Congress that enacted the law. Was this fair? What chance did the pretties have to defend themselves?

"I demand that the 19th amendment be repealed!"

These are strong words, indeed, in the defense of American womanhood. Our next public service advertisement will offer the masculine side of the question. Meanwhile, if you would care to express your opinion on the subject fill out the ballot below and send it to us. We will send you one of the badges shown, depending on which way you vote. And we hope that the men in the audience will continue to buy Rainier Ale if for no other reason than that, as far as is known, no woman has ever been known to drink it. A remarkable record.

310

KEEP TIMES SQUARE GREEN!

(A MODEST REFORESTATION PROPOSAL FROM OREGON'S LARGEST & ONLY BREWERY AS A FITTING PRELUDE TO OREGON'S GLORIOUS 1959 CENTENNIAL CELEBRATION)

Just picture what reforestation will do for Times Square! Cool and green, teeming with game, salmon swimming up-Pepsi Cola sign to spawn. Why, it'll be a little corner of Oregon! But let's start at the beginning . . .

The name of our Beer is Blitz. Perhaps we'd better spell it out for you so you won't claim later that you got us confused with some other beer because we mumbled. Please pay attention now: B-L-I-T-Z. "Beer" is spelled just the way it sounds.

It's hard to say what good this priceless knowledge will do you because you haven't a prayer of getting Blitz in New York or wherever it is you live; unless you live in the Northwest, which we doubt. Especially we like to think of you as living in New York, probably because we've always wanted to get ourselves a nice, old city with marvelous possibilities and do things with it. One thing we won't do is sell you our magnificent Beer of the Bright Cascades (as we say) although it'd very likely be the making of you.

You couldn't afford it. Supposing you rationed yourself to one bottle a day; the air-mail alone would stagger reason. For that kind of money you could move to Oregon and enjoy Blitz postage-free for the rest of your life. And some life! You'd love it. Oh, yes you would, too.

We realize that some of you may not be able to come to Oregon right this minute. To you stranded unfortunates—wherever you are—we will send, absolutely free, an Oregon Do-It-Yourself Kit: an Oregon Fir tree and directions for planting. If you don't have a yard or a window box you might set them out in pots on the street*, though not under marquees; they grow to be a couple of hundred feet tall. Please let us know where you decide.

*Like in front of Lindy's; a delicatessen that may in summer wear a nest of robins in its hair.

SEND FOR YOUR FREE TREE TODAY!

Blitz-Weinhard Company
1133 W Burnside Street, Portland 9, Oregon

Dear Blitz:
I'd love an Oregon Fir, please send one. I'll let you know where I plant it and how it's doing. Give my very best to the gang. Sincerely,

Name_____

Address_____

City_____State_____

P.S. You understand why I can't come to Oregon right now—I can't get out of that thing on Thursday. I'll be there for the '59 Centennial you can bet.

Prescient Promotions. Even Harry Truman got into the act when Gossage had Blitz-Weinhard give away fir trees to celebrate Oregon's Centennial. As for the ad on the left... 311

HOW TO BECOME THE WORLD'S GREA

> *Howard Gossage was invited to address the Awards Luncheon of the Art Directors Club of Los Angeles. Coincidentally, art director Bob Freeman of the agency, Weiner & Gossage, Inc., was also there to accept the medal for the best consumer advertising campaign given to their series for the Eagle Shirtmakers.*

ONE time Stan Freberg was barnstorming through Australia with a troupe, doing one night stands in all principal cities. They got to Adelaide, on the west coast, did a show, and didn't get to bed until three. The next morning, still pooped and half-asleep, they had to present themselves at the God-awful hour of eight to be received by the Lord Mayor and the Council. There they all were in an enormous council room, wood paneled, and lined with books, with rows of pews on each side. There were ornately costumed officials in wigs, and the Lord Mayor and Councillors in their robes of office. The Lord Mayor arose and said: "I'm sure we're very happy to honor the famous American entertainer Mr., uh (referring to notes) Stan Freberg and his company who, I believe, gave a most successful performance at, uh (consulting notes), the Gaiety Theatre last evening to a gathering of uh (notes), it doesn't say, but there must have been many people there. And so to you, Mr. Freeman, and your talented associates, welcome to Adelaide." Stan stood up, looked around at the somber, formal magnificence, cleared his throat, and said: "Thank you for your kind reception, but I won't make my remarks over-long since I know we're all anxious to get on with the reading of the will." Speaking of Mr. Freeman, I'm sure you all know *our* Mr. Freeman, Robert Freeman. I am happy to announce that art direction has at last come into its own. Bob is the new president of our company, bringing the total number up to three. This is because neither Joe Weiner last year, nor I this year could bear to be demoted. Besides, we are too small to have vice-presidents. Robert bridled a bit when the honor was first bestowed on him. He was afraid somebody would think he was a super account executive, and that henceforth he would have to walk around with an attache case full of graphs showing the degree of penetration of outdoor as compared to per capita cat food consumption in Cincinnati. We managed to assuage his fears by pointing out that other great figures in the art world such as Winston Churchill, Dwight Eisenhower, and Jack Roberts—though not necessarily in that order—had assumed the robes of leadership without sacrificing their artistic integrity.

> *At this point Mr. Gossage's nose began to bleed copiously and continued through the rest of his remarks. "Where else," he asked, "but Los Angeles, can you hear a speech and watch a man bleed to death at the same time?"*

Now, the question arises: If it is possible for an art director to become a tycoon, can an account executive or copywriter become an art director? By all means. I would like to sacrifice

TEST UNRECOGNIZED ART DIRECTOR

modesty and use myself as a case in point. People have asked me, "Mr. Gossage, how did you become the world's greatest unrecognized art director?" I always give them the same answer: by being sneaky. The important thing is getting off on the right foot. First, you must make friends with the art director. Oh and Ah whenever he brings anything around for you to look at; even if it is lousy. Go along for months like that; play the waiting game; don't show your hand. Yes, contain yourself until he goes on his vacation, or off on the annual Aspen strength-through-joy free-load. Then strike. You see, all this time you will have been saving up loads and loads of simply wonderful ideas. So while he is gone you ram them through with the help of some scab from the outside who sees eye to eye with you. And then you get them all O.K.'d by the client; not too great a trick since the artist is usually the client's nephew. Then, when the poor AD comes back to the office fresh and invigorated—a condition that will last for about 45 seconds—he has his work all cut out for the next year. It will take him that long to repair the damages. Now, this sounds perfectly simple, doesn't it. And it is, but there are pitfalls you must watch out for. Art directors are a tricky lot. You will find that they profit by experience and will try to henceforth take their vacations at the same time you take yours. Don't let it throw you. What you do is announce in a loud voice that you are going to take your vacation at a certain time. Your spies in the accounting department will tell you whether or not he has bitten; chances are about 100 to one that he will bite. Fine. You say goodbye to him…oh, on the last day, to lull him further into false security, come to the office with your bags, golf clubs, etc., so he will think you are leaving right from work. Of course you don't go at all—*but he does!* Warning: this system will not work more than two years in a row with any but the most simple-minded and gullible art directors. Indeed, I have known of art directors who were so wary that they quit taking vacations at all. This, on the face of it, would seem to defeat the plan, but no, quite the contrary. If you can get an art director so twitchy and nervous that he won't take *any* time off, why, you have him right where you want him. Not only will his spirit be broken from lack of zestful, carefree recreation, but his wife will start grousing at him because she never gets to go anywhere. Trouble at home! You can help this along by having your wife run into his wife somewhere, as if by accident, and telling her what a great time the two of you had at Vegas or Disneyland, or wherever it is account executives spend their holidays. The end result is he becomes cowed and like putty in your hands; you will have the field all to yourself; *you* will have become the art director! If you have to work with several art directors simultaneously you will not, of course, be able to follow this concentrated procedure. You will have to employ day-by-day psychological warfare. I have found that three modes of attack will suffice to reduce even a very large art department to a talentless, quivering blob. One: Whenever a layout incorporating an illustration is presented, merely ask, "Don't you think photography would have more immediacy?" If photography is presented you work it the other way around. You say, "Look, Saul, or whatever your name is, do you really think this gets over the *feeling* of the product as well as an illustration would?" Two: Whatever the art treatment is, you say with a little tired smile, "Well, this is certainly pretty, and I'm sure it will get in the art director's show, but that's not our primary job, is it?" Three: If it is an all-type ad, you say, "Yeah, sure, it looks *great;* but isn't the purpose of this ad to get read?" An alternative to this is to learn the names of a couple of obscure type faces, and no matter what is shoved before you, you say, "gee, I sort of visualized the headline in Hyperthyroid Extended and the body copy in Diner's Club Oldstyle." Any situation not covered by these phrases can be rescued by saying: "Well, what the hell, we can always use it for a trade ad." Well, that concludes my remarks and I want to express my appreciation again for inviting me to, uh (consulting notes), Los Angeles. Thank you.

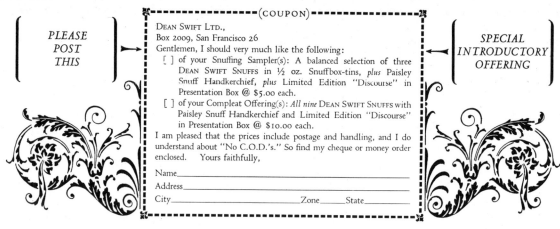
YOU WILL FIND DEAN SWIFT® SNUFF TO BE AT ONCE ELEGANT, ASTONISHING, AND REWARDING

FEW of this age have known the ineffable pleasures of snuffing.

We of DEAN SWIFT LTD. think this a propitious time to reintroduce fancy snuff, hence the offering above. But first the points below:

[1] DEAN SWIFT SNUFF is *sniffing* snuff: dry, floured, aromaticked tobacco. Do not, we implore you, confuse fancy snuff with the unfortunate, orally-induced "snuffs."

[2] It is the most exhilarating form of tobacco ever devised. In the words of Coleridge, ". . . snuff! Perhaps it is the final cause of the human nose."

[3] Because it is extremely satisfying, and much more socially acceptable than smoking, fancy snuffing quite eclipsed it *for over 200 years!* People simply gave up smoking for something more rewarding. Perhaps they will again.

[4] (Smoking's comeback in the 19th Century was apparently due to two phenomena: [A] The revolt against the aristocracy. *Recall that snuff was the hallmark of the aristocrat;* [B] The invention of the "Lucifer" or sulphur match. The heady novelty of "instant fire" demanded conspicuous use. In light of this, the psychological reasons for smoking appear to be balderdash. It is a fad pure and simple.)

[5] As to healthfulness, we cannot suggest that snuff is actually *good* for you, of course. However, there is this: if we are to credit the Surgeon General's remarks, most unpleasantnesses are not present in the tobacco leaf, *but are formed during the burning process.* So much for that.

[6] While, for the present at least, the graceful, cleanly procedures of fancy snuffing could attract you quite an audience at a cocktail party, it can be accommodated without notice anywhere; even at an investiture, one imagines. And one simply sneers at "No Smoking" signs.

[7] DEAN SWIFT SNUFF is not only convenient, it is economical. A half-ounce tin should last the average ex-heavy smoker well over a week!

[8] If you are not presently a snuffer you may not be aware of the enormous range of taste DEAN SWIFT caters to. At the moment we import nine fancy snuffs into this country: DEAN'S OWN,* MRS. SIDDONS'S NO. 3 & 4,* DR. JOHNSON,* CAMELEOPARD NO. 5,* BEZOAR FINE GRIND,* INCHKENNETH,* BOSWELL'S BEST,* WREN'S RELISH,* and SPECIFIC NO. 1.* All are exceptionally agreeable. Since space forbids detailing the properties of each here (and since they possibly wouldn't mean much to you anyway until you have compared at least three snuffs), we shall include descriptive material and reorder forms when we fill your present order. The offerings then:

[9] The $5.00 SNUFFING SAMPLER, in an exceptionally comely presentation box, brings you three assorted mixtures in half-ounce lacquered snuffbox-tins *plus* an imported paisley snuff handkerchief *plus* a numbered copy of the limited edition "A Discourse On Snuff or Its Nature Reveal'd;" with precise instructions in the modes of elegant sniffing.

[10] (It should be mentioned that a proper snuff handkerchief is highly desirable going in.)

[11] The $10.00 COMPLEAT OFFERING is a magnificent unabridged presentation of *all nine* DEAN SWIFT SNUFFS in their extraordinary variety, *plus* the imported paisley snuff handkerchief *and* the "Discourse"! A truly great adventure in snuffing. Definitive.

[12] We shall also send with each order a Free Illustrated Catalogue of snuffboxes in gold, silver, pewter, horn, and precious woods; variously priced.

Thank you for your kind attention. Now back to the coupon; what better way to find out whether you are up to snuff?

*Trademarks of DEAN SWIFT LTD.

©1964, DEAN SWIFT LTD.

Howard and his merry band teamed up to reintroduce a new habit - snuff! Then he wrote an 18th Century brochure, "A Discourse on Snuff or Its Nature Reveal'd."

WINE COLLECTING TAKES UP LESS SPACE THAN ANTIQUE CARS, IS QUIETER THAN HI-FI, AND TASTES BETTER THAN STAMPS

People always say that every man ought to have a hobby but they never mention the real reason, which is: it's the only way he can be alone at home.

Most men, therefore, will choose a hobby that is so bulky, messy, noisy, or boring that no one can bear to be near him; a high price to pay for solitude.

The wise man will forsake these self-tortures and take up wine collecting. It works just as well, no one will bother him: A) children do not drink and so are not interested; B) women love to have wine at the table, but they feel, quite rightly, that the collecting of wine is, like hunting, man's work. And so it is.

Wine collecting has one magnificent advantage over other hobbies: you can drink it. Also, it is neither expensive nor complicated to start. One may begin with two or three different reds and two or three whites; but which ones? To help you we will be happy to send you the labels of all thirteen Paul Masson table wines (plus a description of the delicious differences of each) to give you a collector's feel right away. Write: Paul Masson Vineyards, Dept. Y-1, Saratoga, California.

This ad looks better in color, but we had to share one of our favorite Paul Masson headlines. Here, Howard encouraged another new habit. [Which also tastes better than snuff.]   315

(Wide-open, from **Ford Aardvark** to **Zosterops!**)

EAGLE SHIRTMAKER'S GREAT MAVERICK RE-NAMING CONTEST!

"Ford a few weeks ago let it be known that its cars would come in such colors as Thanks Vermillion and Freudian Gilt. That sparked a new game of thinking up similar names. Suggestions received at Ford: Forever Amber, Unsafe Topaz, Navel Orange."
—NEWSWEEK (Apr. 7, 1969)

WELL, sure, *you* remember Eagle's great color naming contest of five years ago, but who would have thought that a busy company like Ford would? Yet it seemed that all the names (except Thanks Vermillion—and our congratulations to the author) had been selected for this signal honor from our list at left.

Sure enough, when the Maverick was introduced on April 18, there it was in Glorious Eaglecolor, including Original Cinnamon, Hulla Blue, and Anti-Establish Mint. We were in! And no telling how many others they'll pick up in the Fordseeable Fuchsia.

Ford Bored

Now Ford didn't ask us for any favors in return, but we *would* like to express our gratitude, so how about this: If Ford is tired of the same old approach to colors, how must they feel about Thunderbird, LTD, Mustang and the rest? As a matter of fact "Maverick" is defined in Webster's Unabridged as "an unbranded animal," and perhaps that's a big, proud company's way of saying "Help!"

Hence your chance to submit new names for this fine Ford product, win lavish prizes of Eagle Shirts, and help build up another list of consumer-approved, pre-copyrighted names for Ford to browse through the next time they need a better idea.

First off, these names must be usable by Ford, no clever stuff, so here are a few guidelines.

As we see it, Ford is very strong on animal entries, but there's no use sending in "Ford Horse" or "Ford Cow" when they have already made do with the racier "Mustang" and "Maverick."

No Oozers

It may be, of course, that automobile manufacturers don't care *what* the names mean as long as they sound aggressive. Chevrolet's Camaro, for example, is simply Spanish for "shrimp." Be careful, though. The **Ford Teredo** turns out to be a worm. On the whole we'd stay away from anything that oozes around, but nature is still a treasure trove of names.

BIRDS. The **Ford Eagle** (theirs without asking); the **Ford Yunx** (a genus of woodpeckers); the **Ford Zosterops** (much better than Maverick if Ford is after the Volkswagen trade. The Encyclopedia Britannica says: the birds of this group are mostly of unpretending appearance").

SNAKES. They already have the Ford Cobra, but there are deadlier serpents than that. The **Ford Krait,** for example. And many others.

MICROBES. Both **Ford Flagellata** and **Ford Suctoria,** for instance, have a contemporary quality sound.

MISCELLANEOUS. Don't forget the choice pickings in insects, mammals, fruits, fish, vegetables, flowers, monsters **(Ford Thing)** and minerals **(Ford Ore).** The field is wide open!

Rules: Submit any number of names you wish. The first prize will be ½ doz. Eagle Shirts—what the hell, make it a dozen—and the next 99 prizes will be one shirt apiece.

Partners

One other thing. Since we're apparently in this with Ford for good, we here at Eagle would like to consolidate the new partnership. To that end our '69 line of shirts (including the magnificent Pierre Cardin designs and the shaped, colorful Travis McGee numbers—both of which are selling so well we can't keep up with the demand) are hereby dubbed "The Edsel Collection."

Again, we want to thank the Ford Motor Co. for making all of this possible. If they want to go all out **(Ford Whole Hog?),** their dealers can pass out entry blanks too.

EAGLE has a *pretty good idea*

MAVERICK RE-NAMING FORM
Eagle Shirtmakers, Quakertown, Pa. 18951

A) Here is (are) my new name(s) for the Ford Maverick:

_____

_____

B) I can't think of any more, but here are some new color names:

_____

_____

My Name_____

Address_____

City_____State_____Zip_____

Collar Size_____Sleeve Length_____

DOGS, FIREPLUGS AND INSANITY

To begin with I should like to pay my last, public respects to a splendid man who was feared and admired in his world, Nicholas Samstag. I loved him.

Nick's cool sense of cold reality was breathtaking. I recall the first time I met him. It was after a long stimulating correspondence. Even so, he walked into my room tentatively, removing neither his hat nor his coat, as though he first wanted to make up his mind whether I would do. Thus fully garbed, he began pacing up and down, talking of ideas. At one point the subject of children came up and I said a very commonplace thing: that I didn't want my son to go through what I had gone through.

He turned on me and said, "Look, Gossage, would you be satisfied if your son turned out as well as you have?" I thought for a moment and replied, "I'd be absolutely delighted if he did." This answer apparently satisfied Nick, for he took off his coat and hat and remained very close to me the rest of his life.

I have tried this question out on a number of men since, and invariably the answer has been that they would indeed be pleased if their children turned out as well as they. Which leads me to believe that people, on the whole, are more content with themselves than they think they are.

Nick's world was divided into what he called "Mammonoids and Tediophobes." A Mammonoid is a man who is motivated by money and a Tediophobe is one who hates tedium. Mammonoids are usually managers, and tediophobes are artists of one sort or another, talent. He believed that there was no real possibility of them ever getting together because neither of them understands why the other one behaves as he does.

The mammonoid thinks that if he offers the tediophobe enough money, that will do the trick, and he is always baffled because it never does. The tediophobe will take the money, but what he really wants is simply to avoid being bored. So the poor mammonoid is constantly confused and frustrated because his best — and best-paid — tediophobes are always leaving him to go to silly jobs that pay less money.

Whereupon the mammonoid wails the universal cry of the unrequited lover, "How could you do this to me?" And the tediophobe answers with genuine mystification, "Do *what?*"

It is a measure of Nick's versatility that with one illustration he disposed of three of the subjects which concern this symposium: Love, Art, and Money. I should like to talk about the remaining one, Time. I am concerned with Time as it bears on perception and problem-solving.

I can't remember when I first noticed that a very good approach to problem-solving was: if you're stuck with a lemon, make lemonade out of it. Indeed, I was so successful at this method of turning disaster into triumph that, when there wasn't a lemon handy, I'd find myself rummaging around in the

---

A recent issue of New York Magazine described Howard Luck Gossage as "The San Francisco advertising genius who invented Beethoven sweatshirts, The Paper Airplane Book, and Marshall-McLuhan-as-a-marketing-event. The 20th century invented Gossage, or maybe it was the other way around."

This is the full text of an address that Gossage delivered April 9th to the 13th Communications Conference.

HOWARD LUCK GOSSAGE

fruit bowl just so I'd have something to work with. Life — and clients — being what they are, I generally didn't have far to look.

The way it worked was this: if I listened to a client long enough, sooner or later he would come up with his real quandary, the problem he was stuck with. Whereupon I would run an ad for him that said, in effect, "Now here is my quandary," and let the readers help him figure it out. I often included a coupon for their convenience in answering. This frequently succeeded, since there is nothing that people adore so much as giving advice. In their desire to be helpful, many of them went so far as to actually buy the product.

This approach worked out so well that it was several years before I found out anything more about *why* it worked.

Do you remember Charles Lamb's Dissertation On Roast Pig? The hero discovered roast pork, and how delicious it was, when his house burned down with a pig inside it. Being shrewd, he put two and two together. Thereafter, everytime he wanted roast pork, he burned the house down.

Well, it was quite a while before I figured out that it wasn't absolutely necessary to have a disaster or a quandary before making advertising campaigns; that the chief ingredient was simply recognizing what was there instead of wasting time in wishful thinking about what *should* be there, or prying overly much into *why* things were the way they were.

It was about this time that I also concluded that what we usually call creativity consisted mostly of seeing a hundred horses go by and being able to say, "That one there is a zebra." And that originality was being able to ask, "Now, what do you do with 99 non-zebras?"

It wasn't until perhaps six years ago that I discovered that this type of reality perception was a recognized philosophical method and even had a name: "non-teleological thinking." John Steinbeck introduced me to it and I shall always be grateful to him for doing so. In case you're interested, he has written on this concept in his book "The Log From the Sea of Cortez," the chapter called "Easter Sunday." He says it is the most personal writing he has ever done, and I believe him.

"Non-teleological" is not an easy word to bandy about. It means . . . well, first let's define "teleological." It means, more or less, looking at things as having a discoverable cause in the past, a reason for existing now, and an ultimate purpose in the future: things *should* be a certain way and, if they aren't, there ought to be a reason *why*. Now, this seems like an entirely reasonable way of looking at things, doesn't it? Actually, that is the customary way of looking at things — despite the fact that it doesn't often work out very well.

Non-teleological thinking, on the other hand, doesn't ask *why* a thing is the way it is or say that it *should* be some other way. It says, "This is the way it is; now what do we do about it?"

This point-blank method can lead to some rather profound and unexpected conclusions. I will admit that it can also sound like a pretty slipshod way of looking at things. I guess a great deal depends on who is doing the looking — and whether they're really trying to solve a problem. Problems, like beauty, are in the beholder's eye; and some people behold better than others.

As to the futility of asking, "Why," Steinbeck cites a homely example, that of a box of matches. Now, the matches all appear to be the same size, however if you measure them carefully you will find that some of them are heavier or longer than the others. A good teleological question, therefore, might be, "Why are some matches larger than others?"

So far, this sounds like a perfectly logical research project, even typical. The only trouble with it is the trouble with all research projects of this sort: there is no real answer, nor does it

serve any real use except to fill comforting books and security files. When you have gone into the question as deeply as you can, the only answer you're going to come up with ultimately is, "The reason some matches are larger than others is just because they are." Nor will it do any good to insist indignantly that, after all the money that's been put into precision machinery, those matches *should* be the same size.

People who think in this direct fashion are often accused of being cynical or even heartless. On the contrary, I find it a humane way of looking at the world, even though it involves giving up some cherished illusions about what is fitting and right.

Steinbeck tells of an instance when he was living in the Carmel woods, to the south of San Francisco. A woman lived in the house next door and her dog had recently died. So she told the Steinbecks that she had put a dinner bell beside her bed and, if marauders came into the house and cut her telephone wires preparatory to robbing her, she would ring the bell; and, if the Steinbecks heard it, would they please call the police?

Now, this was an improbable contingency and, a man might say, the woman's fears were foolish and even neurotic. The teleological response would have been to point out how unlikely the whole thing was and even to try to reason with the woman so that she would get over her fears. In other words, a sensible person would have told her that she *shouldn't* be frightened and would have told her *why* she shouldn't be frightened. This would have done exactly no good at all, for the fact was that the woman *was* frightened and her fears *were* real. So the non-teleological answer would have been, "Of course we'll listen for the bell; we'll keep the windows open on that side of the house." Then, if you really wanted to solve the woman's problem, you might buy her another dog.

Speaking of dogs, I can give you another example, one which also includes a solution area: the problem of dogs

urinating on fire plugs. No, that's wrong. Dogs don't urinate on fire plugs, they piss on fire plugs. Perhaps dogs *should* urinate on fire plugs but the fact is that they piss on them. Very well.

Now, there are several teleological solutions to this problem of dogs pissing on fire plugs. The arch-conservative solution would probably be to lock up all the dogs, which is plainly impossible. The militant radical solution might be to rip up all the fire plugs; which would work, but might not be worth the inconvenience. Or, I suppose, we could do a thorough, preliminary feasibility study into *why* dogs piss on fire plugs, file it away, and let it go at that.

The non-teleological thinker is likely to look at the problem in quite another fashion. The first thing he would say is, "Dogs piss on fire plugs; that is a fact." Then he might ask, "What else do dogs piss on?" The answer to that is: dogs piss on anything. "Well, in that case," he might say, "why don't we plant a lot of trees? We can't stop dogs from being dogs, but we can spread them around a little bit and at the same time we'll end up with a more beautiful city. And instead of wasting our time stewing about dogs, we'll be doing something for human beings."

Thinking non-teleologically is a very hard discipline to come by and it is very hard to apply all the time. It's tough not to say "should" or ask "why" even when you realize as you say the words that they are not going to do any good whatsoever. However, the non-teleological thinker always has the advantage, especially when he has knowledge and timing on his side — and the power to do something about the situation.

The most brilliant piece of non-teleological thinking any of us is ever likely to see occurred just recently when President Johnson announced that he would not run. Not being a particularly modest man myself, I said to my wife, "If he had hired me to plot this out for him, it couldn't have come off better." This isn't to say that I had guessed beforehand that he would do as he did. No, like the rest of you I was too busy thinking in terms of "why" and "should."

However, I haven't seen anything in the public prints to indicate that any of our leaders or pendits have caught what I believe to be the full implication of his stunningly brilliant maneuver; and I doubt very much that that smart old man is going to spell out the message for them.

I mean, in addition to the surface message which caused that profile in retroactive courage, Robert Kennedy, to leap for joy. I don't know what there is about that boy, but just physically, he's always looked to me like somebody wearing hand-me-downs; his suits *look* nice enough, but you can always tell when they've been cut-down; you know, there's something about the fit?

And I think I'll look at him differently the day I also see him wear an idea that hasn't belonged to somebody else first.

Back to Lyndon B. Johnson, here's what I saw: what he apparently did was to renounce a new Presidential term to start next January. What he actually did was to start a new term as President right then. In other words, he succeeded himself on the spot: he ended the old administration and inaugurated a new one with, in effect, a new man under new auspices.

He is now, I believe, in just about the same position as Eisenhower was when he succeeded Truman, but Johnson's trick is that he did it with himself. That his new administration will last only nine months is beside the point. Nine months is a long time. You can make a baby in nine months, or you can make peace, or you can blow up the world if you're the most powerful man in it; and he is.

Under the circumstances, with no political fences or obligations, he may be at this moment the most powerful man the world has ever seen. I would guess that a good deal of this power stems from his innate knowledge that he has nothing to lose. I also imagine that he is experiencing that peculiar euphoria and clear-headedness reserved for those whose fate is irrevocably sealed. As Samuel Johnson said, "Depend upon it sir, when a man knows he's to be hanged in a fortnight, it concentrates his mind wonderfully."

This is an attitude that Orientals understand perhaps better than we do. They may, as we believe, have less regard for life than we do, but they have a much greater understanding and respect for death — and imminent death. Therefore, I am not surprised that Hanoi responded instantly to the President's peace overtures, nor will I be surprised if they continue to take him seriously as long as he persists in his present mood and the full exercise of his power. And thank you, H. V. Kaltenborn.

Now, if it is more realistic and more effective to think non-teleologically, why is it that our natural tendency is apparently to think the other way — in terms of cause and effect, of *why* and *should?*

And what has all of this got to do with our subject, Time? I'll bet you thought I'd never ask. I think it's got everything to do with our *sense* of time — the way we compartmentalize it in our language and thinking patterns.

To begin with, Past, Present and Future are very sophisticated terms. Man must have evolved millions of years before these abstracts began to govern his life. We know, of course, that time sense will vary from language to language and from nation to nation, but for the most part — in the West, at least — we are settled on more or less uniform concepts of Past, Present, and Future. We generally think of ourselves as facing the future, or marching into the future.

The ancient Greeks apparently didn't look at it that way at all; quite the opposite. It seems that the Greek word for "future" was the same as that for "back," or so I have read. At any rate, the Greeks thought of themselves as facing the past where they could see it — the future was at their back. To visualize this, imagine yourself off on one of those moving sidewalks they have at airports, which for some reason just make the dreary trip out to Gate 142 seem even longer than it is. Anyway, imagine yourself riding backwards on one of them so that you can see where you have been but you can't see where you are going: the past is out in front of you, but you can't see the future there in back.

Personally, I find this a much more logical way of looking at time, but I doubt that it will ever catch on except for perhaps at Republican conventions: ". . . so, with our backs firmly to the future, we stride confidently into the past." Or, if you prefer: ". . . so, with our faces to the past, we back into the future."

The only people I know of in our society who do not think in terms of past, present, and future are either animals, the very young, or philosophers. Philosophers know that time is a continuum; that river that Heraclitus tells us that we can't step into the same one of twice. But I suspect that even for philosophers, it is a Sunday truth, and that they, like the rest of us, are answering queries about their 1965 tax returns even as they put a little something down on their 1968 estimates. Very young children will think of time as a complete unit until they are taught worse. And I should think that animals would have very little sense of time at all beyond reflexes.

Well, this matter of language has everything to do with the way we look at time. "Why" is clearly a past tense concept just as "should" is a notion which can only find fulfillment in the future. And since the present is a very arbitrary distinction, and difficult of definition, it is hard to say what "now" is. Is it a beat or is it a century?

Yes, I suppose we are stuck with past, present, and future, but there ought to be something we can do about the sloppy, wishful thinking that seems to go with them. Since they defy precise, positive definition, perhaps we can nail them down negatively.

Like this: If loss of the future is death, and loss of the past is amnesia, then loss of the present must be insanity. It seems to me that the great disease of our time is epidemic insanity so defined: we have lost the present. I wonder how much time we have to get it back.

THE PRINCE

by Leopold Kohr

In letters and talks, I used to call Howard "My Prince." He took it smilingly, but gently scolded me when I addressed him with "Thou." 🍃 He was a princely apparition – tall, handsome, white-maned, regal, the head of a comet streaking through the night of life, with everyone else arranging himself naturally as part of a long incandescent tail – scholars, politicians, newspapermen, business tycoons, artists, psychiatrists, secretaries, dreamers, theorists. 🍃 Even taxi drivers and waiters, those most unresponsive specimens of modern man, felt electrified by Howard's presence, and for once saw again the glory rather than the humiliation of service.

Like the Renaissance Pope who said: *"Now that God has given Us the papacy, let Us enjoy it,"* Howard delighted in his nature-given principality not because of any lust for power but because of his engaging naivete. 🍃 His was the naivete of Schiller's famous essay on the naive and the sentimental; on the poet whose heart radiates directly back what it receives in undiminished intensity, and the thinker who lets his perception percolate through the cooling and discriminating filter of his mind. Schiller pictured himself in his essay as the sentimental, and Goethe, the greater, as the naive. 🍃 And so was Howard naive, spreading exuberance and joy, because he enjoyed everything himself, as he did when he put on his golden monocle which would have stigmatized others as leg-pullers and fools. 🍃 On the eye of Howard, it was a symbol of his principality as natural as the scepter was for kings.

But he was not only princely – like a prince. He *was* a prince. He combined a quick grasp of earthly things with humor and wit as delightedly as it was delightful. ❧ He tempered an easy command over the affections of others with the most engaging of material generosity. And the most princely of his qualities, he blended the monarch's sense of rightness with the medieval beggar's infinite dignity and humility.

It was one of the graces of my life to travel with "My Prince" through the United States during one of the last months of his – from the excitement of his beloved San Francisco to the Pacific solitude of Timber Cove, from the quixotic romanticism of astral Houston, Texas, to the weird happening that is New York. ❧ He arranged, I lectured. I proposed, he disposed. I advanced themes, he set them to music, and conducted the orchestra as well. And in between, on early mornings or late at night, he gave me the gayest performance of the drama of human existence, acting, singing, initiating, commenting, his eyes now and then wistfully straying into the distance, to his Sally, his Sarah, his Jane. And now and then, they were looking forward with a sad amused glint toward the final curtain.

It seems unreal that his physical life is over. But as Gerry Feigen suggested, his real life is not. ❧ Howard lives on through the transplant of his soul and mind into those who loved him.

What I shall remember best from Howard's many memorable statements are particularly two. One illustrates his philosophy that Greatness adheres to the small, not the large, an idea which, much too late, caused our paths to cross. ❧ He made it during one of our not so fortunate conferences in the Virgin Islands dealing with the fate of Anguilla.

When the exploiters of scale tried to muscle in on the opportunities which Howard's famous one-page advertisement in the *New York Times* had opened for that previously unknown miniature community, he tried to encourage the assembled and wavering leaders of Anguilla by giving them the example of his own firm. *"When we founded 'Shade Tree' a decade ago,"* he said, *"we were eleven members. Now, ten years later,"* he continued with pride and a flash in his eyes, *"we are thirteen — two more. Yet it is we, not the great companies, who have the most wonderful office in all San Francisco — the Fire House. And it is us, not them, who have the best working conditions, the most human of scales, the greatest security, the luxury of leisure, the dearest of friends as our co-workers."* No one else would have seen anything to brag about unless the number of personnel had increased from eleven to five hundred.

The other statement illuminates not Howard's philosphy but his character — his naive spontaneity, his zest, his exuberance — with which he enthralled whomever he met. ❧ After I had identified myself during one of his seminars as an anarchist as well as a monarchist, Howard jumped to his feet and announced to an appreciative audience recruited from the tough world of business and politics: *"Wonderful! I too am an anarchist. I too am a monarchist."* And then, with the suddenness of a thrilling revelation, he added what I could not have said of myself: *"I am a Monarch!"*

And so thou wast, My Prince! Fare thee well!

Leopold Kohr — lawyer, economist, college professor, "apostle of shrink-manship," author of The Breakdown of Nations *and winner of the "Alternative Nobel Prize." He was featured in a series of seminars promoted by Gossage and Dr. Gerry Feigen that began with "A Modest Idea for S.F. Secession" and followed with a lecture tour that took them to Houston and New York. Kohr's seminal thinking was the inspiration for his friend E. F. Schumacher's* Small is Beautiful. *So strongly has his approach caught on in this age of "down-sizing" and "right-sizing," it is hard to reconstruct the initial reaction to his ideas and "size theory."*

[Honoring those who produced this book.]

❧ COLOPHON ❧

THE DESIGN OF THE BOOK

was inspired by Howard and Marget's ads, by way of Keith Longino in Chicago and Rich Silverstein in San Francisco. The type is mostly Adobe Garamond by way of Aldus PageMaker. § Other bits and pieces were designed by *CA Magazine*, Dugald Stermer, *University of Illinois Press* and, of course, Robert Freeman, Marget Larsen and George Dippel. § For the cover, thanks to the patient talent of Roy Sandstrom.

THE PRODUCTION OF THE BOOK

was by human beings who cared about quality. § Dick McKee and Dale Taylor at Malloy Printing, Jim Sanders at Chapter One, Keith Love at RPP, Shi Young at IPG, and Mark Tursi at Mars Litho were key contributors. § Their craftsmanship helped us make this dream come true.

THE CONTENTS OF THE BOOK

came from the likes of Dennis Altman, Bill Huey, Sally Kemp Gossage, Alice and Lewis Lowe, Dagmar Mussey, Jean and Patrick Coyne of *CA Magazine*, Dugald Stermer, Stan Freberg, Kim Rotzoll, *University of Illinois Press*, Wayne Helinski and the Robert Freeman estate. § Each played critical roles in this book's assemblage.

THE COPY WORKSHOP

is the good hearts and great talent of Mairee Ryan, Keith Longino, Claire McDonnell, Judy Ippolito, Trish Hoskins and Andreas Fuchs (our International Intern). § George Burrows was a catalyst who deserves special mention. § And to Lorelei – for the love and magic it takes to make things special.

Bruce Bendinger, Editor

[Okay, one more story...]

CARL ALLY RENTED THE PLANE

and they got on board to honor Howard's final wish. § The plane took off to scatter his ashes over Drake's Bay.

Carl slowed the plane to just above stall speed and gave instructions to Bob Freeman and Howard's son, Eben. § Ease open the door, tilt the urn slightly out of the plane, open it. Scatter the ashes.

Well, things don't always go as planned, and a mischievious bit of wind got into the act. § Howard's ashes flew back into the plane and, as Luck would have it, headed right up the Widow Gossage's dress.

AT WHICH POINT, CARL EXCLAIMED,

"Even after he's dead, he's still trying to get in your knickers!" § Laughter joined the tears and scattered into the air – along with Howard's ashes. § The small plane made a final turn over the Bay and headed back to San Francisco.